AMERICAN
ANTISLAVERY
SONGS

Recent Titles in
Documentary Reference Collections

The Eisenhower Administration, 1953-1961: A Documentary History
Robert L. Branyan and Lawrence Harold Larsen, compilers

Education in the United States: A Documentary History
Sol Cohen, compiler

The Law of War: A Documentary History
Leon Friedan, compiler

The Gallup Poll: Public Opinion 1935-1871
George Horace Gallup

The Gallup International Public Opinion Polls, France: 1939, 1944-1975
George Horace Gallup

The Gallup International Public Opinion Polls, Great Britain: 1937-1975
George Horace Gallup

International Law Governing Communications and Information: A Collection
of Documents
Edward W. Ploman

The League for Industrial Democracy: A Documentary History
Bernard K. Johnpoll

Agriculture in the United States: A Documentary History
Wayne David Rasmussen

Six Plays for Young People from the Federal Theater Project (1936-1939)
Lowell Swortzell, editor

AMERICAN ANTISLAVERY SONGS

A Collection and Analysis

VICKI L. EAKLOR

Documentary Reference Collections

GREENWOOD PRESS
New York • Westport, Connecticut • London

Library of Congress Cataloging-in-Publication Data

Eaklor, Vicki Lynn.
   American antislavery songs : a collection and analysis
/ Vicki L. Eaklor.
     p.   cm. — (Documentary reference collections)
   Bibliography: p.
   Includes indexes.
   ISBN 0-313-25413-3 (lib. bdg. : alk. paper)
   1. Slavery—United States—anti-slavery movements—Songs and
music—History and criticism. 2. Slavery—United States—Anti-
slavery movements—Songs and music—Texts. 3. Songs, English—
United States—History and criticism. I. Title. II. Series.
ML3561.A6E2   1988
784.6'8326—dc19   88-15426

British Library Cataloguing in Publication Data is available.

Library of Congress Catalog Card Number: 88-15426
ISBN: 0-313-25413-3

First published in 1988

Greenwood Press, Inc.
88 Post Road West, Westport, Connecticut 06881

Printed in the United States of America

The paper used in this book complies with the
Permanent Paper Standard issued by the National
Information Standards Organization (Z39.48-1984).

10 9 8 7 6 5 4 3 2 1

Contents

Preface

Antislavery sentiment in America - a sentiment that crystallized into a distinctive movement after 1830 - has been the object of a remarkable amount of scholarly inquiry. Two factors, perhaps, help to explain the lure of antislavery study. First, that the Civil War continues to be viewed not only as the watershed of American history but also as a conflict rooted in (if not caused by) the presence of slavery lends a particular significance to the story of opposition to that institution. In the process of tracing the origins and development of organized antislavery, questions arise regarding the motivations and goals of those involved and the actual relationship of their actions to the coming of the war. Second, the study of this most prominent of antebellum reforms ultimately raises issues beyond the specific topic, but central to interpreting our past: the dynamics of reform in America, the methodologies of change and their relationship to the American political system, and the psychology of the reformers themselves.

As they have sought to gain insight into the mind, spirit, and endurance of the antislavery movement, historians seemingly have left no sources untouched. However, the songs that were written and performed by the participants in the cause have received relatively little attention; indeed almost none, save the inclusion of a few in collections of "protest" or other reform songs. Most likely, the assumption has been either that the songs are too few in number to justify the effort or that, regardless of their number, they are not viable sources. As the present collection illustrates, neither idea is accurate. Rather, antislavery songs constitute a body of work surprisingly large in proportion and revealing in scope.

The manner in which this project was undertaken and finally completed is reflected in my attention to both words and music. The search for songs was begun in 1977 in the course of graduate work in musicology and resulted in a M. A. thesis on the function of music in the American antislavery movement. At that time, my interest was as much the social dynamics and uses of music as the actual content of the songs; many of my findings are incorporated into the Introduction. Until recently the hundreds of songs I collected had been shelved; from Missouri to New York, largely unused and unusable, they gathered dust while I pursued training and a career as an historian of American intellectual and cultural history. In 1985 I reopened the notebooks containing the songs and completed the search through periodicals. Having gained a heightened awareness of words as well as music and a greater appreciation for the potential value of these documents to a variety of readers, I decided to publish them.

In spite of my broadened perspective (or because of it) many difficult decisions were involved in preparing this collection for maximum utility. The term "song" itself is a problematic one, since "song" and "poem" often were interchangeable in the era under consideration. The attempt has been to distinguish between the two, reproduce only the former, and err on the side of inclusion in cases of lingering doubt. Obviously antislavery poems are also valuable sources, but to intersperse them would confuse a major issue here: singing for social reform. Therefore, this compilation contains only songs printed with music, lyrics with designated tunes, and/or lyrics otherwise indicating they were actually sung or intended for singing. (For example, most of the songs in the pamphlet, Songs of the Free, and Hymns of Christian Freedom, [Boston: Isaac Knapp, 1836] were excluded, since no mention of tunes or singing appears. Only those poems in the collection that were set to music or recorded in the periodicals as having been sung are included.) A minimum of one verse was the criterion for the lyrics to be considered a "song," and an attempt was made to match isolated titles or lines mentioned in periodicals to the lyrics collected and include that mention in the footnotes. Further, although undoubtedly the largest single collection of antislavery songs to date, this volume is not intended to be definitive. No attempt was made to include antislavery songs that may appear in other types of song books, primary or secondary, or those few in broadsheet form in various archive collections. Rather, this book contains lyrics from antislavery songsters and periodicals only.

More challenging was the task of organizing the songs in a way historically meaningful as well as simply referential. Either a strictly alphabetical or chronological order was rejected in favor of a topical arrangement. The six sections, each preceded by a brief introduction, represent six variations of antislavery thought and activity and follow a

rough chronology overall, from the colonization effort to the
end of the Civil War.   Within each section the songs are
chronological from year to year, the dating of each song being
its earliest appearance in print. Cases of multiple songs for
a given year presented special problems; the rule was to
maintain chronology whenever possible (when all songs of that
year are from dated periodicals), but to arrange   them
alphabetically by first line in the event of mixed sources
(periodicals and songbooks).   It   is   hoped   that   any
inadequacies resulting from these choices are balanced by the
several indices.

    The songs are numbered consecutively throughout the book
and these numbers, not pages, are used for reference in the
section introductions and the indices. Each set of lyrics is
preceded by information from its first printing: title; when
and where sung, if known (often paraphrased, but as close to
the original as possible); and accompanying or specified tune.
In the few instances where tunes appear to have been composed
specifically for the lyrics rather than borrowed, the word
"original" is used and the composer's name is given. The word
"unidentified" refers to cases in which the lyrics were set to
music in the original, but the tune remains unknown to me (and
to the few authorities I consulted). The author's name is
listed even if the information was gleaned from a later
source.

    Excepting the indentation of lines, use of quotation
marks, and apparent printing errors, the policy was to avoid
standardization in the interest of retaining the sense of the
primary sources and their era. Thus original punctuation,
spelling, and variants of names of authors and tunes have been
duplicated exactly.   In the case of line and verse-chorus
format, the main concern, due to the absence here of printed
music, was to represent accurately the tune or type of tune.
For this reason an "etc." in the original occasionally is
spelled out to clarify the actual lines or sections intended
for repetition.   Conversely, in instances of simple
alternation of verse and chorus the word "chorus" has been
substituted for those lyrics provided they did not change.

    Sources are listed chronologically following each song,
with separate notes used to indicate variations in lyrics,
titles, or tunes. The few notes designated by asterisks are
editorial, as is anything in brackets. In the latter case,
tune names surrounded by brackets are those that have been
identified from actual music accompanying the lyrics, while
those in brackets and followed by a "?" indicate that in the
absence of music, the meter of the lyrics or other information
has been used to make an educated guess as to the tune.

In the eleven years since I began this project many people at many institutions have been of invaluable assistance in locating and obtaining sources and I wish to extend my thanks to them: the Boston Public Library; the Herrick Library of Alfred University (especially Linda Hardy, Trevor Jones, Pamela Lakin, and Mattie Lounsberry); the Library of Congress; the Missouri Historical Society; the Oberlin College Library (especially Mary E. Cowles and Herbert F. Johnson [1977-1979], and Dina Schoonmaker [1987]); the Ohio Historical Society; and the Olin Library and the Gaylord Music Library, both of Washington University in St. Louis.

Of the individuals who have shared their information, time, and support, I would like to thank in particular Walter Coffey, Elizabeth Craven, Peggy Nicholson, Carol Pemberton, Norma L. Peterson, Patrick Railsback, Norris F. Schneider, Deborah Van Broekhoven, and Jo Vermeulen. In addition, I am most grateful to Marilyn Brownstein of Greenwood Press for her patience and her faith in this endeavor, and to Barbara Sanford and Michelle Hendrickson for their remarkably accurate and conscientious typing and proofreading, respectively. To my colleagues in the Division of Human Studies at Alfred University I can say only that I have felt fortunate to count them as friends as well as co-workers in the past four years. I am fortunate as well in having parents who are constantly understanding and supportive. My debt to them, Warren and Josie Eaklor, extends far beyond either the scope of this book or words I can summon to thank them.

Introduction

The songs of antislavery, like all songs, are comprised of two elements with two distinct histories: words and music. Those particular histories converged at a moment in the American experience in which the meaning of "America" itself was as yet unclear. That the nation constituted some sort of grand experiment was understood, but equally understood was the historical lesson that experiments often fail. Within this climate of uncertainty emerged both the debate over slavery and a number of self-conscious efforts at creating an "American" identity through artistic expression. The songs in this volume - words and music - reflect that mood, that debate, and those efforts. Their capacity to reveal the processes of our past to us ultimately depends upon our capacity to grapple with the various contexts in which they were created; those contexts are the subject of this essay.

I. Antislavery in America

The American antislavery movement, although commonly associated with the three decades preceding the Civil War, did not begin in 1830, nor did its principles disappear after 1865. What developed after 1830 was a different kind of antislavery, known as abolitionism, which in turn fostered a variety of responses within and outside the "movement."[1]

Paradoxically, an ideology featuring liberty and equality developed against the background of slavery as a system of labor in the British North American colonies.[2] By the end of the seventeenth century, all of the colonies legally recognized slavery and as the American Revolution began, slaves composed about one-fifth of the colonial population.

Slavery was, then, a real situation for a substantial segment of the society, but it also became an important symbol for any kind of tyranny, oppression, or denial of "natural rights." As a result, those who opposed it did so for reasons as diverse as the meanings of slavery itself.

Apparently Quakers were the first group to organize against slavery, founding, in Philadelphia in 1775, the first society devoted exclusively to abolishing the institution. The preceding year the Virginia Convention had refused to approve an antislavery clause included by Thomas Jefferson in his instructions to the Virginia delegates to the Continental Congress. As Jefferson drafted the Declaration of Independence, he composed a passage that condemned George III for vetoing colonial acts against the slave trade, but it was eventually omitted due to Southern opposition. Even as the colonists went to war with Great Britain, receptivity toward antislavery measures was falling along sectional lines.[3]

As the new country attempted to establish a government, sectionalism became more apparent. Again, Jefferson attempted to stifle the system in an ordinance he drafted in 1784, by which slavery would have been excluded from all Western territories after 1800. The measure lost by one vote, but was the forerunner of the Northwest Ordinance of 1787, which barred slavery from the area north of the Ohio River.

Concessions and compromises are apparent in the ambiguous nature of the Constitution on the subject, and the question often is raised as to the lack of a firmer stand on the part of the authors. The answer, perhaps, is fourfold. First, Southerners comprised a powerful delegation at the Constitutional Convention and to alienate them might have meant, if not the failure of the Convention, a more prolonged struggle. Second, the centrality of property rights in the colonists' ideology and third, a certain amount of racism, both undoubtedly played important roles in the overall attitudes toward slavery and blacks. Finally, as later argued, some Constitutional delegates may have regarded slavery, because economically and/or ideologically unsound, already doomed to extinction. Whether any or all of these reasons reflect the reality of the time, the document's ambiguity did contribute to the development of the "higher law" doctrine later espoused by abolitionists. This view essentially held that above and beyond the Constitution was a set of ideals, from a divine source and symbolized by the Declaration of Independence, which represented the true foundation and heritage of the United States; a "higher law" than the Constitution, or in fact any temporal law. At any rate slavery, although alluded to, is not mentioned by name in the Constitution. The intentions of the drafters, thus left open to debate, eventually became a source of contention between not only pro- and antislavery advocates but among abolitionists themselves.

By 1808, the year that the African slave trade was closed, every Northern state either had abolished slavery or had taken steps toward gradual abolition, but no Southern state had done so. In fact, there were no manumission societies in the South outside the border states, a situation which stimulated the Northern migration of antislavery Southerners throughout the antebellum period. Several, such as Samuel Doak, Edward Coles, Levi Coffin, Sarah and Angelina Grimké, and James G. Birney, would become important leaders of the later movement.

Between the end of this first phase of strong opposition to slavery and the abolitionism of the 1830s were two decades memorable more for frontier expansion and a second war with Great Britain than agitation over slavery. It was during this time that some antislavery (and anti-black) sentiment was funneled into the movement to resettle free blacks in the African colony of Liberia. Founded in 1817, the American Society for the Colonization of the Free People of Color in the United States, better known as the American Colonization Society, had the support of such eminents as John Marshall, James Monroe, Daniel Webster, and Henry Clay. The motives of the founders and supporters will never be known completely, but its critics, then and since, have detected an undercurrent of racism fostering a fear of a growing "inferior" population whose place in American society was undefined and unstable. The significance of the movement lay in its ability to absorb temporarily proslavery sentiments as well as genuine humanitarian and antislavery impulses. Colonization could be espoused as easily as rejected by either side at this time because it was open to interpretation as either a step toward emancipation or as the removal of a population both potentially rebellious and threatening to the survival of slavery. (Indeed, Southern fears were realized when in 1822 free black Denmark Vesey organized an abortive slave insurrection in Charleston, South Carolina.) After 1830 abolitionists, both black and white, vehemently opposed colonization, but the American Colonization Society survived and continued to serve as a median between the extremes of immediatism and "positive good" proslavery.

Although the decade of the 1820s can be characterized largely by the colonization effort, it also opened with an important sectional crisis that foreshadowed the predominance of the free soil issue in political antislavery. Missouri, a slave state, threatened to upset the eleven-eleven balance of free and slave states by applying for admission to the Union. The agreement known as the Missouri Compromise was reached when Maine, a free state, entered the Union with Missouri, and slavery was prohibited above the parallel 36° 30' in the remainder of the Louisiana Territory. In an often-quoted passage, Thomas Jefferson prophetically described the implications of this Compromise when he wrote to Massachusetts Congressman John Holmes in April of 1820 that

> . . . this momentous question, like a
> fire-bell in the night, awakened and filled me with
> terror. I considered it at once as the knell of the
> Union. It is hushed, indeed, for the moment. But
> this is a reprieve only, not a final sentence.[4]

Economic growth, improved methods of transportation and communication, and the beginnings of social reform also characterized the 1820s. Ironically, developments that could have united the nation helped divide it. Economic expansion in the North meant industrialization while in the South it was represented by increased agricultural production. Textiles, the foremost Northern industry, was dependent on cotton from the deep South, a situation which created at least one source of Northern anti-abolition sentiment. Meanwhile, newspapers increased in number and diversity, and early abolitionists were quick to adopt this means of mass communication; the Emancipator, the Abolition Intelligencer, and the Patriot all were founded in the 1820s by border states abolitionists. In 1821 Benjamin Lundy began printing the Genius of Universal Emancipation in Ohio and in 1828 hired as assistant editor in Baltimore a young man named William Lloyd Garrison. Despite the emergence of an abolitionist press and the precedent for organization set by such groups as the American Tract Society and the Temperance Union, antislavery societies were relatively insignificant at this time. Much more vital in shaping the ideology, methods, and enthusiasm of the impending abolition movement was the development of revivalism.

Evangelical Protestantism, or revivalism, swept the frontier both North and South in the early nineteenth century in successive waves collectively called the Second Great Awakening. The outstanding figure of the movement, Charles Grandison Finney, numbered among his "students" several future abolitionist leaders: Samuel J. May, Amos A. Phelps, Joshua Leavitt, Stephen S. Foster, and Theodore D. Weld. Emphasizing a personal relationship with God that began with "conversion" (the sudden revelation of seeing oneself a sinner and desiring repentance), this form of Christianity fostered in its converts attitudes toward morality and sin that would lie at the heart of the abolitionism of the 1830s and after.

On January 1, 1831, William Lloyd Garrison published the first issue of the Liberator and his front-page statement "To the Public" best typifies the urgent spirit of the new phase of antislavery:

> I am aware, that many object to the severity of
> my language; but is there not cause for severity?   I
> <u>will be</u> as harsh as truth, and as uncompromising   as
> justice. On this subject, I do not wish to think, or
> speak, or write, with moderation. No! no! . . .
> I am in earnest - I will not equivocate - I will not
> excuse - I will not retreat a single inch - AND I
> WILL BE HEARD.

Seven months later black preacher Nat Turner led about seventy
followers   in   Virgina   in   the   most   famous   of   slave
insurrections. Although there   had   been   antislavery   before
Garrison   and   rebellions   before   Turner,   tensions   now were
building sufficiently on both sides of the slavery question to
meet   each   action with increasingly violent reaction.   To the
South, its "peculiar institution"   seemed   threatened   indeed,
and   what   resulted   in the 1830s was a sweeping violation, by
anti-abolitionists North as well as   South,   of   many   of   the
civil liberties cherished by Americans.

The   responses   to   these   conditions,   however,   were
characterized   in   the   1830s   by   the   effort to work outside
rather than inside the political system; this would   remain   a
hallmark   of   abolitionism.   In   1832   the   New   England
Anti-Slavery Society was   founded,   and   by   the   end   of   the
following   year   the   American   Anti-Slavery   Society had been
formed in Philadelphia.   In   the   interim   Great   Britain   had
liberated   the slaves in its West Indian possessions, and this
act, effective August 1, 1833, added impetus to   the   American
movement.   These   early   organizations, and many that were to
follow, dedicated themselves to   new   and   radical   principles
that   would   distinguish   post-1830   "abolitionism"   from more
general "antislavery":   immediate emancipation, a rejection of
colonization, and civil rights for blacks.   In the doctrine of
immediate emancipation, or "gradual   emancipation   immediately
begun,"   is   the   influence   of   revivalism most apparent.   To
abolitionists, the first   step   was   a   series   of   individual
"conversions"   to the idea that slavery was a sin, after which
those believers would necessarily work to eradicate it as soon
as possible.   This concept was summarized concisely by William
Lloyd Garrison   when,   in   his   declaration   written   for   the
American   Anti-Slavery   Society,   he wrote, "We shall spare no
exertions nor means   to   bring   the   whole   nation   to   speedy
repentance."

The organization and methods of   abolitionism   also   were
derived largely from evangelism.   Traveling agents, whose task
was to establish local societies affiliated   with   the   parent
group   in   New   York,   were   at   the   heart   of   the   American
Anti-Slavery Society.   Their   effort   to   "spread   the   word,"
however,   both   verbally and in written tracts, often met with
violent opposition - an opposition which   in   turn   stimulated
involvement   in   the   movement by increasing numbers with ever
more diverse fears and goals.

The rights of free speech and free press became intricately involved with the slavery question in the mid-1830s. In the South a mob in Charleston broke into the post office in 1835 and burned a large quantity of abolitionist literature. Less violent censorship of the mail was practiced widely in the South until the War, despite an 1836 federal law that forbade such tampering. Anti-abolition mobs in the North destroyed presses and disrupted meetings in Boston, Utica, New York City, and Cincinnati. In 1837 abolitionist editor Elijah P. Lovejoy was killed in Alton, Illinois by a mob seeking to destory his press. If antislavery lost a mouthpiece with his death, it gained something even more valuable: its first martyr.

Academic freedom also was challenged in this period. Prudence Crandall of Canterbury, Connecticut admitted a black child to her girls' school in 1833 and touched off a series of events which ended in her arrest. Once released from prison, she reopened her school and was met with mob violence. A year later the students at Lane Theological Seminary, under the direction of Theodore Weld, held the "Lane Debates," a series of speeches and prayers which culminated in the rejection of colonization and endorsement of immediatism. Shortly thereafter, concerned trustees forbade any discussion of the subject and ordered that the newly-formed antislavery society be disbanded. Nearly the entire student body withdrew and came to form the core of Oberlin College.

Antislavery again crept into the halls of Congress at this time, but the topic would be stifled until the following decade. The abolitionists conducted nationwide petition campaigns in an attempt to force congressional discussion of slavery. The House of Representatives responded by passing a "gag rule" in 1836 that automatically tabled any antislavery petition - a rule not repealed until 1844. Thus Congress (the Senate already had tabled the subject) chose to ignore the issue at the time but in so doing probably alienated Americans concerned with civil liberties if not the plight of slaves.

In fact, it was most likely the association of the abolitionists' methods with the Constitutional rights of all citizens, more than any real sympathy with their message, that rendered their cause increasingly "popular" or at least visible in the 1830s. Even those who despised the abolitionists themselves or disagreed with their purpose began to question the implications of suppressing discussion and denying rights simply because the subject was controversial. By the close of the decade, even as abolitionists were arguing among themselves, many Northerners began to see the issue in these terms. These considerations would determine the subsequent directions of American antislavery.

If the 1830s was a time of violence and violation of
rights, the 1840s was characterized by division and diffusion
within the movement. The two main political parties, the
Democrats and the Whigs, and two prominent churches, the
Methodist and Baptist, each split over the question of slavery
(the Presbyterian Church had split in 1838, partly over
slavery). The political division was not formal, as in the
case of the churches, but new political parties did emerge and
served to complicate the situation further.

One of the first to feel the effects of dissension,
however, was not a political or religious institution, but the
American Anti-Slavery Society itself. Garrison had been
leading a faction which favored the incorporation of women's
rights into the abolition movement while Theodore Weld and his
followers opposed the idea. The latter group claimed that
abolitionism would be more effective if devoted to that single
topic. It is also probable that women's rights was a subject
even more controversial than slavery and hence viewed as
potentially destructive to the movement. The conflict came to
a head when Garrison nominated Abby Kelly for a seat on the
Executive Committee at the 1840 convention; upon Kelly's
election, the non-Garrisonians left and shortly thereafter
formed the American and Foreign Anti-Slavery Society. The
American Anti-Slavery Society retained its original name and
policies until after the Civil War; advocates of women's
rights would create a voice not only there but in an
increasingly visible separate movement.

Also in 1840 a national antislavery convention was called
in Albany, New York. Here the Liberty Party was formed,
naming James G. Birney as its presidential candidate for that
year; thus was political antislavery born. The significance
of the new party lay less in the number of votes it polled
than in serving to force the issue of antislavery irrevocably
into national politics. After the election of 1844, in which
Birney again ran for the Liberty Party and probably drew
enough votes in New York to cause Polk to be elected, the two
major parties recognized that the topic of slavery could no
longer be ignored. At the same time, these elections taught
the reformers that future success depended on expanding their
platform and defining their position constitutionally.

Just as the pro- and antislavery factions were divided
over the constitutionality of slavery, so were antislavery
supporters themselves. Garrisonians (like the Southerners,
ironically) took the stand that the Constitution did indeed
uphold slavery, basing their reasoning on the three-fifths
clause (Art. I, Sec. 2) and those that accord Congress the
power to suppress insurrections (Art. I, Sec. 8) and provide
for the interstate return of fugitives (Art. IV, Sec. 2).
Even that section implicitly concerning the African slave
trade (Art. I, Sec. 9), they argued, merely protected the
trade until 1808 rather than guaranteeing its abolition.

These passages led the Garrisonians to repudiate the Constitution and thus emphasize the radical nature of their stance.

Political abolitionists, on the other hand, utilized the constitutional powers of Congress over the territories, new states (Art. IV, Sec. 3), and the District of Columbia (Art. I, Sec. 8) to develop a rationale that not only aligned the Constitution with their position, but also later became the basis of the Republican Party's program. Their interpretation called for separating the federal government from slavery: first, slavery was to be confined to states where it already existed, and then excluded or eliminated from areas expressly under congressional jurisdiction.

Events of the 1840s served to crystallize this position. When Texas, an independent republic since 1836, joined the Union as a slave state in 1845, tensions both foreign and domestic were exacerbated. The following year the United States entered a territorial war with Mexico and shortly thereafter President Polk requested a bill for funds to purchase the disputed land. When Representative David Wilmot added an amendment excluding slavery from any such territory, a debate ensued that eventually only another war would resolve.

The Wilmot Proviso may have been defeated but the United States was not, and upon the end of the war in 1848, "free soil" emerged as the central issue in American politics for the next decade. Prior to that year's presidential election "Barnburner" Democrats, "Conscience" Whigs and Liberty Party members met in Buffalo and created the Free Soil Party, a new antislavery coalition devoted to excluding slavery from new territories and states. The election went to Whig Zachary Taylor but votes for Free Soil candidate Martin Van Buren, like those for Birney four years earlier, acted as an important barometer of public opinion. Within a decade the new Republican party would incorporate the moderate antislavery of the Free Soilers in its platform, thereby signalling its "arrival" within the two-party system. The moral crusade had not disappeared in the wake of political antislavery, but for the time being, emancipation and black rights were overshadowed by the power of "free soil, free speech, free labor, free men" to absorb a variety of Northern fears.

As the 1850s began, however, opponents of slavery on moral grounds had another chance to add action to rhetoric and gain more converts in the process. Of the several provisions of the Compromise of 1850, which included California's entrance into the Union as a free state, the prohibition of the slave trade in the District of Columbia, and popular sovereignty in New Mexico and Utah, the new Fugitive Slave Law proved to be the most controversial. A stronger version of the law of 1793, this ordinance required every citizen to aid in the capture and return of fugitive slaves and imposed severe penalties to fugitive and abettor alike. Rather than stifling the activities of the legendary "underground railroad" to the North and Canada, though, this law only proved to be counterproductive to its intent. The efforts of black and white abolitionists to assist runaways, now acquiring an heroic dimension in the face of even greater penalities, received open approbation and stimulated calls for civil disobedience. Individuals and states responded, some of the latter passing personal liberty laws in direct defiance of a government perceived to be controlled by a "Slave Power." Into this atmosphere came Uncle Tom's Cabin which, as it unfolded in serial form from 1851 to 1852, provided Northern imaginations with characters and scenes vivid enough to personify a formerly abstract evil, conventional enough to be widely recognized, and symbolic enough to mediate between the personal and political.

Against this backdrop of heightened emotions - sentiment, anger, fervor on both sides - the debate over "free soil" not only continued but produced violence in the 1850s. When Congress passed the Kansas-Nebraska Act in 1854, repealing the Missouri Compromise and establishing popular sovereignty in those territories, both pro- and antislavery factions sought to secure themselves in Kansas. After a proslavery group sacked the town of Lawrence, John Brown and a few followers murdered five proslavery men in what became known as the Pottawatomie Massacre. Only days before this, Senator Charles Sumner of Massachusetts had been beaten on the floor of the Senate by Representative Preston Brooks of South Carolina, in reaction to Sumner's speech on "The Crime Against Kansas." If these events were not enough to create paranoia on both sides, the Dred Scott decision of 1857, an apparent capitulation to the "Slave Power," intensified Northern apprehensions. Conversely, John Brown's martyrdom, after his attempt in 1859 to arm slaves and incite insurrection, further convinced the South of Northern hostility. From the perspective of these actions and ideas, and those of the thirty years preceding them, perhaps it is less surprising that eleven slave states eventually left the Union in reaction to a Republican presidential victory in 1860 than that it took so long for the secession - and the disaster that followed - to occur.

The war that erupted in the spring of 1861 did not immediately render abolitionism obsolete. As the North mobilized to repair the Union, antislavery agitators recognized that their campaign was not to be relinquished to the battlefield. Notable is the persistence of the abolitionists in their original arguments and activities throughout the conflict, until their goal was accomplished in the Southern defeat and the subsequent adoption of the Thirteenth Amendment. After 1865 something of the spirit and breadth of early abolitionism continued to manifest itself in

the work of individuals who turned their attention to the
freed blacks. The movement to abolish slavery in the United
States was over, but the struggle for human rights was not.

II. Singing for Emancipation

As religious and moral reformers began to transform
antislavery sentiment into an organized movement in the early
1830s they utilized every means available for spreading their
message. Music was central to the purpose. In order to
understand fully why and how abolitionists used music, they
must be considered in the context of their own goals as well
as that of contemporary musical thought and practice.

Why Sing?

In the preface to the first edition of his antislavery
song collection The Liberty Minstrel (1844, [iii]) composer
and compiler George W. Clark wrote:

> All creation is musical - all nature speaks the
> language of song. . . . That music is capable of
> accomplishing vast good, and that it is a source of
> the most elevated and refined enjoyment when rightly
> cultivated and practised [sic], no one who
> understands its power or has observed its effects,
> will for a moment deny. . . . Who does not
> desire to see the day when music in this country,
> cultivated and practised [sic] by ALL - music of a
> chaste, refined and elevated style, shall go forth
> with its angel voice, like a spirit of love upon the
> wind, exerting upon all classes of society a rich
> and healthful moral influence. When its wonderful
> power shall be made to subserve every righteous
> cause - to aid every human effort for the promotion
> of man's social, civil and religious well-being.

Music, to Clark, was a truly "natural" adjunct to moral and
social reforms because of powers considered intrinsic to it.
Similarly, another sympathizer to the cause wrote to the
Liberator, "Music has charms, and is irresistable [sic] to all
the finer feelings of our nature."[5] Among these "finer
feelings" was the desire for freedom, and music, it was
assumed, not only could appeal to this quality but forward its
cause as well. "Music has ever been the handmaid of Liberty,"
declared Clark in the preface to The Free Soil Minstrel (1848,
[iii]) and he went on to say that

> . . . now, when the spirit of '76 is abroad,
> kindling in thousands of hearts the determination to
> stand or fall for the Right and the True, the

emotions thus awakened gush forth as naturally in
song, as the morning orisons of the lark, who soars
up in the sunshine like a thing of light and melody.

If such ideas - that music has the power to convey moral
principles, especially that of freedom - help to explain the
abolitionists' advocacy of its use, even more so does the
notion that music was more effective than other means. As the
movement began, "A Delighted Listener" who had attended a
concert of the Garrison Juvenile Choir (of black children)
wrote, "I do sincerely believe that a concert of that kind,
will do more towards curing people of prejudice, and
consequently of Colonizationism, than the best sermon which
the most able orator could give."[6]   A decade later the same
sentiments were expressed by one who responded to a
performance by writing, "Speechifying, even of the better
sort, did less to interest, purify and subdue minds, than this
irresistible anti-slavery music."[7]

A variation of the idea that song had a greater effect
than oration on listeners was that there were some who could
contribute more to the cause if they sang rather than spoke.
Compiler Jairus Lincoln, for example, asserted that "There are
many who have not the gift of speech-making, but who can, by
song-singing, make strong appeals, in behalf of the slave, to
every community and to every heart."[8]   In a like spirit, but
for a different and revealing reason, free black abolitionist
Joshua Simpson explained:

As soon as I could write, which was not until I was
past twenty-one years old, a spirit of poetry,
(which was always in me,) became revived, and seemed
to waft before my mind horrid pictures of the
condition of my people, and something seemed to say,
"Write and sing about it - you can sing what would
be death to speak." So I began to write and sing.[9]

Although speech, in the form of sermons and lectures,
sometimes was considered less influential than music, such was
not necessarily the case with poetry. Rather, the
abolitionists considered poetry a form of expression not only
more sublime than prose, but usually on the same plane with
music. A volume of John G. Whittier's poetry prompted the
remark that "it is the singing [reciting, in this sense] of
great deeds which more than any thing else, excites to
others," and poet-reformer Maria Weston Chapman once stated,
"In reading and singing hymns of triumph and martyrdom, our
minds receive a general idea of something high and
heroic."[10] Garrison himself felt strongly enough to offer a
resolution at a meeting of the Massachusetts Anti-Slavery
Society to the effect that " . . . anti-slavery has
rejoiced, from the beginning, in the aid of poetry, which is
naturally and instinctively on the side of liberty, - it being
impossible, in the providence of God, that Poetry should ever

stoop her wing to the accursed service of slavery . . ." and he went on to say that "Humanity exults and rejoices in her other natural ally, <u>Music</u> . . ."[11] In so doing he reflected the idea, expressed repeatedly by other abolitionists, of a kinship between the two forms. From this it is but a short and logical step to the concept that together they are more powerful than is each alone. The "spontaneous, original, native power, [of] the combined effect of poetry and song" was mentioned, for example, as was the feeling that "Much, very much does righteous sentiment, joined to appropriate music, move mankind to action."[12]

The abolitionists' assumptions that appropriate music and poetry not only could, but should, serve humans in their quest for "righteousness" places them squarely within the mainstream of antebellum musical thought and practice. Thus they become an important group for a complete consideration of that topic while, conversely, an understanding of that musical culture helps to explain the amount and type of attention to music on the part of abolitionists.

That music possesses certain "natural" powers and functions as a language had been a presumption of Western thought undergoing periodic revival since the time of ancient Greece. In the nineteenth century musical discussions on both sides of the Atlantic focused again on this concept on several levels, providing a basis for developments as diverse as the "purity" of Romantic symphonic music (as the language of the soul) and the introduction of music into American public schools.

If there existed general agreement that music was a language, however, there was less so regarding its place in a hierarchy of languages. The New England Transcendentalists, like the European Romanticists, considered music the highest form of communication; as the "language of feeling" it superceded both prose and poetry and could best fulfill this function if not attached to words. Most American musical theorists, though, whether primarily "musicians" or "reformers," felt that the combination of poetry (the highest verbal language) and music was most powerful and hence most useful. Because the abolitionists, like their contemporaries in church music reform, music education, and the temperance movement, saw music's proper role to be a "handmaid" to moral and social goals, they too promoted the subservience of music to the purpose or message entailed in words.[13] Thus while instrumental music, particularly of bands, appears occasionally in antislavery records, it was less useful for the movement's goals and hence mention is negligible compared to that of singing.[14]

As important as the general notion that music should serve as a moral and social agent in nineteenth-century America was the promotion of both "appropriate" music and

universal   participation.   When   Clark   wrote   in   1844   of a
"chaste, refined and elevated style" of music "cultivated   and
practised   by   ALL,"   he   was   reiterating basic tenets of the
American musical thought of his day.   Church   music   reformers
like   Lowell Mason and Thomas Hastings earlier had spearheaded
a movement to return to   congregational   singing   in   the   New
England churches in reaction to the gradual relegation of this
Christian "duty" to separate choirs.   A concern for widespread
musical   participation   in church in turn formed the basis for
teaching children to sing in the common schools of the region.

In the cases of both church and school, then, all   within
the   institutions   were   encouraged   to sing due to the social
function prescribed for words and music together.   The content
and   "style"   of   each   song   component   continued   to undergo
careful scrutiny as reformers sought   to   maximize   the   moral
rewards of performance.

These principles - that music   is   a   language,   that   it
should   serve a purpose, and that the purpose should serve the
combined Christian and republican ideals of the nation   -   led
the   abolitionists   quite   naturally   to include song in their
arsenal of moral suasion weaponry.   Emerging as they did   from
the   Protestant   tradition,   nothing   was more obvious to them
than music's potential to uplift (and possibly   convert);   and
living   as   they   did   among   musical and social theorists who
sought the perfection of humanity, nothing   was   more   natural
than to utilize music to aid that process.

Occasions and Participants

Abolitionists specified not only why music should be used
for   their   purposes   but   when,   where and, in some cases, by
whom.   Clark, for instance, states in the preface   to   another
of his collections that

> The music in this volume is arranged as   solos,
> duetts,   trios,   quartettes,   choruses,   etc., etc.,
> adapted to use in the domestic   circle,   the   social
> gathering,   the   school,   the   club-room,   the mass-
> meeting, and in short, wherever music is   loved   and
> appreciated - Slavery abhorred,   and liberty held
> sacred.[15]

Similar instructions, though usually more general,   often   are
indicated   in   the   heading   information   for individual songs
printed in periodicals (see songs 1, 22, 108, e. g.), as   well
as   in   prefaces   or   notices   relative   to other collections.
William W. Brown's compilation, The Anti-Slavery   Harp   (1848)
is subtitled, A Collection of Songs for Anti-Slavery Meetings,
while   an   advertisement   for   Jairus   Lincoln's   Anti-Slavery
Melodies   (1843)   states,   "Many   of   the   hymns   are   written
expressly for the work, and are adapted expressly   for   social

meetings and anti-slavery festivals."[16] Intentions, however revealing they may be of the relative importance abolitionists placed on song, are less convincing than evidence of actual use. Fortunately, that evidence abounds in the pages of antislavery publications in the form of information attached to printed lyrics and accounts of antislavery meetings and other events.

Of the 492 songs in this volume, 122, or nearly one-fourth, specify that they indeed were sung at least once (see, e. g., songs 19, 167, 319). When this number is supplemented by information regarding the frequency with which singing is noted in antislavery records, the occasions at which songs were sung, and the people who sang them, the real as well as the prescribed use of music in the movement becomes clearer. Conversely, this same knowledge contributes to a more complete picture of antebellum musical thought and activity.

Meetings of various kinds were at the heart of radical antislavery, and most likely their primary function lay in boosting the morale of the abolitionists.[17] Conventions of local, state, and national organizations were held one to four times yearly and were opportunities for the reiteration of old goals and the discussion of new issues. In addition, there were periodic picnics, fairs, bazaars, and teas, all of which usually included music as part of the program of events. Careful, detailed, records of these gatherings were kept and usually printed, in the Liberator or other antislavery publications, or as separate monographs. Even a brief perusal of these immediately illustrates the place given music in the movement; mention is so frequent, in fact, that its absence is almost more noticeable than its presence.

Singing at antislavery meetings usually occurred after the opening prayer and/or immediately before adjournment.[18] Occasionally, however, records show that music was interspersed throughout the course of a meeting, as at the 1843 gathering of the Worcester County Anti-Slavery Society and that of the Norfolk County Anti-Slavery Society.[19] As stated previously, though, such citations often are vague: mention of "appropriate" hymns or songs, and those "adapted," "selected," or "composed for the occasion," appears, as does the performance of "anti-slavery hymns," "anti-slavery songs," and, sometimes, the antislavery song book used.[20]

More explicitly, titles or first lines are designated, as in these passages:

> . . . all united in singing [at a meeting of the Boston Female Anti-Slavery Society] "with spirit and understanding also," that well-known hymn, "Think of our country's glory All dimm'd with Afric's tears"[21]

Meeting [of the Rhode Island Anti-Slavery Society, 1843] opened by singing "I am an Abolitionist."[22]

The brothers Judson, John and Asa Hutchinson, sang the "Fugitive's Song." It was received with great applause [at a meeting of the Massachusetts Anti-Slavery Society].[23]

Occasions which might be termed "special" included music as regularly as did those discussed above. Rallies, for example, were periodic but less predictable opportunities for abolitionists to convene, elicited by such events as the capture and/or rescue of a fugitive slave, the death of a leader, or the visit of a prominent person (mourning songs can be found in both GET OFF THE TRACK! and AMERICAN UNION; songs of welcome are in GET OFF THE TRACK! and those about specific fugitive slaves can be found in AMERICAN UNION; see also the introductions for those sections and refer to the Subject Index for a complete list of occasions and persons relating to the songs). The two most notable of the special occasions, however, quickly took their place alongside the society meetings as regularly scheduled events for the reaffirmation of abolition: the fourth of July and the first of August.

Independence Day, being a commemoration of freedom, became a particularly convenient occasion for abolitionists to restate their purposes and simultaneously remind the nation that not all were free. In this respect, it was chosen as a day to compare the stated ideals of the nation, as expressed in the Declaration of Independence, with the real situation in the United States. The resulting gap was emphasized by the meetings themselves and in the many lyrics written for and sung on that occasion.[24] Records were kept of these meetings too, and in them music appears to play a role comparable to that in all other gatherings of abolitionists. Finally, one entire songbook, Hartley Wood's Anniversary Book of Music, is subtitled, for the Fourth of July, Temperance, and Anti-Slavery Occasions (Boston, 1843), a mixture revealing the mentality of an era that conceived of liberty as (the Preface states, p. [2]) "Freedom from Tyrany [sic], Alcohol and Slavery."

August 1, the anniversary of the emancipation of the slaves in the British West Indies, also served as occasion for comparing goals with reality. On this day abolitionists reminded each other, and the nation, that the British (ironically, the "oppressors" of the Revolution) were living up to the American ideal of freedom better than America itself. In this way citizens were challenged to follow the example set by Great Britain. Music, especially in the form of songs written for the event each year, again was an important part of the ceremonies.[25]

The occasions for the use of music were, then, any and all events which brought abolitionists together. In 1859, in fact, it could be stated that an afternoon meeting of the New England Colored Citizens' Convention was "opened by the customary prelude of singing."[26] Besides providing additional evidence of its importance within the movement, the pervasive use of music adds insight into its role at meetings and concerts. The purposes of song, like those of the gatherings themselves, were to reinforce the commitment of those in the movement and to convert listeners sympathetic enough to attend.

Corresponding to the individual reason for each singing occasion was the identity, number, and function of those who wrote and performed antislavery songs. As might be expected, the majority of those who penned and sang lyrics devoted to emancipation were reformers first and musicians second (if at all).[27] In this respect the influence of the abolitionists' religious background is apparent, since they borrowed directly from church practice their means of utilizing music: amateur soloists, choirs, and especially congregational singing. Further, many of those associated with antislavery music were involved in several capacities, ranging from compiling to composing and performing the music.

The cause did attract a few persons who could be considered professional or semi-professional musicians at the time, but their commitment to abolition clearly was no less than that of their many audiences. In the 1840s, brothers John, Judson, and Asa Hutchinson and their sister Abby began to tour the country singing the popular ballads and folk songs of their day. Another brother, Jesse, traveled with the troupe as manager, wrote lyrics to some of their songs (including Get Off the Track, song 255) and occasionally performed. A precedent had been set by European singing families touring the United States at this time, and the Hutchinsons and others after them capitalized on the popularity of such groups. In fact, they often were referred to as the "New Hampshire Rainers," after the family from the Tyrolean Alps, and included songs in their programs depicting the beauties and virtues of a pastoral life, as did their European counterparts.

Early in their career, the Hutchinsons espoused many of the reforms of their era, including temperance, women's rights, and especially abolition, and began including a few songs on these subjects in their programs for popular audiences. On these occasions, concerts for the public, antislavery songs possibly had the greatest chance of being heard by non-abolitionists and so could serve a truly propagandist function. In addition, the Hutchinsons adopted minstrel as well as folk tunes for these lyrics (a topic discussed more fully in part III), probably in an effort to maximize the appeal of the songs. Thus the original

Hutchinson Family (John and Asa each performed later with their own families) combined entertainment and purpose in a way not only consistent with assumptions already established in American musical culture, but also in a manner that set a significant precedent for "protest singers" since their time.[28]

In January of 1843, the Family, at the invitation of John A. Collins, sang at the Eleventh Annual Meeting of the Massachusetts Anti-Slavery Society and thereafter were in great demand as performers at similar functions. Soon they became the main attraction, or at least featured, at numerous antislavery gatherings of all kinds and on all geographic levels.[29] While their concerts were perhaps potentially more influential than appearances at meetings in spreading antislavery propaganda to non-abolitionists, boosting the morale of those already "converted" seemed to be the most vital utilization of performers and songs alike.

Another well known musician of the cause was George W. Clark, editor of three large song collections in which he not only set his own and others' poems to music of his selection, but also composed original music for lyrics.[30] That Clark was a singer as well as poet, compiler and composer is borne out by evidence of his performances at several antislavery meetings. A record of an 1855 meeting in Syracuse, New York, for example, states in part that "One good singer was there, Geo. W. Clark, who seems to have improved even upon himself, and greatly enlivened our Convention with his sweet and joyous music, in prediction of the improved condition of things "a hundred years hence."[31] Similarly, notice is given Clark's singing at the New England antislavery convention in Boston in 1860 at which, in addition to an "anti-slavery song," he "sang with much expression an appropriate song of progress."[32]

Just as Clark was involved in various phases of the production of antislavery music, so was the black abolitionist quoted previously, Joshua Simpson. A graduate of Oberlin College and free resident of Zanesville, Ohio, Simpson is unique in that he acted as author, rather than compiler, of all poetry in his three collections. As yet, he is the only person, black or white, known to have done so.[33] Further, he may be in fact the most prolific poet of the movement, as his antislavery works total fifty-five, forty of which are in this volume.[34] Among them, the largest number (twenty-three, in GONE, SOLD AND GONE) concern the evils of slavery, often from the slave's perspective; nearly half describe the activities of fugitive slaves and/or the legendary underground railroad. While these songs may offer a rare "insider's" view of contemporary events (Simpson probably was a "conductor" for the infamous railroad), the remainder of his songs are equally significant for the opposite reason: rather than singular they are truly representative of the movement and antislavery song writing as a whole, utilizing as they do every major rationale for opposing slavery. Finally, besides his contributions to the cause as poet and activist, he was known also to sing on occasion.[35]

Most other individuals, unlike Clark and Simpson, served the movement in a single capacity and of those, excepting figures like John G. Whittier, John Pierpont, or Maria W. Chapman, little or nothing is known of them. George W. Putnam, for example, author of four antislavery poems (see the Author Index), is reported to have sung an antislavery song at the twenty-third annual meeting of the Massachusetts Anti-Slavery Society, but is not mentioned elsewhere in either capacity.[36] Even less specifically, and more typically, the reader is told only that "Misses Fuller and Mr. Richardson" performed at a celebration of August 1 at Dedham (see songs 71, 156) and that "a young friend of the cause" sang "I am an Abolitionist" (song 240) at the annual gathering of the Worcester County Anti-Slavery Society.[37]

Mentioned more often than soloists at antislavery occasions are various groups or choirs which, like those of the church, presumably were drawn from the ranks of the believers. For that reason their identity, unless already achieved separately (as with the Hutchinsons), usually remains uncertain except for some special feature of their composition. A "Quartette Club," for example, sang at the annual convocation of the Massachusetts Anti-Slavery Society, while "Friends from Hingham" performed at several regional meetings. More commonly, records show that a convention opened with an antislavery song from "the friends of the cause," or that singing was done by a "volunteer choir," or just "a choir."[38] There exist also, however, several citations mentioning choirs consisting entirely of blacks or children. At one Independence Day celebration, "The music was performed principally by a colored choir, under the direction of Mr. Hill, and added much to the interest of the occasion," and a "juvenile choir" is noted in relation to at least two separate events.[39] Also, choirs consisting of black children gave concerts similar to those of the Hutchinson Family, in which an abolitionist song or two was interspersed with popular songs. An advertisement for such a program, by the Garrison Juvenile Choir, was printed in the Liberator and is reproduced below (emphasis indicates antislavery songs):

A JUVENILE CONCERT of the Colored Children,
constituting the Primary School, No. 6, under the
direction of Miss Susan Paul, will be given at
COLUMBIAN HALL on TUESDAY EVENING NEXT,
February 4, 1834, at 7 o'clock.

ORDER OF EXERCISES

Overture - Marseilles Hymn.
  PART I
1. Duet & Chorus - If Ever I See.
2. Chorus - In School We Learn.
3. Duet & Chorus - The Lark.
4. Duet & Chorus - Ye Who in Bondage Pine [song 39].
5. Duet & Chorus - Pleasures of Innocence.
6. Chorus - This, This is Our Home [song 5].
7. Solo & Chorus - Strike the Cymbal [song 231?].

  Grand Symphony

  PART II
1. Chorus - O Speed Thee, Speed Thee.
2. Recitative & Chorus - Suffer Little Children to
Come Unto Me.
3. Chorus - Little Wanderer's Song.
4. Chorus - The Little Weaver.
5. Solo & Chorus - Prayer for the Commonwealth.
6. Duet & Chorus - Good Night. [40]

Children, in fact, were considered a vital part of the
movement, and so a focus on them as real or potential
performers of antislavery music is much in keeping with the
tactics of these reformers. Two song collections used for
this volume were directed specifically or partially at youth:
John A. Collins' Anti-Slavery Picknick of 1842, "Intended for
Use in Schools and Anti-Slavery Meetings"; and H. S. Gilmore's
Collection of 1845, "for the Use of the Cincinnati High
School" (see the Bibliography for full citations). In light
of the contemporaneous public school movement and the use of
music therein, the preface to the former (p. [3]) seems an
appropriate summary of the many ideals and assumptions
specific to the time:

    This work is designed to interest the young in
the anti-slavery cause. . . . Every possible
effort should be made to secure their confidence and
enlist their sympathies.

    The corrupting influences of the age have
filled their minds, to a great extent, with strong
prejudices against the colored man. They naturally
love freedom and hate oppression, and their
unbiassed [sic] feelings instinctively lead them to
sympathise [sic] with the wronged and the outcast.

> The impressions of the nursery will, to a great
> extent, influence the mind through life. It should
> be our object, then, to encourage every movement
> which shall impress upon their minds the beauty of
> freedom, and the impolicy and wickedness of slavery.

Oddly, although women were vital to the antislavery
movement, often initiating the concern in their communities,
forming and retaining separate societies, and writing many of
the lyrics included here, there is little evidence of females
performing, singly or in groups.[41] At first glance, one
might assume this absence was in keeping with the polarization
of gender roles associated with the "domestic cult" then
developing. Closer inspection, though, reveals that
performing music in public, like teaching children, nursing,
and involvement in reform, was by no means proscribed for
women as long as it was perceived as an extension of their
"natural" role of moral guardian of the nation. Indeed
middle-class women not only were allowed, but at times
expected, to sing or play in their parlors music that would
uplift as well as entertain. That they were permitted to
carry this role outside the home is exemplified by the the
unprecedented promotion and acceptance in America of Jenny
Lind, the "Swedish Nightingale" who became wildly popular by
combining "proper" music with the image of virtuous womanhood
in her concerts.[42] Therefore it is somewhat surprising that
apparently few women served as singers as well as the more
questionable roles of speakers and organizers for the
movement.

Overall, it is safe to assume that the most common
performers of antislavery music were probably all those
attending the meetings, although there is relatively little
evidence to the effect. Just as the most frequent indication
of music is in general terms ("singing," "song," "hymn," etc.)
any persons involved usually are referred to simply as the
audience or congregation.[43] Again the influence of church
practice and the contemporaneous movement for more
congregational participation is evident, as is the premise
that, if only those practices out of the ordinary were worth
recording, songs were included more often than noted and
usually were sung by the entire assembly.

III. The Songs

Less than a month after the American Anti-Slavery Society
was formed in December of 1833, a poem by one James Scott
(song 17) appeared in the _Liberator_ with this preface:

At a late lecture on Slavery, in Pawtucket, Ray Potter, the Lecturer, remarked, that such had heretofore been the remissness of Christians on that subject, he knew not a single hymn adapted to the occasion. If the following will in any degree help to supply that defect, it is at the service of the pious friends of emancipation.[44]

Although Mr. Potter was not entirely correct about the complete lack of topical hymns at that time, his concern - and Scott's effort - are symbolic of the ideas and assumptions that lay behind the large number of antislavery songs written and sung in the antebellum period. These songs are as varied in ideas, approach, and style as the people of the movement, but like those people also, they had one purpose that superceded (if not transcended) individual differences: to end slavery in the United States. Thus the songs written against slavery are invaluable documents on the popular level, and as such are both representative and revealing of the movement, the era, and the ongoing development of the culture itself.

Words

At the time that Scott sent his "Hymn on Slavery" to editor William Lloyd Garrison, several such lyrics had been written and even sung; the Liberator already had included a few, and an occasional song could be found in the earlier Genius of Universal Emancipation and in colonization papers. By the end of the 1830s, however, some sixty additional songs (after Scott's) were in print. The total produced would increase drastically in the 1840s and then dwindle toward the end of the Civil War, following in rationale as well as number the patterns of change and conflict in antislavery agitation.[45]

That relatively few songs can be found before the early 1830s, for instance, corresponds with both the organization of a movement and the new ideals of that movement. After the abolitionists adopted the evangelical concept of immediatism and rejected the colonization of blacks in Liberia as a solution, antislavery songs changed topics as they increased in number. Although colonization was treated musically throughout the era, the songs are so few in number (twelve, in LIBERIA) that they are significant more for the general lack of attention to that subject, even in opposition to it, than for the words themselves.

Once the change to "abolition" was accomplished, at least two major argumentative bases were established and used consistently to convince others of the wrongness of slavery: Christianity and patriotism. In effect, slavery was posited as a sin and a national one at that. Owning human beings, the abolitionists declared, was a practice inconsistent with Christian principles of brotherhood and sisterhood as well as the most fundamental American principle of liberty. In a throwback to Puritan ideas, it was believed that God's punishment would be exacted not on individuals, but rather on the entire group, for allowing these transgressions to occur. By the nineteenth century, of course, the "group" in question was the United States, which had adopted a national ideology assuming a covenant with God to preserve freedom as a Christian as well as a classically liberal concept. Though the lyrics vary in emphasis upon religious and patriotic values, rarely can they be entirely separated, and the presence of both in the majority of songs reflects the prevailing "civil religion" of the period. The sections GOD AND LIBERTY and MY COUNTRY contain these rationale but not exclusively; they can be found throughout the other sections in this volume.

Indeed Christian morality, with or without reference to America, is the most pervasive theme and appears on several levels. When Scott's poem was published, it was still common simply to sing religious hymns at antislavery gatherings, a practice that continued throughout the period. Like Scott, though, others began to write new lyrics for known hymns which would emphasize slavery specifically but retain their religious tone. By 1836, the first collection of hymns specifically for use in the movement was compiled by Maria Weston Chapman and significantly titled, Songs of the Free, and Hymns of Christian Freedom. It included both general and antislavery hymns and reflects the evangelical origins of the abolitionists and the predominance of that mentality in the 1830s.

By 1840, however, mention of the cause and its goals was included in nearly every hymn, indicating a slight shift from the use of hymns to the penning of antislavery hymns. In that year, Freedom's Lyre: or, Psalms, Hymns, and Sacred Songs, for the Slave and His Friends was published, and the lyrics therein consist mainly of prayers - for slaves, slave-holders, and fellow abolitionists. Interestingly, in the preface to that collection (p. [iii]), Edwin F. Hatfield states that it "was undertaken, at the request of the Executive Committee of the American Anti-Slavery Society," and that "A work of this character has, for a long time, been called for, by those who have been accustomed to meet and pray for the Emancipation of the Slave." These remarks suggest that not only was Potter's (and Scott's) challenge taken seriously but also that demand was yet outstripping supply. Such would not be the case as the decade progressed.

To claim that the movement, or the United States, was transformed from "religious" to "secular" would be to oversimplify an important dynamic, and place the phenomenon in too early a period as well. True, "secular" songs begin to

appear in abundance in this decade, but this is more an
indication of the variations emerging in the movement than of
a simple change in values or arguments on the part of
Americans, abolitionists or otherwise. Radical abolition
based in evangelical Protestantism would continue, but by its
side arose political antislavery and its songs. With the
division of the movement itself in 1840, and the formation by
some of the Liberty Party in that year and the Free Soil Party
in 1848, came an outpouring of poetic effusions antislavery in
tenor but political in purpose. The year 1842 saw the
production of at least two collections, while in 1843 Jairus
Lincoln's Anti-Slavery Melodies was published because "The
abolitionists need now a larger book."46 In an effort to
meet an apparently insatiable demand, George W. Clark compiled
the first edition of his Liberty Minstrel in 1844, which went
through seven editions to 1848. In the latter year alone 101
songs appeared for the first time, most of them in collections
and most, not surprisingly, political in orientation. Even
then, black poet William Wells Brown introduced his own
compilation, The Anti-Slavery Harp, by saying (p. [3]):

> The demand of the public for a cheap
> Anti-Slavery Song-Book, containing Songs of a more
> recent composition, has induced me to collect
> together, and present to the public, the songs
> contained in this book. . . . the larger portion
> of these songs has never before been published; some
> have never been in print.

Slavery, of course, had become a national concern by that
time and the polarization of opinion on the subject was well
underway. The abolitionists were no more loved North or South
than they had been fifteen years earlier (that mobs disrupted
their efforts to meet is also recorded in song; see 114 and
401), but the cry of "free soil, free labor, free men," and
the fear of a "Slave Power" in Congress ready to curtail the
rights of all had combined to win more converts to
"antislavery." Here again the songs, in their lyrics, reflect
these developments and new concerns. In this case the vote,
if not replacing prayer as an answer, is clearly regarded as a
powerful tool for reform.

If antislavery, as represented in its songs, seems to
focus more on national figures and events after 1848, perhaps
it is more a reflection of the reverse: that the history of
the nation, as recorded in most textbooks from then to now, is
increasingly interwoven with that of antislavery. This
parallel gives many of the songs from 1848 to 1865 a broader
character, so that they seem simply to record the "important"
developments that led to war: the underground railroad that
went public after the Fugitive Slave Law in 1850, the
Kansas-Nebraska Act that resulted in "bleeding Kansas," the
Sumner-Brooks affair in the halls of Congress, the martyrdom
of John Brown, and the outbreak and conduct of the war itself.

These and other events are included in AMERICAN UNION. At the same time, though, abolitionists continued to meet separately to revitalize their commitments to each other (as seen in GET OFF THE TRACK!) and to voice both their abstract moral argument against slavery as a sin and their more concrete emphasis upon the slaves as brother and sister human beings, whose persons and families were violated continually under the system (the section GONE, SOLD AND GONE consists entirely of the latter rationale).

Songs may not be merely reflective of history already known, however. Viewed again with an interest in the dynamics as well as the "facts" of the past, they offer opportunities to surmise the origins and development of ideas and experiences which only later become part of a fixed picture. The image of American history itself, for example, is revealing as it unfolds through these lyrics. Here one sees that preoccupation with the revolutionary past and its heroes that became central to the American self-image by 1860. Here too is the merging of Pilgrims, Puritans, and rebels into one vague group - "Founders" - which telescopes all colonial history into a single experience and blurs distinctions even as it creates the myth that "freedom," especially of religion, was a goal of the country from the beginning. Finally, also apparent, in at least one case (song 340), is the confusion between the Declaration of Independence and the Constitution, in wording and hence actual function, reflecting the presence of a now common misconception about "equality" in the early republic.

In similar fashion, one must ask whether the rhetoric of family values on which the abolitionists capitalized was only effect or at least partial cause of the now famous nineteenth-century "domestic cult" and its attendant public/private dichotomy according to gender. These lyrics, several of which are directed at women, at times outline both implicitly and explicitly separate "spheres" of influence for men and women within the movement and tailor the argument accordingly. Especially prominent in this category are arguments that slave families were at stake and that slave mothers suffered when children were lost to them (as no doubt they did). On the one hand, this rhetoric reflects the importance of women to the movement generally and indicates early efforts at a consciousness of "sisterhood" among women black and white. On the other hand, they support the idea that females do (or should) have different concerns by appealing specifically to women as mothers in various contexts. To be sure, such values and role divisions predated the antislavery movement, but it is possible that these devices helped to reinforce an ongoing popular ideological evolution; in short, that the words acted as part of a process and not just as a mirror of inorganic concepts.[47]

Music

It is perhaps a surprising feature of this volume that, although it contains several indices for the reader's use, it does not include a listing of composers. This absence, rather than an oversight or product of fatigue, is significant in what it reflects about antislavery songs, their function, and the dynamics of antebellum musical culture. Of the lyrics herein only 39 are set to music probably written for the lyrics, and of those original tunes the vast majority (31) were composed by a single person, George W. Clark (see the Tune Index under "original"). A traditional interpretation would leap to a popular conclusion that this is yet more evidence of the "inferiority" of American music before the twentieth century; that few "good" composers existed at the time anyway and given that fact one could not expect these poets to be "musicians" too. These assumptions, whether true or false, fail to address either the purposes of the songs or the societal role of music in nineteenth-century America.

The adaptation of tunes already known for songs of persuasion was a practice already well established in the West by the nineteenth century. One need only recall the Protestant Reformation and its attendant hymnody, for example, to find antecedents of such borrowing. Even the Protestants were preceded in this by many "composers" of late medieval Church motets, who sometimes combined popular secular tunes (and lyrics!) with liturgical chant in the same piece. The goal, one must bear in mind, was not the originality that became a hallmark of nineteenth-century European Romantic thought but rather the conveying of certain ideas and images to a wide audience. Puritans in England and the colonies continued the tradition in the context of sacred music, as did the revivalists of both Awakenings who set Christian texts to folk melodies. By the mid-nineteenth century, according to one scholar, "any tune that appealed to the taste of the day, whatever its origin, was likely to be adapted for a hymn."[48] From this perspective, the abolitionists' efforts were part of a long tradition in Europe and America established by those who assumed that music, especially singing, was primarily a "handmaid" of religious reform. As the religious impulse was "secularized," or channeled into causes slightly more broad but still based in Christian-American morality, the musical ideas and uses followed.

This is not to say, however, that controversy did not arise, especially over what tunes were "appropriate" for various goals. As the culture became more self-conscious (in terms of both morality and identity), musical and social reformers alike were faced with a dilemma between the need for well-known tunes on the one hand and the "character" of those same tunes on the other. Increasingly, in fact, the more popular the tune, the more likely it was to possess associations (a powerful and pervasive concept at the time) unacceptable from the standpoint of the reformers' moral and musical assumptions. Songs of the theater, tavern, and later the minstrel show came under particular scrutiny as such people as church musicians and early music educators (often the same persons) discussed the relative effects of words and music on the minds of singers and listeners. Indeed even music of seemingly unspotted "character" was questioned at the time, as when Reverend Edward B. Kirk asserted that "'no part, or passage, of Handel's Messiah is sacred music.'"[49] In response George W. Lucas asked, "Now what makes music sacred?" and answered:

> Certainly nothing in its mechanical construction. This is plain to all. Nor does its connection with inspired language or sentiments; for these, as they often have been, may be perverted to mere amusement. . . . When consecrated to the service of the church and made the medium through which our pious and emotions flow, it is sacred, whatever may be the form of its notation. A musical performance is sacred or secular, according to its design, or purpose. . . . The use in divine praise of such tunes as Auld Lang Syne, &c. never have been objected to on the ground that when thus appropriated they were not sacred, but because they were associated with scenes which should not be remembered, especially in divine service.[50]

The controversy raged on during the era and was left largely unresolved, ultimately affecting realms outside church music.

The abolitionists' selection of tunes reflects the ongoing debate and attendant dilemma while also offering a valuable index to the musical taste of the day. Even taking into account the 61 tunes unidentified (most are hymns but the names are unknown to this editor and the authorities consulted), the very number of different melodies adapted for antislavery songs justifies a closer inspection, as does their range in origin and style. A consideration of only the four tunes used most often, for instance, reveals an eclecticism suggestive of both the musical life of the era and the needs and methods of the abolitionists. The patriotic America heads the list (twenty times), followed closely by Scots Wha Hae (or Bruce's Address, nineteen times), a Scottish folk tune. Next is none other than the somewhat sullied Auld Lang Syne (sixteen uses, three of them by Garrison) and in fourth place is the hardly questionable Missionary Hymn (or From Greenland's Icy Mountains, for nine songs) of Lowell Mason. A partial list of tunes used at least four times exhibits a similarly variegated pattern: Old Hundred (psalm tune); Old Granite State (itself adopting a revival melody); The Marseilles (French patriotic); Old Dan Tucker (minstrel); John Brown's Body (marching song from a revival hymn); Zion (hymn); Dandy Jim (minstrel).

On the most basic level, such a list can be considered a fairly accurate representation of the most popular tunes of antebellum America, since to utilize melodies already well known to first-time hearers would expedite the goal of conversion through participation. In short, the memorable tunes simply were more in line with the songs' propagandist function (and possibly that of morale-boosting as well) than were considerations of creativity.

Borrowed tunes can offer more than a general sense of popular culture in a given era, though. Not surprisingly, as taste in music changed over time so did the kinds of melodies thought useful for antislavery. Like the variations that emerged within antislavery after 1840, though, the newer tunes, like the newer arguments, represent less a supplanting of the old than a coexistence alongside it.

Among the cultural developments of the 1840s, perhaps none is more significant, in terms of questions raised, than the rise of minstrelsy. From the first appearance in 1843 of the Virginia Minstrels, a quartet in blackface, the minstrel show evolved into the most popular entertainment form of the entire century. The songs of the shows, written by white composers like Dan Emmett and Stephen Foster, contained elements of black culture in both words and music and, despite confusion regarding their "authenticity" (or due to it), they soon were incorporated into American popular culture and performed in a variety of contexts.[51]

Antislavery agitators were quick to capitalize upon the popularity of minstrelsy and its music even as they recognized it as a controversial act. Joshua Simpson, for example, explained that

> In offering my first little production to the public, I am well aware that many superstitious, prejudiced, and perhaps many good, conscientious well-meaning christians [sic] will have serious objections to the "Airs" to which my poetry is set. My object in my selection of tunes, is to kill the degrading influence of those comic Negro Songs, which are too common among our people, and change the flow of those sweet melodies into more appropriate and useful channels.[52]

Notable here is not just that Simpson, a free black, would use tunes that he considered to exert a "degrading influence" but especially his assumption that altering the "flow" of those tunes would destroy that influence. In a larger context, it becomes clearer that he did not mean a literal change in tempo or rhythm (though one example, not Simpson's, exists of this [song 447]) but rather that their association with new words would render them acceptable. He was proven correct, it seems, by both the relatively enormous popularity of the

antislavery song, <u>Get Off the Track!</u> which was set to the
tune, <u>Old Dan Tucker</u>, and the more famous example of words
adapted to a tavern song eventually becoming the American
national anthem.

The phenomenon of borrowing tunes - sacred, folk, and
popular - if lacking in originality did correspond perfectly
with the purposes of those who pictured a better world and
sought to use music to gain that end. Whatever the perceived
faults are of the abolitionists, as composers, poets, or
moralistic reformers, they clearly believed that change in
America could be effected by persuasion of an emotional and
rational nature; that if they wrote words and sang them to
other Americans they might bring about the end of slavery and
thus better fulfill the American dreams of liberty and
equality for "all." In the end war accomplished (in part) what
they could not through song, but one cannot help admire their
more pacifist, if naive, efforts.

NOTES

1. Many works on American antislavery have influenced
this study both generally and more specifically in the
introduction; please refer to the Bibliography for a complete
listing of sources.

2. This paradoxical relationship is the subject of
Edmund S. Morgan, <u>American Slavery, American Freedom</u> (New
York: W. W. Norton and Co., 1975).

3. Several works examine wholly or partially the issue
of slavery as it relates to the American Revolution and
developments of the early republic. Among them are Bernard
Bailyn, <u>The Ideological Origins of the American Revolution</u>
(Cambridge, MA: Harvard University Press, 1967); Duncan J.
MacLeod, <u>Slavery, Race and the American Revolution</u> (New York:
Cambridge University Press, 1974); and Robert McColley,
<u>Slavery in Jeffersonian Virginia</u> (Urbana: University of
Illinois Press, 1973).

4. Merrill D. Peterson, ed., <u>The Portable Thomas
Jefferson</u> (New York: Viking Press, 1975), pp. 567-568.

5. Letter of Leonard Chase, March 31, 1843, p. 50.

6. Letter to the <u>Liberator</u>, December 28, 1833, p. 207.

7. "New England Anti-Slavery Convention," reprinted from the Practical Christian in the Liberator, June 30, 1843, p. 102.

8. Preface to Anti-Slavery Melodies: for the Friends of Freedom (Hingham: Elijah B. Gill, 1843), p. [3].

9. Preface to The Emancipation Car (Zanesville: E. C. Church, 1854; Sullivan and Brown, 1874), pp. iii-iv.

10. The response to Whittier's poetry is from an unsigned review, Quarterly Anti-Slavery Magazine, July, 1837, p. 447; the source for Chapman is Songs of the Free, and Hymns of Christian Freedom (Boston: Isaac Knapp, 1836), p. 90.

11. Liberator, February 3, 1843, p. 19.

12. Letter of H. W. Carter to the Liberator, March 28, 1845, p. [49]; minutes of the Worcester County North Division Anti-Slavery Society quarterly meeting, Liberator, July 23, 1847, p. 119.

13. American musical ideas and practices of this era, particularly as they relate to reform movements both musical and moral, are treated extensively in Vicki L. Eaklor, "Music in American Society, 1815-1860: An Intellectual History" (unpublished Ph. D. dissertation, Washington University in St. Louis, 1982). Also, the reader is asked to refer to the bibliography of that work for sources on American church music and music education, which are too numerous and tangential to be listed here. For information on Transcendentalism and music see, in addition to the above, Daniel E. Rider, "The Musical Thought and Activities of the New England Transcendentalists" (unpublished Ph. D. dissertation, University of Minnesota, 1964), and for temperance music see George W. Ewing, The Well-Tempered Lyre: Songs and Verse of the Temperance Movement (Dallas: Southern Methodist University Press, 1977).

14. For mention of instrumental music at antislavery meetings see, e. g., Liberator, August 11, 1843, p. 127; October 23, 1846, p. 171; July 27, 1855, p. 118; December 9, 1859, p. 196; and May 20, 1864, p. [81].

15. The Harp of Freedom (New York: Miller, Orton and Mulligan, 1856), p. iv.

16. Liberator, July 21, 1843, p. 115.

17. Ronald G. Walters, in The Antislavery Appeal: American Abolitionism After 1830 (Baltimore: The Johns Hopkins University Press, 1978; New York: W. W. Norton and Co., 1984), argues persuasively that the kinds of meetings and

celebrations discussed here served more to revitalize committed reformers than to win new converts (pp. 23-24).

18. See, e. g., Liberator, September 2, 1842, p. 138; January 19, 1844, p. 10; July 4, 1845, p. 107; and April 16, 1847, p. 63.

19. Liberator, March 10, 1843, p. 38; November 17, 1843, p. 183. For additional examples see these issues of the Liberator: May 26, 1843, p. 81; June 30, 1843, p. 102; and April 19, 1844, p. 62.

20. For examples of vague references see Liberator, May 28, 1836, p. 87; March 24, 1843, p. 46; July 23, 1847, p. 119; and June 8, 1860, p. 90.

21. Report of the Boston Female Anti-Slavery Society (Boston: published by the Society, 1836), p. 73; the reference is to song 36.

22. Liberator, May 5, 1843, p. [69]; the reference is to song 240.

23. Twenty-First Annual Report Presented to the Massachusetts Anti-Slavery Society by its Board of Managers (n. p.: Massachusetts Anti-Slavery Society, 1853; Westport, CT: Negro Universities Press, 1970), p. 100. The song mentioned may be number 341.

24. The twenty-five songs about July 4 are in MY COUNTRY while the twenty-seven sets of lyrics sung on that day are interspersed throughout this volume; see the Subject Index for a complete listing of both. It is also interesting to note that one song written for July 4 [song 462] was read rather than sung on that day, "as it was not possible to arrange music for it at the time," a stated intention which reinforces the general sense here of the importance and widespread use of music at antislavery meetings (Liberator, July 27, 1860, p. 118).

25. Like the July 4 songs, those about August 1 are in MY COUNTRY (total of twenty-one) while those written for, sung on, or read on that day (total of twenty-eight) are distributed among the various sections according to the subject of the lyrics; see the Subject Index for a complete listing.

26. Liberator, Aug. 26, 1859, p. 136 (emphasis added).

27. See Eaklor, "Music in American Society," for the argument that most "musicians" were in fact "reformers" of one kind or another.

28. The Hutchinson Family is mentioned in most surveys of American music. For more extensive information see Carol Brink, Harps in the Wind: The Story of the Singing Hutchinsons (New York: Macmillan, 1947); John Wallace Hutchinson, Story of the Hutchinsons (Tribe of Jesse), ed. Charles E. Mann, 2 vols. (Boston: Lee and Shepard, 1896; New York: Da Capo Press, 1977); and Philip D. Jordan, Singin' Yankees (Minneapolis: University of Minnesota Press, 1946).

29. For mention of the Hutchinsons, see, e. g., Liberator, May 26, 1843, p. [81]; July 14, 1843, p. 110; April 19, 1844, pp. 62 and [63]; and December 9, 1859, p. 196. See also the Twenty-Second Annual Report of the American Anti-Slavery Society (New York: Dorr & Butterfield, 1855; New York: Kraus Reprint Co., 1972), pp. 123, 131.

30. See the Bibiography for Clark's collections; see also the Author Index for Clark's poems and the Tune Index under "original" for his musical compositions.

31. Radical Abolitionist, August, 1855, p. 7; the reference is to song 295.

32. Liberator, June 30, 1860, p. 90; for additional references to Clark as singer see songs 161 and 272, and Radical Abolitionist (extra edition), June 2, 1856, p. 94.

33. For Simpson's collections please refer to the Bibliography, and for more information on Simpson see Vicki L. Eaklor, "The Songs of The Emancipation Car: Variations on an Abolitionist Theme," Bulletin of the Missouri Historical Society, January, 1980, pp. 92-102.

34. Fifteen songs were not included here in the interest of consistency according to source and an ending date of 1865; five of Simpson's songs exist in broadsheet form only and ten were published only in the 1874 edition of The Emancipation Car.

35. Simpson himself states that he sang (in the preface to The Emancipation Car, 1874) and, according to an article concerning a celebration in Zanesville of the adoption of the Fifteenth Amendment, "Dr. McSimpson sang a war song of his own composition." (Thomas W. Lewis, "Colored Folk of City Joyous Over New Amendment," Zanesville Sunday Times Signal, June 6, 1925, in which the primary source cited is The [Zanesville?] Courier but with no other information.) Simpson's full name was Joshua McCarter Simpson and it commonly appears as "McSimpson." The "Dr." refers to his practice in herb medicine.

36. Proceedings of the Massachusetts Anti-Slavery Society at the Annual Meetings Held in 1854, 1855, & 1856 . . (n.p., n.d.; Westport, CT: Negro Universities Press, 1970), p. 37.

37. Liberator, March 10, 1843, p. 38.

38. See, e. g., records relative to the Massachusetts Anti-Slavery Society: its Fifteenth Annual Report (n. p.: Massachusetts Anti-Slavery Society, 1847; Westport, CT: Negro Universities Press, 1970), p. 93; and its Eighteenth Annual Report (1850), p. 88. See also Proceedings of the American Anti-Slavery Society, at its Third Decade (New York: American Anti-Slavery Society, 1864), pp. 60, 62, 65, and Liberator, November 17, 1843, p. 183; July 23, 1847, p. 119; and November 5, 1847, p. 179.

39. Liberator, July 6, 1833, p. 107; February 3, 1843, p. 19; and August 11, 1843, p. 127. For additional references to choirs of black and white performers see the First Annual Report of the American Anti-Slavery Society (New York: Dorr & Butterfield, 1834; New York: Kraus Reprint Co., 1972) p. 3; and song 111. See song 112 for reference to children singing.

40. February 1, 1834, p. 19. Other citations for this group include Liberator, December 21, 1833, p. 203; and December 28, 1833, p. 207.

41. See the Subject Index under "women" for female performers. For female poets see the Author Index; nearly one-third of the poets listed, due to incomplete information, are of unknown gender, while about one-fifth of the total are women.

42. Since Barbara Welter's "The Cult of True Womanhood: 1820-1860" appeared in 1966 (American Quarterly, Summer, pp. 151-174), the concept and terminology have become fairly standard when discussing middle class Victorian women on both sides of the Atlantic. For Jenny Lind in America see especially Neil Harris, Humbug: The Art of P. T. Barnum (Chicago: University of Chicago Press, 1973; 1981), pp. 113-141; and W. Porter Ware and Thaddeus C. Lockard, Jr., P. T. Barnum Presents Jenny Lind: The American Tour of the Swedish Nightingale (Baton Rouge: Louisiana State University Press, 1980. Also, it is interesting to note that song 198 was written "For Jenny Lind to sing to the American People."

43. See, e. g., songs 9 and 10, and Liberator, November 19, 1847, p. [185]; July 10, 1857, p. 110; and August 19, 1859, p. 132.

44. January 25, 1834, p. 16.

45. A breakdown by decade of the songs in this volume
reveals the peak in the 1840s: 1820s, 8; 1830s, 72; 1840s,
239; 1850s, 126; 1860s, 47.

46. The quotation is from p. [3]; please refer to the
Bibliography for complete information on the works mentioned.

47. See the Subject Index under "women" for songs about
and/or directed at women. For the development of "republican
motherhood" prior to the nineteenth century see Linda K.
Kerber, Women of the Republic: Intellect and Ideology in
Revolutionary America (Chapel Hill: University of North
Carolina Press, 1980; New York: W. W. Norton and Co., 1986);
and Mary Beth Norton, Liberty's Daughters: The Revolutionary
Experience of American Women, 1750-1800 (Boston: Little,
Brown and Co., 1980).

48. Gilbert Chase, America's Music: From the Pilgrims
to the Present, rev. 2nd ed. (New York: McGraw-Hill, 1966),
p. 156.

49. Quoted in George W. Lucas, Remarks on the Musical
Conventions in Boston, &c. (Northampton: printed for the
author, 1844), p. 13.

50. Lucas, ibid., pp. 13-14; and see Eaklor, "Music in
American Society" for a fuller treatment of this debate.

51. Robert C. Toll, in Blacking Up: The Minstrel Show
in Nineteenth-Century America (New York: Oxford University
Press, 1974; 1977) provides a particularly insightful study of
the subject. For the music of minstrelsy, see especially Hans
Nathan, Dan Emmett and the Rise of Early Negro Minstrelsy
(Norman: University of Oklahoma Press, 1962).

52. Original Anti-Slavery Songs (Zanesville: printed
for the author, 1852), p. [3]. Nicholas E. Tawa discusses
the objection of middle-class Americans to minstrel songs and
states that the source of concern was less the music than the
use of Negro dialect ("The Parlor Song in America, 1790-1860"
[unpublished Ph. D. dissertation, Harvard University, 1974],
I, pp. 136-145). Irwin Silber notes the use of minstrel
tunes for campaign songs (Songs America Voted By [Harrisburg,
PA: Stackpole Books, 1971], p. 50; and William W. Austin
suggests briefly both the irony and the possible effects of
adapting these tunes to antislavery purposes in "Susanna,"
"Jeanie," and "The Old Folks at Home": The Songs of Stephen
C. Foster from His Time to Ours (New York: Macmillan, 1975),
p. 35.

Bibliography

Primary

<u>Song Sources</u>: <u>Collections</u>

Brown, William W., comp. <u>The Anti-Slavery Harp</u>. Boston:
Bela Marsh, 1848; Philadelphia: Rhistoric Publications,
1969.

[Chapman, Maria Weston, comp.]. <u>Songs of the Free, and Hymns</u>
<u>of Christian Freedom</u>. Boston: Isaac Knapp, 1836.

[Clark, George W., comp.]. <u>The Free Soil Minstrel</u>. New
York: Martyn and Ely, 1848.

Clark, George W., comp. <u>The Harp of Freedom</u>. New York:
Miller, Orton and Mulligan, 1856.

Clark, George W. <u>The Liberty Minstrel</u>. 7 eds. New York:
published by the author, 1844-1848.

Collins, John A., comp. <u>The Anti-Slavery Picknick: A</u>
<u>Collection of Speeches, Poems, Dialogues and Songs;</u>
<u>Intended for Use in Schools and Anti-Slavery Meetings</u>.
Boston: H. W. Williams, 1842.

Gilmore, H. S. comp. <u>A Collection of Miscellaneous Songs,</u>
<u>from the Liberty Minstrel, and Mason's Juvenile Harp;</u>
<u>for the Use of the Cincinnati High School</u>. Cincinnati:
Sparhawk and Lytle Printers, 1845.

Hatfield, Edwin F., comp. Freedom's Lyre: or, Psalms, Hymns, and Sacred Songs, for the Slave and His Friends. New York: S. W. Benedict, 1840; Miami: Mnemosyne Publishing Co., Inc., 1969.

Hymns and Songs for the Friends of Freedom. Middletown: C. H. Pelton, 1842.

Lincoln, Jairus, comp. Anti-Slavery Melodies: for the Friends of Freedom. Hingham: Elijah B. Gill, 1843.

Simpson, J[oshua] McC[arter]. The Emancipation Car. Zanesville: E. C. Church, 1854; Zanesville: Sullivan and Brown, 1874.

Simpson, J[oshua] McC[arter]. Original Anti-Slavery Songs. Zanesville, O.: printed for the author, 1852.

Wood, Hartley. Hartley Wood's Anniversary Book of Music, for the Fourth of July, Temperance, and Anti-Slavery Occasions. Boston: Musical Visitor Office, 1843.

Song Sources: Periodicals

The African Repository and Colonial Journal. Washington City: American Colonization Society, 1825-1892.

The American Anti-Slavery Almanac for 1844. D. L. Child, comp. New York: American Anti-Slavery Society, 1844.

American Anti-Slavery Reporter. n.p.: American Anti-Slavery Society, 1834; Westport, CT: Negro Universities Press, 1970.

Anti-Slavery Tracts. [New York: American Anti-Slavery Society, 1855-1862]; Westport, CT: Negro Universities Press, 1970.

Douglass' Monthly. Frederick Douglass, ed. Rochester, N.Y., 1859-1863; New York: Negro Universities Press, 1969.

Genius of Universal Emancipation. Benjamin Lundy, ed. Baltimore, et al., 1821-1839.

The Liberator. William Lloyd Garrison, ed. Boston, 1831-1865.

The Liberty Bell. Boston: American Anti-Slavery Society, 1839-1858, except 1840, 1850, 1854, 1855, and 1857.

National Anti-Slavery Standard. Nathaniel P. Rogers,
     Lydia Maria Child, eds. New York: American Anti-Slavery
     Society, 1840-1872; Westport, CT: Negro Universities
     Press, 1970.

Report of the Boston Female Anti-Slavery Society. Boston:
     published by the Society, 1836.

Additional Sources Consulted

American Jubilee. William Goodell, ed. & publ. New
     York, 1854-1855; Westport, CT: Negro Universities
     Press, 1970.

Annual Report of the American Anti-Slavery Society. New
     York: Dorr & Butterfield, 1834-1840, 1855, 1856, 1859-
     1861; New York: Kraus Reprint Co., 1972.

Annual Report of the American and Foreign Anti-Slavery
     Society. New York, 1851.

Annual Report Presented to the Massachusetts Anti-Slavery
     Society, by its Board of Managers. n.p.: Massachusetts
     Anti-Slavery Society, 1833-1856; Westport, CT: Negro
     Universities Press, 1970.

The Anti-Slavery Examiner. New York: American Anti-
     Slavery Society, 1836-1845.

The Anti-Slavery Record. New York: American Anti-Slavery
     Society, 1835-1837.

The Emancipator. Jonesborough, TN: Elihu Embree, 1820;
     Nashville, TN: B.H. Murphy, 1932.

The Non-Slaveholder. Abraham L. Pennock, et al., eds.
     Philadelphia, 1846-1854; Westport, CT: Negro
     Universities Press, 1970.

Proceedings of the American Anti-Slavery Society, at its
     Third Decade. New York, 1864.

Quarterly Anti-Slavery Magazine. Elizur Wright, Jr., ed.
     New York: American Anti-Slavery Society, 1835-1837.

Radical Abolitionist. William Goodell, ed. New York,
     1855-1858; New York: Negro Universities Press, 1969.

Whittier, John G. "The Anti-Slavery Convention of 1833,"
     Old South Leaflets. No. 81. Boston: Directors of
     the Old South Work, n.d.

Secondary

Sources Cited in Introduction

Austin, William W. "Susanna," "Jeanie," and "The Old Folks
    at Home": The Songs of Stephen C. Foster from His Time
    to Ours. New York: Macmillan, 1975.

Bailyn, Bernard. The Ideological Origins of the American
    Revolution. Cambridge, MA: Harvard University Press,
    1967.

Brink, Carol. Harps in the Wind: The Story of the Singing
    Hutchinsons. New York: Macmillan, 1947.

Chase, Gilbert. America's Music from the Pilgrims to the
    Present. Rev. 2nd ed. New York: McGraw-Hill, 1966.

Eaklor, Vicki L. "Music in American Society: An Intellectual
    History." Ph. D., Washington University in St. Louis,
    1982.

Eaklor, Vicki L. "The Songs of The Emancipation Car:
    Variations on an Abolitionist Theme." Bulletin of the
    Missouri Historical Society, January, 1980, pp. 92-102.

Ewing, George W. The Well-Tempered Lyre: Songs and Verse of
    the Temperance Movement. Dallas: Southern Methodist
    University Press, 1977.

Harris, Neil. Humbug: The Art of P. T. Barnum. Chicago:
    University of Chicago Press, 1973; 1981.

Hutchinson, John Wallace. Story of the Hutchinsons (Tribe
    of Jesse). Ed. Charles E. Mann. 2 vols. Boston: Lee
    and Shepard, 1896; New York: Da Capo
    Press, 1977.

Jordan, Philip D. Singin' Yankees. Minneapolis: University
    of Minnesota Press, 1946.

Kerber, Linda K. Women of the Republic: Intellect and
    Ideology in Revolutionary America. Chapel Hill:
    University of North Carolina Press, 1980; New York:
    W. W. Norton and Co., 1986.

Lewis, Thomas W. "Colored Folk of City Joyous over New
    Amendment." Zanesville Sunday Times Signal, June 6,
    1925.

MacLeod, Duncan J. Slavery, Race and the American Revolution.
    New York: Cambridge University Press, 1974.

McColley, Robert. Slavery and Jeffersonian Virginia. 2nd
    ed. Urbana: University of Illinois Press, 1973.

Morgan, Edmund S. American Slavery, American Freedom: The
    Ordeal of Colonial Virginia. New York: W. W. Norton
    and Co., 1975.

Nathan, Hans. Dan Emmett and the Rise of Early Negro
    Minstrelsy. Norman: University of Oklahoma Press,
    1962.

Norton, Mary Beth. Liberty's Daughters: The Revolutionary
    Experience of American Women, 1750-1800. Boston:
    Little, Brown and Co., 1980.

Peterson, Merrill D., ed. The Portable Thomas Jefferson.
    New York: Viking Press, 1975.

Rider, Daniel E. "The Musical Thought and Activities of the
    New England Transcendentalists." Ph.D., University of
    Minnesota, 1964.

Silber, Irwin. Songs America Voted By. Harrisburg, PA.:
    Stackpole Books, 1971.

Tawa, Nicholas E. "The Parlor Song in America, 1790-1860."
    2 vols. Unpublished Ph.D. dissertation, Harvard
    University, 1974.

Toll, Robert C. Blacking Up: The Minstrel Show in
    Nineteenth-Century America. New York: Oxford
    University Press, 1974; 1977.

Walters, Ronald G. The Anti-Slavery Appeal: American
    Abolitionism After 1830. Baltimore: The Johns Hopkins
    University Press, 1978; New York: W. W. Norton and Co.,
    1984.

Ware, W. Porter and Thaddeus C. Lockard, Jr. P. T. Barnum
    Presents Jenny Lind: The American Tour of the Swedish
    Nightingale. Baton Rouge: Louisiana State University
    Press, 1980.

Welter, Barbara. "The Cult of True Womanhood: 1820-1860,"
    American Quarterly, Summer, 1966, pp. 151-174.

Selected Additional Sources: Antislavery

Barnes, Gilbert Hobbs. The Anti-Slavery Impulse 1830-1844.
    n.p.: American Historical Association, 1933;
    Gloucester, MA: Peter Smith, 1973.

1   BIBLIOGRAPHY

Bonham, Milledge L., Jr. "A Rare Abolitionist Document,"
     Mississippi Valley Historical Review, 8 (December,
     1921), 266-273.

Dillon, Merton L. The Abolitionists: The Growth of a
     Dissenting Minority. DeKalb: Northern Illinois
     University Press, 1974.

Duberman, Martin, ed. The Antislavery Vanguard: New Essays
     on the Abolitionists. Princeton: Princeton University
     Press, 1965.

Dumond, Dwight Lowell. Antislavery. Ann Arbor: University
     of Michigan Press, 1961.

Dumond, Dwight Lowell. Antislavery Origins of the Civil War
     in the United States. n.p.: University of Michigan
     Press, 1939; n.p.: University of Michigan Press, 1969.

Filler, Louis. The Crusade Against Slavery 1830-1860.
     New York: Harper & Brothers, 1960.

Foner, Eric. Free Soil, Free Labor, Free Men. New York:
     Oxford University Press, 1970.

Hopkins, Geraldine. "'A Rare Abolitionist Document,'"
     Mississippi Valley Historical Review, 18 (June, 1931),
     60-64.

Kraditor, Aileen S. Means and Ends in American Abolitionism.
     New York: Pantheon Books, 1969.

Lerner, Gerda. The Grimke Sisters from South Carolina.
     New York: Schocken Books, 1971.

Quarles, Benjamin. Black Abolitionists. New York: Oxford
     University Press, 1969.

Richards, Leonard L. "Gentlemen of Property and Standing":
     Anti-Abolition Mobs in Jacksonian America. New York:
     Oxford University Press, 1970.

Sorin, Gerald. Abolitionism: A New Perspective. New
     York: Praeger Publishers, 1972.

Stewart, James Brewer. Holy Warriors: The Abolitionists and
     American Slavery. New York: Hill and Wang, 1976.

Selected Additional Sources: Music

Foner, Philip S. American Labor Songs of the Nineteenth
     Century. Urbana: University of Illinois Press, 1975.

Fowke, Edith and Joe Glazer. Songs of Work and Protest.
    New York: Dover Publications, Inc., 1973.

Greenway, John. American Folksongs of Protest.
    Philadelphia: University of Pennsylvania Press, 1953.

Hitchcock, H. Wiley. Music in the United States: A
    Historical Introduction. Englewood Cliffs, N.J.:
    Prentice-Hall, Inc., 1969.

Lawrence, Vera Brodsky. Music for Patriots, Politicians,
    and Presidents. New York: Macmillan, 1975.

Levy, Lester S. Grace Notes in American History. Norman:
    University of Oklahoma Press, 1967.

Mellers, Wilfrid. Music in a New Found Land. London:
    Barrie and Rockliff, 1964.

Rosen, David M. Protest Songs in America. [Westlake
    Village, CA]: Aware Press, 1972.

Tatham, David. The Lure of the Striped Pig. Barre, MA:
    Imprint Society, 1973.

Key to Song Sources

(See Bibliography for full citations)

Song collections:

Anniversary — Hartley Wood's Anniversary Book of Music, for the Fourth of July, Temperance, and Anti-Slavery Occasions, 1843.

Car — The Emancipation Car, 1854; 1874.

Collection — A Collection of Miscellaneous Songs, from The Liberty Minstrel, and Mason's Juvenile Harp; for the Use of the Cincinnati High School, 1845.

Free Soil — The Free Soil Minstrel, 1848.

Freedom — The Harp of Freedom, 1856.

Harp — The Anti-Slavery Harp, 1848.

Hymns — Hymns and Songs for the Friends of Freedom, 1842.

Liberty — The Liberty Minstrel, 1848.

Lyre — Freedom's Lyre: or, Psalms, Hymns, and Sacred Songs for the Slave and His Friends, 1840.

Melodies — Anti-Slavery Melodies: for the Friends of Freedom, 1843.

Original — Original Anti-Slavery Songs, 1852.

Picknick   The Anti-Slavery Picknick: A Collection of
                     Speeches, Poems, Dialogues and Songs;
                     Intended for Use in Schools and Anti-
                     Slavery Meetings, 1842.

Songs   Songs of the Free, and Hymns of Christian
                     Freedom, 1836.

Periodicals:

African   The African Repository and Colonial Journal,
                     1825-1892.

Almanac   The American Anti-Slavery Almanac for 1844.

Douglass   Douglass' Monthly, 1859-1863.

Genius   Genius of Universal Emancipation, 1821-1839.

Liberator   Liberator, 1831-1865.

Liberty Bell   The Liberty Bell, 1839-1858.

Report   Report of the Boston Female Anti-Slavery
                     Society, 1836.

Reporter   American Anti-Slavery Reporter, 1834.

Standard   National Anti-Slavery Standard, 1840-1872.

Tracts   Anti-Slavery Tracts, No. 12, 1855-1856.

The Songs

LIBERIA

Not poor and empty handed,
As first to us they came,
With superstition branded,
And want, and woe, and shame,
Are we the race returning
Back to their native sod;
But with our laws, our learning,
Our freedom and our God!

The twelve songs in this section span the entire antebellum era and represent the two opposing arguments regarding colonization. On the one hand, they illustrate the ideas behind the colonization movement itself, which remained active from the formation of the American Colonization Society in 1817 until shortly after the Civil War. On the other hand, the very lack of songs on the general subject, for or against, reflects the rejection of colonization on the part of both black and white abolitionists that became one of the distinguishing features of post-1830 antislavery sentiment.

The strength of the Christian appeal is revealed in the fact that it is present in nine of the twelve sets of lyrics and prominent in five. One of the earliest examples of the combination of patriotism and Christianity that constitutes a major abolitionist device (see the section, GOD AND LIBERTY) is number 5, the first of the anti-colonization songs.

Something of the attitudes of the colonizers is revealed in the songs written and sung for specific pro-colonization organizations and/or events (1-4, 9-11), which constitute a slight majority. Especially apparent is the belief that colonization was a means of "enlightening" a "benighted" people (light and dark metaphors pervade this literature for obvious reasons); that the goal was as much the happiness of

the colonists as the colonizers. Not unlike the justification
for more traditional imperialism, these arguments no doubt
reflect varying degrees of sincerity on the part of the
authors and thus lend insight into the range of motives
involved in the movement. More surprising than the
ethnocentrism of the pro-colonization songs is the early
appearance of the argument that (contrary to the sentiment of
song 10, quoted in part above) the United States, not Africa,
is the true home of American blacks (song 5, 1832). The
remainder are somewhat more cynical in tone, particularly
those of Joshua Simpson, (8, 12) a free black resident of
Zanesville, Ohio. All anti-colonization songs, it should be
noted, appeared in the Liberator and/or in antislavery song
collections, while the pro-colonization songs are from
periodicals either earlier or specific to that cause.

1. HYMN

Written for the anniversary of
the Norfolk Colonization Society.

Author: unspecified
Tune: unspecified

THERE is a land for ages past
O'erlook'd by God above;
(For so it seem'd) but now at last
Remembered in his love.

O! She hath drunk the wine of woe
And of astonishment!
But all her tears shall cease to flow,
And all her chains be rent.

For, "Go, ye ransom'd slaves," He cries,
"Across the swelling sea;
Go, seek ye again your sunny skies,
Where ye shall flourish free.

And ye shall teach your rudest race
All good and gentle arts,
And that true gospel of my grace
That healeth human hearts.

And I will plant you on the shore,
And lead you thro' the land,
And will enlarge you more and more,
And help you with my hand.

And I, who am the KING OF KINGS,
Will cover you in peace,
Ev'n as an Eagle, with my wings,
Protecting your increase.

And men shall wonder to behold
The things that I will do,
Beyond whate'er I did of old,
To raise and comfort you."

ALMIGHTY GOD! we hear thy voice,
And welcome thy decree:
And thou, poor Africa, rejoice!
And we'll rejoice with thee.

African, December, 1825, p. 320.

2. ODE

Sung at an annual meeting of the Auxiliary
Colonization Society of Portsmouth, Va.

Author: V.
Tune: unspecified

Rise, sun of Afric! from thy cloud,
And shine upon thine own;
From land to land the summons loud
On wings of joy has flown.

'Tis not the trumpet's war-like voice,
Though Freedom wakes the strain,
That bids the African rejoice -
His hope's no longer vain.

No; 'tis the sound of Jubilee -
Th' auspicious morn is near;
Columbia wakes with joy to see
The dawn of life appear.

She wakes to see yon day-star rise,
That flames on Afric's shore;
And gilds with hope those kindling skies,
That frown'd so dark before.

On young Liberia's willowed stream
Its rays of promise shine,
Where hope and joy and freedom beam,
In harmony divine.

Far through the desert's deep profound
The spreading light shall run,
Till Ethiopia's wilds resound
The wonders God has done.

Yes, there "the desert shall rejoice,"
Its fragrant verdure rise,
While ransom'd millions lift their voice,
Adoring, to the skies.

Then let the waking summons loud
From land to land be thrown,
Rise, sun of Afric! from thy cloud,
And shine upon thine own.

Genius, March 24, 1827, p. 168.

3. HYMN

Sung in the public meeting in Hartford, Connecticut,
on the 4th of July, to aid the American Colonization Society.

Author: Lydia H. Sigourney
Tune: unspecified

When injured Afric's captive claim,
Loads the sad gale with startling moan,
The frown of deep indignant blame,
Bend not on Southern climes alone.

Her toil, and chain, and scalding tear,
Our daily board with luxuries deck,
And to dark slavery's yoke severe,
Our fathers help'd to bow her neck.

If slumbering in the thoughtful breast,
Or justice or compassion dwell,
Call from their couch the hallowed guest,
The deed to prompt, the prayer to swell.

Oh, lift the hand, and Peace shall bear
Her olive where the palm tree grows,
And torrid Afric's desert share
The fragrance of salvation's rose.

But if with Pilate's stoic eye,
We calmly wash when blood is spilt,
Or deem a cold, unpitying sigh,
Absolves us from the stain of guilt;

Or if, like Jacob's recreant train,
Who traffick'd in a brother's woe,
We hear the suppliant plead in vain,
Or mock his tears that wildly flow;

Will not the judgments of the skies,
Which threw a shield round Joseph sold,
Be roused by fetter'd Afric's cries,
And change to dross the oppressor's gold?

Genius, new series, October 9, 1829, p. 36.

Songs, pp. 49-50, as "Self-Reproof"; no tune specified.

4. HYMN

Sung at the anniversary of the colonization
society of Kenyon College, 1830.

Author: H. C.
Tune: unspecified

Captives in exile growing
'Neath slavery's galling chains!
Heathens in darkness roaming
O'er Afric's thirsty plains!
Christians of every nation!
Friends of the wretched slave!
O shout with adoration,
For Jesus comes to save.

Praise him with songs of gladness,
Let every tear be dry,
He comes to banish sadness,
And 'stablish equity;
He comes in peace from heaven
To burst each bond in twain,
To save the blinded heathen,
And break the captive's chain.

Full many a bark is steering
O'er ocean's heaving breast,
Full many an exile bearing
To peace, and home, and rest;
Soon Afric's darkest nation
Thy name, O Lord, shall hear;
The rose of thy salvation
Shall bloom unfading there.

Soon rivers gently flowing
The burning land shall bless,
The roses ever blowing
Deck the wild wilderness;
While in soft dews descending,
The spirit from above
Shall spread the never ending -
The blissful reign of love.

O Jesus! let thy story
Throughout the world be known,
Awake the song of glory,
And break the heart of stone,

Till every soul is lighted,
Till every slave is free,
Till every realm benighted
Bows down, O Lord, to thee.

Genius, Ser. 3, October, 1830, pp. 107-108.

5. HYMN

Proper to be sung on all occasions by people of
color who do not intend to emigrate to Africa.

Author: W. J. Snelling
Tune: Sweet Home

Great God, if the humble and weak are as dear
To thy love as the proud, to thy children give
ear.
Our brethren would drive us in deserts to
roam;
Forgive them, O Father, and keep us at home.
Home, sweet home!
We know of no other; this, this is our home.

Here, here our loved mothers released from
their toils
To watch o'er our cradles and joy in our
smiles:
Here the bones of our fathers lie buried, and
here
Are friends, wives, and children, ay, all we
hold dear.
Home, sweet home!
We know of no other; this, this is our home.

Here is law, here is learning, and here we may
move,
Most merciful God, in the light of thy love.
Boasts Afric such blessings? oppressors,
declare:
Oh, no, we may seek but shall not find them
there.
Home, sweet home!
We know of no other; this, this is our home.

Columbia, dear land of our birthright, may He
Who made us a people, rain blessings on thee:
From thy bosom no pleading shall tempt us to
roam;
Till force drives us from it, this, this is
our home.
Home, sweet home!
Till force drives us from it, this, this is
our home.

Liberator, October 13, 1832, p. 163.

Songs, p. 41, as "Home"; no tune specified, with the note:
"This Hymn is expressive of the sentiments of our colored
brethren with regard to the wild and cruel scheme of the
American Colonization Society."

Picknick, pp. 105-107, as "Colored Man's Opinion of Colonization," to the same tune.

6. MR. PREJUDICE

Sung at the New England Anti-Slavery
Convention, May 27-29 [1834].

Author: unspecified
Tune: unspecified

Pray who is Mr. Prejudice,
We hear so much about,
Who wants to spoil our pleasant songs,
And keep the white folks out?

They say he runs along the streets,
And makes a shocking noise,
Scolding at little colored girls,
And whipping colored boys.

We never yet have met the wretch,
Although our mothers say,
That colored folks, both old and young,
He torments every day.

A colonizing agent hired,
We're told he has a whip,
With which he flogs our honest friends,
And drives them to the ship.

The colonizers tell us all
They hate this wicked man -
Yet ask him every day to dine,
And flatter all they can.

He must be very tall and stout,
Quite dreadful in a rage,
For strongest colored men they say,
He'll toss out of a stage.

We wish that we could catch him here,
We think he'd hold his tongue,
If he should see our smiling looks,
And know how well we've sung.

However strong the rogue may be,
Kind friends, if you'll unite,
Should he peep in, oh, never fear,
We'll banish him tonight.

Liberator, May 31, 1834, p. 87, preceded by the information that it was sung by Miss [Susan] Paul's Juvenile Colored
Choir, and "elicited great applause."

                7. COLONIZATION SONG
            TO THE FREE COLORED PEOPLE

                Author: unspecified
              Tune: Spider and the Fly

Will you, will you be colonized?
Will you, will you be colonized?

"Tis a land that with honey
And milk doth abound,
Where the lash is not heard,
And the scourge is not found.
CHORUS:
Will you, will you be colonized?
Will you, will you be colonized?

If you stay in this land
Where the white man has rule,
You will starve by his hand,
In both body and soul.
CHORUS

For a nuisance you are,
In this land of your birth,
Held down by his hand,
And crushed to the earth.
CHORUS

My religion is pure,
And came from above,
But I cannot consent
The black negro to love.
CHORUS

It is true there is judgment
That hangs o'er the land,
But 't will all turn aside,
When you follow the plan.
CHORUS

You're ignorant I know,
In this land of your birth,
And religion though pure,
Cannot move the curse.
CHORUS

But only consent,
Though extorted by force,
What a blessing you'll prove,
On the African coast.
CHORUS

Harp, pp. 17-18.

8. OLD LIBERIA IS NOT THE PLACE FOR ME

Author: Joshua Simpson
Tune: Come to the Old Gum Tree

Come all ye Colonizationists,
My muse is off today -
Come, listen while she's singing
Her soft and gentle lay.
Before she's done you'll understand,
Whoever you may be,
That Old Liberia
Is not the place for me.

Although I'm trodden under foot
Here in America -
And th' right to life, and liberty,
From me you take away,
Until my brethren in the South,
From chains are all set free -
The Old Liberia
Is no place for me.

Although (as Moses Walker* says;)
"There children never cry:"
And he who can well act the hog,
For food will never die;
"For there the yams and cocoa-nuts,
And oranges are free;"
Yet old Liberia
Is not the place for me.

You say "it is a goodly land,
Where milk and honey flow;
And every Jack will be a man
Who there may choose to go."
You say that "God appointed there
The black man's destiny;"
Yet old Liberia
Is not the place for me.

The sweet potatoes there may grow,
And rice in great supplies;
And purest waters ever flow,
Which dazzle quite your eyes.
Tho' there they have the sugar-cane;
Also the coffee tree,
Yet old Liberia
Is not the place for me.

Three million slaves are in the South!
And suffering there today:
You've gag'd them; yea, you've stop'd their
mouth,
They dare not even pray!
We who in art and enterprise,
Are trudging on our way,
You'd have us all to colonize,
In old Liberia.

"Give joy or grief - give ease or pain,
Take life or friends away;"
I deem this as my native land,
And here I'm bound to stay.

I have a mind to be a man
Among white men and free;
And OLD LIBERIA!
Is not the place for me!!

My muse has chanted now too long,
And spent her breath in vain -
In singing of that Negro Den,
Across the raging main.
Our blood is now so far dispers'd
Among the Anglo-race,
To rid this country of the curse
Would need a larger space.

And old Liberia
Is rather far away:
I'd rather find a peaceful home
In Old America!

Original, pp. 24-27; and Car, pp. 69-72.

*Simpson explains that Walker is "a colored man who has
recently returned from Liberia, where he has been on a SPYING
tour, and has been since his return, tickling the ears of the
Colonizationists in many parts of our State [Ohio], with the
'joyous' report of the glorious prospect of Liberia becoming a
great nation. . . ."

                    9. HYMN

          Sung at the Twentieth Anniversary of the
          New York State Colonization Society.

                  Author: L. Wilder
                  Tune: America

          Father in Heaven above,
          Fountain of light and love,
          God over all;
          Bless thou this cause we plead,
          In all our counsels lead;
          Guide thou in word and deed;
          Oh, hear our call.

          Look thou on man below,
          Teach him thy will to know,
          Love and obey;

Thy breath can chase away
Dark shades of error's way;
O'er sins benighted way,
Open the day.

To every land oppressed,
Thy light and promised rest
Do thou restore;
Then Afric's grateful lays
Shall swell that song of praise
Which ransomed nations raise
For evermore.

African, June, 1852, p. 185.

10. LIBERIA

Sung at the Twentieth Anniversary of the
New York State Colonization Society.

Author: Miss Margaret Junkin
Tune: unspecified

From bosoms warmly beating,
We send across the sea
An elder sister's greeting,
Liberia! to thee!
With firm and steady patience,
Thou hast maintained thy way,
Till one among the nations
We see thee stand today.

Thy beacon we are hailing;
Its radiance clear and bright
Across the waves is trailing
A stream of living light.
With fond and filial yearning,
Where e'er they rest or roam,
Thy children are returning,
Called by that signal home.

Home, where the hopes now centre
That once were vague and vain;
Where bondage cannot enter
To bind them down again;
Home, free from all oppressors;
Home, where the palm tree waves;
Home, to their own possessions,
Home, to their grandsires' graves!

> Not poor and empty handed,
> As first to us they came,
> With superstition branded,
> And want, and woe, and shame,
> Are we the race returning
> Back to their native sod;
> But with our laws, our learning,
> Our freedom and our God!

African, June, 1852, p. 189.

11. [UNTITLED]

Sung by the Ladies' Literary Institute
at a meeting for President J. J. Roberts
upon his return from England to Monrovia, Liberia.*

Author: unspecified
Tune: unspecified

> But we not unmindful be,
> Of God who gives the victory,
> Let us to him our voices raise
> In songs of gratitude and praise.
>
> And let Liberia's sons rejoice,
> And every daughter lend her voice,
> To spread the cheering truth abroad,
> Jehovah is our friend and God.

African, October, 1853, p. 304.

*Joseph Jenkins Roberts (1809-1876) was elected first
President of Liberia when that nation became a republic
in 1847.

12. COME TO OLD LIBERIA

Author: Joshua Simpson
Tune: [Massa's in the Cold, Cold Ground?]

> O! don't you hear the white man singing?
> Hear ye what they say?
> Like a thousand mighty trumpets ringing,
> All through America.

Ho! all of you despised, black "niggers,"
Turn your eyes this way -
No longer wear your galling fetters -
Come away to Africa.

Cold wind and snow will not upbraid you,
On that pleasant shore;
Nor never will the white man there degrade you
Freedom you'll enjoy evermore.
Why will you tarry here any longer?
Why not haste away?
Know ye not your chains are growing stronger
Stronger every hour you stay.

O! how our hearts for you are swelling,
With our enterprise,
How we feel for you there is no telling,
O, darkey now be wise.
This is a land of milk and honey,
Now to you we show,
And we will give you clothes and money,
Go, Darkey; we say go!

There you can raise the big sweet potatoes
And great fields of rice,
There you can see the big Alligators,
And every other thing that's nice.
There you'll always be befriended,
Rest from all your toils,
Then when your days on earth are ended,
Die upon your native soil.

There you can cut a fine great figure,
Swell like big, black toads,
No one will dare to call you "nigger,"
Neither need you work on the roads;
There you can wear the highstanding collars
And the long-tailed blue,
All your pockets will be chuck full o'
dollars,
O! Darkey, who then cut you?

Car, pp. 89-91.

GOD AND
LIBERTY

God is our guide from field and wave,
From plough, from anvil, and from loom;
We come to liberate the slave,
And speak the factious despot's doom;
And, hark! we raise from sea to sea,
The watchword - "God and Liberty!"

The combination "God and Liberty" (song 51) has been
particularly influential in the development of the American
self-image. No other phrase, perhaps, summarizes so concisely
the concept of the American past, present, and future that
governed not only the activities of reformers but the
perceptions of most of their contemporaries as well. From the
Puritans' "city on a hill" to George Bancroft's ten-volume
explanation of United States history as the unfolding of a
divine plan (published 1834-1874), God and American destiny
were assumed to be irrevocably paired. The bond that united
them, however, had been transformed gradually from a specific
and well-defined Protestant covenant into a contract whose
central tenet, the preservation of God-given liberty among His
chosen people, made it paradoxically simpler yet more diffuse.

As the debate over slavery intensified, "liberty," it
turned out, could be interpreted a number of ways depending
upon what, whose, and how much were involved. To the
abolitionists especially a major issue was the possible
judgment upon a nation that defined itself as the main
depository of this most precious natural right yet denied that
right to a large segment of the populace. For this reason,
and due to the specifically evangelical origins of the
movement itself, God is present in the majority of antislavery
song lyrics.

    What distinguishes this section, then, is the degree   and
explicit   nature   of that presence.   In these ninety-one songs
the primary rationale for abolition is the sin of slavery   and
the   necessity   of   redemption for the nation as a whole.   One
finds not only the expected Biblical   imagery   but   also   the
frequent   use   of   simply   "Hymn"   as a title, the use of hymn
tunes, arguments regarding the humanity of   the   slave   (as   a
brother   or   sister   under   the   same   God),   and   prayers for
guidance, strength and, ultimately, of praise and   thanks   for
victory   (examples   of the latter are song 98, celebrating the
Emancipation Proclamation, and 103, celebrating the Thirteenth
Amendment).   The onset of the War, from this perspective, was
interpreted as punishment at the very least and, by   many,   as
Armageddon.   The most famous song from the era, and one of the
best known in American history, in fact, clearly reflects this
mentality: Julia Ward Howe's "Battle Hymn of the Republic" of
1861, set to a revival tune known by   then   as   "John   Brown's
Body"   (its   very   notoriety and the fact that it was found in
none of the antislavery   sources   used   for   this   compilation
precluded   its   inclusion   here).   An interesting variation of
that song is Garrison's "Our National Visitation" (97),   which
appeared   in print five months after Howe's poem was published
in the Atlantic Monthly.

13. INVOCATION

Sung at the Park Street Church, Boston, on July 4.

Author: Rev. John Pierpont
Tune: [America?]

With thy pure dews and rains,
Wash out, O God, the stains
From Afric's shore;
And, while her palm trees bud,
Let not her children's blood
With her broad Niger's flood
Be mingled more!

Quench, righteous God, the thirst
That Congo's sons hath cursed -
The thirst for gold!
Shall not thy thunders speak,
Where Mammon's altars reek,
Where maids and matrons shriek,
Bound, bleeding, sold?

Hear'st thou, O God, those chains,
Clanking on Freedom's plains,
By Christians wrought!
Them, who those chains have worn,
Christians from home have torn,
Christians have hither borne,
Christians have bought!

Cast down, great God, the fanes
That, to unhallowed gains,
Round us have risen -
Temples, whose priesthood pore
Moses and Jesus o'er,
Then bolt the black man's door,
The poor man's prison!

Wilt thou not, Lord, at last,
From thine own image, cast
Away all cords,
But that of love, which brings
Man, from his wanderings,
Back to the King of kings,
The Lord of lords!

Genius, new series, September 2, 1829, p. 3, preceded by
an introduction by "W. L. G."[Garrison], calling the piece
"beautiful and thrilling . . . admirably adapted to be spoken

at the exhibition of public schools, and should be treasured up in the memory of every reader."

Songs, pp. 47-49, as "Prayer for the Oppressed"; no tune specified.

Picknick, pp. 102-103, as "Prayer for the Oppressed," to an unidentified tune.

Melodies, pp. 32-33, as "Hymn 19," to an unidentified tune.

14. HYMN

Sung at Hartford, July 4, 1829.

Author: unspecified
Tune: unspecified

Awake! O Afric! desolate, forlorn;
Behold thy day of Jubilee is come;
Arise! and hail the bright and cheering morn,
That calls thy exiled, captive children home.

Call on thy sons the joyful song to raise,
Of heaven-born freedom, for they now are men;
The song of triumph, gratitude and praise,
To Him whose hand has burst their galling
chain.

No more need gentle Pity mourn thy woes;
Nor kind Humanity thy lot deplore;
The Voice of Justice breaks its long repose,
And pleads thy sacred cause from shore to
shore.

In silent sadness, sit no more alone;
The God of nations will thy right maintain;
Awake! Arise! Ascend thy long lost throne,
And widely o'er thy new born empires reign.

Soon shall the Gospel o'er thy darkness shed
Its noon day glory, like a mighty flood;
Thy farthest realms shall rise, as from the
dead,
And Ethiopia stretch her hand to God.

Genius, new series, November 6, 1829, p. 68.

15. HYMN

Sung at the editor's [Garrison's] address at Boylston Hall.

Author: Wm. J. Snelling, Esq.
Tune: unspecified

Today, O God, in praise to thee,
A nation's voices, thankful, rise;
A grateful people bow the knee,
And shouts of joy ascend the skies.

Thanks! thanks! whate'er mankind can need
Thy law, earth's choicest fruits and flowers,
And LIBERTY, of thought and deed,
Thy dearest gift, all, all are ours -

Yet, father, hear! to thee, in heaven,
By earth contemn'd, a race complains;
Our hymns of thanks for freedom given
Are mingled with the clank of chains.

Thou inv'st the right, and hat'st the wrong -
Then grant this asking of the free,
That Afric's sons may have, ere long,
As much to thank thee for as we.

Liberator, July 7, 1832, p. 107.

16. [UNTITLED]

Sung at the Hartford Beneficent Society for Colored Children.

Author: L. H. S.
Tune: unspecified

Oh, if to Afric's sable race,
A fearful debt we justly owe,
If Heaven's dread book record the trace
Of every deed and thought below -

And if for them the Christian's prayer
Implore of God to guide and save,
Then let these helpless suppliants share
From mercy's store, the mite they crave -

Touch deep for them the pitying breast,
Bid bounty's stream flow warm and free,
For who can tell among the blest
How sweet their harps of praise may be?

Liberator, June 8, 1833, p. 91.

Songs, pp. 74-76, as "Appeal for the Samaritan Asylum";
no tune specified.

17. HYMN ON SLAVERY

Author: James Scott
Tune: unspecified

O Lord! whose forming hand one blood
To all the tribes and nations gave,
And gives to all their daily food,
Look down in pity on the slave.

Fetters and chains and stripes remove,
And freedom to their bodies give;
And pour the tide of light and love
Upon their souls, and bid them live.

Oh, kindle in our hearts a flame
Of zeal, thy holy will to do;
And bid each child, who loves thy name,
To love his bleeding brother too.

We send to foreign shores thy word,
To guide to Thee the steps that roam;
Shall we forget the myriads, Lord,
Who sit in darkness here at home?

Bend the proud hearts, the iron hands,
That vex thy sable children so,
Till they undo the heavy bands,
And let their sighing captives go.

Through all thy temples, let the stain
Of prejudice each bosom flee;
And hand in hand, let Afric's train,
With Europe's children, worship thee.

Liberator, January 25, 1834, p. 16, preceded by these
remarks from the author to Garrison: "At a late lecture on
Slavery, in Pawtucket, Ray Potter, the Lecturer, remarked,
that such had heretofore been the remissness of Christians

on that subject, he knew not a single hymn adapted to the
occasion. If the following will in any degree help to supply
that defect, it is at the service of the pious friends of
emancipation."

Freedom, p. 318, as "O Lord, Whose Forming Hand"; no
tune specified.

18. 182 SELECT HYMN

Sung at the first annual meeting of the Old Colony,
Plymouth County Anti-Slavery Society, July 4, 1835.

Author: unspecified
Tune: unspecified

Soon Afric's long enslaved sons
Shall join with Europe's polished race,
To celebrate in different tongues,
The glories of redeeming grace.

From east to west, from north to south,
Emmanuel's kingdom shall extend,
And every man and every face,
Shall meet a brother and a friend.

Liberator, July, 11, 1835, p. 110, indicating that these are
the last two verses.

19. HYMN

Sung at the Addison County Anti-Slavery Convention,
Middlebury, Vt., July 6, 1835.

Author: Zebulon Jones
Tune: Zion

To thy throne, O God of nations,
Hear the voice of millions cry.
Whom the power of earthly stations
Dooms in bondage still to sigh:
"Princely Saviour,
Speak our Freedom from the sky."

"Long these chains have bound this image,
Which the God of nature made;
Long have masters bought and sold us,
Making this a nation's trade:
Princely Saviour,
Speak our Freedom from the sky."

Hark! from Heaven's triumphal arches,
Lo! the shouts of Angels come:
Slave! the gory chains are falling;
Thou shalt rest at Freedom's home;
Purest glory
Still shall shine on Afric's name.

Land of Freemen! hear the message,
Break the chains of fettered hands,
Free the mind of shrouding darkness,
Heed the voice of God's commands:
Quickly sever
Proud oppression's cruel bands.

Liberator, July 11, 1835, p. 111.

20. ORIGINAL HYMN

Sung at Salem, July 4, 1835.

Author: unspecified
Tune: unspecified

Who are the free? The Sons of God,
That hate oppression, strife, and blood;
Who are the slaves? The men that sell
God's image for the gains of hell!

They scourge the frame, the sinews bind;
They trample on th' immortal mind:
Earth can endure the guilt no more,
And God rolls on th' avenging hour.

The clouds of judgment round he spreads,
Th' oppressor in the dust he treads: -
The year of his redeemed is come!
He calls the toil-worn captive home!

He moves in strength and righteousness,
To save th' oppressed of Afric's race;
He opes the weary prisoner's door,
And brings salvation to the poor.

Proclaim his truth, spread forth his laws;
Strike at the sin his soul abhors:
Break every yoke, the slave release,
Let chains, and stripes, and bondage cease.

Thus shall the earth resemble heaven;
Oppression back to hell be driven;
And LOVE shall bind, in sweet accord,
ALL NATIONS, RANSOMED OF THE LORD!

Liberator, July 11, 1835, p. 112.

Songs, p. 97, as "The Truly Free", no tune specified.

Freedom, p. 319, as "Who Are the Free?"; no tune specified.

21. ORIGINAL HYMN

Sung by the children of the Belknap St. Sabbath School,
July 4, 1835, while celebrating the national jubilee.

Author: unspecified
Tune: unspecified

Soon shall the trump of freedom
Resound from shore to shore;
Soon, taught by heavenly wisdom,
Man shall oppress no more:
But every yoke be broken,
Ev'ry captive wretch set free -
And every heart shall welcome
This day of jubilee.

Then tyrant's crowns and sceptres,
And victors' wreaths, and cars
And galling chains, and fetters,
With all the pomp of wars,
Shall in the dust be trodden,
Till time shall be no more,
And peace, and joy, from heaven
The LORD on earth shall pour.

Liberator, July 18, 1835, p. 116.

Songs, pp. 199-200, as "The Day of Jubilee"; no tune
specified.

Melodies, pp. 46-47, as "Hymn 30," to an unidentified tune.

22. HYMN

For the Rhode Island Anti-Slavery Society Convention.

Author: M. W. Chapman
Tune: Old Hundred

"Awake my people!" saith your God!
"Your brother's blood the land profanes!
Ye bend beneath the oppressor's rod -
He binds your spirits in his chains."

"With breaking heart and tortured nerve,
Your brother drains the accursed cup!
Now in the name of him ye serve -
The living God of hosts - come up!"

"While faith each fervent spirit fills,
Arise! with hope and triumph crown'd!
Shout FREEDOM through your hundred hills
Till banded hosts come surging round!"

Our God! we come at thy commands; -
Thy people offer willingly!
No swords are in our peaceful hands, -
From wrath and doubt our hearts are free.

Vowed to the cause of awful TRUTH,
As erst our Pilgrim Fathers came,
With maid and matron, age and youth,
We throng round FREEDOM'S kindling flame.

Liberator, February 6, 1836, p. 23.

Songs, pp. 88-89, as "Convention"; no tune specified.

23. HYMN FOR THE MONTHLY CONCERT

Author: unspecified
Tune: unspecified

"Break every yoke," the Gospel cries,
"And let the oppressed go free";
Let every captive taste the joys
Of peace and liberty.

Lord, when shall man thy voice obey,
And rend each iron chain,
O when shall love its golden sway
O'er all the earth maintain.

Send thy good Spirit from above,
And melt the oppressor's heart,
Send sweet deliverance to the slave,
And bid his woes depart.

With freedom's blessings crown his day -
O'erflow his heart with love,
Teach him that strait and narrow way,
Which leads to rest above.

Songs, pp. 203-204.

Hymns, p. 9; Free Soil, p. 175; Liberty, p. 159; and
Freedom, p. 175, as "Break Every Yoke," to the tune,
"O No, We Never Mention Her."

Anniversary, p. 30, as "Break Every Yoke"; no tune
specified.

24. PREJUDICE REPROVED

Author: Lydia H. Sigourney
Tune: unspecified

God gave to Afric's sons
A brow of sable dye, -
And spread the country of their birth
Beneath a burning sky, -
And with a cheek of olive, made
The little Hindoo child,
And darkly stained the forest tribes
That roam our Western wild.

To me he gave a form
Of fairer, whiter clay, -
But am I, therefore, in his sight,
Respected more than they? -
No. - 'Tis the hue of deeds and thoughts
He traces in his book, -
'Tis the complexion of the heart,
On which he deigns to look.

Not by the tinted cheek,
That fades away so fast,
But by the color of the soul,
We shall be judged at last.
And God, the Judge, will look at me
With anger in His eyes,
If I, my brother's darker brow
Should ever dare despise.

Songs, pp. 138-140.

Melodies, p. 34, as "Hymn 20," to an unidentified tune.

25. CONVENTION

Author: M. W. Chapman
Tune: unspecified

Hark! Hark, to the trumpet call -
"Arise in the name of God most high!"
On ready hearts the deep notes fall,
And firm and full is the strong reply:

The hour is at hand to do and dare! -
Bound with the bondsmen now are we!
We may not utter the patriot's prayer,
Or bend in the house of God the knee!

Say! shall the blood of the martyred slain,
Sink vainly to the attesting earth?
To prison and exile, scourge and chain,
Shall the faithful and the just go forth?

Throng, throng, from your mountains green!
Pour like a flood from your hill-tops white!
With kindling hearts and voices keen,
Swell high the song of truth and right.

A mighty sound the region fills -
An awful voice from our fathers' graves!
It comes from the brows of a thousand hills -
"Woe to the lords of a land of slaves!"

Rise, for a slandered gospel's sake;
Nor rest till the notes be heard again,
That erst on the Savior's birth-night brake,
Of peace on earth - good will towards men.

Hark! Hark, to the trumpet call,
And firm and full be the glad reply:
On ready hearts the deep notes fall -
"Arise in the name of God most high!"

Songs, pp. 189-191.

26. SYMPATHY AND FAITH

Author: unspecified
Tune: unspecified

Hark! I hear the voice of anguish,
In my own, my native land;
Brethren doomed in chains to languish,
Lift to heaven the fettered hand,
And despairing,
Death to end their grief demand.

Let us raise our supplication,
For the scourged and suffering slave -
All whose life is desolation,
All whose hope is in the grave;
God of mercy!
From thy Throne, O hear and save.

Those in bonds we would remember,
Lord! our hands with theirs are bound;
With each helpless suffering member,
Let our sympathies be found,
Till our labors
Spread the smile of freedom round.

Even now the word is spoken:
"Tyrants' cruel power must cease -
From the slave the chain be broken -
Captives hail the kind release":
Then in splendor
Christ shall reign, the Prince of Peace!

Songs, pp. 143-145.

Collection, p. 34; Free Soil, pp. 56-57; and Freedom,
pp. 236-237, as "Hark! I Hear a Sound of Anguish," to
the tune, "Calvary."

27. HYMN FOR THE MONTHLY CONCERT

Author: W. H. Hayward
Tune: unspecified

Holy Father, God of love,
Send thy spirit from above;
Help us thy great name to sing,
God of mercy, heavenly King.

For the burdened slave would we
Ask the gift of liberty;
For the weary souls oppressed,
We would ask thy peace and rest.

In thy gracious love arise, -
See his burden, - hear his cries, -
Rend his fetters, - set him free
From oppression's tyranny.

Then his thankful voice shall raise
Songs to thee of grateful praise:
Thy great love shall be his theme,
He shall own thee, Lord, Supreme.

Songs, p. 198.

Melodies, p. 40, as "Hymn 26," to an unidentified tune.

28. THE HOUR OF FREEDOM

Author: William Lloyd Garrison
Tune: unspecified

The hour of freedom! come it must -
O, hasten it in mercy, Heaven!
When all who grovel in the dust,
Shall stand erect, their fetters riven!

When glorious freedom shall be won
By every caste, complexion, clime;
When tyranny shall be o'erthrown,
And color cease to be a crime!

Friend of the poor - long suffering Lord!
This guilty land from ruin save!
Let Justice sheath her glittering sword,
And Mercy rescue from the grave!

And ye who are like cattle sold,
And vilely trodden like the earth,
And bartered constantly for gold -
Your souls debased from their high birth:

Bear meekly still your cruel woes;
Light follows darkness - comfort, pain:
So time shall give you sweet repose,
And sever every hateful chain.

Not by the sword your liberty
Shall be obtained, in human blood;
Not by revolt or treachery, -
Revenge did never bring forth good:

God's time is best - 't will not delay -
E'en now your cause is blossoming,
And rich shall be the fruit: - the day
Of your redemption loudly sing!

Songs, pp. 32-33.

Melodies, p. 9, as "Hymn 3," to the tune, "Wells."

29. THE LAST NIGHT OF SLAVERY

Author: unspecified
Tune: unspecified

Let the floods clap their hands!
Let the mountains rejoice!
Let all the glad lands
Breathe a jubilant voice:
The sun that now sets on the waves of the sea,
Shall gild with his rising the land of the
Free.

Let the islands be glad,
For their King in his might,
Who his glory hath clad
With a garment of light;
In the waters the beams of his chambers hath
laid,
And in the green waters his pathway hath made.

No more shall the deep
Lend its awe-stricken waves
In their caverns to steep
Its wild burden of slaves:
The Lord sitteth King; - sitteth King on the
flood,
He heard, and hath answered the voice of their
blood.

Dispel the blue haze,
Golden fountain of morn!
With meridian blaze
The wide ocean adorn!
The sunlight has touched the glad waves of the
sea,
And day now illumines the land of the Free.

Songs, pp. 214-215.

Picknick, pp. 138-139, under the same title, to an
unidentified tune.

Hymns, pp. 14-15; Free Soil, pp. 165-166; and Freedom,
pp. 165-166, under the same title, to the tune, "Cherokee
Death Song."

30. LORD DELIVER

Author: E. L. Follen
Tune: unspecified

Lord Deliver! thou canst save,
Save from evil, Mighty God; -
Hear! oh hear the kneeling slave; -
Break, oh break the oppressor's rod.

That captive's prayer - may it fill
All the earth, and all the sky;
Every other voice be still,
While he pleads to God on high.

He whose ear is every where,
Who doth silent sorrow see,
He will hear the captive's prayer -
He can set the captive free.

From the tyranny within,
Save thy children, Lord, we pray;
Chains of iron, chains of sin -
Let them all be cast away.

> Love to man, and love to God,
> These must all our weapons be;
> These can break the oppressor's rod,
> These will set the captive free.

Songs, pp. 168-169.

Melodies, p. 37, verse four omitted, as "Hymn 23," to an unidentified tune.

Tracts, p. 7, under the same title; no tune specified, but with the following verses:

> Lord deliver! Thou canst save.
> Save thy children, mighty God!
> Hear, O hear the kneeling slave!
> Break, O break the oppressor's rod!
>
> Shall the tyrant reign forever?
> Shall we always suffer wrong?
> When wilt Thou our race deliver?
> Must we wait? "O God, how long?"
>
> O, how long, with blood and tears,
> Shall we till the oppressor's soil?
> When shall end these heavy years?
> When shall cease our hopeless toil?
>
> Robbed of manhood, knowledge, all;
> Father, we have nought but Thee.
> Hear us, when on Thee we call!
> God of mercy, set us free!
>
> Not on Afric's distant strand
> Shall our people exiled be.
> Here, within our native land,
> Give us back our liberty!
>
> Still we watch the passing hour
> Patiently through sorrow's night;
> Till the Lord shall give us power
> Here to vindicate our right.
>
> He whose power is everywhere,
> Who doth lowly sorrow see;
> He will hear the captive's prayer.
> He will set the captive free.

31. ADVENT OF CHRIST

Author: Reginald Heber
Tune: unspecified

The Lord will come! the earth shall quake,
The hills their fixed seat forsake;
And, withering, from the vault of night
The stars withdraw their feeble light.

The Lord will come! but not the same
As once in lowly form he came,
A silent lamb to slaughter led,
The bruised, the suffering, and the dead.

The Lord will come! a dreadful form,
With wreath of flame and robe of storm:
Master and slave alike shall find
An equal judge of human kind.

Can this be he who wont to stray
A pilgrim on the world's highway;
By power oppressed, and mocked by pride?
Oh God! is this the crucified?

Go, tyrants! to the rocks complain!
Go, seek the mountain's cleft in vain:
But faith, victorious o'er the tomb,
Shall sing for joy - the Lord is come!

Songs, pp. 9-11.

Melodies, p. 13, as "Hymn 7," to an unidentified tune
from Carmina Sacra.

32. HYMN

Sung at the quarterly meeting of the Massachusetts
Anti-Slavery Society, March 28, 1836.

Author: Mrs. H. G. Chapman
Tune: unspecified

The memory of the faithful dead
Be on their children's hearts this day!
Your father's God, their host that led,
Will shield you through the stormy way.

Your Saviour bids you seek and save
The trampled and the oppressed of earth,
At his command the storm to brave,
Faithful and true! come boldly forth!

Their suffering though your souls must share -
Though pride oppress and hate condemn,
Stand up! and breathe your fearless prayer
For those in bonds as bound with them.

Unheeded falls the fierce command
That bids the struggling soul be dumb!
Shout with a voice to rouse a land!
Bid the free martyr spirit come!

Searcher of hearts, to thee we bow -
Uphold us with thy staff and rod.
Our fervent hearts are ready now -
We come to do thy will, Oh God!

Liberator, April 2, 1836, p. 55.

Songs, pp. 121-122, as "Devotion to the Cause of Christ";
no tune specified.

33. PRAYER FOR THE SLAVE

Author: Wesley
Tune: unspecified

O Let the prisoners' mournful sighs,
As incense in thy sight appear!
Their humble wailings pierce the skies,
If haply they may feel thee near.

The captive exiles make their moans,
From sin impatient to be free:
Call home, call home thy banished ones!
Lead captive their captivity!

Out of the deep regard their cries,
The fallen raise, the mourners cheer;
O Son of Righteousness arise,
And scatter all their doubt and fear!

Stand by them in the fiery hour,
Their feebleness of mind defend;
And in their weakness show thy power,
And make them patient to the end.

Relieve the souls whose cross we bear,
For whom thy suffering members mourn:
Answer our faith's effectual prayer;
And break the yoke so meekly borne!

Songs, p. 26.

Free Soil, pp. 90-91; and Freedom, pp. 90-91, under the
same title, to the tune, "Hamburgh."

34. HYMN

Sung on the evening of the 9th inst. [March, 1836],
at which time the Abington Anti-Slavery Society was formed.

Author: A gentleman of East Abington
Tune: unspecified

O, Thou, who from thy throne on high,
Dost deign to lend a listening ear
To the young ravens, when they cry,
O! condescend our voice to hear.

We, unto Thee, our crimes confess,
With our most aggravated sin
Of disregarding the distress
Of those who wear a darker skin.

Long hast thou blest our happy land
With Freedom's mild and cheering light;
May we, with cheerful heart and hand,
Extend to all, this sacred right.

May Freedom's universal reign
Fill earth, as waters fill the sea,
Break the oppressor's iron chain,
And let the oppressed all go free.

Then shall earth's darkest regions ring,
And shouts of joy, shall rend the sky;
And all th' enslaved shall rise and sing,
"All glory be to God on high."

Liberator, March 19, 1836, p. 48.

35. DUTY OF THE FREE

Author: unspecified
Tune: unspecified

Rise, freemen, rise! the call goes forth;
List to the high command -
Obedience to the word of God,
Throughout this mighty land.

Rise, free the slave! oh, burst his chains!
His fetters cast ye down;
Let virtue be your country's pride,
Her diadem and crown, -

That the blest day may soon arrive,
When equal all shall be,
And freedom's banner waving high
Proclaim that all are free.

Songs, p. 40.

Melodies, p. 21, as "Hymn 13, to an unidentified tune.

Free Soil, p. 114; and Freedom, p. 114, as "Rise, Freemen,
Rise," to original music by G. W. C.

36. PATRIOTISM AND SYMPATHY

Author: E.M. Chandler
Tune: unspecified

Think of our country's glory,
All dimm'd with Afric's tears -
Her broad flag stained and gory,
With the hoarded guilt of years.

Think of the frantic mother,
Lamenting for her child,
Till falling lashes smother
Her cries of anguish wild!

Think of the prayers ascending,
Yet shrieked, alas! in vain,
When heart from heart is rending,
Ne'er to be joined again!

Shall we behold unheeding,
Life's holiest feelings crush'd?
When woman's heart is bleeding,
Shall woman's voice be hush'd?

Oh, no! by every blessing,
That heaven to thee may lend -
Remember their oppression,
Forget not, sister, friend.

Songs, p. 28.

Hymns, pp. 3-4, under no title, to the tune, "Missionary
Hymn."

Mentioned in Liberator, August 8, 1856, p. 126, as being
sung at a celebration of August 1.

37. CHRISTIAN RESOLUTION

Author: Caroline Weston
Tune: unspecified

To Freedom's cause, the cause of truth,
With joy we dedicate our youth;
To Freedom's holy altar bring
Fortune and life as offering.

Temptations sore and deadly foes,
Our onward progress would oppose;
And conflict stern we still must wage
With bigot hate and tyrant rage.

With scorn the foes of God and man
Our number and our weakness scan,
Feeble and few and distant far,
'T is ours to wage unequal war.

Yet are we strong, Oh God of might!
Ours are thy words of truth and right;
And armed with these, in vain thy foes
Their thronging numbers may oppose.

In vain with blood-stained hands they rear,
Their proud abodes of grief and fear!
Shaking their glories to the ground,
Thy trumpet blast of truth we sound!

> In earnest hope we wait the hour,
> Foretold us by prophetic power,
> When all shall come to thee, and own
> The glorious kingdom of thy son.

Songs, pp. 207-208.

Picknick, pp. 100-101, under the same title, to an
unidentified tune.

38. WHERE IS THY BROTHER

Author: E. L. F.
Tune: unspecified

> What mean ye that bruise and bind
> My people, saith the Lord,
> And starve your craving brother's mind,
> That asks to hear my word?
>
> What mean ye that ye make them toil
> Through long and dreary years,
> And shed like rain upon your soil
> Their blood and bitter tears?
>
> What mean ye that ye dare to rend
> The tender mother's heart;
> Brothers from sisters, friend from friend,
> How dare you bid them part?
>
> What mean ye, when God's bounteous hand
> To you so much has given,
> That from the slave who tills your land
> You keep both earth and heaven?
>
> When at the judgment God shall call,
> Where is thy brother? say,
> What mean ye to the Judge of all,
> To answer on that day?

Report, p. 107.

Songs, pp. 20-21; and Tracts, p. 1, under the same
title; no tune specified.

Melodies, p. 18, as "Hymn 10," to an unidentified tune.

Hymns, p. 7; Harp, p. 46; Free Soil, pp. 214-215; and
Freedom, p. 318, as "What Mean Ye?" to the tune "Ortonville."

Mentioned in Liberator, May 21, 1852, p. 82, as being
sung at the Eighteenth Annual Meeting of the American
Antislavery Society.

39. HOPE AND FAITH

Author: William Lloyd Garrison
Tune: unspecified

Ye who in bondage pine,
Shut out from light divine,
Bereft of hope;
Whose limbs are worn with chains,
Whose tears bedew our plains,
Whose blood our glory stains,
In gloom who grope:

Shout! for the hour draws nigh,
That gives you liberty!
And from the dust, -
So long your vile embrace, -
Uprising, take your place
Among earth's noblest race,
By right, the first!

The night - the long, long night
Of infamy and slight,
Shame and disgrace,
And slavery, worse than e'er
Rome's serfs were doomed to bear,
Bloody beyond compare -
Recedes apace!

Speed, speed the hour, O Lord!
Speak, and, at thy dread word,
Fetters shall fall
From every limb - the strong
No more the weak shall wrong,
But Liberty's sweet song
Be sung by all!

Songs, pp. 50-51.

Mentioned under the title, "Ye Who in Bondage Pine," in
Liberator, May 31, 1834, p. 87, as having been sung at
the New England Anti-Slavery Convention, May 27-29, by
Miss [Susan] Paul's Juvenile Colored Choir.

Mentioned in <u>Liberator</u>, January 28, 1837, p. 19, as "Ye
Who in Bondage Pine," in a notice of a future Juvenile
Concert.

<u>Hymns</u>, pp. 39-40, under no title, to the tune, "America."

<u>Picknick</u>, p. 104, as "Rise, Sons of Afric!" to an unidentified
tune.

<u>Melodies</u>, pp. 30-31, as "Hymn 18," to an unidentified tune.

<u>Liberator</u>, February 7, 1851, p. 22, as "Ye Who in Bondage
Pine," to the tune, "America."

40. HYMN

Sung at the third anniversary of the West India
Emancipation, in the Broadway Tabernacle,
New York, August, 1837.

Author: J. G. Whittier
Tune: unspecified

O, holy Father! just and true
Are all thy words, and works, and ways,
And unto Thee alone are due
Thanksgiving and eternal praise!
As children of thy gracious care,
We veil the eye - we bend the knee,
With broken words of praise and prayer,
Father and God, we come to thee!

For thou hast heard, O God of right,
The sighing of the island slave:
And stretched for him the arm of might,
Not shorten'd that it could not save.
The laborer sits beneath his vine -
The shackled soul and hand are free:
Thanksgiving! for the work is thine -
Praise! for the blessing is of thee.

And O, we feel thy presence here;
Thy awful arm in judgment bare!
Thine eye hath seen the bondman's tear -
Thine ear hath heard the bondman's prayer.
Praise! for the pride of man is low,
The cousels of the wise are nought;
The fountains of repentance flow -
What hath our God in mercy wrought?

Speed on thy work, Lord God of Hosts! -
And, when the bondman's chain is riven,
And swells from all our guilty coasts,
The anthem of the free to Heaven,
O, not to those, whom thou hast led,
As with thy cloud and fire before,
But, unto THEE, in fear and dread,
Be praise and glory evermore!

Genius, fifth series, October, 1837, p. 90; and Liberator,
August 31, 1838, p. 40, indicating that it was sung at that
year's August 1 celebration in the Broadway Tabernacle.

41. [UNTITLED]

Sung at the semi-annual meeting of the Plymouth County
Anti-Slavery Society at Hingham, at a collation prepared
by the Female Anti-Slavery Society.

Author: unspecified
Tune: Auld Lang Syne

No boastful chorus now shall rise
To Thee, Almighty God!
Our song shall be the captive's cries,
Beneath th' oppressor's rod.
Oh hear them, Thou who hearest prayer;
Oh hear them, God above;
And oh, th' oppressor's heart prepare
To obey the law of love.

"They touch our shore, their shackles fall";
Old England's glorious strain!
What answer from this land of thrall?
The clankings of the chain!
Oh hear them, etc.

And must these clankings rend the skies,
Where we have full control?
Must still the captive's plaints arise
In our own Capital?
Oh hear them, etc.

Liberator, November 16, 1838, p. 181.

42. ORIGINAL HYMN

Sung at the Annual Meeting of the Abington
Anti-Slavery Society, June 11, 1839.

Author: unspecified
Tune: unspecified

Ye heralds of Freedom! ye noble and brave,
Who dare to insist on the rights of the slave;
Go onward - go onward - your cause is of God,
And He will soon sever the oppressor's strong
rod.

The finger of slander may now at you point -
That finger will soon lose the strength of its
joint;
And those who now plead for the rights of the
slave,
Will soon be acknowledged the good and the
brave.

Though thrones, and dominions, and kingdoms,
and powers,
May now all oppose you, the victory is yours;
The banner of Jesus will soon be unfurled,
And He will give FREEDOM and PEACE to the
world.

Go under His standard, and fight by His side -
O'er mountains and billows you'll then safely
ride;
His gracious protection will be to you given,
And bright crowns of glory He'll give you in
heaven.

Liberator, July 5, 1839, p. 108.

Melodies, pp. 48-49; Free Soil, pp. 99-100; and Freedom,
pp. 99-100, as "Ye Heralds of Freedom," to the tune, "I Would
Not Live Always" (see song 316).

Harp, pp. 31-32, as "Ye Heralds of Freedom"; no tune
specified.

43. [UNTITLED]

Sung at the celebration of August 1 in West Amesbury.

Author: Mary Jackman
Tune: unspecified

Eternal Father, thou hast made
A numerous family thy care;
Nor sable hue, nor caste, nor grade,
Excludes the meanest from his share.

Of kindred blood, and flesh the same,
In thy pure sight of equal worth;
Then why should one the sceptre claim,
And crush his brother to the earth?

Why should the sighing bondman grope,
A cheerless journey to the tomb;
No star to guide - no ray of hope,
To shine upon the darksome gloom.

Wilt thou not hear, and set them free,
The down-cast slaves for whom we plead;
And make our land as it should be,
A free and happy land indeed?

Liberator, August 16, 1839, p. 132.

Melodies, p. 11, as "Hymn 5," to an unidentified tune from
Carmina Sacra.

44. [UNTITLED]

Sung at the celebration of August 1 in West Amesbury.

Author: Mary Jackman
Tune: unspecified

See yon glorious star ascending,
Brightly o'er the Southern sea,
Truth and peace to earth portending,
Herald of a Jubilee;
Hail it, freemen,
'Tis the star of liberty.

Dim at first - but widely spreading,
Soon 'twill burst supremely bright,
Life and health and comfort shedding
O'er the shades of mortal night.
Hail it, bondmen,
Slavery cannot bear its light.

Few its rays, - 'tis but the dawning
Of the reign of truth and peace,
Joy to slaves, - yet sad forewarning,
To the tyrants of our race;
Tremble, tyrants,
Soon your cruel power will cease.

Earth enlightened by the glory
Of its mild and peaceful rays,
Ransomed slaves shall tell the story,
See its light and sing its praise;
Hail it, Christians,
Harbinger of better days.

Liberator, August 16, 1839, p. 132.

Hymns, pp. 15-16, under no title, to the tune, "Greenville."

Picknick, pp. 90-91, as "The Harbinger," to an unidentified tune.

Melodies, pp. 26-27, as "Hymn 16," to an unidentified tune.

Free Soil, pp. 173-174; and Freedom, pp. 173-174, as "Harbinger of Liberty," to original music by G. W. C.

45. HYMN

Written for and sung at the celebration of the
First of August, by the National Anti-Slavery
Convention at Albany.

Author: Rev. John Scoble
Tune: unspecified

Hasten, O Lord, we pray
The great and glorious hour,
When from the river to the sea,
The earth shall own thy power;

When thy pure Gospel light
Shall brighten every Isle,
And, gilded by its radiance bright,
The wilderness shall smile;

When from the Plains below,
Unto the Heights above,
The heart of every man shall glow
With LIBERTY and LOVE;

When solemn praise and prayer
To thee shall ever rise,
And Earth itself become once more
A blissful Paradise.

Liberator, August 23, 1839, p. 136.

46. ODE

Sung at the celebration of the first of August,
in Belknap-Street Church, Boston, 1840.

Author: M. W. Chapman
Tune: America

Wake with a song, my soul!
Free from all base control,
Wake with a song!
Glad let the people be -
Darkness and bondage flee!
Glory and praise to thee,
Oh! God, belong!

Rouse ye! true-hearted ones -
Liberty's faithful sons!
Let your glad shout,
Mingling with theirs who sing
Liberty's welcoming,
Over the waters ring
Joyously out!

Vainly, oh! vainly ye
Ask song of Jubilee
Of our sad band:
Still must our voices fail -
Still must the tones of wail
O'er the gay feast prevail -
In Slavery's land.

Still our free souls must weep
While the land's tyrants keep
Their wearing chain
Cold on our brother's heart,
Bidding his peace depart,
While, on the crowded mart,
They scorn his pain.

Rise for your brothers, then,
Noble but trampled men!
And God, who gave
Rights to the human race,
Shall from his holy place,
Grant us the might and grace
To free the Slave!

Liberator, August 7, 1840, p. 128.

47. PRAYER FOR THE SLAVE

Author: J. Pierpont
Tune: Missionary Hymn

Almighty God, thou Giver
Of all our sunny plains,
That stretch from sea to river,
Hear'st thou thy children's chains?
See'st thou the snapper'd lashes
That daily sting afresh?
See'st thou the cowskin's gashes,
Cut through the quivering flesh?

See'st thou the sores that rankle,
Licked by no pitying dog,
Where, round the bondman's ankle,
They've riveted a clog?
Hear'st thou the curse he mutters?
See'st thou his flashing eye?
Hear'st thou the prayers he utters,
That thou would'st let him die?

God of the poor and friendless,
Shall this unequaled wrong,
This agony, be endless?
How long, O Lord, how long
Shall man set, on his brother,
The iron heel of sin,
The Holy Ghost to smother -
To crush the God within!

Call out, O God, thy legions -
The hosts of love and light!
Ev'n in the blasted regions
That slavery wraps in night,
Some of thine own anointed
Shall catch the welcome call,
And, at the hour appointed,
Do battle for the thrall.

Let press, let pulpit thunder,
In all slave-holders' ears,
Till they disgorge the plunder
They've garnered up, for years;
Till Mississippi's valley,
Till Carolina's coast,
Round Freedom's standard rally,
A vast, a ransomed host!

Picknick, pp. 128-129.

48. REMEMBER THEM THAT ARE IN BONDS

Author: E. M. Chandler
Tune: Lincoln

Christian mother, when thy prayer
Trembles on the twilight air,
And thou askest God to keep,
In their waking and their sleep,
Those, whose love is more to thee
Than the wealth of land or sea;
Think of those who wildly mourn
For the loved ones from them torn.

Christian daughter, sister, wife,
Ye who wear a guarded life,
Ye, whose bliss hangs not, thank God,
On a tyrant's word or nod,
Will ye hear, with careless eye,
Of the wild despairing cry,
Rising up from human hearts,
As their latest bliss departs?

Blest ones, whom no hands on earth
Dare to wrench from home and hearth,
Ye, whose hearts are shelter'd well,
By affection's holy spell,

Oh, forget not those, for whom
Life is nought but changeless gloom,
O'er whose days, so woe-begone,
Hope may paint no brighter dawn.

Picknick, pp. 135-137.

Melodies, pp. 54-55, as "Hymn 32," to the same tune.

Liberty, p. 80; and Freedom, p. 217, as "Christian Mother," to the same tune.

49. THE THINGS WHICH ARE CAESAR'S

Author: unspecified
Tune: unspecified

ETERNAL Sov'reign of the sky,
And Lord of all below:
We mortals, to thy majesty,
Our first obedience owe.

Our souls adore thy throne supreme,
And bless thy providence
For magistrates of meaner name,
Our glory and defense.

The rulers of these states shall shine
With rays above the rest,
While laws and liberties combine
To make a nation blest.

Kingdoms on firm foundations stand,
While virtue finds reward;
And sinners perish from the land,
By justice and the sword.

Let Caesar's due be ever paid
To Caesar and his throne;
But consciences and souls were made,
To be the Lord's alone.

Hymns, pp. 38-39.

50. [UNTITLED]

Author: unspecified
Tune: Uxbridge

FATHER of all the human race! -
The white or color'd, bond or free -
Thanks for thy gifts of heavenly grace,
Vouchsaf'd through Jesus Christ to me.

'Tis this, 'mid ev'ry cruel wrong,
Has borne my sinking spirits up,
Made sorrow joyful - weakness strong,
And sweeten'd Slavery's bitter cup.

Hath not a Saviour's dying hour
Made e'en the yoke of thraldom light?
Hath not thy Holy Spirit's pow'r
Made bondage freedom - darkness bright?

Thanks, then, O Father! for the gift,
Thou in thy Son to me hath given;
Which thus, from bonds and earth, can lift
The soul to liberty and heav'n.

But not the less I mourn their shame,
Who, heedless of Thy gracious will;
Call on a Father's - Saviour's name,
Yet keep their brethren bondsmen still!

Forgive them, Lord! for Jesus sake,
And when thou hast the slave unbound;
The chains which bind th' oppressor break,
And be thy love's last triumph crown'd.

Hymns, pp. 21-22.

51. GOD AND LIBERTY

Author: unspecified
Tune: unidentified

God is our guide from field and wave,
From plough, from anvil, and from loom;
We come to liberate the slave,
And speak the factious despot's doom;
And, hark! we raise from sea to sea,
The watchword - "God and Liberty!"

We draw no devastating sword,
No war's destructive fires we light,
By reason and the living word
Of God, we put our foes to flight;
And, hark! we raise from sea to sea,
The watchword - "God and Liberty!"

We come with blessings in our train,
To spread them with a bounteous hand;
To wipe away the guilty stain
Of Slavery, from this much-lov'd land;
And, hark! we raise from sea to sea,
The watchword - "God and Liberty!"

Picknick, pp. 112-113.

52. CHILDREN PLEADING FOR THE SLAVE

Author: C. W. Dennison
Tune: unidentified

God of the wide creation -
Of air, and earth and sea!
Accept the young oblation,
We children bring to thee;
We come, thy sons attending,
And join our notes with theirs;
At mercy's footstool bending,
We lift our youthful prayers.

And will the Lord of glory,
Who dwells beyond the sky,
Regard our humble story,
And answer from on high?
He will; for he hath told us
In his eternal word,
He always doth behold us,
His ears have ever heard.

When Samuel bow'd before him,
And clasp'd his hands and pray'd,
God taught him to adore him,
And heard the pray'r he said;
Now, Samuel's God is near us,
Where we have met today;
He bows his ear to hear us,
And teaches us to pray.

Then bless, Great God of heaven!
The helpless, bleeding slave;
Let light and truth be given,
His darken'd soul to save;
And speed, good Lord! the season,
When Slavery's reign shall end,
And masters, sway'd by reason,
Shall call the slave their friend.

Picknick, pp. 94-95.

Melodies, pp. 44-45, without verse three, as "Hymn 29," to
the tune, "Missionary Hymn."

53. HAIL TO THE CAUSE OF LIBERTY

Author: C. W. Dennison
Tune: Hail to the Chief

Hail to the cause that in triumph advances,
Pouring the light of its glory afar;
Banner'd and plum'd, lo! the sheen of its
lances
'Lumines the steeds and the prow of its car.
Hark hear it rolling on,
Trumping of battles won;
Won o'er the hosts that have set it at bay!
Shout! it is marching now;
Shout! see its foemen bow!
"God and our cause!" we are winning the day.

Lo! o'er the field mark! the foe is preparing
Rank upon rank for another attack;
While God and right he is wickedly daring;
Who from the conflict turns cowardly back?
March to the battle-field!
Never, no! never yield,
Dark through the cloud of the enemy lowers!
Strike! and be valiant, then;
Stand to your posts like men;
"GOD AND OUR CAUSE!" soon the triumph is ours!

Weapons of war we have cast from the battle;
TRUTH is our armor - our watchword is LOVE;
Hushed be the sword and the musketry's rattle;
All our equipments are drawn from above;
Praise, then, the God of Truth,

Hoar age and ruddy youth!
Praise Him, who flock for our army's increase!
Long may our rally be
"LOVE, LIGHT, AND LIBERTY," -
Ever our banner the banner of peace!

<u>Picknick</u>, pp. 125-127.

54. [UNTITLED]

Author: unspecified
Tune: unspecified

HARK the chain - the clanking chain,
With our triumph blending -
Sighs of sorrow, groans of pain,
O'er our songs ascending.
Lo! our injur'd brother man,
Crush'd beneath the scourge - the ban -
Still a wretched slave must be;
Him proud freedom will not free.

Hear the slave, with lifted hands,
Mid his anguish raving:
On his neck proud freedom stands,
All her banners waving.
She hath cut the tyrant's cord,
Driv'n away the foreign lord,
Yet her foot's contemptuous thrust
Tramples millions to the dust.

Hark the chain - the loosen'd chain,
From its victim falling: -
Wake - Oh! wake a loftier strain,
Glorious days forestalling.
Love and mercy sweetly plead,
Justice urges to the deed,
Reason's mighty voice is heard,
Loud is God's commanding word.

Heav'n has heard the stifled cry,
Hearts from sleep awaken;
Freedom, with uplifted eye,
Owns herself mistaken:

See! 'tis done - the slave is free -
Raise the song of Jubilee!
Let it sound o'er land and sea!
Love hath conquer'd - man is free.

<u>Hymns</u>, pp. 30-32.

55. [UNTITLED]

Author: unspecified
Tune: unspecified

HIGH as the heav'ns above the ground,
Reigns the Creator God;
Wide as the whole creation's bound,
Extends his awful rod.

Let princes of exalted state
To him ascribe their crown;
Render their homage at his feet,
And cast their glories down.

Know that his kingdom is supreme,
Your lofty thoughts are vain;
He calls you gods: that awful name:
But ye must die like men.

Then let the sov'reigns of the globe
Not dare to vex the just;
He puts on vengeance like a robe,
And treads the worms to dust.

Ye judges of the earth: be wise,
And think of heav's with fear;
The meanest saint, whom you despise,
Has an Avenger there.

<u>Hymns</u>, pp. 37-38.

56. GOD SPEED THE RIGHT

Author: unspecified
Tune: unidentified

Now to heav'n our pray'rs ascending,
God speed the right!
In a noble cause contending,
God speed the right!
Be their zeal in heav'n recorded,
With success on earth rewarded,
God speed the right,
God speed the right.

Be that pray'r again repeated,
God speed the right!
Ne'er despairing, though defeated,
God speed the right!
Like the good and great in story,
If they fail, they fail in glory;
God speed the right,
God speed the right.

Patient, firm and persevering,
God speed the right!
Ne'er th' event nor danger fearing,
God speed the right!
Pain, nor toils, nor trials heeding,
And in Heav'n's own time succeeding,
God speed the right,
God speed the right.

Still their onward course pursuing,
God speed the right!
Every foe at length subduing,
God speed the right!
Truth thy cause, whate'er delay it,
There's no power on earth can stay it,
God speed the right,
God speed the right.

Picknick, p. 97.

Freedom, pp. 44-45, under the same title, to the same tune.
In this version, it is noteworthy that "our" is substituted
for "their," "thy," and "thine," a stronger message replaces
line six of verse three ("Millions in their chains are bleeding"), and verse two is as follows:

May this truth be kept before us,
God speed the right!
Freedom's cause is just and glorious,
God speed the right!
Like the good and great in story,
If we fail, we fail with glory,
God speed the right!
God speed the right!

57. HYMN FOR AN ANTI-SLAVERY MEETING

Author: E. S.
Tune: Liberia

O'er the southern plains of darkness,
Christian, see your countrymen,
Far from hope and bowed in sadness,
Doomed to toil in slavery's chain;
Blessed jubilee - blessed jubilee,
Hasten on fair Freedom's reign.

Let the poor despairing bondman,
With his wife and children see,
That divine and glorious conquest,
To be won for liberty;
Day of Freedom - Day of Freedom,
Dawn, and every slave set free.

Afric's sons, so long neglected,
Grant them, Lord, the glorious light,
Now from northern coast to southern,
Truth and Freedom chase the night;
God of Justice - God of Justice,
Break the bands of slavery.

Fly abroad, thou mighty spirit,
Win and conquer - never cease,
Tire not on thy blessed pinions,
Banish sin and prejudice,
All united - all united,
May we see the reign of peace.

Liberator, December 23, 1842, p. 204.

58. [UNTITLED]

Author: unspecified
Tune: Zion

On the mountain tops appearing,
Lo the sacred herald stands;
Welcome news to pris'ners bearing,
Pris'ners long in hostile lands:
Mourning captive:
God himself will loose thy bands.

Has thy night been long and mournful,
All thy friends unfaithful prov'd?
Have thy foes been proud and scornful,
By thy sighs and tears unmov'd?
Cease thy mourning,
Africa is well-beloved.

God, thy God will now restore thee,
He himself appears thy friend;
All thy foes shall flee before thee,
Here their boasts and triumphs end;
Great deliv'rance
Zion's King vouchsafes to send.

Peace and joy shall now attend thee,
All thy warfare now is past,
God, thy Saviour, shall defend thee.
Peace and joy have come at last;
All thy conflicts
End in everlasting rest.

Hymns, pp. 34-35.

59. [UNTITLED]

Author: unspecified
Tune: Belville

"The ox, that treadeth out the corn,
Thou shalt not muzzle." - Thus saith God.
And will ye muzzle the free-born, -
The man - the owner of the sod, -
Who "gives the grazing ox his meat,"
And you, - his servants here, - your seat?

There's a cloud, blackening up the sky!
East, west, and north its curtains spread;
Lift to its muttering folds your eye!
Beware, for, bursting on your heads,
It hath a force to bear you down;
'Tis an insulted people's frown.

A weapon that comes down as still
As snow-flakes fall upon the sod;
But executes a freeman's will
As lightning does the will of God;
And from its force, nor doors nor locks
Can shield you; - 'tis the ballot box.

Black as your deed shall be the balls
That from that box shall pour like hail!
And when the storm upon you falls,
How will your craven cheeks turn pale?
For, at its coming though ye laugh,
'Twill sweep you from your hail like chaff.

Not woman, now, - the people pray,
Hear us, or from us ye will hear!
Beware! - a desperate game ye play!
The men that thicken on your rear, -
Kings though ye be, - may not be scorn'd.
Look to your move! your stake! Ye're warned.

Hymns, pp. 17-18.

60. PRAYER OF THE ABOLITIONIST*

Author: John Pierpont
Tune: unidentified, by G. A. Hewes

We ask not that the slave should lie,
As lies his master, at his ease,
Beneath a silken canopy,
Or in the shade of blooming trees.

We mourn not that the man should toil;
'Tis nature's need, 'tis God's decree;
But let the hand that tills the soil,
Be, like the wind that fans it, free.

We ask not, "eye for eye," that all,
Who forge the chain and ply the whip,
Should feel their torture; while the thrall
Should wield the scourge of mastership.

We only ask, O God, that they,
Who bind a brother, may relent:
But, Great Avenger, we do pray
That the wrong-doer may repent.

Picknick, p. 124.

Melodies, p. 5, as "Hymn 1," to the tune, "Old Hundred."

Almanac, p. 31, as "Hymn"; no tune specified.

*This song is widely referred to in secondary sources as
"The Abolitionist Hymn."

61. COMMITTING ALL TO GOD

Author: unspecified
Tune: unspecified

Why should I vex my soul and fret,
To see the wicked rise?
Or envy sinners waxing great,
By violence and lies?

As flow'ry grass cut down at noon,
Before the evening fades;
So shall their glories vanish soon,
In everlasting shades.

Then let me make the Lord my trust,
And practice all that's good;
So shall I dwell among the just,
And he'll provide me food.

I to my God my ways commit,
And cheerful wait his will;
Thy hand, which guides my doubtful feet,
Shall my desires fulfill.

Hymns, pp. 22-23.

62. ARMING, BUT NOT WITH CARNAL WEAPONS

Author: unspecified
Tune: unidentified

Ye spirits of the free,
Can ye forever see
Your brother man,
A yok'd and tortur'd slave,
Scourg'd to an early grave,
And raise no hand to save,
E'en when you can?

Shall tyrants from the soul
That they in pomp may roll,
God's image tear,
And call the wreck their own;
While, from th' eternal throne,
They shut the stifled groan,
And bitter prayer?

Shall he a slave be bound,
Whom God hath doubly crowned
Creation's lord?
Shall men of Christian name,
Without a blush of shame,
Profess their tyrant claim
From God's own word?

NO! at the battle-cry,
A host, prepared to die,
Shall arm for fight:
But not with martial steel,
Grasped with a murd'rous zeal;
No arms their foes shall feel,
But LOVE and LIGHT.

Firm on Jehovah's laws,
Strong in their righteous cause,
They march to save;
Vain is th' oppressor's mail,
Against their battle-hail,
Till cease the woe and wail
Of every slave.

Picknick, pp. 98-99.

Collection, pp. 23-24; Free Soil, pp. 127-128; Harp, p. 16;
and Freedom, pp. 127-128, as "Ye Spirits of the Free," to the
tune, "My Faith Looks Up to Thee."

63. HYMN 11

Author: Montgomery
Tune: unidentified

Daughter of sadness, from the dust
Exalt thy fallen head,
In thy Redeemer firmly trust:
He calls thee from the dead.

Awake, awake, put on thy strength,
Thy beautiful array;
The day of freedom dawns at length,
The Lord's appointed day.

> Rebuild thy walls - thy bounds enlarge,
> And send thy heralds forth;
> Say to the South, "Give up thy charge,
> And keep not back, O North."

Melodies, p. 19.

64. HYMN 25

Author: unspecified
Tune: unidentified

> Hear us, Father, while we cry,
> Pleading for an injur'd race;
> Make the bolts asunder fly,
> By thine own resistless grace.
>
> Let the captives all go free,
> Let the oppressor cease to reign;
> And the arm of tyranny,
> Never more be rais'd again.
>
> Crush the system in the dust,
> Ere another year be past,
> Every chain and fetter burst,
> Which have been around them cast.
>
> Then will shrieks be turn'd to praise,
> As the gory whip departs;
> And the ransom'd daily raise,
> Songs of joy from grateful hearts.

Melodies, p. 39.

65. HYMN 21

Author: unspecified
Tune: unidentified

> How long shall Afric's sons,
> Be sons of grief and pain,
> How long shall slavery curse the earth,
> And mercy plead in vain.

Lift up your voice today,
In Freedom's holy cause,
Till all the world in love obey
Their maker's righteous laws.

Then in your blissful songs,
Shall bond and free unite.
His praise to spread, to whom belongs
All majesty and might.

Melodies, p. 35.

66. SONG

Sung at the late Nantucket Anti-Slavery Fair.

Author: Mrs. A. H.
Tune: Sandy and Jenny

How long will the friend of the slave plead in
vain?
How long e'er the Christian will loosen the
chain?
If he, by our efforts, more hardened should
be,
O Father, forgive him! we trust but in thee.

That "we're all free and equal," how senseless
the cry,
While millions in bondage are groaning so
nigh;
O where is our freedom? equality where?
To this none can answer, but echo cries,
where?

O'er this stain on our country we'd fain draw
a veil,
But history's page will proclaim the sad tale,
That Christians, unblushing, could shout, "we
are free,"
Whilst they the oppressor of millions could
be.

They can feel for themselves, for the Pole
they can feel,
Towards Africa's children their hearts are
like steel;
They are deaf to their call, to their wrongs
they are blind;
In error they slumber, nor seek truth to find.

Though scorn and reproach on our pathway
attend,
Despised and reviled, we the slave will
befriend;
Our Father, thy blessing! we look but to thee,
Nor cease from our labors till all shall be
free.

Should mobs in their fury with missiles
assail,
The cause it is righteous, the truth will
prevail;
Then heed not their clamors, though loud they
proclaim
That freedom shall slumber, and slavery reign.

Liberator, January 13, 1843, p. 8.

Free Soil, p. 67; and Freedom, p. 229, as "How Long! O!
How Long!"; no tune specified.

67. HYMN 6

Author: Rev. Dr. Willard
Tune: unidentified

Let freeborn empires offer prayer,
Lord, God of Hosts, around thy throne.
The sons of toil are equal there
With those who boast a royal crown.

Beneath the guardian eye of heaven,
Th' unchanging rights of men we claim;
Our sires th' oppressive yoke have riven,
And mark'd our way to pow'r and fame.

Let Afric's children, dear to God,
Expire in galling chains no more;
Nor grasping av'rice, stain'd with blood,
Columbia's elder sons devour.

Let reason guide each patriot band,
And love exert her mild control;
The tyrant yield to thy command,
And freedom reign from pole to pole.

Melodies, p. 12.

68. GOD IS JUST

Author: unspecified
Tune: unspecified

Oh righteous God! whose awful frown
Can crumble nations to the dust,
Trembling we stand before thy throne,
When we reflect that thou art just.

Dost thou not see the dreadful wrong,
Which Afric's injured race sustains?
And wilt thou not arise ere long,
To plead their cause, and break their chains?

Must not thine anger quickly rise
Against the men whom lust controls,
Who dare thy righteous laws despise
And traffic in the blood of souls?

Anniversary, p. 30.

Free Soil, p. 91; and Freedom, p. 91, as "Remembering That
God is Just"; no tune specified.

69. HYMN 27

Author: W. L. Garrison
Tune: unidentified

Savior, though by scorn requited,
Oft'ner than by gratitude;
Still on earth thy soul delighted
Constantly in doing good.

As the way to glory leading,
As the truth that sets us free,
As the light from heaven proceeding,
Chiefly do we honor thee.

"Follow me," - Yes precious Savior!
In thy footsteps we will tread;
By thy grace, our whole behavior
Shall be worthy of our head.

Help us ev'ry chain to sever,
Ev'ry captive to set free -
And our guilty land deliver
From the curse of slavery.

Melodies, p. 41.

70. HYMN 22

Author: Mrs. Sigourney
Tune: unidentified

This day doth music rare
Swell through our nation's bound;
But Afric's wailing mingles there,
And heaven doth hear the sound.

Almighty God! we turn
In penitence to thee;
Bid our lov'd land the lesson learn,
To bid the slave be free.

Melodies, p. 36.

71. HYMN

Sung at the Dedham A. S. Picknick
[celebrating August 1].

Author: Rev. J. Pierpont
Tune: unspecified

Thy voice, O God, is on the air,
As it stirs the leaves of every tree,
That stands around us, while at prayer,
For the negro captive's liberty.
That's well! That's well!
For, louder is thy voice, O God,
Than the voice of all, who ply the rod.

Thy hand, O God, hath raised the grove,
That, above us, lifts its leafy shield,
While, in our armor, - truth and love -
We are here, on Freedom's battle-field.

That's well! That's well!
For, stronger is thy hand, O God,
Than the hand of all, who ply the rod.

Thy smile, O God, is in the light,
That around us shines, from all the sky,
When, or at noontide or at night,
To the slave we speak of liberty.
That's well! That's well!
For, brighter is thy smile, O God,
Than the smile of all, who ply the rod.

Thy word, O God, "Well done! Well done."
Is forever heard, nor heard in vain,
When MAN casts off, and tramples on
His iron yoke, and broken chain.
That's well! That's well!
For, mightier is thy word, O God,
Than the word of all, who ply the rod.

Thy frown, O God, on him doth rest,
Who returneth, bound, the hunted thrall;
Though in a robe of ermine drest,
And the highest in a judgment hall.
That's well! That's well!
Though darker is thy frown, O God,
Than the hue of all who feel the rod.

Liberator, August 4, 1843, p. 124.

Liberator, August 11, 1843, p. 126, indicates that this song
was sung by "Misses Fuller and Mr. Richardson" at the occasion
noted above.

72. WHO IN GOD'S SIGHT IS HOLY

Author: Miss Almira Seymour
Tune: Morning Light is Breaking

Who in God's sight is holy?
What lips shall dare to pray,
Our Father! let thy kingdom
Be hastened on its way?
Shall hands, that forge the fetters,
Which clasp the living limb,
Stained with a brother's life-blood,
Be raised in prayer to Him?

Shall lips breathe forth His praises,
That, in their impious pride,
Contemn His sacred image,
And mercy's claims deride?
Shall tongues exhort to virtue
The erring steps of men,
That to earth's darkest vices
Millions of souls condemn?

Forbid it, blest Religion!
All holy things and true!
And, Father! O forgive them,
They know not what they do.
O, purify thy churches,
Throughout this sinful land;
Let justice, truth and mercy
Beside thy altar stand.

Chase from thy holy temple,
All which ensnares, deceives,
And let thy house, no longer,
Be as a den of thieves;
Fill it with thy own presence,
Life-giving as thou art,
Till largest love becometh,
The life of every heart.

Melodies, pp. 58-59.

73. THE CLARION OF FREEDOM

Author: unspecified
Tune: unspecified

The clarion - the clarion of Freedom now
sounds,
From the east to the west Independence
resounds;
From the hills, and the streams, and the far
distant skies,
Let the shout independence from Slavery arise.

The army - the army have taken the field,
And the hosts of Freemen never, never will
yield;
By free principles strengthened, each bosom
now glows
And with ardor immortal the struggle they
close.

The armor, the armor that girds every vreast,
Is the hope of deliverance for millions
oppressed;
O'er the tears, and the sighs, and the wrongs
of the slave,
See the white flag of freedom triumphantly
wave.

The conflict - the conflict will shortly be
o'er,
And the demon of slavery shall rule us no
more;
And the laurels of victory shall surely reward
The heroes immortal who've conquered for God.

Collection, p. 29.

Free Soil, pp. 17-18; and Freedom, pp. 266-267, under the
same title, to the tune, "The Chariot."

74. ANTI-SLAVERY HYMN

Author: D. S. Whitney
Tune: Sparkling and Bright

Fairer than light, to the human sight,
Is the freedom God has given;
And every man, in tribe or clan,
Receives this boon from heaven.
O then renounce all claim at once,
To every sister, brother;
There's nothing so base in the human race,
As enslaving one another.

Loathsome as death is Slavery's breath,
To every human creature;
They shun its blight, they hate its sight,
In every form and feature.
O then renounce, etc.

Wide as the land its bold command,
For all to pay it allegiance;
And few indeed abjure the deed,
Or refuse to bow in obedience.
O then renounce, etc.

The Democrat kneels, and the Whig too yields,
To Slavery as their master;
And then unite against the right,
To crush our liberties faster.
O then renounce, etc.

The Church it claims to sanction its chains,
And the priest at the altar serving;
And a godless crew its pleasures do,
In spite of the true and unswerving.
O then renounce, etc.

The learned and great, in Church and State,
Have made with hell an alliance,
And think to find in all a mind
To yield a ready compliance.
O then renounce, etc.

But it will not hold, the compact bold,
Though Church and State pledge together;
For true souls feel the cruel steel,
That pierces the heart of a brother.
O then renounce, etc.

In God we trust, the true and just,
Who ne'er will forsake the needy;
To Him we'll pray by night and day,
To send them deliverance speedy.
O then renounce, etc.

On to the charge, free hearts and large,
In truth's bright armor shining!
In God's great might, we'll strike for the
right,
And deliver the bond-slave pining!
O then renounce, etc.

Liberator, April 25, 1845, p. 68.

75. PATRIOTIC SONG

Author: unspecified
Tune: unspecified

Friends, we bid you welcome here,
Freedom's sacred cause revere;
Daily breathe a breath sincere,
For them who suffer wrong.

Fear not lest your hope should fail.
Truth is strong and must prevail.
What though foes our cause assail,
They'll never prosper long.

Who is he devoid of shame,
Justice for himself would claim,
Yet deny to all the same,
Through vain and selfish pride?
Friends, you long our hearts have known,
You're not left to fight alone;
We will make the cause our own,
For Heaven is on our side.

Who would live, to live in vain,
Live alone for worldly gain?
Spending days and nights in pain
For some ignoble end?
We would hope to leave behind,
Better times than now we find;
Better be it for mankind,
That we have lived their friend.

Collection, p. 18.

76. LINES

Read at a celebration of August 1 at Waltham.

Author: James Russell Lowell
Tune: unspecified

Let others strive for fame and gold,
And make God's earth and air and sea
Their own mean prison, dark and cold, -
We only toil to set men free.

Men make themselves the serfs of pelf,
And feed the worms of living graves;
But 'tis the ugly demon self
That helps us make our brothers slaves.

One chain the politician wears,
The priest another, forged full strong;
But he the heaviest fetter bears,
Who doth a human being wrong.

We fain would break the bands of all,
Making both slave and tyrant free,
And carving on each dungeon's wall,
That brotherhood is liberty.

Tears rust some bitter gyves in twain,
Fear makes some conquests for the right,
Force breaks some chains, but soon again
The sundered links more firm unite.

But God hath given to us a charm,
Whereby all fetters melt like snow, -
Love needs but touch th' oppressor's arm,
And straight he lets the captive go.

Liberator, August 8, 1845, p. 127, preceded by the statement,
"It was originally designed that they [the lines] should be
sung by the Hutchinsons, but those friends were engaged at a
similar festival in their own State."

77. SING ME A TRIUMPH SONG

Author: unspecified
Tune: [America?]

Sing me a triumph song,
Roll the glad notes along,
Great God, to thee!
Thine be the glory bright,
Source of all power and might!
For thou hast said, in might,
Man shall be free.

Sing me a triumph song,
Let all the sound prolong,
Air, earth, and sea,
Down falls the tyrant's power,
See his dread minions cower;
Now, from this glorious hour,
Man will be free.

Sing me a triumph song,
Sing in the mighty throng,
Sing Jubilee!
Let the broad welkin ring,
While to heaven's mighty King,
Honor and praise we sing,
For man is free.

Collection, p. 46.

Free Soil, p. 128; and Freedom, p. 128, under the same
title; no tune specified.

78. HYMN FOR CHILDREN

Author: W. S. Abbott
Tune: Miss Lucy Long

While we are happy here,
In joy and peace and love,
We'll raise our hearts with holy fear
To thee, great God, above.

God of our infant hours!
The music of our tongues,
The worship of our nobler powers,
To thee, to thee belongs.

The little trembling slave
Shall feel our sympathy;
O God! arise with might to save
And set the captive free.

No parent's holy care
Provides for him repose,
But oft the hot and briny tear,
In sorrow freely flows.

The God of Abraham praise;
The curse he will remove;
The slave shall welcome happy days,
With liberty and love.

Pray without ceasing, pray,
Ye saints of God Most High,
That all who hail this glorious day,
May have their liberty.

Collection, p. 43; Free Soil, p. 215; and Freedom, p. 320.

79. SONG, FOR THE FRIENDS OF FREEDOM

Faneuil Hall, Twelfth Anti-Slavery Fair.

Author: Eliza Lee Follen
Tune: unspecified

HEART to heart, and hand in hand
Bound together let us stand,
Storms are gathering o'er the land,
Many friends are gone!
Still we never are alone,
Still we bravely march right on,
Right on! right on! right on!

To the Pilgrim spirit true
Which nor slave nor master knew,
Onward! faithful, fearless few,
Liberty's the prize!
Full of hope that never dies,
Spirits of the free arise!
Arise! arise! arise!

Will you your New England see
Crouching low to slavery?
Rise and say it shall not be!
More than life's at stake!
Rise and every fetter break!
Every free-born soul awake!
Awake! awake! awake!

Listen to our solemn call,
Sounding from old Faneuil Hall,
Consecrate yourselves, your all
To God and Liberty!
On your spirit's kindred knee,
Swear your country shall be free,
Be free! be free! be free!

Heed not what may be your fate,
Count it gain when worldlings hate,
Naught of hope, or heart abate,
Victory's before!
Ask not that your toils be o'er
Till all slavery is no more,
No more! no more! no more!

Welcome, then, the crown of thorns
Which the faithful brow adorns;
All complaint the brave soul scorns,
Burdens are its choice, -

While within it hears a voice
Ever echoing, rejoice!
Rejoice! rejoice! rejoice!

Soon, to bless our longing eyes,
Freedom's glorious sun shall rise;
Now it lights those gloomy skies
Faintly from afar, -
Faith and love her heralds are,
See you not her morning star?
Hurra! hurra! hurra!

Liberty Bell, 1846, pp. 65-67.

Liberator, January 9, 1846, p. 8, under the same title; no
tune specified.

Liberator, February 18, 1859, p. 26, as "Verses"; no tune
specified.

80. NATIONAL ANTISLAVERY HYMN

Written for, and sung at the Dedham
Anti-Slavery Pic Nic on the 4th [of July] inst.

Author: T. W. Higginson
Tune: unspecified

The land our fathers left to us
Is foul with hateful sin: -
When shall, O Lord, this sorrow end,
And hope and joy begin?

What good, though growing wealth and strength
Shall stretch from shore to shore,
If thus the fatal poison-taint
Be only spread the more?

Wipe out, O God, the nation's guilt -
Then swell the Nation's power;
But build not high our yearning hopes
To wither in an hour!

No outward show, nor fancied strength,
From thy stern justice saves;
There is no liberty for them
Who make their brethren slaves!

Liberator, July 17, 1846, p. 116.

81. ANTI-SLAVERY ODE

Sung by the Barker family at a Ladies' Meeting in Lynn
for the reception of Frederick Douglass, May 1, 1847.

Author: Alonzo Lewis
Tune: unspecified

To God on high, the glory
Of this glad moment be!
Send out the joyful story
O'er hill-top and o'er sea!
Columbia's lovely daughters
Have raised the kindly hand,
That fettered limbs and slaughters
No more may mar our land.

When truth and right affection
Our pathway shall reveal,
We need no sword's protection,
No cannon's thunder peal!
In Heaven's persuasive manner,
Our hosts shall take the field;
Love is our only banner,
And truth our safest shield!

When dangers are impending,
They only are the brave,
Whose souls, to heaven ascending,
Rely on God to save!
When true hearts shall assemble,
And Heaven's assistance call,
Then tyrant hearts shall tremble,
Then iron chains shall fall.

Is not the Lord Almighty
As strong in power today,
As when, with breath so flighty,
Th' Assyrian fell away?
Will not the God of heaven
His aid to us bestow,
As when, by trumpet riven,
Fell down old Jericho?

But where are all the preachers
Of God's most holy word;
That, for their fellow creatures,
Their voices are not heard?
When Polk's loud cannon rattles,
They're making their long prayers
To their great god of battles,
Who ne'er a foeman spares!

And where are all the Christians?
Some in the fosses lurk,
To aid, with their assistance,
Brave Taylor's bloody work!
And some in bonds of slavery
Hold souls with all their might;
While pleaders for their knavery
Pray they may hold them tight!

And some hang up their brothers,
Their love for God to show!
To spread the gospel, others
Are fighting Mexico!
A few, from thraldom parted,
Are here with us today;
And for them, the true-hearted,
Our thanks to heaven we pay!

When duty is revealing
The way to end each wrong,
Let all, with hearts of feeling,
In God's great name be strong!
The coward soul may falter,
The traitor heart may flee;
But we will never alter,
Till all the world is free!

Liberator, May 7, 1847, p. 75.

82. THE LAW OF LOVE

Author: A Lady
Tune: original, by G. W. C.

Blest is the man whose tender heart
Feels all another's pain,
To whom the supplicating eye
Was never raised in vain,
Was never raised in vain.

Whose breast expands with generous warmth,
A stranger's woe to feel,
And bleeds in pity o'er the wound,
He wants the power to heal,
He wants the power to heal.

He spreads his kind supporting arms,
To every child of grief;
His secret bounty largely flows,
And brings unasked relief,
And brings unasked relief.

To gentle offices of love
His feet are never slow;
He views, through mercy's melting eye,
A brother in his foe,
A brother in his foe.

To him protection shall be shown,
And mercy from above
Descend on those, who thus fulfill
The perfect law of love,
The perfect law of love.

Free Soil, pp. 135-136.

83. THE MERCY SEAT

Author: Mrs. Sigourney
Tune: original, by G. W. C.

From every stormy wind that blows,
From every swelling tide of woes,
There is a calm a sure retreat -
Our refuge is the Mercy seat.

There is a place where Jesus sheds
The oil of gladness on our heads,
A place than all beside more sweet -
We seek the blood-bought Mercy seat.

There is a spot where spirits blend,
Where friend holds fellowship with friend;
Though sundered far, by faith we meet,
Around one common Mercy seat.

Ah! whither could we flee for aid,
When hunted, scourged, oppressed, dismayed, -
Or how our bloody foes defeat,
Had suffering slaves no Mercy seat!

Oh! let these hands forget their skill,
These tongues be silent, cold, and still,
These throbbing hearts forget to beat,
If we forget the Mercy seat.

Free Soil, pp. 137-138; and Freedom, pp. 137-138.

84. COME AND SEE THE WORKS OF GOD

Author: unspecified
Tune: unspecified

Lift up to God the shout of joy,
Let all the earth its powers employ,
To sound his glorious praise;
Say, unto God - "How great art thou!
Thy foes before thy presence bow!
How gracious are thy ways!"

To thee all lands their homage bring,
They raise the song, they shout, they sing
The honors of thy name.
Come! see the wondrous works of God;
How dreadful is his vengeful rod!
How wide extends his fame!

He made a highway through the sea,
His people, long-enslaved, to free,
And give them Canaan's land;
Through endless years his reign extends,
His piercing eye to earth he bends -
Ye despots! fear his hand.

O! bless our God, lift up your voice
Ye people! sing aloud - rejoice -
His mighty praise declare;
The Lord hath made our bondage cease,
Broke off our chains, brought sure release,
And turned to praise our prayer.

Free Soil, p. 144.

85. THE LIBERTY ARMY

Author: unspecified
Tune: [America?]

Our brother, lo! we come!
But not with sounding drum
We come to thee.
No bloody flag we bear;
No implements of war,
Nor carnage red shall mar
Our victory.

Our flag is spotless white,
Our watch-word, "Freedom's Right
To all be given."
Our emblem is the dove,
Our weapons, Truth and Love,
Our Captain, God above,
Who rules in heaven.

Behold! Salvation's King
On the dark tempest's wing
In haste comes down.
Oppression's cheek is pale,
And despots blanch and quail;
The parting clouds reveal
Jehovah's frown!

Exult ye valleys now!
Ye melting mountains flow
To meet your King!
Let Slavery's knell be rung!
Oppression's dirge be sung!
And every bondman's tongue
Of freedom sing!

Free Soil, p. 194.

Freedom, p. 195, under the same title; no tune specified.

86. PRAISE AND PRAYER

Author: Miss Chandler
Tune: unidentified

Praise for slumbers of the night,
For the wakening morning's light,
For the board with plenty spread,
Gladness o'er the spirit shed;
Healthful pulse and cloudless eye,
Opening on the smiling sky.
Healthful pulse and cloudless eye,
Opening on the smiling sky.

Praise! for loving hearts that still
With life's bounding pulses thrill;
Praise, that still our own may know -
Earthly joy and earthly woe.
Praise for every varied good,
Bounteous round our pathway strew'd!
Praise for every varied good,
Bounteous round our pathway strew'd!

Prayer! for grateful hearts to raise
Incense meet of prayer and praise!
Prayer, for spirits calm and meek,
Wisdom life's best joys to seek;
Strength 'midst devious paths to tread -
That through which the Saviour led.
Strength 'midst devious paths to tread -
That through which the Saviour led.

Prayer! for those who, day by day,
Weep their bitter life away;
Prayer, for those who bind the chain
Rudely on their throbbing vein -
That repentance deep may win
Pardon for the fearful sin!
That repentance deep may win
Pardon for the fearful sin!

Liberty, p. 167.

87. TO-NIGHT

Author: unspecified
Tune: original, by G. W. C.

Tonight, the bondman, Lord,
Is bleeding in his chains;
And loud the falling lash is heard,
On Carolina's plains!

Tonight is heard the shriek
Of pain and anguish wild;
And one by one her heart-strings break,
As Rachel mourns her child!

Tonight, with stealthy tread,
While doors and locks are barr'd,
The slave devours the crumb of bread,
The dogs left in the yard!

Tonight, in swamp or brake,
The fugitive, Oh God!
Hears baying blood-hounds on his track,
Eager to drink his blood!

Oh, may no cloud arise
To hide the pole-star's ray,
Which smiles and beckons from the skies,
To cheer him on his way.

Whilst he pursues his flight
With bleeding heart and limb -
Shall we petition Thee, tonight,
And not remember him?

O God! do thou provide,
And sure assistance give;
And in thy dark pavilion hide
The trembling fugitive.

Free Soil, p. 207.

Freedom, p. 193, as "The Trembling Fugitive," to the same
tune.

88. HOLY TIME

Author: unspecified
Tune: Somerville

What's "holy time?" what's "holy time?"
There is no time too pure
To win the erring back from crime,
The wav'ring to secure;
To whisper to the doubting soul,
"The tempting draught beware!
Touch not, touch not the sparkling bowl
Touch not - for death is there!"

To raise the bondman from the dust,
Where he hath suffer'd long,
To bid him hope with joyful trust,
Take courage, and be strong;
To pledge to him our heart and hand,
That firmly by his side,
Shoulder to shoulder we will stand,
As brethren true and tried.

The light of home again to shed
O'er many a dreary hearth;
To raise once more the tones long fled -
The tones of joy and mirth,
For this the Sabbath's hours were given,
For this was it designed,
That we therein might worship Heaven,
By toiling for mankind.

Free Soil, pp. 203-204; Liberty, pp. 206-207; and Freedom,
pp. 203-204.

89. PLEA FOR THE FUGITIVE

Author: unspecified
Tune: Lightly Row

Christians, say - Christians, say -
Was the sacred Sabbath day
Made for man, made for man,
As the Savior saith?
Then, with confidence we come,
Pleading for the wronged and dumb;
And our plea, and our plea,
Is a "prayer of faith."

Christians, see! Christians, see!
Southern "goods," by law, was he -
Human law, human law -
Is it law divine?
Is it not a burning shame
To the hallowed Christian name,
That the Church - that the Church
Does her work resign?

Does she live, does she live,
When the panting fugitive
Cries for aid, cries for aid,
And she hears him not?
Still, with confidence we come,
Pleading for the wronged and dumb,
And our plea, and our plea
Will not be forgot.

Liberator, June 29, 1849, p. 104.

90. HYMN

Written for and sung at the celebration of
the Twentieth Anniversary of the Liberator.

Author: George W. Putnam
Tune: Hebron

The land was wrapped in moral night,
The Slave was to the Tyrant given,
When Freedom's lonely signal light
Streamed trembling up the blackened heaven.

Startling Oppression in its lair,
And Conscience 'neath its triple pall,
A voice upon the heavy air
Pierced like a Prophet's warning call.

Sustained by Freedom's little band,
Braving all obloquy and shame,
From master mind and iron hand,
The dauntless "LIBERATOR" came!

Choosing the Christian's better part,
Turning away from Life's bright dreams,
The pure of soul and true of heart
Looked in upon ethereal scenes.

And when God's hand drew back the veil,
Where the eternal cycles roll,
That lonely band, awe-struck and pale,
Scanned the vast circuit of the soul!

Then, weary, cursed, and forlorn,
They toiled along their upward path,
And 'mid the driving storm of scorn,
They bridged with Faith the Sea of Wrath.

On darkened eyes they sent the ray
Of truths the lowly Jesus taught;
And, clothed with light, they stand today,
The centre of a sea of thought.

Paul stood upon the hill of Mars -
Before him Error's mantle fell;
Bursting the Spirit's prison bars,
Came Luther from the convent cell.

Not less your work, O, faithful band!
Who, while Sin kept her bloody throne,
Proclaimed throughout a darkened land,
A God of mercy all unknown!

God! keep these fearless pioneers!
World! cherish thou their honored name,
Who, walking 'mid a night of tears,
Behind them leave a path of flame!

And Thou! O leader of the brave!
Behold! with Freedom's seal and sign,
Stretches the army of the slave
From morning to the sunset line!

Still go where leadeth Truth's bright form,
Oppression long shall fear thy face;
And thunder still, above the storm,
Scion of Boanerges' race!

Liberator, January 31, 1851, p. 18.

91. HYMN

Sung at services commemorating the Anniversary
of the Kidnapping of Thomas Sims.*

Author: Rev. Theodore Parker
Tune: [Scots Wha Hae?]

Sons of men who dared be free,
For Truth and Right who crossed the sea!
Hide the trembling poor that flee
From the land of slaves.

Men that love your Fathers' name,
Ye who prize your country's fame,
Wipe away the public shame
From your native land.

Men that know the Mightiest Might,
Ye who serve th' Eternal Right,
Charge the darkness into light,
Let it shine for all.

Now's the day, and now's the hour;
See the front of Thraldom lower;
See advance the Southern power,
Chains and slavery.

See! the kidnappers have come!
Southern chains surround your home;
Will you wait for harsher doom?
Will ye wear the chain?

By yon sea that freely waves,
By your Fathers' honored graves,
Swear you never will be slaves,
Nor steal your fellow-man.

By the Heaven whose breath you draw,
By the God whose Higher Law
Fills the Heaven of Heavens with awe,
Swear for Freedom now.

Men whose hearts with pity move,
Men that trust in God above,
Who stoutly follow Christ in love,
Save your Brother Men!

Liberator, April 16, 1852, p. 62.

*Thomas Sims was a fugitive slave whose seizure in Boston
in 1851 intensified hostilities between opponents of the
Fugitive Slave Law and legal officials.

92. [UNTITLED]

Written for and sung at a celebration of August 1
in the Baptist Church, Fitzwilliam, N. H.

Author: unspecified
Tune: unspecified

See! ye who dwell in Slavery's night,
And sorrowing, weep forlorn,
The breaking of the glorious light
That ushered in the morn,
The morn, the morn, the cheerful morn,
When thousands found themselves free-born.

And solemn was that silent hour,
Before the break of day,
When Tyranny must lose its power,
And Freedom claim her sway;
Her sway, her sway, fair Freedom's sway,
O'er minds that long in darkness lay.

That solemn hour has passed; and then,
From swelling hearts, the voice
Of prayer and praise of earnest men,
Bade al the land rejoice;
Rejoice! rejoice! with song and mirth,
Before the Lord of heaven and earth.

When shall th' auspicious day-star rise,
Columbia! o'er thy soil,
To cheer the heart, make glad the eyes,
Of all the sons of toil?
Of toil, of toil; and ours the toil
From Tyranny to rend the spoil.

That was a glorious work, indeed!
The anti-slavery cause;
When men to men their rights concede,
And ordain righteous laws;
The cause, the cause, our worthy cause,
Blessed by high Heaven with its applause.

For such, the host of angels sung
At the Redeemer's birth;
Good-will the sons of men among,
And peace diffused on earth;
O'er all the earth, the wide-spread earth,
Be known of men sweet Freedom's birth.

Liberator, August 26, 1853, p. 136.

93. TO THE WHITE PEOPLE OF AMERICA

Author: Joshua Simpson
Tune: Massa's in the Cold, Cold Ground

O'er this wide extended country,
Hear the solemn echoes roll,
For a long and weary century,
Those cries have gone from pole to pole;
See the white man sway his sceptre,
In one hand he holds the rod -
In the other hand the Scripture,
And says that he's a man of God.
Hear ye that mourning?
'Tis your brother's cry!
O! ye wicked men take warning,
The day will come when you must die.

Lo! ten thousand steeples shining
Through this mighty Christian land,
While four million slaves all pining
And dying 'neath the Tyrant's hand.
See the "blood-stained" Christian banner
Followed by a host of saints(?)
While they loudly sing Hosannah,
We hear the dying slave's complaints:

Hear ye that mourning?
Anglo-sons of God,
O! ye Hypocrites take warning,
And shun your sable brother's blood.

In our Legislative members,
Few there are with humane souls,
Though they speak in tones of thunder
'Gainst sins which they cannot control,
Women's rights and annexation,
Is the topic by the way,
While poor Africa's sable nation
For mercy, cry both night and day.
Hear ye that mourning?
'Tis a solemn sound,
O! ye wicked men take warning,
For God will send his judgment down.

Tell us not of distant Islands -
Never will we colonize:
Send us not to British Highlands,
For this is neither just nor wise,
Give us equal rights and chances,
All the rights of citizens -
And as light and truth advances,
We'll show you that we all are men.
Hear ye that mourning?
'Tis your brother's sigh,
O! ye wicked men take warning,
The judgment day will come by and by.

Car, pp. 13-15.

94. ACRES AND HANDS

Author: Duganne
Tune: [original?], by T. Wood

The earth is the Lord's and the fullness
thereof
Says God's most holy word:
The water hath fish and the land hath flesh.
And the air hath many a bird;
And the soil is teeming o'er the earth
And the earth hath numberless lands,
Yet millions of hands want acres,
While millions of acres want hands,
While millions of acres want hands.

Sunlight and breeze and gladsome flowers
Are o'er the earth spread wide,
And the good God gave these gifts to men,
To men who on earth abide;
Thousands are toiling in poisonous gloom
And shackl'd with iron bands,
While millions of hands want acres,
While millions of acres want hands,
While millions of acres want hands.

Never a rood hath the poor man here,
To plant with a grain of corn;
And never a plot where his child may cull
Fresh flowers in the dewy morn;
The soil lies fallow, the woods grow rank,
But idle the poor man stands,
Ah! millions of hands want acres,
And millions of acres want hands,
And millions of acres want hands.

'Tis writ that "ye shall not muzzle the ox
That treadeth out the corn"
Yet, behold! ye shackle the poor man's limbs,
Who hath all Earth's burdens borne.
The land is the gift of the bounteous God,
And the labor his word commands;
Yet millions of hands want acres,
And millions of acres want hands,
And millions of acres want hands.

Who hath ordained that the few shall hoard
Their millions of useless gold;
And rob the earth of its fruits and flowers,
While profitless soil they hold.
Who hath ordained that a parchment scroll
Shall fence around miles of Land;
While millions of hands want acres,
And millions of acres want hands,
And millions of acres want hands.

'Tis a glaring lie on the face of day,
'Tis robbery of men's rights:
'Tis a Lie that the word of the Lord disowns -
'Tis a curse that burns and blights.
And 'twill burn and blight 'till the people
rise,
And swear - while they burst their bands -
That the hands henceforth shall have acres,
And the acres henceforth have hands,
And the acres henceforth have hands.

Freedom, pp. 17-19.

95. TO ONE AS WELL AS ANOTHER

Author: unspecified
Tune: original, by G. W. C.

"Keep it before the people,"
That earth was made for man,
That the flowers were strown,
And the fruits were grown,
To bless and never to ban;
That the sun and rain,
And the corn and grain,
Are yours and mine, my brother;
Free gift from heaven,
And freely given,
To one as well as another,
To one as well as another.

"Keep it before the people,"
That famine, and crime, and woe,
Forever abide,
Still side by side,
With luxury's dazzling show;
That Lazarus crawls
From Dives' halls,
And starves at his gate, my brother,
Yet life was given,
By God from heaven,
To one as well as another,
To one as well as another.

"Keep it before the people,"
That the laborer claims his meed -
The right of soil,
And the right to toil,
From spur and bridle freed;
The right to bear,
And the right to share,
With you and me, my brother -
Whatever is given
By God from heaven,
To one as well as another,
To one as well as another.

Freedom, pp. 75-77.

96. ANTI-SLAVERY HYMN

Sung at the New England Anti-Slavery Convention.

Author: George W. Stacy
Tune: Lenox

O, Father, from above,
Send thy good spirit here;
The spirit of thy love,
That "casteth out all fear."
O may we stand,
By truth set free,
A noble band
For Liberty!

Why should we halt and wait?
Our work so well begun;
And know we not our fate,
If work is left undone?
O give us heart,
To run the race:
Nor may we part
With heavenly grace.

Ah, what an hour is this!
How pregnant with our fate!
Say, is it woe or bliss,
For which the millions wait?
Who long have borne
The galling chain,
With flesh all torn
'Mid sweat and pain!

The night is near at hand,
And what a night 'twill be,
If God's divine command,
To set his people free,
Shall still remain
Unheard and blank,
And every chain
Our death-knell clank!

No! by the help of God,
We'll set the captive free;
We must obey the word, -
That word is LIBERTY!
A word of right
For every soul
That sees the light,
Or feels earth's roll.

                    Still ONWARD! is the cry -
                    The battle must be won!
                    Raise, raise the standard high,
                    Unfurl it to the sun!
                    Shout, shout and sing,
                    Nor cease the voice,
                    Till earth shall ring,
                    And man rejoice!

Liberator, June 6, 1862, p. 92.

                    97. OUR NATIONAL VISITATION

        Written for and sung at the Anti-Slavery Celebration
            at Framingham, (Mass.) July 4th, 1862.

                        Author: W. L. G.
                    Tune: John Brown Song

                For the sighing of the needy, to deliver the
                oppressed,
                Now the Lord our God arises, and proclaims his
                high behest;
                Through the Red Sea of his justice lies the
                Canaan of rest;:
                Our cause is marching on!
                Glory, glory, hallelujah!
                Glory, glory, hallelujah!
                Glory, glory, hallelujah!
                Our cause is marching on!

                Hark! the tumult of the battle, as it rages
                through the land!
                There is weeping, there is wailing, there is
                death on every hand!
                Before His fiery judgments what tyrant-force
                shall stand?
                Our cause is marching on!
                Glory, glory, etc.
                Our cause is marching on!

                For her manifold transgressions is our nation
                scourged and torn;
                She has forged the galling fetter - doomed a
                helpless race to mourn;
                And now she writhes in anguish, of her pride
                and glory shorn -
                For God is marching on!
                Glory, glory, etc.
                For God is marching on!

No longer let her safety seek in refuges of
lies!
No longer with oppression make a sinful
compromise!
Let the trump of jubilee echo through the
vaulted skies,
As she goes marching on!
Glory, glory, etc.
For Truth is marching on!

Then blood shall flow no longer, and all
dissensions cease;
For ruin, high prosperity - for horrid war,
sweet peace;
And Heaven shall smile upon us, and give us
large increase,
As we go marching on!
Glory, glory, etc.
As we go marching on!

Liberator, July 11, 1862, p. 112.

98. ARMY HYMN

Sung at a concert in Boston
celebrating the Emancipation Proclamation.

Author: Dr. Holmes
Tune: [original?], by Mr. [Otto] Dresel

O Lord of Hosts! Almighty King!
Behold the sacrifice we bring!
To every are Thy strength impart,
Thy spirit shed through every heart!

Wake in our hearts the living fires,
The holy faith that warmed our sires;
Thy hand hath made our nation free:
To die for her is serving Thee.

Be thou a pillared flame to show
The midnight maze, the silent foe;
And when the battle thunders loud,
Still guide us in its moving cloud.

God of all nations! Sovereign Lord!
In Thy dread name we draw the sword,
We lift the starry flag on high,
That fills with light our stormy sky.

No more its flaming emblems wave
To bar from hope the trembling slave;
No more its radiant glories shine
To blast with woe a child of Thine!

From treason's rent, from murder's stain,
Guard Thou its fold till peace shall reign,
Till fort and field, till shore and sea
Join our loud anthem, Praise to Thee!

Liberator, January 9, 1863, p. 7.

99. [UNTITLED]

Sung at a celebration of August 1 at Abington.

Author: George S. Burleigh
Tune: Old Hundred

God reaps his judgment-field today,
And sifts the darnel from the wheat;
A whirlwind sweeps the chaff away,
And fire the refuge of deceit.

In vain a nation's bloody sweat,
The sob of myriad hearts in vain,
If the scotched snake may live to set
Its venom in our flesh again.

The lords of treason and the whip
Have called to us the dread appeal,
From the loud cannon's fevered lip,
And the wide flash of bristling steel.

If now the echo of that voice
Shake down their prison-house of wrong,
They have their own perfidious choice,
For God is good, and Truth is strong.

Their steel draws lightning, and the bolt
But fires their own volcanic mine;
God in their vineyard of Revolt
Treads out his sacramental wine!

Be this our conquest - as they gave
Their all to Treason and the Chain,
We snap the fetter from the slave,
And make our sole revenge their gain!

Liberator, August 7, 1863, p. 126.

100. [UNTITLED]

Sung at the celebration of the 31st Anniversary
of the American Anti-Slavery Society.

Author: unspecified
Tune: unspecified

GOD made all his creatures free;
Life itself is liberty:
God ordained no other bands
Than united hearts and hands.

Sin the primal charter broke -
Sin, itself earth's heaviest yoke;
Tyranny with sin began,
Man o'er brute, and man o'er man.

But a better shall be,
Life again be liberty,
And the wide world's only bands
Love-knit hearts and love-linked hands.

Liberator, May 20, 1864, p. 82.

101. [UNTITLED]

Sung at the celebration of the 31st Anniversary
of the American Anti-Slavery Society.

Author: Theodore Tilton
Tune: unspecified

O Thou, before whose throne we fall,
Who bendest to the bended knee,
Who spurnest none, who lovest all, -
How long, O God, from land and sea,
Shall yet the groaning nations call?

O Thou, by whom the lost are found,
Whose Cross, upraised, forever stands,
When shall its shadow on the ground
Spread East and West through all the lands,
Until it gird the world around?

O Thou, who makest kingdoms Thine,
When shall thy mighty arms outreach
From Southern palm to Northern pine,
To bind each human heart to each,
And each to Thee as branch to vine?

O Thou, who cleanest human sin,
For whom the whole creation waits,
When shall thy reign on earth begin? -
O be ye lifted up, ye gates,
And let the King of Glory in!

Liberator, May 20, 1864, p. 81.

102. [UNTITLED]

Sung at the celebration of the 31st Anniversary
of the American Anti-Slavery Society.

Author: unspecified
Tune: unspecified

Out of the dark the circling sphere
Is rounding onward to the light;
We see not yet the full day here,
But we do see the paling night;

And Hope, that lights her fadeless fires,
And Faith, that shines, a heavenly will,
And Love, that courage re-inspires -
These stars have been above us still.

Look backward, how much has been won!
Look round, how much is yet to win!
The watches of the night are done;
The watches of the day begin.

O Thou, whose mighty patience holds
The night and day alike in view,
Thy will our dearest hopes enfolds;
O keep us steadfast, patient, true!

Liberator, May 20, 1864, p. 81.

103. [UNTITLED]

Sung at the Boston Music Hall at a celebration
of the passage of the Thirteenth Amendment.

Author: unspecified
Tune: Old Hundred

Giver of all that crowns our days,
With grateful hearts we sing thy praise!
Through deep and desert, led by Thee,
Our Canaan's promised land we see!

Ruler of Nations, judge our cause!
If we have kept thy holy laws,
The sons of Belial curse in vain
The day that rends the captive's chain.

Thou God of Vengeance! Israel's Lord!
Break in their grasp the shield and sword,
And make thy righteous judgments known
Till all thy foes are overthrown!

Then, Father, lay Thy healing hand
In mercy on our stricken land;
Lead all its wanderers to the fold,
And be their Shepherd as of old!

So shall our Nation's song ascend
To Thee, our Ruler, Father, Friend;
While Heavens' wide arch resounds again
With peace on earth, good will to men!

Liberator, February 10, 1865, p. 23.

MY COUNTRY

My country, 'tis for thee,
Dark land of slavery,
For thee I weep;
Land where the slave has sighed,
And where he toiled and died,
To serve a tyrant's pride -
For thee I weep.

The discrepancy between the boasted freedom of the United States and the presence of slavery in the nation was a favorite target of the antislavery reformers, and the popular song, "America," provided an ideal means of expressing it. First sung on July 4, 1832, "America" captured in the first verse alone important tenets of the American national faith:

My country 'tis of Thee
Sweet land of liberty;
Of thee I sing.
Land where my fathers died
Land of the Pilgrims' pride
From every mountain side
Let freedom ring.

It was not long before abolitionists began to satirize the song. An even earlier version than "My Country" (187, quoted above) appeared in the Liberator in 1839 with some revealing opening remarks (see 130 for the entire song):

. . . In the popular little hymn, entitled 'America,' written by S. F. Smith, and often sung with great eclat, there is such a manifest unlikeness to our true condition as a nation, which it was the author's design to depict, that if it

were divested of its caption and the author's
signature, it would be difficult to guess the
original. In order to bring out some great and
shameful truths in relation to our national
character and condition, which are concealed by this
otherwise beautiful production, I send you for
publication the following parody.

> My country! 'tis of thee,
> Strong hold of Slavery -
> Of thee I sing:
> Land, where my fathers died;
> Where men man's rights deride;
> From every mountain-side,
> Thy deeds shall ring.

In the 1850s yet two more versions were written, the first by
black poet Joshua Simpson, appropriately entitled "Song of the
'Aliened American'" (209) and the second, "The Patriot's Hymn"
(218), signed only "S. G. C."

Although not as blatantly as the parodies, most of the
songs in this largest section refer to the central idea of
"America": the country as a "land of liberty." As in the
previous group, many of these lyrics combine liberty - and
American history - with God (as does "America" itself), but
God's presence often is more implicit and even overshadowed by
the focus on American heritage. Here is American history at
its most romantic, with repeated images of the "fathers" of
the past, whether Pilgrims, Revolutionary soldiers, or simply
"noble sires" fighting for freedom (it is noteworthy that song
116 appeals rather to the "daughters" than the "sons" of these
men and that song 220 commemorates "The Colored American
Heroes of 1776"). A typical American ambivalence toward the
Founders is revealed in the alternating tendencies to revere
them and expose perceived hypocrisies; an example of the
latter is song 134, "Jefferson's Daughter." Hypocrisy came
under most severe attack, however, in the twenty-five songs
written about July 4 which are interspersed throughout this
section, while August 1, Emancipation Day in the British West
Indies, similarly was a subject inviting not only praise and
hope but also unfavorable comparisons.

104. HYMN

The following was sung at a meeting of colored
people, on the 4th of July last, in New York.

Author: unspecified
Tune: unspecified

Afric's sons, awake, rejoice!
To you this day sounds freedom's voice;
This day to us our birthright's given;
United raise your thanks to heaven.

May every son, with grateful heart,
This day from others set apart:
The hour that first proclaimed us free,
Shall be our lasting jubilee.

When history unrolls her page
Of Afric's degraded age,
Then shall the dawn of freedom's light
A radiance shed o'er slavery's night.

Come, raise your thankful voice to Heaven;
To us Religion's truths are given;
In lands where late the heathen trod,
Now Ethiopia seeks her God.

O! may He guide our rugged way;
Our flame by night, our cloud by day;
Our injuries let all forgive,
And by the Gospel's precepts live.

Genius, new series, September 8, 1827, p. 80.

105. INDEPENDENCE ODE

Sung at the celebration of our national
independence, in Danville, Kentucky.

Author: Velasco
Tune: Ode to Science

When Freedom, in the Eastern world,
Was from her temple-altars hurl'd,
And Slavery round her standard curl'd,
In mock'ry of her heav'n born pride,

Through the dark mists of Gothic night,
In Western climes, a land of light,
Burst forth, in glory, on her sight,
With nature's choicest gifts suppli'd.
She came high-bounding o'er the wave,
Encompass'd by the free and brave,
Who scorn'd the lordling and the slave,
The curses of a land so fair:
She rais'd her azure banner high,
Streak'd with the morning's crimson dye,
And call'd the eagle from the sky,
To perch in matchless glory there.

The baldrick of the milky way,
Shed on its folds its starry ray,
While thousands blest the happy day,
That gave to them this symbol bright, -
That they henceforth should ever [be],
The greatest great, the freest free,
The hope of earth, the pride of sea,
The friends of truth and equal right.
When hostile footsteps press'd our strand,
Around this standard flock'd a band,
The choicest spirits of our land,
To free us from despotic power:
They check'd the foeman's siroc race,
With "steel to steel," and face to face,
On every spot in Freedom's place,
From Mountain height to sylvan bower.

At length, above war's tempests rose
The glowing rainbow of repose,
That spoke a quiet on our woes, -
The ensign bright of victory:
Then on the breeze was borne along,
In language free, and accents strong,
A new born nation's choral song -
The thrilling notes of liberty.
Hail to the day, when freedom broke
The vassal's chain, the bondsman's yoke,
And into new existence spoke,
Another nation of the earth!
Let every heart with rapture beat -
Let every tongue in music sweet,
The dear, the joyous tale repeat, -
The story of our country's birth!

Genius, new series, December 1, 1827, p. 176.

106. SLAVERY

Author: Richard Wright
Tune: unspecified

Columbians! whilst blest with the bounties of
heaven,
Whilst your National flag is unfurl'd,
Whilst proud that your Colony-fetters are
riven -
Your fame spreading wide through the world;
Whilst free as the waves of the fathomless
ocean,
And boasting each well-informed mind -
Do your bosoms ne'er heave with the rising
emotion
Of shame! as ye tread on your kind? -

Is Consistency banish'd from Liberty's
charter?
Is Honour a thing but of name?
Is your high Independence a license to barter
What cupidity only would claim?
Is Reason so poor or so weak that she falters,
If required to break SLAVERY'S chain?
Is Religion denouncing the blackest
defaulters,
Unheard, or but heard on the main?

Columbians! let not Albion's Island surpass
you,
Whose magical shore frees the slaves;
Let not the red Indian, in mockery, class you
As flesh-dealing white man, though brave.
If, as holding inferior each Afric-descendant,
Humanity's pleadings be vain,
Yet Character, sure, on which Fame is
dependent,
Should lead to break SLAVERY'S chain.

Genius, new series, October 25, 1828, p. 48.

107. SONG FOR THE FOURTH OF JULY

Sung in various places on the 4th instant.

Author: unspecified
Tune: unspecified

The trumpet of Liberty sounds thro' the world,
And the universe starts at the sound;
Her standard Philosophy's hand has unfurl'd,
And the nations are thronging around.
Fall, tyrants, fall!
These are the days of Liberty,
Fall, tyrants, fall!

How noble the ardor that seizes the soul!
How it bursts from the yoke and the chain!
What pow'r can the fervor of Freedom control,
Or its terrible vengeance restrain?
Fall, tyrants, fall! etc.

Ye stern towers of despots! ye dungeons and
cells!
The tempest shall sweep you away:
From west to the east the dread hurricane
swells,
And the tyrants grow pale with dismay.
Fall, tyrants, fall! etc.

The slave, on whose neck the proud despot had
trod,
Now feels that himself is a man;
And his lordly usurper, who ruled with a rod,
Hides his head 'midst his servile divan.
Fall, tyrants, fall! etc.

The cruel dominion of Priestcraft is o'er,
Its thunders, its faggots, its chains:
Mankind will endure the vile bondage no more,
While Religion her freedom maintains.
Fall, tyrants, fall! etc.

The hymn of the free shall Americans hear
With a cold and insensible mind?
No! each freeman his part of the chorus shall
bear,
And contend for the rights of mankind.
Fall, tyrants, fall! etc.

Liberator, July 9, 1831, p. 109.

Liberator, January 19, 1849, p. 12, with the introduction: "In
1831, the following incendiary effusion was widely printed in
the newspapers - South as well as North - reckless of its
application to American slavery."

108. ODE FOR THE FOURTH OF JULY

Written for the New-England Anti-Slavery Society.

Author: J. E.
Tune: Auld Lang Syne

Shall Afric's children be forgot,
And never brought to mind?
That "much enduring race," who long
In slavery have pined?
Oh no! they shall not be forgot -
We'll ever bear in mind
The millions of our fellow men
Who still in slavery pine.

Shall we our country's freedom [bow] at,
Forgetful of the sigh
Breathed from two million countrymen,
That gives our boast the lie?
Two million of our countrymen
By countrymen oppressed!
Grief, shame and indignation swell
Each true and generous breast.

Shall woes unequalled be forgot,
Which slavery's victims bear?
The toil compelled, the hunger, stripes,
The anguish and despair!
By tyrant power asunder torn,
Bereft of all that's dear,
When husbands, wives, and brethren weep,
Have we no answering tear?

See childless parent, orphan's child,
Though child and parent live!
Live, still the kindred tie to feel,
The parting still to grieve.
Oh no! their woes we'll ne'er forget,
We'll do, as well as feel;
Their utter, hopeless, helplessness
Shall be their strong appeal.

Shall we the days gone by forget?
Our nation's infant song,
That "all men free and equal are,"
Which burst from every tongue?
Like auld lang syne this truth we hold,
And never will resign;
Our brethren's rights we'll still declare,
For auld lang syne.

> Then give a hand each freeman true,
> And here's a hand of mine -
> This holy cause must sure succeed,
> If all true hearts will join.
> Then here we join each heart and hand,
> Resolved we'll ne'er despair;
> Nor cease our brethren's cause to plead,
> Till they our freedom share.

Liberator, June 30, 1832, p. 103.

109. ODE FOR THE FOURTH OF JULY

Written for the New-England Anti-Slavery Society.

Author: J. E.
Tune: Scots Wha Hae

> Ye who liberty revere!
> Hold it far than life more dear -
> Ye who boast from year to year,
> Free and equal laws!
> In the name of the oppress'd,
> In the name of the distress'd,
> We demand their wrongs redress'd -
> Who will aid our cause?
>
> Who, when freedom he commends,
> Freedom but for self intends,
> Let him rest in selfish ends,
> Selfish liberty.
> Who for others' wo or weal,
> As his own can strongly feel -
> Let him hark the slave's appeal
> To his sympathy.
>
> To boast our country free, how vain!
> Freemen will the boast disdain,
> While two million countrymen
> Pine in slavery.
> By our country's sacred name,
> By her glory and her shame,
> Hence be it our solemn aim
> From her shame to free.
>
> By oppression's woes and pains,
> By our brethren's servile chains,
> We will still, while life remains,
> War with slavery.

Yet no battle's storm shall lower,
Truth shall claim the day and hour,
And religion's holy power
Gain our victory!

Liberator, June 30, 1832, p. 103.

110. SONS OF COLUMBIA! AWAKE!

Author: C. W. D.
Tune: Portuguese Hymn

Sons of Columbia! Awake from your sleeping!
Awake! lest your slumbers be those of the
grave!
See, yonder, the Genius of Liberty weeping,
And pointing, through tears, to the chains of
the slave!

Love ye your blessings! your blood-purchased
glory?
Plucked forth 'neath the Lion of Albion's
mane?
Long ye to live in the pages of story,
When monarchs and sceptres in darkness shall
wane?

Then waken! And fling from your bondmen
forever,
The fetters now galling, on many a limb!
GOD gave ye your freedom: and never-no-never
Forbear to obey - or confide ye in HIM!

And now, boasting freemen! give ear to His
thunder -
His voice loud careering 'mid tempests on
high!
Obey! lest in wrath He should tear ye asunder,
And cast ye like dust on the winds of the sky!

"UNDO THE SLAVE'S BURDENS! LET HIS YOKE BE
BROKEN!
KNOCK OFF EVERY CHAIN! LET YOUR BROTHER GO
FREE!
Do this: and from Heaven shall glean out a
token
Of union to you - of forgiveness from ME!"

Sons of Columbia! awake from your sleeping!
Awake! lest your slumbers be those of the
grave!
See, yonder, the Genius of Liberty weeping,
And pointing, through tears, to the chains of
the slave!

Liberator, October 26, 1833, p. 171.

111. ORIGINAL HYMN

Sung [twice, to different tunes] on the
4th of July, at the Chatham Street Chapel.

Author: John G. Whittier
Tune: Old Hundred and Wells

Oh, Thou, whose presence went before
Our fathers in their weary way,
As with Thy chosen moved of yore
The fire by night - the cloud by day!

When from each temple of the free
A nation's song ascends to Heaven,
Most Holy Father! - unto Thee
May not our humble prayer be given?

Thy children all - though hue and form
Are varied in Thine own good will -
With Thy own holy breathings warm,
And fashioned in Thine image still.

We thank Thee, Father! - hill and plain
Around us wave their fruits once more,
And clustered vine, and blossomed grain
Are bending round each cottage door,

And peace is here - and hope and love
Are round us as a mantle thrown,
And unto Thee, supreme above,
The knee of prayer is bowed alone.

But, Oh, for those, this day can bring
As unto us - no joyful thrill.
For those, who, under FREEDOM'S wing,
Are bound in SLAVERY'S fetters still: -

For those to whom thy living word
Of light and love is never given,
For those whose ears have never heard
The promise and the hope of heaven!

For broken heart - and clouded mind,
Whereon no human mercies fall,
Oh, be thy gracious love inclined,
Who, as a father, pitiest all! -

And grant, Oh, Father! that the time
Of Earth's deliverance may be near,
When every land and tongue and clime
The message of Thy love shall hear -

When, smitten as with fire from Heaven,
The captive's chain shall sink in dust
And to his fettered soul be given
THE GLORIOUS FREEDOM OF THE JUST!

Genius, fourth series, July, 1834, pp. 104-105; Liberator,
July 12, 1834, p. 110; and Reporter, July, 1834, p. 112.

Hymns, pp. 28-29, four verses only, as "Seeking Independence
for the Captives"; no tune specified.

Melodies, pp. 16-17, four verses only, as "Hymn 9," to an
unidentified tune.

112. HYMN

Sung at the Rev. Howard Malcom's
Church, on the fourth of July.

Author: unspecified
Tune: unspecified

Dwell there a child upon this land
Who joins not with the festive band;
Who strikes no note of jubilee,
On this bright day of liberty?

Yes, - the poor SLAVE in silence pines,
And weeps, and moans - for on him shines
From FREEDOM'S SUN no Heaven-born ray,
No moral light; no mental day.

Sad brother - sister - would that we
Could rend thy chains, and set the free;
Could warm thy heart with virtue's flame,
Could teach thee our blest SAVIOUR'S name.

Father in Heaven! Eternal King!
Of liberty, thou art the spring;
In pity, then, - in mercy save
From tyranny, the helpless slave.

Liberator, July 19, 1834, p. 116.

Mentioned in Liberator, July 18, 1835, p. 116, as having been
sung by the children of the Belknap St. Sabbath School on July
4, 1835, "while celebrating the national jubilee."

113. ODE

Sung by the choir of Rev. Mr. White's Church,
after the delivery of an Anti-Slavery Discourse.

Author: A gentleman of East Sudbury
Tune: unspecified

America! extatic [sic] sound,
To freemen dear;
Thy name's a spell to summon round,
From Liberty's enchanted ground,
All who, to love of Freedom bound,
Have sought her here;
Our Fathers' blood has seal'd thy fame,
Then let their sons thy glorious name
Revere.

Against oppression's iron hand,
They nobly fought;
A fearless, mighty, conquering band,
They swore to live in Freedom's land,
To fall as men, or nobly stand,
As freemen ought;
Proud victors in the glorious strife,
Our freedom with their blood, their life,
They bought.

And is there then no slavery here,
America?
Go! see that Afric Mother's tear -
Go! see that Sister weeping near -
Go! if thou more wouldst know, and hear
That Maiden's sigh;

Her lover's gone she wists not where,
But lays her down, in cold despair,
To die.

"Mother! why sad and abject?" "Why?
I weep a son."
(She raises not her eyes on high,
She points not to the upper sky,
Her grief is not for those who die),
"My son has gone;
He's now upon the ocean's wave,
Your freemen took him for a slave -
He's gone."

And does thy soil a slave contain,
America?
Oh! blot it out, thy glory's stain;
Rise, freemen! burst the galling chain,
Break thro' the bonds his soul restrain,
Free the oppressed -
Fear not, for God protects the right;
Then onward in the glorious fight -
'Tis won!

Awake! arise! ye patriot band;
Ye boasted free;
Rise! seize your brethren by the hand,
Their God, their souls, your aid demand;
Burst, burst their chains; make this a land
Of Liberty;
Resolve it shall not hold a Slave;
But Freedom's home, or Freedom's grave,
Shall be.

Liberator, February 21, 1835, p. 32.

114. HYMN FOR THE CONVENTION

Author: S. T. S.
Tune: Scots Wha Hae

Children of the glorious dead,
Who for freedom fought and bled,
With, her banner o'er you spread,
On to victory.

Not for stern ambition's prize,
Do our hopes and wishes rise;
Lo, our Leader, from the skies,
Bids us do or die.

Ours is not the tented field -
We no earthly weapons wield -
Light and Love, our sword and shield,
Truth our Panoply.

This is proud oppression's hour;
Storms are round us: Shall we cower?
While beneath a despot's power
Groans the suffering slave?

While on every southern gale
Comes the helpless captive's tale,
And the voice of woman's wail,
And of man's despair?

While our homes and rights are dear,
Guarded still with watchful fear,
Shall we coldly turn our ear
From the suppliant's prayer?

Never! by our country's shame -
Never! by a Saviour's claim
To the men of every name,
Whom he died to save.

Onward, then, ye fearless band -
Heart to heart, and hand to hand;
Yours shall be the patriot's stand -
Or the martyr's grave.

Liberator, November 7, 1835, p. 180, preceded by this introduction: "The following hymn, for the use of the Utica Convention, was composed, a few nights previous, by a young lady,
recently converted to the cause of immediate emancipation.
The circumstances of the meeting of course prevented any exercise of singing." [On October 21, 1835, an anti-abolitionist
mob disrupted the attempt of the Utica Anti-Slavery Society to
form a state organization.]

Songs, pp. 147-151, as "Convention"; no tune specified.

Lyre, pp. 180-181, three verses only, under no title; no tune
specified.

Hymns, pp. 5-7, under no title, to the same tune.

Melodies, pp. 52-53, as "Hymn 34," to the same tune.

Picknick, pp. 108-109; Harp, p. 33; and Liberty,
p. 83, as "On to Victory," to the same tune.

Free Soil, p. 30; and Freedom, p. 277, as "Children of the
Glorious Dead," by Mrs. S. T. Martyn; no tune specified.

115. THE FIRST OF AUGUST

Author: Montgomery
Tune: unspecified

Blow ye the trumpet abroad o'er the sea,
Britannia hath triumphed, the Negro is free;
Sing for the pride of the tyrant is broken,
His scourges and fetters, all clotted with
blood,
Are wrenched from his grasp; - for the word
was but spoken,
And fetters and scourges were sunk in the
flood:
Blow ye the trumpet abroad o'er the sea,
Britannia hath triumphed, the Negro is free.

Hail to Britannia, fair Liberty's isle!
Her frown quailed the tyrant, the slave caught
her smile,
Fly on the winds to tell Afric the story:
Say to the mother of mourners, "Rejoice!"
Britannia went forth in her beauty, her glory,
And slaves sprung to men at the sound of her
voice:
Praise to the God of our fathers; - 'twas He,
Jehovah, that triumphed, Britannia, by thee.

Songs, p. 54.

Hymns, pp. 33-34, as "Sound the Loud Timbrel"; no tune
specified.

Picknick, pp. 114-117, as "Sound the Loud Timbrel," to the
tune, "Britannia Hath Triumphed."

Melodies, pp. 6-7, as "Blow Ye the Trumpet," to the tune,
"Sound the Loud Timbrel."

116. THE AMERICAN FEMALE SLAVE

Author: Elizabeth M. Chandler
Tune: unspecified

Daughters of the Pilgrim Sires,
Dwellers by their mould'ring graves,
Watchers of their altar fires,
Look upon your country's slaves!

Look! 'tis woman's streaming eye,
These are woman's fettered hands,
That to you, so mournfully,
Lift sad glance, and iron bands.

Scars are on her fettered limbs,
Where the savage scourge hath been;
But the grief her eye that dims,
Flows for deeper wounds within.

For the children of her love,
For the brothers of her race,
Sisters, like vine-branches wove,
In one early dwelling place -

For the parent forms that hung
Fondly o'er her infant sleep,
And for him to whom she clung,
With affection true and deep -

By her sad forsaken hearth,
'Tis for these she wildly grieves!
Now all scattered o'er the earth,
Like the wind-strewn autumn leaves!

Ev'n her babes so dear, so young,
And so treasured in her heart,
That the cords which round them clung,
Seemed its life, its dearest part -

These, ev'n these were torn away!
These, that when all else were gone,
Cheered the heart, with one bright ray,
That still bade its pulse beat on!

Then to still her frantic woe,
The inhuman scourge was tried,
Till the tears that ceased to flow,
Were with redder drops supplied.

And can you behold unmoved,
All the crushing weight of grief,
That her aching heart has proved,
Seeking not to yield relief?

Are not woman's pulses warm,
Beating in that anguished breast?
Is it not a sister's form,
On whose limbs those fetters rest?

Oh then save her from a doom,
Worse than aught that ye may bear;
Let her pass not to the tomb,
Midst her bondage and despair.

Songs, pp. 154-157.

Melodies, p. 38, as "Hymn 24," to an unidentified tune.

117. FOURTH OF JULY

Author: Mary Ann Collier
Tune: unspecified

Heard ye the mighty rushing?
As a storm-waked sea it came;
'Twas a nation's deep rejoicing
For her proud and spotless name.

Land of my sleeping fathers!
O'er thee no chain is flung;
Through all thy verdant vallies
The shout of joy is rung.

Wide o'er thy rolling rivers,
Thy fair and sunny plains,
And up thy woody mountains,
The soul of freedom reigns.

Land of my sleeping fathers!
O'er thee no chain is flung?
Through all thy verdant vallies
The shout of joy is rung.

And is there then no shadow
To dim this hallowed mirth?
And shall thy name, my country,
Be the watch-word o'er the earth?

Are all the captives loosened?
The fettered slave set free?
Is his crushed spirit gladdened
On this gay jubilee?

Say to the captive toiling
In freedom's proud abode,
"Cast off thy fetters, brother,
Take back the gift of God."

Let not oppression linger
Where starry banners wave;
Swell high the shout of freedom,
Let it echo for the <u>slave</u>.

<u>Songs</u>, pp. 102-105.

<u>Anniversary</u>, pp. 34-40, as "Echo for the Slave," to music by
<u>Lowell Mason</u>.

118. EXTENSION OF SLAVERY IN THE UNITED STATES

Author: S. Ripley
Tune: unspecified

Weep, sons of Freedom! your honor is low;
'Tis bleeding in liberty's desolate fane:
They whom ye trusted have bowed to the foe!
Oppression has conquered your country again.

Weep, sons of Freedom! your scutcheon is
stained;
"The star-spangled banner" waves proudly no
more:
"The land of the free" has been foully
profaned;
Again hath the tyrant prevailed on her shore!

Weep, sons of Freedom, o'er Liberty crushed!
Yet strive to deliver the down trodden slave;
Though the foes of mankind bid your voices be
hushed;
Though the poor of the land it is treason to
save!

Weep, sons of Freedom! for yet there is hope;
The tears of repentance are pleasing to Him
Who casteth ye down, or lifteth ye up; -
Let the cup of repentance be filled to the
brim.

Haste! sons of Freedom! the burdens undo;
Break the yoke of your bondmen, and bid them
be free:
Then your light shall break forth as the
morning anew; -
Your peace "like a river" that flows to the
sea.

<u>Songs</u>, pp. 163-164.

Hymns, p. 26, under no title, to the tune, "Alknomook."

Liberator, July 22, 1859, p. 114, as "The Gathering of the Free"; no tune specified, but with George N. Allen rather than Ripley implied as the author. The song was sung at a "welcome home" celebration for antislavery minister and educator Horace Bushnell at Oberlin.

119. FOURTH OF JULY

Author: Lydia H. Sigourney
Tune: unspecified

We have a goodly clime,
Broad vales and streams we boast,
Our mountain frontiers frown sublime,
Old Ocean guards our coast;
Suns bless our harvest fair,
With fervid smile serene,
But a dark shade is gathering there -
What can its blackness mean?

We have a birth-right proud,
For our young sons to claim -
An eagle soaring o'er the cloud,
In freedom and in fame.
We have a scutcheon bright,
By our dead fathers bough:
A fearful blot disdains its white -
Who hath such evil wrought?

Our banner o'er the sea
Looks forth with starry eye,
Emblazoned glorious, bold and free,
A letter on the sky -
What hand with shameful stain
Hath marred its heavenly blue?
The yoke, the fasces, and the chain,
Say, are these emblems true?

This day doth music rare
Swell through our nation's bound,
But Afric's wailing mingles there,
And Heaven doth hear the sound:
O God of power! - we turn
In penitence to thee,
Bid our loved land the lesson learn -
To bid the slave be free.

Songs, pp. 204-206.

Free Soil, pp. 125-126; and Freedom, pp. 125-126, under
the same title, to original music by G. W. C.

120. HYMN

Sung at the annual meeting of the Plymouth County
Anti-Slavery Society, on the 4th of July.

Author: George Russell
Tune: [America?]

Sons of the noble sires!
Who brav'd proud ocean's waves,
For freedom's sake:
Say, will ye quench those fires,
Their faith and love inspires,
And while amid their graves,
Their ways forsake?

Shall freedom find a grave,
On fair Columbia's soil?
Must we be slaves?
Shall we our lives to save,
No boon of mercy crave,
But with the bondman toil,
Branded as knaves?

Shall Despotism sway,
Its iron sceptre here,
Our lips to close?
Sons of the pilgrims! say!
Will ye proud lords obey,
And ask them when ye may
The truth disclose?

Say! will ye wear the yoke,
And shut your mouths for fear
Of Mobs or Death?
If truth our foes provoke,
Must it then ne'er be spoke?
Shall Jesus' law be broke,
To save our breath?

No! No! then answer No!
Nor fear the truth to speak,
While breath remains:
Did Christ our Teacher so?
Would He the truth forego?
Or did He struggle through,
Mindless of pain?

While then a <u>slave</u> remains,
To weep, and <u>groan</u>, and bleed,
We'll speak, and "pray":
We'll wear the bondman's chains;
We'll bear the bondman's pains;
We'll hear when he complains;
We'll <u>do</u>, and <u>say</u>.

<u>Liberator</u>, August 4, 1837, p. 128.

121. THEY SING OF FREEDOM

Author: J. P.
Tune: unspecified

They sing of Freedom! Afric's sons
Their notes of joyance sing;
And every hill and every dale
With Freedom's echoes ring!
All sing - the children at their play,
The laborers at their toil,
They chant a merry roundelay,
And bless the fertile soil.
They sing of Freedom! Afric's sons
Their notes of joyance sing;
And every hill and every dale
With Freedom's echoes ring!

All sing! the mountains and the plains,
And sounding shores reply,
In murmurs and melodious strains,
To hymns of liberty!
The rustling lime-groves learn the song,
And fields of waving cane,
And spring breezes waft along
A grateful, loud Amen!
They sing of Freedom, etc.

All sing! the master and the slave,
The servant and the lord;
And each a thankful offering give,
For Liberty restored.
In crowds they throng the house of God,
On bended knee they pray;
Mercy has broke the oppressor's rod,
And wiped their tears away.
They sing of Freedom, etc.

All sing! how beautiful is love
Within the tropic clime!
Beneath the golden orange-grove,
The myrtle and the lime!
Beneath the fragrant cooling shade,
Where spicy breezes blow,
The hill-top and the flowery glade,
Where sparkling waters flow.
They sing of Freedom, etc.

All sing! around these sea-girt isles
Content and safety dwell;
Abundance decks the land with smiles,
And all betokens well.
The gorgeous Amidarid birds,
Their glossy plumes display;
With sweet sounds the air is stirred,
To hail the rising day.
They sing of Freedom, etc.

All sing! the children at their play,
The laborers at their toil;
They chant a merry roundelay,
And bless the fertile soil.
They sing of Freedom! Afric's sons
Their notes of joyance sing;
And every hill and every dale
With Freedom's echoes ring.

Liberator, June 29, 1838, p. 104.

Hymns, pp. 20-21, under no title, to the tune, "Ortonville."

122. ORIGINAL HYMN

Sung at Marlboro' Chapel, July 4, 1838.

Author: P. H. Sweetser
Tune: unspecified

Who fought their country to redeem
From stern Oppression's iron hand,
And braved the tyrant's savage power,
To purchase freedom for this land?

Who, side by side with Washington,
For equal blessings did contend?
And who with Warren bled and died,
Their country's honor to defend?

The blood of Afric's sable sons
Has redden'd many a tented field!
The trophies of the fights they won
Are blazen'd on our country's shield!

They shrunk not in that fearful hour,
When sternest patriotism quailed;
They smote Oppression's hateful form,
And Freedom smiled, and Truth prevailed!

But hark! what means that cry of woe?
Man is transformed into a fiend!
Fair Freedom's sons are captive now
To those whom their own sires redeemed!

Weep, Mercy, weep! the corner stone
Of Freedom's temple rests in blood -
While vile attorneys shout, Amen!
And priests obey "the brotherhood!"

But truth and right will soon prevail,
And law and justice be restored -
And men of every caste shall know,
And love, and fear, and trust the Lord!

Shout, Freedom, shout! Oppression dies!
The monster, Slavery, gasps for life!
Sword of the Spirit, now awake,
And stay the foe, and end the strife!

Liberator, July 13, 1838, p. 110.

123. LINES

Sung at a meeting of the Westford
Anti-Slavery Society on the 4th of July.

Author: Claudius Bradford
Tune: unspecified

Behold, behold, how earth and sky
Are green and bright;
How spring and summer seem to vie
To yield delight;
But ah! there's something dims it all,
And checks my verse,
That hangs o'er Nature's face its pall,
'Tis Slavery's curse!

Hark! how the birds their gentle notes
Of Freedom raise;
How all around the anthem floats
Of prayer and praise;
But ah! there's something, something jars
With horrid tone,
And all the lovely music mars, -
'Tis Slavery's Groan!

"Shall Mercy's tears no longer flow?"
Can Pity die?
Can man forget his brother's wo,
And woman's sigh?
Oh no; - while Reason holds her seat,
And life remains,
We'll pledge our highest efforts yet,
To rend his chains.

Liberator, July 20, 1838, p. 116.

Melodies, pp. 56-57, as "Hymn 33," to an unidentified tune.

124. HYMN

Sung at East Bradford, on the 4th of July.

Author: M. P. Atwood
Tune: unspecified

Bright dawns a nation's jubilee,
With peaceful light o'er land and sea;
Freemen, awake and hail its dawn,
Welcome with joy, this glorious morn.

Sacred to liberty should be
The birth-day of a nation free;
Rise, then, the rights of man assert,
And from th' oppress'd the scourge avert.

Past is the hour of fearful strife,
When "fortune, sacred honor, life,"
Were pledged against oppression's might,
By patriot sires for freedom's right.

Yet, though for all the boon was sought,
Those rights for which they bravely fought,
Slavery their pure, their brightening fame,
Has clouded with its hateful name.

Rise, then, in freedom's holy cause,
Maintain your country's injured laws,
And brightly let her fires still glow,
On altars rent and prostrate now.

Let freedom's sun, all pure and bright,
Long shed its pure and radiant light
On freemen, not in name alone,
But most by deeds of virtue known.

Liberator, July 20, 1838, p. 116.

125. HYMN

Sung at the Anti-Slavery celebration
in Charlestown on the 4th of July.

Author: F. Howe
Tune: unspecified

Now joyous hail the genial light,
The day once more we see,
Which speaks of glorious deeds, and bright,
And tells us, WE ARE FREE.

But while our fathers' God we praise,
For freedom, choicest boon,
Our humble voices let us raise
For Libya's injur'd son.

While warm from Southern plains the gale
Is wafted to our ears,
'Tis mingled with the negro's wail,
And moistened with his tears.

The cutting lash and clanking chain,
In dread array arise;
The galling yoke and wasting pain,
With tender children's cries.

We to their wails will ope our ear,
Attentive hear their cries,
For them will shed the pitying tear,
With them will sympathise.

We'll firm remain an active band,
Those injured ones to save,
Till in Columbia's happy land
There breathes no fettered slave.

Liberator, July 20, 1838, p. 116.

126. ORIGINAL ODE

Sung at Marlboro' Chapel, August 1, 1838.

Author: unspecified
Tune: unspecified

Loud Hosannas,
Wave your banners,
Sound the trump of Jubilee!
Thousands springing
Forth are singing
Sweet is Freedom - WE ARE FREE!

From the mountain,
Vale and fountain,
From each shady grove and dell,
List! arising,
Joy surprising,
Which shall Britain's glory swell.

Oh the glory
Of the story,
Freemen, hail the blissful morning,
See ye not the heavenly dawning,
Tyrants quiver,
Shackles shiver,
Freedom's triumph hath begun!

Glorious hour,
Which the power,
Of thine arm, O Lord, hath given,
Soon shall waken
Those forsaken,
Those whose spirits STILL are riven.

Holy Father, speed the day,
Hold thee on thy conquering way,
Then from grateful hearts shall rise,
Hallelujahs to the skies!

We'll praise Thee, we'll praise Thee,
Thou glorious conquering One!
We'll praise Thee, we'll praise Thee,
Thou glorious conquering One!
Hosanna! Hosanna! Hosanna!

Liberator, August 10, 1838, p. 128.

127. ODE

Sung at the celebration of the
first of August, in Deerfield, Mass.

Author: unspecified
Tune: unspecified

Once more is heard the funeral knell
Of tyranny accursed!
Her idols and her temples down
Are crumbling into dust!
All Hail, Britannia, honored land!
Hail, Freedom's holy birth!
And Hail, ye happy, sea-girt isles,
The noble of the earth!

Welcome the sacred Jubilee,
Across Jamaica's wave,
Which from her Constitution blots
The ignoble name of slave!
All Hail, etc.

Joyful Antigua, thou hast felt
The worth of freemen's hands,
Yet loud and merry peal shalt ring,
For light in sister lands!
All Hail, etc.

Nor deaf shall be your watchful ears,
Ye lands of slavery,
For joy shall fill the bondman's heart,
At thought of what shall be!
All Hail, etc.

O, bright shall be that glorious morn,
And glad, for bond and free,
When fair Columbia's sons can say,
As natives o'er the sea:

All Hail, our country, honored land!
Hail, Freedom's holy birth!
No tyrant-chains, no slavish toils,
Oppress thy smiling earth!

Liberator, August 24, 1838, p. 136.

128. HYMN

Sung at the celebration of the
first of August, in Deerfield, Mass.

Author: unspecified
Tune: unspecified

A voice of joy, a rapturous sound
Comes pealing o'er the distant sea;
It speaks the prisoner's chain unbound -
The fetters broke, the captive free.

The slave may lift his chainless hand,
Assert at length his equal birth;
Beside his brother freely stand,
A man, upon his Maker's earth.

O, happy England, thou art free;
Thy children sigh in chains no more;
At home, and o'er the far blue sea,
The plague of slavery is o'er.

But thou, Columbia, who could'st see
Of freedom's boon, the peerless worth,
How can'st thou longer brook to be
A blot upon the beauteous earth?

Rise, O my country, cleanse thy hands
From those foul stains, that dim thee now;
Unbind oppression's iron bands,
And lay the tyrant, slavery, low.

Liberator, August 24, 1838, p. 136.

129. JAMAICA'S JOY AND PRAISE AT THE ABOLITION OF SLAVERY

Author: unspecified
Tune: Falcon Street

The day is come at last,
The first of August's come,
The reign of slavery is past,
The act of freedom's done.
Praise ye the Lord, Hallelujah.

Behold the ocean's waves,
All haste to greet our shore;
They leap upon the land, it loves -
A land of slaves no more!
Praise ye the Lord, Hallelujah.

Behold the clouds on high,
Embrace the mountain tops;
They promise, from the peaceful sky,
Their fertilizing drops.
Praise ye the Lord, Hallelujah.

Behold the cane-fields smile,
In living green arrayed;
They wave their flags, and sing meanwhile
"Our laborers are paid."
Praise ye the Lord, Hallelujah.

Behold the stately palms,
They wave their branches high;
And, 'midst the breezes and the calms,
Joy in our liberty.
Praise ye the Lord, Hallelujah.

Praise Him, the Lord of Hosts,
And sound abroad his fame,
Yes, spread thro' all your island coasts,
The honors of his name.
Praise ye the Lord, Hallelujah.

Liberator, September 14, 1838, p. 148.

130. AMERICA - A PARODY

Author: Theta
Tune: America

My country! 'tis of thee,
Strong hold of Slavery -
Of thee I sing:
Land, where my fathers died;
Where men man's rights deride;
From every mountain-side,
Thy deeds shall ring.

My native country! thee -
Where all men are born free,
If <u>white</u> their skin:
I love thy hills and dales,
Thy mounts and pleasant vales;
But hate thy <u>negro</u> sales,
As foulest sin.

Let <u>wailing</u> swell the breeze,
And <u>ring from</u> all the trees
The <u>black</u> man's wrong:
Let <u>every</u> tongue awake,
Let <u>bond</u> and free partake,
Let <u>rocks</u> their silence break,
The sound prolong.

Our father's God! to thee -
Author of Liberty!
To thee we sing;
<u>Soon</u> may our land be bright, -
<u>With holy Freedom's</u> light -
Protect us by thy might,
Great God, our King.

<u>Liberator</u>, May 3, 1839, p. 72; and <u>Melodies</u>, pp. 28-29.

131. HYMN FOR THE FOURTH OF JULY

Author: Wm. J. Snelling
Tune: The Marseilles Hymn

Heirs of the brave, who live in story,
In peace enjoy what valor won,
Remembrance of your country's glory,
Bequeathed from patriot sire to son.
Lo! fields of plenty bloom around us,
And Freedom's sons, a sacred band,
The guardians of their country stand,
Where Freedom's choicest gifts surround us!
Rejoice, this day rejoice!
Proclaim it to land and sea,
Tell to the skies, with one vast voice,
Our father-land is free!

Lo! on the prophet's rapt eye gleaming,
What visions of the future rise!
The stars that light a nation beaming,
While God accords what man denies;
The power and pride of despots taming,
What earth has never known before,

That man is man and none is more,
To man of every hue proclaiming!
United, hand in hand,
Hear us, O earth and sea,
Tell all the world our father-land
Was, is and shall be free!

Liberator, July 5, 1839, p. 107.

132. LIBERTY

Author: Vattel
Tune: I See Them on Their Winding Way

I see them on their toilsome way,
Their faces wear no smiles today;
The white man's note of revelry
Blends with the captive's wailing cry;
And waving arms and banners bright,
Are glancing in the noon-day light; -
But not for them this jubilee;
Waves not for them the banner free;
And at the contrast, fainter still,
The sinking captives mount the hill.

Crack, crack, the whip! - the cruel lash
Leaves on their shoulders many a gash;
Weeping and chained, along they drag,
Above them waves fair Freedom's flag,
And, from the crowded Court-house near,
The white man's hymn of joy they hear.
Forth, forth, and meet them on their way,
Their bleeding feet brook no delay;
Strike off their fetters, make them free,
Then raise your songs of Liberty.

Liberator, July 19, 1839, p. 116, preceded by this introduction: "Scene - a town in South Carolina; drums beating - guns
firing - colors flying - 4th of July; a coffle of slaves are
seen in the distance; four sons of liberty on horseback, with
long whips, acting as drivers."

133. ODE

Author: J. Pierpont
Tune: When the Trump of Fame

Let the trump of Fame
Now to their memory swell,
Who, in Freedom's name,
Fought and bravely fell!
On the heroes moved,
With death on every side: -
For the land they loved
They died - they died. -
Round the names of all,
Shall Honor's chaplets green,
Here, in Freedom's Hall,
Freshly wreathed be seen,
Till all the nations raise
The shout, like ocean's roar,
That RIGHT our sceptre sways,
And SLAVERY reigns no more!

When the patriot dead,
Who, in their glory rest,
From their lowly bed,
In ghostly garments drest,
Came up, and at our call,
Their festive board surround -
Shall they see this Hall
In wassail drowned?
Can man, to Freedom true,
Prove false to Virtue's laws? -
In our father's view,
Come, Pledge the TEMPERANCE CAUSE.
Wine is Freedom's foe!
Hence let the recreant fly,
Lest by the traitor's blow,
She, in HER CRADLE, die!

Liberator, July 19, 1839, p. 116.

134. JEFFERSON'S DAUGHTER

Author: unspecified
Tune: unspecified

Can the blood that, at Lexington, poured o'er
the plain,
When the sons warred with tyrants their rights
to uphold,
Can the tide of Niagara wipe out the stain?
No! Jefferson's child has been bartered for
gold!

Do you boast of your freedom? Peace, babblers
- be still;
Prate not of the goddess who scarce deigns to
hear;
Have ye power to unbind? Are ye wanting in
will?
Must the groans of your bondman still torture
the ear?

The daughter of Jefferson sold for a slave!
The child of a freeman for dollars and francs!
The roar of applause, when your orators rave,
Is lost in the sound of her chain, as it
clanks.

Peace, then, ye blasphemers of Liberty's name!
Though red was the blood by your forefathers
spilt,
Still redder your cheeks should be mantled
with shame,
Till the spirit of freedom shall cancel the
guilt.

But the brand of the slave is the tint of his
skin,
Though his heart may beat loyal and true
underneath;
While the soul of the tyrant is rotten within,
And his white the mere cloak to the blackness
of death.

Are ye deaf to the plaints that each moment
arise?
Is it thus ye forget the mild precepts of
Penn, -
Unheeding the clamor that "maddens the skies,"
As ye trample the rights of your dark
fellow-men?

When the incense that glows before Liberty's
shrine,
Is unmixed with the blood of the galled and
oppressed, -
O, then, and then only, the boast may be
thine,
That the stripes and stars wave o'er a land of
the blest.

Liberator, March 6, 1840, p. 40.

Liberator, May 26, 1848, p. 84, under the same title; no tune
specified.

Harp, pp. 23-24, under the same title; no tune specified. An introduction quoted from the [London] Morning Chronicle states, "It is asserted, on the authority of an American Newspaper, that the daughter of Thomas Jefferson, late President of the United States, was sold at New Orleans for $1,000."

135. HYMN

Author: C. W. Dennison
Tune: Missionary Hymn

Our countrymen are dying
Beneath their cankering chains,
Full many a heart is sighing,
Where nought but slavery reigns.
No note of joy and gladness,
No voice with freedom's lay;
Falls on them in their sadness
To wipe those tears away.

Where proud Potomac dashes,
Along its northern strand,
Where Rappahannock lashes
Virginia's sparkling sand;
Where Eutaw, famed in story,
Flows swift to Santee's stream,
There, there, in grief and gory
The pining slave is seen!

And shall New England's daughters,
Descendants of the free,
Beside whose far famed waters
Is heard sweet minstrelsy,
Shall they when hearts are breaking,
And woman weeps in wo,
Shall they all listless waiting
No hearts of pity show?

No! let the shout for freedom
Ring out a certain peal,
Let sire and youthful maiden,
All who have hearts to feel,
Awake! and with the blessing
Of Him who came to save,
A holy, peaceful triumph,
Shall greet the kneeling slave!

Standard, September 24, 1840, p. 64.

Free Soil, pp. 48-49; and Freedom, pp. 244-245, as "Our
Countrymen"; and Liberty, pp 94-95, as "Our Countrymen are
Dying," all to the same tune.

136. INDEPENDENCE DAY

Author: Wm. Lloyd Garrison
Tune: Auld Lang Syne

The bells are ringing merrily,
The cannon loudly roar;
And thunder-shouts for liberty
Are heard from shore to shore;
And countless banners to the breeze
Their "stars and stripes" display: -
What call for sights and sounds like these?
'Tis Independence day!

Our fathers spurned the British yoke,
Determined to be free;
And full of might they rose and broke
The chains of tyranny!
O! long they toiled, with zeal unfeigned,
And kept their foes at bay,
Till by their valorous deeds they gained
Our Independence day!

They fought not for themselves alone,
But for the RIGHTS OF ALL,
Of every caste, complexion, zone,
On this terrestrial ball:
To God they made their high appeal,
In hope, not in dismay;
For well they trusted He would seal
Their Independence day!

Their creed how just - their creed how grand!
"ALL MEN ARE EQUAL BORN!"
Let those who cannot understand
This truth, be laughed to scorn!
Cheers for the land in which we live,
The free, the fair, the gay!
And hearty thanks to Heaven we'll give,
For Independence day!

O God! what mockery is this!
Our land, how lost to shame!
Well may all Europe jeer and hiss
At mention of her name!

For, while she boasts of liberty,
'Neath SLAVERY'S iron sway
Three millions of her people lie,
On Independence day!

She may not, must not, thus rejoice,
Nor of her triumphs tell:
Hushed be the cannon's thundering voice,
And muffled every bell!
Dissolved in tears, prone in the dust,
For mercy let her pray,
That judgments on her may not burst
On Independence day!

Lo! where her starry banner waves,
In many a graceful fold -
There toil, and groan, and bleed her slaves,
And men, like brutes, are sold!
Her hands are red with crimson stains,
And bloody is her way;
She wields the lash, she forges chains,
On Independence day!

Friends of your country - of your race -
Of freedom - and of GOD!
Combine oppression to efface,
And break the tyrant's rod:
All traces of injustice sweep
By moral powers away;
Than a glorious jubilee we'll keep
On INDEPENDENCE day!

Liberator, June 18, 1841, p. 99; and Standard, July 1, 1841,
p. 16.

Anniversary, pp. 13-14, five verses only (1-4 and 8), under
the same title, to the same tune.

137. [UNTITLED]

Author: unspecified
Tune: Yarmouth

ALAS! the bondmen's story,
With cruel injuries fraught,
Has trac'd our nation's glory,
With deep damnation's blot:

His tears have stain'd our banner,
Made dim our early fame,
And on our nation's honor
Stamp'd infamy and shame.

And shall this freeborn nation
Still trade in human souls?
While men of every station
The lust of gold controls?
Shall freemen foster slavery,
And wield oppression's rod,
And ruin by their knavery
"The noblest work of God?"

Shall man, in worth outshining
Peruvian gems and gold,
In slavery's chains be pining -
Like brutes be bought and sold?
Shall he be taught by scourges,
Be driven by the blow,
Who, through eternal ages,
In intellect shall grow?

Ah! no; this freeborn spirit
Above its chains shall rise,
And after death inherit
A crown beyond the skies:
'Tis free as ours forever,
It cannot be confin'd;
E'en Slavery's fetters never
Can wholly crush the mind.

Hymns, pp. 24-25.

138. [UNTITLED]

Author: unspecified
Tune: Indian Philosopher

But art thou, still, my country, free?
The land which heaven born Liberty
Hath honored with her name!
Lo! from the South there comes a cry,
Where foul Oppression's victims lie
In bondage, woe and shame.

The land the Pilgrim Fathers trod,
The highly favored land of God,
Is sunk in infamy;
E'en on this consecrated soil
Afric's three millions hopeless toil,
For Freedom vainly sigh.

No pity warms the Oppressor's heart,
But deeper still he drives the dart,
And binds the chain more fast,
Till worn with misery and with grief,
The injured captive finds relief,
In heaven a home at last.

Arise! ye children of the light,
And tear away this withering blight
That mars your country's fame.
Oh! wipe away vile Slavery's stains!
Strike off the fettered negro's chains,
Your everlasting shame.

Kind heaven will your efforts bless,
And crown your labors with success,
Restore lost liberty;
and then shall Freedom's banner wave
Triumphant o'er Oppression's grave,
And every slave be free.

Hymns, pp. 16-17.

139. THE WEST INDIES EMANCIPATED

Author: unspecified
Tune: unspecified

HAIL to the brightness of freedom's glad
morning!
Join, all the earth, in an anthem of praise;
Day - joyful day - in its glory is dawning,
Light is dispensing its soul cheering rays.
See, how 'tis gilding those isles of the ocean
Hark to the echoing songs of their joy -
Brighter is burning the flame of devotion,
Music far sweeter than angels employ.

Thousands long buried in deep degradation,
Rise to the sphere which their Maker assign'd;
Bearing glad triumph to God's free salvation,
Sent from above, by "good will to mankind."

Now may the Gospel exert its dominion
Over the beings now treated as men;
Borne from the dust upon Freedom's blest
pinion,
God may behold his own image again.

Joy to those Islands! the cloud has pass'd
o'er them,
Brightly the rain-bow encircles the skies;
Heaven is smiling and spreads out before them,
Fadeless and pure its own glorious prize.
When will our land thus arouse from its
slumber,
And be delivered from tyrany's stain?
When will redemption reach all that vast
number,
Fettered so long by dark Slavery's chain?

Speed on thou herald of freedom! Oh, hasten
Such a proud era for us to proclaim;
Fain to those tidings of joy would we listen,
Fain would we witness the conqueror's fame.
Hail, then, thrice hail to this glorious
morning:
Hail to the myriads from bondage releas'd;
Hope's gilded beams, the horizon adorning,
Tell us the night of oppression hath ceas'd.

Hymns, pp. 32-33.

140. FREEMEN, AWAKE!*

Author: Maria W. Chapman
Tune: unidentified

Hark! hark! it is the trumpet call,
"Rise in the name of God Most High!"
On ready hearts the accents fall,
And firm and full they make reply;

"The hour hath come to do and dare,
Bound with the bondmen now are we;
We'll pour aloft the mighty prayer,
We'll bend in God's own house the knee."

Stream forth from all your mountains green,
Pour like a flood from ev'ry height;
With kindling hearts and voices keen,
Swell high the song of truth and right.

A mighty sound the region fills,
A voice from all our fathers' graves,
It comes from all these thousand hills
"Woe to the land of human slaves!"

Picknick, p. 87.

Melodies, p. 10, as "Hymn 4," to an unidentified tune from
Boston Academy.

*Astute readers will note the similarity between these verses
and song 25 in the previous section; they are substantially
the same, but the omission of the original third, sixth, and
seventh verses in the version above changed the emphasis
enough to be classified as slightly more "patriotic" than
"Christian." To facilitate indexing, the two versions are
treated as separate songs except in the Author Index.

141. [UNTITLED]

Author: unspecified
Tune: Clarence

HARK - hark the voice of anguish,
Borne over freedom's plains;
A groan from those who languish
In slavery and in chains!
'Tis wafted o'er the mountains,
From Camden's sacred field,
From Eutaw's hallowed fountains,
Where patriot blood was spill'd!

Hark - hark the clank of fetters,
From shady grove and dell,
A shriek where freedom's martyrs
In glorious combat fell!
What! stripes and chains and fetters,
In freedom's boasted land,
Where Liberty's proud altars,
And tow'ring temples stand?

Is this the Home of freedom,
Of truth and holy light?
Where millions grope in thraldom,
Depriv'd of ev'ry right! -
A refuge from oppression
For Europe's sons to share;
While for a dark complexion
Her own the chain must wear?

Say, is that a voice of wailing -
That undissembled cry -
That tale the slave is telling -
Not worth a single sigh?
And shall their many sorrows
Be heard by us in vain?
No - no! - we'll end their horrors,
We'll break off ev'ry chain.

Hymns, pp. 23-24.

142. [UNTITLED]

Author: unspecified
Tune: Flower When Evening Gathers Round Thee

Hear ye not the voice of anguish,
In our own - our native land?
Brethren, doom'd in chains to languish,
Lift to heaven the fetter'd hand.

Let us raise our supplication,
For the scourg'd, the suffering slave -
All whose life is desolation,
All whose hope is in the grave.

Those in bonds we would remember;
Lord! our hands with theirs are bound:
With each helpless, suff'ring member,
Let our sympathies be found.

Even now the word is spoken:
"Lo! the tyrant's power must cease:
From the slave the chain be broken:
Captives! hail the kind release."

Hymns, pp. 27-28.

143. [UNTITLED]

Author: unspecified
Tune: unspecified

Lift up our country's banner high,
And fling abroad its gorgeous sheen,
Unroll its stripes upon the sky,
And let its lovely stars be seen!
Blood - blood is on its spangled fold:
Yet from the battle comes it not;
But all the waters oceans hold,
Cannot wash out the guilty spot.

Up, freemen! up; determine, do
What Justice claims, what freemen may;
What frowning heav'n demands of you,
While yet its muttering thunders stay:
That ye, forever from this soil,
Bid SLAVERY'S with'ring blight depart,
And to the wretch restore the spoil,
Though ye cannot the broken heart.

Lift up your brother from the dust,
And speak his long crush'd spirit FREE;
That millions, by your avarice curst,
May sharers in your blessings be:
Then to the universe wide spread
Your glorious stars without a stain;
Bend from your skies, illustrious dead -
The land ye won is free again.

Hymns, pp. 29-30.

        144. A HYMN FOR THE FIRST OF AUGUST

            Author: W. L. Garrison
            Tune: unspecified

Lo! the bondage of ages has ceased!
The chains of the tyrant are riven!
No more as a chattel or beast,
Shall man to his labor be driven:
Where the groans and the shrieks of despair
From heart-broken victims were heard,
Songs of rapturous joy fill the air,
More sweet than the notes of a bird!

Lo! the gloom and the blackness of night
Have suddenly vanished away,
And all things rejoice in the light
Of Freedom's meridian day!

Restored to their sight are the blind -
No longer they grope for the wall;
All who seek may with certainty find,
For clear is the vision of all!

Hark! a voice from the Isles of the Sea!
Its echoes are heard round the world;
O! joyful its message - "WE ARE FREE!
To the dust Oppression is hurled!
We are free as the waves of the deep,
As the winds that sweep o'er the earth;
And therefore we jubilee keep,
And hallow the day of our birth!"

Praise, praise to the name of the Lord!
What wonders his right hand hath done!
How mighty and sure is his word!
How great is the victory won!
The power that Jehovah defied,
In ruin and infamy lies; -
O, spread the intelligence wide -
For marvellous 'tis in all eyes.

Columbia! O shame on thee now!
Repent thee in ashes and dust!
There is blood on thy hands - on thy brow -
And thou art by slavery cursed!
Thy millions of vassals set free,
Away with the scourge and the rod -
Then join with the Isles of the Sea,
In a shout of thanksgiving to God!

Picknick, pp. 140-141.

Melodies, pp. 64-65, with verse four omitted, as "Lo the
Bondage of Ages Has Ceased," to an unidentified tune.

145. SONG FOR THE FIRST OF AUGUST

Author: unspecified
Tune: Away the Bowl

Our grateful hearts with joy o'erflow,
Hurra, Hurra, Hurra,
We hail the Despot's overthrow,
Hurra, Hurra, Hurra,
No more he'll raise the gory lash,
And sink it deep in human flesh,
Hurra, Hurra, Hurra, Hurra,
Hurra, Hurra, Hurra.

We raise the song in Freedom's name,
Hurra, Hurra, Hurra,
Her glorious triumph we proclaim,
Hurra, Hurra, Hurra,
Beneath her feet lie Slavery's chains,
Their power to curse no more remains,
Hurra, Hurra, Hurra, Hurra,
Hurra, Hurra, Hurra.

With joy we'll make the air resound,
Hurra, Hurra, Hurra,
That all may hear the gladsome sound,
Hurra, Hurra, Hurra,
We glory at Oppression's fall,
The Slave has burst his deadly thrall,
Hurra, Hurra, Hurra, Hurra,
Hurra, Hurra, Hurra.

In mirthful glee we'll dance and sing,
Hurra, Hurra, Hurra,
With shouts we'll make the welkin ring,
Hurra, Hurra, Hurra,
Shout! shout aloud! the bondsman's free!
This, this is Freedom's jubilee!
Hurra, Hurra, Hurra, Hurra,
Hurra, Hurra, Hurra.

Picknick, pp. 122-123.

Harp, p. 12, as "Jubilee Song," to the same tune.

146. FREEMEN ASSERTING THEIR OWN RIGHTS

Author: unspecified
Tune: unidentified

Spirit of Freemen, wake;
No truce with Slavery make,
Thy deadly foe;
In fair disguises dressed,
Too long hast thou caress'd
The serpent in thy breast,
Now lay him low.

Must e'en the press be dumb?
Must truth itself succumb?
And thoughts be mute?

Shall law be set aside,
The right of prayer denied,
Nature and God decried,
And man called brute?

What lover of her fame
Feels not his country's shame,
In this dark hour?
Where are the patriots now,
Of honest heart and brow,
Who scorn the neck to bow
To Slavery's power?

Sons of the Free! we call
On you, in field and hall,
To rise as one;
Your heaven-born rights maintain,
Nor let Oppression's chain
On human limbs remain; -
Speak! and 'tis done.

Picknick, pp. 132-133.

Harp, p. 13, as "Spirit of Freemen, Wake," to the tune,
"America."

Free Soil, p. 194; and Freedom, p. 195, first and last
verses only, as "Spirit of Freemen, Awake," to the tune,
"America."

147. FREEDOM'S WAR

Author: unspecified
Tune: Bonny Boat

They gather for the coming strife,
Not as of yore, with drum and gun,
And bugle's blast and sound of fife,
And pealing clarion;
But with a step as firm as they,
And with a heart as true and brave,
They march to tear the yoke away
That bows to dust the slave.

See! rank on rank the stalwart men
Come swarming from the forest shades,
From lofty hill and lowly glen
And mountain everglades;

The veteran, bowed with years and toil,
Whose young blood flowed for freedom, when
A foreign foe profaned our soil,
Speeds to the fight again!

A deadlier monster roams the strand,
Than England's Lion fierce for blood,
A wilder wailing through the land
Goes upward unto God;
Young hearts his iron hoofs have crushed,
Young forms his cruel fangs have torn,
And blood like purple wine hath gushed
Till shore and ocean mourn.

Shall we, the sons of noble sires,
Who gave to us their names and graves,
On hills where blazed their beacon fires,
Behold our brethren, SLAVES?
SLAVES, crouching on the very dust
That patriots hallowed when they fell,
Victims of mammon, hate and lust,
That makes of earth a hell!

Hark! from old Bunker's glory bed
Where loudest freedom's trumpet pealed,
From Camden's garden of the dead,
And Eutaw's haunted field,
From Bennington's oak-shaded hill,
And Saratoga's field of snow,
And Erie's waters, dark and chill,
The DEAD give answer, NO!

The LIVING catch the answer, NO, -
And round the winter hearth at eve,
While tears of child and mother flow,
And gray-haired matrons grieve,
STRONG MANHOOD nerves his heart and hand,
And from Ohio to the sea,
A million voices fill the land,
"THE FETTERED SHALL BE FREE!"

Hymns, pp. 11-13.

148. FOR THE FIRST OF AUGUST

Author: John Pierpont
Tune: unidentified, by Baker

Where Britannia's emerald isles
Gem the Caribbean sea,
And an endless summer smiles,
Lo! the negro thrall is free!
Yet not, on Columbia's plains,
Hath the sun of Freedom risen;
Here, in darkness and in chains,
Toiling millions pine in prison.

Shout, ye islands disenthralled!
Point the finger, as in scorn,
At a country that is called
Freedom's home - where men are born,
Heirs, for life, to chains and whips;
Bondmen, who have never known
Wife, child, parent, that their lips,
Ever dared to call their own.

Yet a Christian land is this!
Yea, and ministers of Christ,
Slavery's foot in homage kiss,
And their brother, who is priced
Higher than their Saviour, even,
Do they into bondage sell;
Pleading thus the cause of Heaven,
Serving thus the cause of Hell.

Holy Father, let thy word,
Spoken by thy prophets old,
By the pliant priest be heard;
And let lips, that now are cold,
(Chilled by Mammon's golden wand,)
With our nation's burden glow,
Till the free man and the bond,
Shout for Slavery's overthrow.

Picknick, pp. 88-89.

149. AROUSE, NEW-ENGLAND'S SONS

Author: Miss M. L. Gardner
Tune: unidentified

Arouse, New-England's sons, arouse!
Wake from your coward sleep,
The tyrant's hand is on your neck,
And shall his fetters keep,

In bondage, men whom freedom nursed,
In her own chosen home?
Where patriot's blood was freely poured
In holy martyrdom?

Arouse, New-England's sons, arouse!
A clinging curse on thee!
If here supinely ye will sleep,
Dreaming that ye are free.
Arouse, and see how false the name,
Which ye so fondly claim,
Free are ye! while ye bear about
The tyrants' galling chain?

Free! while the halls ye rear are burned?
Free! while your sons are driven
By slavery's mobs, because they dare
To speak for truth and heaven?
Free! while the very homes you've made
Beside your fathers' graves,
Are pillaged if ye dare to aid
The panting, flying slave?

Arouse, New-England's sons, arouse!
And lay oppression low,
And strike for freedom and for God,
An earnest manly blow.
Nail up your banner to the wall,
In God's name let it wave,
Until beneath its ample folds
Shall crouch no wretched slave.

Melodies, pp. 78-79.

150. COME ALL WHO CLAIM THE FREEMAN'S NAME

Author: James H. Wilder
Tune: unidentified

Come all who claim the freeman's name,
Come join in earnest song:
In freedom's praise your voices raise,
And loud the strain prolong.
Ring out the shout, the land throughout,
No room be here for craven doubt,
In trust arouse, with truthful vows,
Arouse, arouse, arouse.

From "British yoke and galling chain"
Our fathers loosed the land -
But other yokes and bonds remain,
Their sons with shame to brand.
For chains and bars and whips and scars
Now mingle with Columbia's stars,
To change for shame her banner's fame,
For shame, for shame, for shame.

Sons of the free! shall these thing be
Where th' eagle's scream is heard?
Beneath a sky where gleams the eye
Of freedom's mountain bird?
Shall former emblems only be
The epitaphs of Liberty?
Then thunder no! let th' outcry go,
Oh no! oh no! oh no!

While justice, honor, mercy, love,
Are aught but empty sounds,
We'll strive foul slavery's curse to drive
Beyond our nation's bounds.
For right we'll fight, with all our might,
While truth sheds down her full clear light,
"Let all be free," the cry shall be,
Be free, be free, be free.

On this fair land let freedom stand,
And wide her banner wave,
Nor ever be our blood-bought soil,
Her hapless, hopeless grave.
While beams the star that shews the North,
While bondmen dream of freedom's worth,
They'll flee away, at rest to stay,
Away, away, away.

O God of love! look from above
In mercy on the slave.
Let blessed peace bring his release,
Let truth be strong to save.
When comes the day, as come it must,
That chains shall crumble into dust,
We'll all hurra, both near and far,
Hurra, hurra, hurra.

Melodies, pp. 84-85.

Mentioned in Liberator, May 21, 1852, p. 82, as having been
sung at the Eighteenth Annual Meeting of the American Anti-
Slavery Society.

151. HYMN FOR THE FIRST OF AUGUST

Author: Frances H. Green
Tune: Judah

Glory to God! Let joyful songs
Through Heaven's high arches ring!
While ransomed slaves the strain prolong
And Freedom's children sing!

Shout for the day when chains were broke!
Triumphant Liberty
The glorious mandate only spoke; -
And bondmen stood up free!

Joy! - for the sun of Truth is up!
The cloud hath passed away!
And thousands drink of Freedom's cup,
To bless this holy day!

Joyfully sing, SOULS OF THE FREE!
Send up your shouts again,
For Liberty's sweet jubilee
[When CHATTELS] were made MEN!

Glory to God! for every chain
His power shall yet destroy! -
[Let heaven] and earth repeat the strain,
And swell the echoing joy!

Liberator, August 4, 1843, p. 124.

152. THE TRUMPET OF FREEDOM

Author: unspecified
Tune: unidentified

Hark! hark! to the TRUMPET of FREEDOM!
Her rallying signal she blows:
Come, gather around her broad banner,
And battle 'gainst Liberty's foes.

Hurra, for the old-fashioned doctrine,
That men are created all free!
We ever will boldly maintain it,
Nor care who the tyrant may be.

Our forefathers plighted their honor,
Their lives and their property, too,
To maintain in defiance of Britain,
Their principles, righteous and true.

We're foes unto wrong and oppression,
No matter which side of the sea;
And ever intend to oppose them,
Till all of God's image are free.

Melodies, pp. 66-67.

Liberty, pp. 157-158, under the same title; and Free Soil,
pp. 13-14, and Freedom, pp. 262-263, as "The Home of the
Free," all to the tune, "Rosin the Bow," with the following
added verses:

We'll show to the world we are worthy
The blessings our ancestors won,
And finish the temple of Freedom,
That HANCOCK and FRANKLIN begun.

When Poland was fighting for freedom,
Our voices went over the sea,
To bid her God-speed in the contest -
That Poland, like us, might be free.

When down-trodden Greece had up-risen,
And battled the Mohomet crew;
We rejoiced in the glorious issue,
That Greece had her liberty, too.

Repeal, do we also delight in -
Three cheers for the "gem of the sea!"
And soon may the bright day be dawning,
When Ireland, like us, shall be free.

Like us, who are foes to oppression;
But not like America now.
With shame do we blush to confess it,
Too many to slavery bow.

Some tell us because men are colored,
They should not our sympathy share;
We ask not the form or complexion -
The seal of our Maker is there!

Success to the old-fashioned doctrine,
That men are created all free!
And down with the power of the despot
Wherever his strongholds may be.

We're proud of the name of a freeman
And proud of the character, too;
And never will do any action,
Save such as a freeman may do.

We'll finish the Temple of Freedom,
And make it capacious within,
That all who seek shelter may find it,
Whatever the hue of their skin.

For thus the Almighty designed it,
And gave to our fathers the plan;
Intending that liberty's blessings,
Should rest upon every man.

Then up with the cap-stone and cornice,
With columns encircle its wall,
Throw open its gateway, and make it
A HOME AND A REFUGE FOR ALL!

153. ODE FOR THE FOURTH OF JULY

Author: unspecified
Tune: unidentified

Hark how the loud, deep cannon's roar,
Insults the peaceful dawn,
And beat of drums and chime of bells
Marshals the early morn.

A country vowed to liberty,
And vowed to slavery too,
And striving with a half-way soul
To do and to undo.

Let the day see the pageant show,
Float banners to the breeze,
Bid liberty all hail! throughout
Columbia's lands and seas.

Yes, rally brave America,
Thy noble hearts and free,
Around the eagle as he soars -
Sunward - in majesty.

Melodies, p. 94.

154. HYMN

Written for the 1st of August.

Author: Mary L. Gardner
Tune: unidentified

Is there one here within whose soul
Lingers a spark of Freedom's fire,
One, who would boast with honest pride
The spirit of his patriot sire,
One who would scorn the tyrant rod,
The iron yoke, the galling chain,
Who will not swell the joyous song
That comes today across the main?

List! list! the wind exulting bears
The thrilling note upon its wing;
Eight hundred thousand ransom'd souls
Th' inspiring song of freedom sing.
Long had they bow'd beneath the yoke,
Long "welter'd in a living grave,"
Their chains are broke, and Britain's isles
Now bear no impress of a slave.

Wake! wake the chorus! shall their shout
Upon New England's hill-tops die,
Where freedom first with trumpet tone
Sent forth her wild and fearless cry?
No! let it ring o'er hill and vale,
From Greenland to the southern plain,
Where even now the soil is cursed
By Slavery's dark and hateful stain.

O, Father! may thy word go forth,
From India to the western sea,
Till millions now in dreadful thrall,
Can swell the anthem of the Free;
Till over Afric's sable race,
No more is waved oppression's rod, -
And man no longer dares for gold
To sell the image of his God.

Melodies, pp. 14-15.

155. HYMN

Author: Mary Ann Collier
Tune: unidentified

Land of my sleeping fathers!
O'er thee no chain is flung;
Through all thy verdant vallies,
The shout of joy is rung;
Wide o'er thy rolling rivers,
Thy fair and sunny plains,
And up thy rocky mountains,
The soul of Freedom reigns.

But is there then no shadow,
To dim this hallow'd mirth?
Is not thy name, my country!
A by-word on the earth?
Are all the captives loosen'd?
The fetter'd slave set free?
Is his crush'd spirit gladden'd,
On this gay Jubilee?

Say to the captive toiling,
In Freedom's proud abode:
"Cast off thy fetters, brother!
Take back the gift of God."
Let not oppression linger,
Where starry banners wave;
Swell high the shout of Freedom,
And give it to the slave.

Melodies, pp. 42-43.

156. ARE YE TRULY FREE?

Author: J. R. Lowell
Tune: Martyn

Men! whose boast it is that ye
Come of fathers brave and free;
If there breathe on earth a slave,
Are ye truly free and brave?
Are ye not base slaves indeed,
Men unworthy to be freed?
If ye do not feel the chain,
When it works a brother's pain.

Women! who shall one day bear
Sons to breathe God's bounteous air,
If ye hear without a blush,
Deeds to make the roused blood rush

Like red lava through your veins,
For your sisters now in chains;
Answer! are ye fit to be
Mothers of the brave and free?

Is true freedom but to break
Fetters for our own dear sake,
And, with leathern hearts forget
That we owe mankind a debt?
No! true freedom is to share
All the chains our brothers wear,
And with hand and heart to be
Earnest to make others free.

They are slaves who fear to speak
For the fallen and the weak;
They are slaves, who will not choose
Hatred, scoffing, and abuse,
Rather than, in silence, shrink
From the truth they needs must think;
They are slaves, who dare not be
In the right with two or three.

Liberator, August 4, 1843, p. 123.

Liberator, August 11, 1843, p. 126, indicates that this song
was sung by "Misses Fuller and Mr. Richardson" at a celebration of August 1 at Dedham.

Free Soil, pp. 156-157; Harp, pp. 44-45; and Freedom,
pp. 156-157, under the same title, to the same tune.

157. FREEDOM'S BANNER

Author: R. C. Waterston
Tune: unidentified

My country, shall thy honored name
Be as a byword through the world?
Rouse! for (as if to blast thy fame,)
This keen reproach is at thee hurled,
"The banner that above thee waves,
Is floating o'er three million slaves."

That flag, my country, I had thought,
From noble sires was given to thee,
By the best blood of patriots bought,
To wave alone above the Free!
Yet now, while to the breeze it waves,
It floats above three million slaves.

The mighty dead that flag unrolled,
They bathed it in the heaven's own blue.
They sprinkled stars upon each fold,
And gave it as a trust to you;
And now that glorious banner waves,
In shame, above three million slaves.

Oh, by the virtues of our sires,
And by the soil on which they trod,
And by the trust their name inspires,
And by the hope we have in God,
Arouse, my country, and agree
To set thy captive children free.

Arouse! and let each hill and glen
With prayer to the high heavens ring out
Till all our land, with free-born men,
May join in one triumphant shout,
That freedom,s banner does not wave
Its fold above a single slave.

Melodies, pp. 72-73.

Harp, pp. 38-39, under the same title, to the tune, "Freedom's Banner."

158. SPIRIT OF FREEDOM, AWAKE

Author: unspecified
Tune: O Lady, Sweet Lady

O Freedom, sweet Freedom,
O Freedom, sweet Freedom, return, return,
Thy stars are dim, thy light is gone,
Thy stars are dim, thy light is gone.
This hour's for thee, for thee alone,
O hear our prayers.
Spirit of Freedom, awake, awake,
Sound the loud trump of Jubilee.
Till, at its note, the nation shake,
And proclaim the captive free.
Spirit of Freedom, awake, awake.
Fa la la lal la la fa la la la
Fa la la lal la la la
Fa la la lal la la fa la la la
Fa la la lal la la la.

Melodies, pp. 80-83.

159. THE PILGRIMS ARE LAUNCHED

Author: Henry Ware, Jr.
Tune: The Wild Hunt of Lutzow

The Pilgrims are launched on the wild winter
main,
Their bark on the foam madly tossing:
The tempest is high; but its threats they
disdain;
They are fleeing from tyranny's sceptre and
chain,
It is Liberty's sea they are crossing.
Hark! loud rings their cry o'er the stormy
wave,
"Freedom! Death or Freedom!
Freedom, or ocean our grave!
Death or Freedom!
Freedom! or ocean our grave!"

Borne high on the breath of the soft summer
gale,
The slave ship is proudly careering.
What sighs of despair, and what voices of
wail!
What anguish and madness beneath that fair
sail,
To hopeless captivity steering!
Hark! hark, from the black hold the stifled
cry,
"Freedom! Death or Freedom!"
Hear how it pierces the sky!
"Death or Freedom."
Hear how it pierces the sky.

In the darkness and rain of the chill autumn
night,
The slave from the cane-fields is striding;
Thro' hunger and hardship he urges his flight,
Nor perils dismay him, nor blood-hounds
affright,
By the North-star his weary feet guiding.
Help! help for him! answer his earnest cry!
"Freedom! Freedom! Freedom!"
Tell him that rescue is nigh;
"Freedom! Freedom!"
Tell him that rescue is nigh.

Up, up with your banners to honor the brave!
O'er your forefathers' tombs be they flying!
And hail to the hero, tho' black and a slave,
Who shrinks from oppression, but fears not the grave,
And throws off his fetters by dying.
Join, join in the shout that he flings on high,
"Freedom! Death or Freedom!"
Join; - 'twas your Forefathers' cry;
"Death or Freedom!"
Join; - 'twas your Forefathers' cry.

Melodies, pp. 74-76.

160. NEW ENGLAND, AWAKE!

Author: J. G. Whittier
Tune: [original?], by S. S. Wardwell

Pride of New England!
Soul of our fathers!
Shrink we all craven-like,
When the storm gathers?
What tho' the tempest be
Over us lowering,
Where's the New-Englander
Shamefully cowering?
Graves green and holy
Around us are lying,
Free were the sleepers all,
Living and dying.

Back with the Southerner's
Padlocks and scourges,
Go - let him fetter down
Ocean's free surges!
Go - let him silence
Winds, clouds and waters,
Never New-England's own
Free sons and daughters!
Free as our rivers are
Ocean-ward going,
Free as the breezes are
Over us blowing.

Up to our altars, then,
Haste we and summon
Courage and loveliness,
Manhood and woman!

Deep let our pledges be:
Freedom forever!
Truce with oppression,
Never, oh! never.
By our own birth-right gift,
Granted of heaven,
Freedom for heart and lip,
Be the pledge given.

If we have whispered truth,
Whisper no longer:
Speak as the tempest does,
Sterner and stronger.
Still be the tones of truth
Louder and firmer,
Startling the haughty South
With the deep murmur.
God and our charter's right,
Freedom forever.
Truce with oppression,
Never, oh! never.

Melodies, pp. 91-93.

161. WE ARE COMING

Author: John E. Robinson
Tune: unspecified

We are coming, we are coming! Freedom's battle
is begun!
No head shall furl our banner, ere her victory
be won!
Our shields are locked for Liberty, and Mercy
goes before:
Tyrants, tremble in your citadel! Oppression
shall be o'er.

We have hatred, dark and deep, for the fetter
and the thong;
We bring light for prisoned spirits; for the
captive's wall, a song;
We are coming, we are coming ! and, "NO LEAGUE
WITH TYRANT MAN,"
Is blazoned on our banner, while Jehovah leads
the van!

We are coming, we are coming! but we wield no
battle-brand:
We are armed with Truth and Justice, with
God's charter in our hand;
And our voice, which swells for freedom -
freedom now and ever more -
Shall be heard as Ocean's thunders, when they
burst upon the shore.

Be patient, O, be patient! ye suffering ones
of earth!
Denied a glorious heritage, - our common right
by birth;
With fettered limbs and spirits, your battle
shall be won!
O, be patient - we are coming! suffer on,
suffer on!

We are coming, we are coming! not as comes the
tempest's wrath,
When the frown of Desolation sits brooding
o'er its path;
But with Mercy, such as leaves His holy
signet-light upon
The air in lambent beauty, when the darkened
storm is gone.

O, be patient in your misery! Be mute in your
despair!
While your chains are grinding deeper, there's
a voice upon the air!
Ye shall feel its potent echoes, ye shall hear
its lovely sound -
We are coming! we are coming! bringing freedom
to the bound!

Liberator, August 9, 1844, p. 128, with the note, "Suggested
by a song sung by George W. Clarke, at a recent convention."

Collection, pp 31-32, as "We're For Freedom Through the Land";
no tune specified.

Free Soil, pp. 185-188; and Freedom, pp. 185-188, as "We're
For Freedom Through the Land," to the tune, "Old Granite
State."

162. FREEDOM'S LYRE

Author: Mrs. Mary H. Maxwell
Tune: The Mellow Horn

Attune the chords of freedom's lyre,
To bounding notes of glee;
And swell upon each burning wire,
The anthems of the free!
Strike, strike again the notes of old,
That swept these hills along!
Where freedom's sons her flag unrolled,
And shouted freedom's songs!

Wake! wake, the tones of victory, now,
For freedom's heart beats high!
And triumph sits on manhood's brow,
And speaks from woman's eye.
The sun that rose on cloud and gloom,
Now beams in radiance bright;
And in meridian splendor, soon
Shall blaze with freedom's light.

When Slavery's night shall pass away,
And wide over land and sea
Again on every breeze shall play,
The banner of the free!
Then true the lyre - let music sweep
Our hills and vales along!
While ocean's waves in gladness leap,
And dance to freedom's song!

Liberator, August 23, 1844, p. [136; printed as 132].

163. THE STAR-SPANGLED BANNER

New version of the National Song.

Author: E. A. Atlee
Tune: The Star-Spangled Banner

Oh, say do you hear, at the dawn's early
light,
The shrieks of those bondmen, whose blood is
now streaming
From the merciless lash, while our banner in
sight
With its stars, mocking freedom, is fitfully
gleaming?
Do you see the backs bare? do you mark every
score
Of the whip of the driver trace channels of
gore?

And say, doth our star-spangled banner yet
wave
O'er the land of the free, and the home of the
brave?

On the shore, dimly seen thro' the mists of
the deep,
Where Afric's race in false safety reposes,
What is that which the breeze, o'er the
towering steep,
As it heedlessly sweeps, half conceals, half
discloses?
'Tis a slave ship that's seen, by the
morning's first beam,
And its tarnished reflection pollutes now the
stream:
'Tis our star-spangled banner! Oh! when shall
it wave
O'er the land of the free, and the home of the
brave!

And where is the band, who so valiantly bore
The havoc of war, and the battle's confusion,
For Liberty's sweets? We shall know them no
more:
Their fame is eclipsed by foul Slavery's
pollution.
No refuge is found on our unhallowed ground,
For the wretched in Slavery's manacles bound;
While our star-spangled banner in vain boasts
to wave
O'er the land of the free, and the home of the
brave!

Shall we ne'er hail the day when as freemen
shall stand
The millions who groan under matchless
oppression?
Shall Liberty's shouts, in our heaven-rescued
land,
Ne'er be shared by the slave in our
blood-guilty nation?
Oh, let us be just, ere in God we dare trust;
Else the day will o'ertake us when perish we
must;
And our star-spangled banner at half mast
shall wave
O'er the death-bed of Freedom - the home of
the slave.

Liberator, September 13, 1844, p. 148.

164. SONG FOR THE PEOPLE

Author: George Donald
Tune: Let's Seek the Bower of Robin Hood

I love to sing of liberty - I love the true
and free,
Though steeped to the very lips in poverty
they be;
I love to sing of freedom, 'twas the earliest
strain I sung,
And freedom's song shall be the last that
trembles on my tongue.

Let rank and riches, pride and power, against
me fret and frown,
I laugh at all their feeble aims to break my
spirit down;
Let friends and fortune me forsake, or chains
my body bind,
Of this I cannot be bereft - the freedom of my
mind!

Hail, Liberty! thou first and beat of earthly
blessings given,
To elevate the human race; - thou dearest gift
of heaven!
Inspirer of the truly good, the noble, and the
great,
The terror of the tyrant, and the slavish
coward's hate!

In evil days, my native land was thrall'd by
wicked men,
But, my fathers sought the mountain side, the
cave and heathy glen,
And boldly raised their altars to freedom and
to God,
And kindled up those fires that now are
spreading fast abroad.

A little while, and there shall be, on every
mountain top,
A flag of triumph waving to confirm the
patriot's hope;
The moral war is raging now, and Reason leads
the fight,
That soon must terminate in life, and liberty,
and light!

On, then, ye millions, in the strife! be weary
not, nor faint!
Why should you idly waste your time in
impotent complaint?
The spoilers tremble!   onward, then!   your
rights as men demand,
And the Charter of your freedom soon shall
flourish in your land.

I love to sing of Liberty - I love the true
and free,
Though steeped to the very lips in poverty
they be;
I love to sing of freedom, 'twas the earliest
strain I sung,
And freedom's song shall be the last that
falters on my tongue.

Liberator, October 25, 1844, p. 172.

165. HYMN FOR EMANCIPATION

Author: Oliver Johnson
Tune: The Wild Hunt of Lutzow

The Bondmen are free in the Isles of the Main!
The chains from their limbs they are flinging!
They stand up as MEN - never tyrant again
Their God-given rights in proud scorn shall
profane!
It is LIBERTY'S song they are singing:
Hark! loud swells their strain o'er the
foaming sea -
"Freedom, holy Freedom! Freedom, our joy is in
thee!"

That shout of the Freedmen bursts sweet on our
ears!
Their hymn full of joy hear it swelling!
Their hearts throb with pleasure, their eyes
fill with tears,
As ends the hard bondage of many long years;
Now, exultant with pride, they are telling -
"Free, free are we from the slave's hard yoke!
Freemen, faithful Freemen - Freemen our
fetters have broke!"

Now praise to JEHOVAH! the might of His Love
At length o'er the foe is prevailing;
His Truth was the weapon, and by it we strove,
In the light of His Spirit sent down from
above -
E'en His Love and His Truth never failing;
Thanks, thanks unto God! now the Slave is
free!
Freedom! holy Freedom! FATHER, our thanks are
to Thee!

Alas! that today on Columbia's shore
The groans of her Slaves are resounding!
On plains of the South their rich life-blood
they pour!
O Freemen! blest Freemen! your help they
implore!
It is Slavery's wail that is sounding!
Hark! loud comes the cry on the southern gale
"Freedom! Death or Freedom! Freedom or Death
must prevail!"

O ye who are blest with fair LIBERTY'S light,
With courage and hope all abounding,
With Weapons of Love be ye bold for the Right;
By the preaching of Truth put Oppression to
flight;
Then, your altars triumphant surrounding,
Loud, loud let the anthem of joy ring out!
"Freedom! holy Freedom!" let all the world
hear the shout!

O fairest of Isles! your example shall shine,
A star in the firmament gleaming!
A beacon of light whose ray is Divine,
Giving hope unto all who in bondage may pine.
Now, ye Nations! awake from your dreaming!
Blow, blow loud, the trumpet of Jubilee!
Bondmen! weary Bondmen! Bondmen, YE ALL
SHALL BE FREE!

Liberator, August 8, 1845, p. 127. Three verses appear
earlier, in Liberator, August 11, 1843, p. 128, with no other
information except mention that the song was sung at the
Dedham Picnic.

Free Soil, p. 155; and Freedom, p. 155, as "Holy Freedom,"
to the same tune.

Mentioned in Liberator, July 27, 1855, p. 118, in a program of
events for a celebration of August 1 to be held in Cincinnati
by that city's "Colored Citizens."

166. THE LIBERTY BALL

Author: G. W. C.
Tune: Rosin the Bow

Come all ye true friends of the nation,
Attend to humanity's call;
Come aid the poor slave's liberation,
And roll on the liberty ball -
And roll on the liberty ball -
And roll on the liberty ball,
Come aid the poor slave's liberation,
And roll on the liberty ball.

The Liberty hosts are advancing -
For freedom to all they declare;
The down-trodden millions are sighing -
Come, break up our gloom of despair.
Come break up our gloom of despair, etc.

Ye Democrats, come to the rescue,
And aid on the liberty cause,
And millions will rise up and bless you
With heart-cheering songs of applause.
With heart-cheering songs, etc.

Ye Whigs forsake slavery's minions,
And boldly step into our ranks;
We care not for party opinion,
But invite all the friends of the banks.
And invite all the friends of the banks, etc.

And when we have formed the blest union
We'll firmly march on, one and all -
We'll sing when we meet in communion,
And roll on the liberty ball.
And roll on the liberty ball, etc.

How can you stand halting while virtue
Is sweetly appealing to all;
Then haste to the standard of duty,
And roll on the liberty ball.
And roll on the liberty ball, etc.

The question of test is now turning,
And freedom or slavery must fall,
While hope in the bosom is burning,
We'll roll on the liberty ball.
We'll roll on the liberty ball, etc.

Ye freemen attend to your voting,
Your ballots will answer the call;
And while others attend to log-rolling,
We'll roll on the liberty ball.
We'll roll on the liberty ball, etc.

Collection, p. 8; Free Soil, pp. 12-13; and Liberty,
pp. 156-157.

Harp, p. 10, under the same title, to the same tune, but
without the last three verses.

Freedom, pp. 261-262, under the same title, to the same tune,
with these lyrics substituted for verse four:

Ye Fogies quit Slavery's minions,
And boldly renounce your old pranks;
We care not for party opinions,
But invite you all into our ranks.
And invite you all into our ranks, etc.

167. SONG

Written to be sung at the New-England
Anti-Slavery Convention, May, 1845.

Author: J. R. Lowell
Tune: Scots Wha Hae

Friends of freedom! ye who stand
With no weapon in your hand,
Save a purpose stern and grand
To set all men free;
Welcome! Freedom stands in need
Of true men in thought and deed,
Men who have this only creed -
That they will not flee.

Women, come! your gentleness
Thrice our holy cause shall bless;
Strength is mighty, but no less
Needs Love's crystal shield;
Ho! the Harvest stands in sight;
Though your hands be soft and white,
Yet have all an equal might,
Toiling in God's field.

From the land of bondage come!
Let the Red sea's angry foam
Howl between us and our home,
Yet we will not dread;
God doth lead us; he will make
Pathway for his children's sake,
And the meeting waves shall break
O'er the oppressor's head.

Though we were but two or three,
Sure of triumph we should be;
We our promised land shall see,
Though the way seem long;
Every fearless word we speak
Makes Sin's stronghold bend and creak,
Tyranny is always weak,
Truth is young and strong.

All the hero-spirits vast,
Who have sanctified the past,
Bearing witness to the last,
Fight upon our part;
We can never be forlorn;
He, who in a manger born,
Bore the Priest's and Levite's scorn,
Gives us hope and heart.

Liberator, July 4, 1845, p. 108.

168. SONG

Written for and sung at an antislavery picnic at Danvers.

Author: unspecified
Tune: Old Dan Tucker

Our Fathers fought on Bunker's Hill
For liberty and independence,
And Freedom fires are glowing still,
Deep in the souls of their descendants.
Rouse up the flame - rouse up the flame -
Rouse up the flame, throughout the nation,
Death to slavery and oppression!

The glorious victories they won,
Shall perish from our memories never,
And Yorktown, Concord, Bennington,
On History's page shall live forever.

Rouse up the flame - rouse up the flame -
Rouse up the flame, throughout the nation,
Death to slavery and oppression!

Confusion to those recreant sons,
An Arnold's fame they richly merit,
The Pickenses and Athertons,
Who sell the birthright they inherit!
Shame on the men - shame on the men -
Shame on the men, throughout the nation,
Trucklers base to foul oppression!

How long shall pampered priests for hire
The Gospel precepts dare to libel,
On Freedom's altars quench the fire,
With texts misquoted from the Bible?
Send up the cry - send up the cry -
Send up the cry throughout the nation,
God abhors the foul oppression!

The host of Slavery! See, it comes
With gory scourges, clanking fetters,
Led on by furious Quattlebums,
And Northern vile dough-faced abettors!
Gird on your arms - gird on your arms -
In Freedom's rank take honored station,
Drive the tyrant's from the nation!

For Freedom's conflict then prepare,
Nor cowardly await invasion;
The weapons of our warfare are
The Ballot-box and Moral Suasion.
Stand to your arms - stand to your arms -
Stand to your arms, throughout the nation -
Hurl the tyrants from their station!

Then to the earth's remotest clime,
The voice of Fame shall waft the story,
Proclaiming till the end of time,
That Freedom is the nation's glory
Send up the shout - send up the shout -
Let distant lands repeat the story,
Freedom is the nation's glory!

Liberator, August 8, 1845, p. 127.

169. STRIKE FOR LIBERTY

Author: unspecified
Tune: Scots Wha Hae

Sons of Freedom's honored sires,
Light anew your beacon fires,
Fight till every for retires
From your hallowed soil.
Sons of Pilgrim Fathers blest,
Pilgrim Mothers gone to rest,
Listen to their high behest,
Strike for Liberty.

Ministers of God to men,
Heed ye not the nation's sin?
Heaven's blessing can ye win
If ye falter now?
Men of blood now ask your vote,
O'er your heads their banners float;
Raise, Oh raise the warning note,
God and duty call!

Men of justice, bold and brave,
To the ballot-box and save
Freedom from her opening grave -
Onward! brothers, on!
Christian patriots, tried and true,
Freedom's eyes now turn to you;
Foes are many - are ye few?
Gideon's God is yours!

Collection, pp. 19-20; and Liberty, pp. 82-83.

170. WAKE, SONS OF THE PILGRIMS

Author: unspecified
Tune: M'Gregor's Gathering

Wake sons of the Pilgrims, and look to your
right!
The despots of Slav'ry are up in their might;
Indulge not in sleep, it's like digging the
graves
Of blood-purchased freedom - 'tis yielding
like slaves.
Then halloo, halloo, halloo, to the contest,
Awake from your slumbers, no longer delay,
But struggle for freedom, while struggle you
may -
Then rally, rally, rally, rally, rally, rally,
While our forests shall wave or while rushes a
river,
Oh, yield not your birth-right! maintain it
forever!

Wake, Sons of the Pilgrims! why slumber ye on?
Your chains are now forging, your fetters are done;
Oh! sleep not, like Samson, on Slavery's foul arm,
For, Delilah-like, she's now planning your harm.
Then halloo, halloo, halloo, to the contest!
Awake from your sleeping - nor slumber again,
Once bound in your fetters, you'll struggle in vain;
Then rally, rally, rally, rally, rally, rally -
While your eye-balls may move, O wake up now, or never -
Wake, freemen! awake, or you're ruined forever!

Yes, freemen are waking! we fling to the breeze,
The bright flag of freedom, the banner of Peace;
The slave long forgotten, forlorn, and alone,
We hail as a brother - our own mother's son!
Then halloo, halloo, halloo, to the contest!
For freedom we rally - for freedom to all -
To rescue the slave, and ourselves too from thrall.
We rally, rally, rally, rally, rally, rally -
While a slave shall remain, bound, the weak by the stronger,
We will never disband, but strive harder and longer.

Collection, p. 29; Free Soil, pp. 129-130; and Freedom, pp. 129-130.

171. SONG FOR THE FIRST OF AUGUST

Written for and sung at an antislavery picnic at Danvers.

Author: A. R. Potter*
Tune: Auld Lang Syne

Welcome the day we celebrate,
Welcome this jubilee!
Let every voice shout, shout aloud,
Great Britain's slaves are free!

Then let the sound go far and wide,
O'er mountain height and sea,
Victoria's realms no more are curst
With chattel slavery.

The whip, the fetter, and the chain,
Are buried in the earth;
And cries, and groans, and wailings now,
Are changed to joy and mirth.
Then let the word go far and wide,
O'er mountain height and sea,
Great Britain once held many slaves,
But now hath set them free.

Now let us turn to our own land,
That claims to be so free,
And yet three million souls are held
In abject slavery.
Then let the word go far and wide,
O'er mountain height and sea,
That fair Columbia's soil is dyed
In blackest slavery.

Shame, shame on our America,
Whose steeples tower on high,
And prayers from gilded altars rise,
In anthems to the skies;
Whose banners, waving to the breeze,
O'er mountain height and sea,
Falsely proclaiming far and wide
Our countrymen are free.

O, let those banners wave no more,
Until our land is free;
Nor prayers, nor songs ascend on high,
In solemn mockery.
But let the truth go far and wide,
O'er mountain height and sea,
This boasted land of Freedom is
Still curst with slavery.

Up, then! for freedom and for right,
And get a glorious name;
And wipe from our escutcheon bright
The foul and damning stain.
Then shall the truth go far and wide,
O'er mountain height and sea,
Columbia, our happy land,
Is now forever free.

Liberator, August 1, 1845, p. 123.

*Liberator, August 8, 1845, p. 127, mentions this song and
designates the author as "Mr. A. R. Porter."

172. WE'RE COMING! WE'RE COMING!

Author: G. W. C.
Tune: Kinloch of Kinloch

We're coming, we're coming, the fearless and
free,
Like the winds of the desert, the waves of the
sea!
True sons of brave fathers who battled of
yore,
When England's proud lion ran wild on our
shore!
We're coming, we're coming, from mountain and
glen,
With hearts to do battle for freedom again;
The slave power is trembling as trembled
before,
The Slavery which fled from our fathers of
yore.

We're coming, we're coming, with banners
unfurled,
Our motto is FREEDOM, our country the world;
Our watchword is LIBERTY - tyrants beware!
For the Liberty army will bring you despair!
We're coming, we're coming, we'll come from
afar,
Our standard we'll nail to humanity's car;
With shoutings we'll raise it, in triumph to
wave,
A trophy of conquests, or shroud for the
brave.

Then arouse ye, brave hearts, to the rescue
come on!
The man-stealing army we'll surely put down;
They are crushing their millions, but soon
they must yield,
For freemen have risen and taken the field.
Then arouse ye! arouse ye! the fearless and
free,
Like the winds of the desert, the waves of the
sea;
Let the north, west, and east, to the
sea-beaten shore,
Resound with a liberty triumph once more.

Collection, pp. 28-29; Free Soil, pp. 21-22; Harp, p. 32;
and Freedom, pp. 264-265.

173. YE SONS OF FREEMEN

Author: Mrs. J. G. Carter
Tune: Marseilles Hymn

Ye sons of freemen wake to sadness,
Hark! hark, what myriads bid you rise;
Three millions of our race in madness
Break out in wails, in bitter cries,
Break out in wails, in bitter cries;
Must men whose hearts now bleed with anguish,
Yes, trembling slaves, in freedom's land
Endure the lash, nor raise a hand?
Must nature 'neath the whip-cord languish?
Have Pity on the slave,
Take courage from God's word;
Pray on, pray on, all hearts resolved these
captives shall be free,
Pray on, pray on, all hearts resolved these
captives shall be free.

The fearful storm - it threatens lowering,
Which God in mercy long delays;
Slaves yet may see their masters cowering,
While whole plantations smoke and blaze!
While whole plantations smoke and blaze!
And ye may now prevent the ruin,
Ere lawless force with guilty stride
Shall scatter vengeance far and wide -
With untold crimes their land embruing.
Have pity on the slave;
Take courage from God's word;
Pray on, pray on, all hearts resolved these
captives shall be free,
Pray on, etc.

With luxury and wealth surrounded,
The southern masters proudly dare,
With thirst of gold and power unbounded,
To mete and vend God's light and air!
To mete and vend God's light and air;
Like beasts of burden, slaves are loaded,
Till life's poor toilsome day is o'er;
While they in vain for right implore;
And shall they longer still be goaded?
Have pity on the slave;
Take courage from God's word;
Toil on, toil on, all hearts resolved these
captives shall be free,
Toil on, etc.

O Liberty! can man e'er bind thee?
Can overseers quench thy flame?
Can dungeons, bolts, or bars confine thee,
Or threats thy Heaven born spirit tame?
Or threats thy Heaven born spirit tame?
Too long the slave has groaned bewailing
The power these heartless tyrants wield;
Yet free them not by sword or shield,
For with men's hearts they're unavailing.
Have pity on the slave;
Take courage from God's word;
Vote on! vote on! all hearts resolved these
captives shall be free!
Vote on, etc.

Collection, pp. 6-7; Free Soil, pp. 158-162; Harp, pp. 8-9;
and Freedom, pp. 158-162.

174. THE LIBERTY BELL

Author: Oliver Wendell Withington
Tune: The Campbells Are Coming

An anthem of wailing
Goes up on the air,
Man's spirit is failing,
And Hope fadeth there;
No arm is extended
To succor and save,
No action is blended
With prayer for the slave.

But, hark! there's a murmur,
Subdued and yet deep,
It comes from a Spirit,
That starts from its sleep -
Hearts noble and gallant,
Act truly and well,
And we hear the low clang
Of the Liberty Bell.

Oh! long may it echo
O'er earth and o'er sea,
Till man, in God's image,
Stands holy and free;
Till Love's great achievement
Is faithfully done,
And man, with his brother,
United, is one.

There's a voice on the waters,
A song in the air,
The sons and the daughters
Of Freedom are there -
All hail to the echo
From mountain and dell!
Hurrah for the music
Of Liberty Bell!

Oh! long may it revel
O'er mountain and sea,
Till man, in God's image,
Stands gallant and free;
Till Love's bright achievement
Is faithfully done,
And man, with his brother
And sister, is one.

Some voices at present
Blend not in the cry;
They'll think it quite pleasant
To join by and by!
Some talk, too, of Treason -
However it be -
We know it is Reason -
Ay, just to a T.

Some rail at the fetter,
But like not our war -
"Then, come and do better,"
Friend Parker would say
The day-star, in beauty,
Is weaving its spell,
And cheers us while ringing
The Liberty Bell.

Liberator, January 14, 1848, p. 7.

175. AROUSE! AROUSE!

Author: unspecified
Tune: unspecified

Arouse, arouse, arouse!
Ye bold New England men!
No more with sullen brows,
Remain as ye have been:

Your country's freedom calls,
Once bought by patriots' blood
Rouse, or that freedom falls
Beneath the tyrant's rod!

Three million men in chains,
Your friendly aid implore;
Slight you the piteous strains
That from their bosoms pour?
Shall it be told in story,
Or troll'd in burning song,
New England's boasted glory
Forgot the boundman's wrong?

Shall freeman's sons be taunted,
That freedom's spirit's fled;
That what the fathers vaunted,
With sordid sons is dead?
That they in grovelling gain
Have lost their ancient fire,
And 'neath the despot's chain,
Let liberty expire?

Oh no, your father's bones
Would cry out from the ground;
Ay e'en New England's stones
Would echo on the sound:
Rouse, then, New England men!
Rally in freedom's name!
In your bosoms once again
Light up the sleeping flame!

Free Soil, p. 164; and Freedom, p. 164.

176. LIBERTY BATTLE-SONG

Author: unspecified
Tune: Our Warrior's Heart

Arouse, ye friends of law and right,
Arouse, arouse, arouse!
All who in Freedom's cause delight,
Arouse, arouse, arouse!
The time, the time, is drawing near,
When we must at our posts appear;
Then clear the decks for action, clear!
Arouse, arouse, arouse!

Awake, and couch Truth's fatal dart,
Awake! awake! awake!
Bid error to the shades depart,
Awake! awake! awake!
Prepare to deal the deadly blow,
To lay the power of Slavery low,
A ballot, lads, is our veto;
Awake! awake! awake!

Arise! ye sons of honest toil,
Arise! arise! arise!
Ye freeborn tillers of the soil,
Arise! arise! arise!
Come from tour workshops and the field,
We've sworn to conquer ere we'll yield;
The ballot-box is Freedom's shield,
Arise! arise! arise!

Unite and strike for equal laws,
Unite! unite! unite!
For equal justice! that's our cause,
Unite! unite! unite!
Shall the vile slavites win the day?
Shall men of whips and blood bear sway?
Unite, and dash their chains away!
Unite! unite! unite!

March on! and vote the hirelings down,
March on! march on! march on!
Our blighted land with blessings crown,
March on! march on! march on!
Shall Manhood ever wear the chain?
Shall Freedom look to us in vain?
Up to the struggle! Strike again!
March on! march on! march on!

Free Soil, pp. 33-34; and Freedom, pp. 272-273.

Liberty, p. 128, first verse only, under the same title, to
the same tune.

177. RAISE A SHOUT FOR LIBERTY

Author: unspecified
Tune: Old Granite State

Come all ye sons and daughters,
Raise a shout from freedom's quarters,
Like the voice of many waters,
Let it echo through the land:

And let all the people,
And let all the people,
And let all the people,
Raise a shout for liberty.

We have long been benighted,
And the cause of freedom slighted,
But we now are all united
To reform our native land:
And we mean to conquer,
And we mean to conquer,
And we mean to conquer,
With a shout for liberty!

Let us raise a song of gladness,
To subdue the tyrant's madness,
Let us cheer the bondman's sadness,
With the chorus of the free;
And let all the people,
And let all the people,
And let all the people,
Raise a shout for liberty!

Let Liberty awaken,
And never be forsaken,
Till the enemy is taken,
And the victory is won: -
Then will all the people,
Then will all the people,
Then will all the people,
Raise a shout for liberty!

Come and join our holy mission,
Whatsoever your condition,
Let each honest politician
Come and labor for the slave
We will bid you welcome,
We will bid you welcome,
We will bid you welcome,
With a shout for liberty!

With the flag of freedom o'er us,
And the light of truth before us,
Let all freemen raise the chorus,
And the nation shall be free,
Then will all the people,
Then will all the people,
Then will all the people,
Raise a shout for liberty!

Then spread the proclamation,
Throughout this guilty nation,
And let every habitation
Be a dwelling of the free!

> And let all the people,
> And let all the people,
> And let all the people,
> Raise a SHOUT FOR LIBERTY.

Free Soil, p. 189; Liberty, pp. 212-213; and Freedom,
p. 189 and pp. 304-305.

178. THAT'S MY COUNTRY

Author: unspecified
Tune: Martyn

> Does the land, in native might,
> Pant for Liberty and Right?
> Long to cast from human kind
> Chains of body and of mind -
> That's my country, that's the land
> I can love with heart and hand,
> O'er her miseries weep and sigh,
> For her glory live and die.

> Does the land her banner wave,
> Most invitingly, to save;
> [Wooing] to her arms of love,
> Strangers who would freemen prove?
> That's the land to which I cling,
> Of her glories I can sing,
> On her altar nobly swear
> Higher still her fame to rear.

> Does the land no conquest make,
> But the war for honor's sake -
> Count the greatest triumph won,
> That which most of good has done -
> That's the land approved of God;
> That's the land whose stainless sod
> O'er my sleeping dust shall bloom,
> Noblest land and noblest tomb!

Free Soil, p. 157; and Freedom, p. 157.

179. THE FLAG OF THE FREE

Author: G. W. C.
Tune: Carrier Dove

Fling abroad its folds to the cooling breeze,
Let it float at the most-head high;
And gather around, all hearts resolved,
To sustain it there or die:
An emblem of peace and hope to the world,
Unstained let it ever be;
And say to the world, where'er it waves,
Our flag is the flag of the free!

That banner proclaims to the list'ning earth,
That the reign of base tyrants is o'er,
The galling chain of the cruel lord,
Shall enslave mankind no more:
An emblem of hope to the poor and crushed,
O place it where all may see;
And shout with glad voice as you raise it
high,
Our flag is the flag of the free!

Then on high, on high let that banner wave,
And lead us the foe to meet,
Let it float in triumph o'er our heads,
Or be our winding sheet:
And never, oh, never be it furled,
'Till it wave o'er earth and sea;
And all mankind shall swell the shout
Our flag is the flag of the free.

Free Soil, p. 149; and Freedom, p. 149.

Liberty, p. 114, as "The Liberty Flag," to the same tune.

180. SONG OF THE FREE

Author: G. W. C.
Tune: Lutzow's Wild Hunt

From valley and mountain, from hill-top and
glen,
What shouts thro' the air are rebounding!
And echo is sending the sounds back again,
And loud thro' the air they are sounding,
And loud thro' the air they are sounding:
And if you ask what those joyous strains?
'Tis the songs of bondmen now bursting their
chains.

And who through our nation is waging the
fight?
What host from battle is flying?
Our true hearted freemen maintain the right,
And the monster oppression is dying,
And the monster oppression is dying:
And if you ask what you there behold?
'Tis the army of freemen, the true and the
bold.

Too long have slave-holders triumphantly
reigned.
Too long in their chains have they bound us;
To freedom awaking, no longer enchained,
The goddess of freedom has saved us,
The goddess of freedom has saved us:
And if you ask what has made us free?
'Tis the vote that gave us our liberty.

Free Soil, pp. 153-155; and Freedom, pp. 153-155.

181. HAIL THE DAY!

Author: unspecified
Tune: Wreathe the Bowl or Yankee Doodle

Hail the day
Whose joyful ray
Speaks of emancipation!
The day that broke
Oppression's yoke -
The birth-day of a nation!

When England's might
Put forth for right,
Achieved a fame more glorious
Than armies tried,
Or navies' pride,
O'er land and sea victorious!

Soon may we gain
An equal name
In honor's estimation!
And righteousness
Exalt and bless
Our glorious happy nation!

Brave hearts shall lend
Strong hands to rend
Foul slavery's bonds asunder,
And liberty
Her jubilee
Proclaim, in tones of thunder

We hail afar
Fair freedom's star,
Her day-star brightly glancing;
We hear the tramp
From freedom's camp,
Assembling and advancing!

No noisy drum
Nor murderous gun,
No deadly fiends contending;
But love and right
Their force unite,
In peaceful conflict blending.

Fair freedom's host,
In joyful boast,
Unfolds her banner ample!
With Channing's fame,
And Whittier's name,
And BIRNEY'S bright example!

Come join your hands
With freedom bands,
New England's sons and daughters!
Speak your decree -
Man shall be free -
As mountain winds and waters!

And haste the day
Whose coming ray
Speaks our emancipation!
Whose glorious light,
Enthroning right,
Shall bless and save the nation!

Liberty, p. 180.

Freedom, p. 300, under the same title, to the same tunes, but
with verses six and seven omitted.

182. RIGHT ON

Author: unspecified
Tune: Lenox

Ho! children of the brave,
Ho! freemen of the land,
That hurl'd into the grave
Oppression's bloody band;
Come on, come on, and joined be we
To make the fettered bondman free.

Let coward vassals sneak
From freedom's battle still,
Poltroons that dare not speak
But as their priests may will;
Come on, come on, and joined be we
To make the fettered bondman free.

On parchment, scroll and creed,
With human life blood red,
Untrembling at the deed,
Plant firm your manly tread;
The priest may howl, and jurist rave,
But we will free the fettered slave.

The tyrant's scorn is vain,
In vain the slanderer's breath,
We'll rush to break the chain,
E'en on the jaws of death;
Hurrah! Hurrah! right on go we,
The fettered slave shall yet be free.

Right on, in freedom's name,
And in strength of God,
Wipe out the damning stain,
And break the oppressor's rod;
Hurrah! Hurrah! right on go we,
The fettered slave shall yet be free.

Harp, pp. 35-36.

This song is mentioned in the Liberator as having been sung
on several occasions in the 1850s: an antislavery celebration
at Abington (July 9, 1852, p. 110); a West Indian emancipation celebration in Framingham (August 6, 1852, p. 126); at
a July 4 meeting of the Massachusetts Anti-Slavery Society at
Framingham (July 13, 1855, p. 111); and at the New England
Colored Citizens' Convention (August 19, 1859, p. 132).

183. THE WATCHWORD OF THE FREE

Author: unspecified
Tune: Auld Lang Syne

Hurrah to the note that rising swells
From lake to rolling sea!
Of truth and victory it tells -
'Tis the watchword of the Free.
That watchword comes o'er hill and plain,
From western lands afar;
Our ocean waves repeat the strain -
Hurrah! hurrah! hurrah!

The star our fathers watched of yore,
To guide their steps aright,
Though long bedimm'd, displays once more
Its rays of peerless light.
It shines on many a hill and plain
Of Western lands afar;
It gleams upon the rocks of Maine -
Huzza! huzza! huzza!

And sunnier climes the anthem spread
O'er their time-honored graves,
To tell us Freedom's light is shed,
E'en on a land of slaves.
Our free note from Iowa's plain,
Where sinks the evening star,
Is echoing from the rocks of Maine,
Hurrah! hurrah! hurrah!

Hail to the tillers of the land,
Whose brave hearts beating free,
Disdain with fettered slaves to stand,
And bend the suppliant knee.
Their watchword from Iowa's plain,
Borne on the breeze afar,
Is echoing from the rocks of Maine -
Huzza! huzza! huzza!

We vow by all the rights of toil,
And by our fathers' graves,
The air that floats o'er Freedom's soil,
Shall not be breathed by slaves!
Our free note from Iowa's plain,
Where sets the western star,
Is echoing from the rocks of Maine -
Hurrah! hurrah! hurrah!

Hail to our "Empire's" honor'd one -
One loud acclaim for thee!
Hail to our Adams' gifted son,
Apostles of the Free!

It comes from many a western plain
Borne on the breeze afar;
It rings amid the rocks of Maine -
Hurrah! hurrah! hurrah!

Free Soil, pp. 221-222.

Freedom, pp. 307-308, with the last verse omitted, as "Echo
from the Rocks of Maine," to the same tune.

184. STANZAS FOR THE TIMES

Author: J. G. Whittier
Tune: original, by G. W. C.

Is this the land our fathers loved,
The freedom which they toiled to win?
Is this the soil whereon they moved?
Are these the graves they slumber in?
Are we sons by whom are borne,
The mantles which the dead have worn?

And shall we crouch above these graves,
With craven soul and fettered lip?
Yoke in with marked and branded slaves,
And tremble at the driver's whip?
Bend to the earth our pliant knees,
And speak - but as our masters please?

Shall outraged Nature cease to feel?
Shall Mercy's tears no longer flow?
Shall ruffian threats of cord and steel -
The dungeon's gloom - th' assassin's blow,
Turn back the spirit roused to save
The Truth - our Country - and the Slave?

Of human skulls that shrine was made,
Round which the priests of Mexico
Before their loathsome idol prayed -
Is Freedom's altar fashioned so?
And must we yield to Freedom's Gid
As offering meet, the negro's blood?

Shall tongues be mute, when deeds are wrought
Which well might shame extremest Hell?
Shall freemen lock th' indignant thought?
Shall Mercy's bosom cease to swell?
Shall Honor bleed? - Shall Truth succumb?
Shall pen, and press, and soul be dumb?

No - by each spot of haunted ground,
Where Freedom weeps her children's fall -
By Plymouth's rock - and Bunker's mound -
By Griswold's stained and shattered wall -
By Warren's ghost - by Langdon's shade -
By all the memories of our dead!

By their enlarging souls, which burst
The bands and fetters round them set -
By the free Pilgrim spirit nursed
Within our inmost bosoms, yet, -
By all above - around - below -
Be ours the indignant answer - no!

No - guided by our country's laws,
For truth, and right, and suffering man,
Be ours to strive in Freedom's cause,
As Christians may - as freemen can!
Still pouring on unwilling ears
That truth oppression only fears.

Free Soil, pp. 104-106; and Freedom. pp. 104-106.

185. THE PLEASANT LAND WE LOVE

Author: N. P. Willis
Tune: Carrier Dove

Joy to the pleasant land we love,
The land our fathers trod!
Joy to the land for which they won
"Freedom to worship God."
For peace on all its sunny hills,
On every mountain broods,
And sleeps by all its gushing rills,
And all its mighty floods.

The wife sits meekly by the hearth,
Her infant child beside;
The father on his noble boy
Looks with a fearless pride.
The grey old man, beneath the tree,
Tales of his childhood tells;
And sweetly in the hush of morn
Peal out the Sabbath bells.

And WE ARE free - but is there not
One blot upon our name?
Is our proud record written fair
Upon the scroll of fame?

Our banner floateth by the shore,
Our flag upon the sea;
But when the fettered slave is loosed,
We shall be truly free!

Free Soil, pp. 147-149; and Freedom, pp. 147-149.

186. MARCH TO THE BATTLEFIELD

Author: G. W. C.
Tune: Oft in the Stilly Night

March to the battlefield,
The foe is now before us;
Each heart is freedom's shield,
And heaven is smiling o'er us.
The woes and pains
Of slavery's chains,
That bind their millions under;
In proud disdain we'll burst in twain,
And tear each link asunder.
March, etc. [repeat first four lines]

Who for his country brave,
Would fly from her invader?
Who his base life to save
Would traitor like degrade her?
Our hallowed cause -
Our homes and laws,
'Gainst tyrant hosts sustaining,
We'll win a crown of bright renown,
Or die, man's rights maintaining.
March, etc.

Free Soil, pp. 150-152; Liberty, pp. 115-117; and Freedom,
pp. 150-152.

187. MY COUNTRY

Author: unspecified
Tune: America

My country, 'tis for thee,
Dark land of slavery,
For thee I weep;

Land where the slave has sighed,
And where he toiled and died,
To serve a tyrant's pride -
For thee I weep.

My native country! thee
Land of the noble free -
Of liberty -
My native country weep!
A fast in sorrow keep;
The stain is foul and deep
Of slavery.

From every mountain side,
Upon the ocean's tide,
They call on thee;
Amid thy rocks and rills,
Thy woods and templed hills,
I hear a voice which thrills -
Let all go free.

Arise! break every band,
And sound throughout this land,
Sweet freedom's song;
No groans their song shall break,
But all that breathe partake,
And slaves their silence break -
The sound prolong.

Our fathers' God! to thee,
Author of liberty,
To thee we pray:
Soon may our land be pure,
Let freedom's light endure,
And liberty secure,
Beneath thy sway.

Free Soil, pp. 193-194; and Freedom, pp. 194-195.

Liberator, September 27, 1861, p. 155, with minor changes,
as "Song for the National Fast," to the same tune.

188. BRIGHT IS THE DAYBREAK

Author: unspecified
Tune: Rory O'More

Oh, bright is the daybreak, and thrilling the
sight
Of America's rally for freedom and right;

Her sons and her daughters she calls from
afar,
To hail the bright advent of Liberty's star.
Old Maine standeth firm with breast to the
floods;
Her sons' hearts as high as their tall piny
woods;
And shoulder to shoulder New Hampshire is
there,
With lots of brave freemen, enough and to
spare!
Vermont, who shall count all her Green
mountain boys?
When Liberty raiseth her clarion voice;
Massachusetts, God bless her! When freedom's
at stake,
Every soul of her children are up and awake!

Rhode Island is little, but goeth it strong;
And Connecticut too, who don't "calculate"
wrong;
New York! no mistake, she will take up the
Van;
When New Jersey arises, beat her if you can.
Pennsylvania is ready, the old State of Penn -
How can she do other than succor free men?
And Delaware, too, with old Maryland yet;
For free soil and freemen will a precedent
set!
Illinois, Indiana, Iowa, and all,
With Ohio for freedom will stand or will fall;
And soon thro' the length and the breadth of
our land;
Not a heart shall be cold, not a recreant
hand!

Free Soil, pp. 23-25; and Freedom, pp. 289-291.

189. YOUR BROTHER IS A SLAVE

Author: unspecified
Tune: unspecified

O weep, ye friends of Freedom, weep!
Shout liberty no more;
Your harps to mournful measures sweep,
Till slavery's reign is o'er.

O, furl your star-lit thing of light -
That banner should not wave
Where, vainly pleading for his right,
Your Brother toils - a Slave!

O pray, ye friends of Freedom, pray
For those who toil in chains,
Who life their fettered hands to day
On Carolina's plain!
God is the hope of the Oppressed;
His arm is strong to save;
Pray, then, that freedom's cause be blest,
Your Brother is a Slave!

O toil, ye friends of Freedom, toil!
Your mission to fulfil, -
That Freedom's consecrated soil
Slaves may no longer till;
Ay, toil and pray from deep disgrace
Your native land to save;
Weep o'er the miseries of your race,
Your Brother is a Slave!

Harp, pp. 39-40.

190. OUR COUNTRYMEN IN CHAINS

Author: Whittier
Tune: Beatitude

Our fellow countrymen in chains,
Slaves in a land of light and law!
Slaves crouching on the very plains
Where rolled the storm of Freedom's war!
A groan from Eutaw's haunted wood -
A wail where Camden's martyrs fell -
By every shrine of patriot blood,
From Moultrie's wall and Jasper's well.

By storied hill and hallow'd grot,
By mossy wood and marshy glen,
Whence rang of old the rifle-shot,
And hurrying shout of Marion's men!
The groan of breaking hearts is there -
The falling lash - the fetter's clank!
Slaves - SLAVES are breathing in that air,
Which old De Kalb and Sumter drank!

What, ho! - our countrymen in chains!
The whip on WOMAN'S shrinking flesh!
Our soil yet reddening with the stains,
Caught from her scourging, warm and fresh!
What! mothers from their children riven!
What! God's own image bought and sold!
AMERICANS to market driven,
And barter'd as the brute for gold!

Speak! shall their agony of prayer
Come thrilling to our hearts in vain?
To us, whose fathers scorn'd to bear
The paltry menace of a chain;
To us, whose boast is loud and long
Of holy Liberty and Light -
Say, shall these writhing slaves of wrong,
Plead vainly for their plunder'd Right?

Shall every flap of England's flag
Proclaim that all around are free,
From "farthest Ind" to each blue crag
That beetles o'er the Western sea?
And shall we scoff at Europe's kings,
When Freedom's fire is dim with us,
And round our country's altar clings
The damning shade of Slavery's curse?

Just God! and shall we calmly rest,
The Christian's scorn - the Heathen's mirth -
Content to live the lingering jest
And by-word of a mocking Earth?
Shall our own glorious land retain
That curse which Europe scorns to bear?
Shall our own brethren drag the chain
Which not even Russia's menials wear?

Down let the shrine of Moloch sink,
And leave no [traces] where it stood;
No longer let its idol drink
His daily cup of human blood:
But rear another altar there,
To Truth and Love, and Mercy given,
And Freedom's gift, and Freedom's prayer
Shall call an answer down from Heaven!

Free Soil, pp. 119-120; and Freedom, pp. 119-120.

The last verse appears in the Liberator, May 20, 1864, p. 82,
with the indication that it was sung at the thirty-first
annual meeting of the American Anti-Slavery Society.

191. OUR PILGRIM FATHERS

Author: Pierpont
Tune: Minstrel Boy

Our Pilgrim Fathers - where are they?
The waves that brought them o'er,
Still roll in the bay, and throw their spray
As they break along the shore;
Still roll in the bay, as they rolled that
day,
When the Mayflower moored below;
When the sea around was black with storms,
And white the shore with snow.

The mists that wrapped the Pilgrim's sleep,
Still brood upon the tide;
And his rocks yet keep their watch by the
deep,
To stay its waves of pride.
But the snow-white sail, that she gave to the
gale
When the heavens looked dark, is gone;
As an angel's wing, through an opening cloud,
Is seen, and then withdrawn.

The Pilgrim exile - sainted name!
The hill, whose icy brow
Rejoiced when he came in the morning's flame,
In the morning's flame burns now.
And the moon's cold light, as it lay that
night,
On the hill-side and the sea,
Still lies where he laid his houseless head;
But the Pilgrim - where is he?

The Pilgrim Fathers are at rest;
When Summer's throned on high,
And the world's warm breast is in verdure
dressed,
Go, stand on the hill where they lie.
The earliest ray of the golden day,
On that hallowed spot is cast;
And the evening sun as he leaves the world,
Looks kindly on that spot last.

The Pilgrim spirit has not fled -
It walks in noon's broad light;
And it watches the bed of the glorious dead,
With the holy stars, by night.

It watches the bed of the brave who have bled,
And shall guard this ice-bound shore,
Till the waves of the bay, where the Mayflower
lay,
Shall foam and freeze no more.

Free Soil, pp. 101-103; and Freedom, pp. 101-103.

192. PILGRIM SONG

Author: Geo. Lunt
Tune: Troubadour

Over the mountain wave
See where they come;
Storm-cloud and wintry wind
Welcome them home;
Yet where the sounding gale
Howls to the sea,
There their song peals along,
Deep toned and free.
Pilgrims and wanderers,
Hither we come:
Where the free dare to be,
This is our home.

England hath sunny dales,
Dearly they bloom;
Scotia hath heather-hills,
Sweet their perfume:
Yet through the wilderness
Cheerful we stray,
Native land, native land -
Home far away!
Pilgrims, etc.

Dim grew the forest path,
Onward they trod:
Firm beat their noble hearts,
Trusting in God!
Gray men and blooming maids,
High rose their song -
Hear it sweep, clear and deep
Ever along!
Pilgrims, etc.

Not theirs the glory-wreath,
Torn by the blast;
Heavenward their holy steps,
Heavenward they passed!

Green be their mossy graves!
Ours be their fame,
While their song peals along,
Ever the same!
Pilgrims, etc.

Free Soil, pp. 123-124.

193. EMANCIPATION HYMN OF THE WEST INDIAN NEGROES

For the First of August Celebration.

Author: unspecified
Tune: unspecified

Praise we the Lord! let songs resound
To earth's remotest shore!
Songs of thanksgiving, songs of praise -
For we are slaves no more.

Praise we the Lord! His power hath rent
The chains that held us long!
His voice is mighty, as of old,
And still His arm is strong.

Praise we the Lord! His wrath arose,
His arm our fetters broke;
The tyrant dropped the lash, and we
To liberty awoke!

Praise we the Lord! let holy songs
Rise from these happy isles! -
O! let us not unworthy prove,
On whom His bounty smiles.

And cease we not the fight of faith
Till all mankind be free;
Till mercy o'er the earth shall flow,
As waters o'er the sea.

Then shall indeed Messiah's reign
Through all the world extend;
Then swords to ploughshares shall be turned,
And Heaven with earth shall blend.

Harp, pp. 10-11.

194. ROUSE UP, NEW ENGLAND

Author: A Yankee
Tune: original, by G. W. C.

Rouse up, New England! Buckle on your mail of
proof sublime,
Your stern old hate of tyranny, your deep
contempt of crime;
A traitor plot is hatching now, more full of
woe and shame,
Than ever from the iron heart of bloodiest
despot came.

More slave States added at a breath! One
flourish of a pen,
And fetters shall be riveted on millions more
of men!
One drop of ink to sign a name, and slavery
shall find
For all her surplus flesh and blood, a market
to her mind!

A market where good Democrats their fellow men
may sell!
O, what a grin of fiendish glee runs round and
round thro' hell!
How all the damned leap up for joy and half
forget their fire,
To think men take such pains to claim the
notice of God's ire.

Is't not enough that we have borne the sneer
of all the world,
And bent to those whose haughty lips in scorn
of us are curled?
Is't not enough that we must hunt their living
chattels back,
And cheer the hungry bloodhounds on, that howl
upon their track?

Is't not enough that we must bow to all that
they decree, -
These cotton and tobacco lords, these pimps of
slavery?
That we must yield our conscience up to glut
Oppression's maw,
And break our faith with God to keep the
letter of Man's law?

But must we sit in silence by, and see the
chain and whip
Made firmer for all time to come in Slavery's
bloody grip!
Must we not only half the guilt and all the
shame endure,
But help to make our tyrant's throne of flesh
and blood secure?

Is water running in our veins? Do we remember
still
Old Plymouth rock, and Lexington, and glorious
Bunker Hill?
The debt we owe our Fathers' graves? and to
the yet unborn,
Whose heritage ourselves must make a thing of
pride or scorn?

Grey Plymouth rock hath yet a tongue, and
Concord is not dumb,
And voices from our fathers' graves, and from
the future come;
They call on us to stand our ground, they
charge us still to be
Not only free from chains ourselves, but
foremost to make free!

Awake, New England! While you sleep the foes
advance their lines;
Already on your stronghold's wall their bloody
banner shines;
Awake! and hurl them back again in terror and
despair,
The time has come for earnest deeds, we've not
a man to spare.

Free Soil, pp. 111-113; and Freedom, pp. 111-113.

195. THE SPIRIT OF THE PILGRIMS

Author: unspecified
Tune: Be Free, Oh, Man, Be Free

The spirit of the Pilgrims
Is spreading o'er the earth,
And millions now point to the land
Where freedom had her birth:

Hark! Hear ye not the earnest cry
That peals o'er every wave?
"God above,
In thy love,
O liberate the slave!"

Ye heard of trampled Poland,
And of her sons in chains,
And noble thoughts flashed through your minds,
And fire flowed through your veins.
Then wherefore hear ye not the cry
That breaks o'er land and sea? -
"On each plain,
Rend the chain,
And set the captive free!"

Oh, think ye that our fathers,
(That noble patriot band,)
Could now look down with kindling joy,
And smile upon the land?
Or would a trumpet-tone go forth,
And ring from shore to shore; -
"All who stand,
In this land,
Shall be free for evermore!"

Great God, inspire thy children,
And make thy creatures just,
That every galling chain may fall,
And crumble into dust:
That not one soul throughout the land
Our fathers died to save,
May again,
By fellow-men,
Be branded as a Slave!

Liberty, pp. 181-182 ; and Freedom, pp. 301-302.

196. FREEDOM'S GATHERING

Author: Whittier
Tune: original, by G. W. C.

A voice has gone forth, and the land is awake!
Our freemen shall gather from ocean to lake,
Our cause is as pure as the earth ever saw,
And our faith we will pledge in the thrilling
huzza.

Then huzza, then huzza,
Truth's glittering falchion for freedom we
draw.

Let them blacken our names and pursue us with
ill,
Our hearts shall be faithful to liberty still;
Then rally! then rally! come one and come all,
With harness well girded, and echo the call.

Thy hill-tops, New England, shall leap at the
cry,
And the prairie and far distant south shall
reply;
It shall roll o'er the land till the
farthermost glen
Gives back the glad summons again and again.

Oppression shall hear in its temple of blood,
And read on its wall the handwriting of God;
Niagara's torrent shall thunder it forth,
It shall burn in the sentinel star of the
North.

It shall blaze in the lightning, and speak in
the thunder,
Till Slavery's fetters are riven asunder,
And freedom her rights has triumphantly won,
And our country her garments of beauty put on.
Then huzza, then huzza,
Truth's glittering falchion for freedom we
draw.

Let them blacken our names, and pursue us with
ill,
We bow at thy altar, sweet liberty still!
As the breeze f'm the mountain sweeps over the
river,
So, chainless and free, shall our thoughts be,
for ever.

Then on to the conflict for freedom and truth;
Come Matron, come Maiden, come Manhood and
youth,
Come gather! come gather! come one and come
all,
And soon shall the altars of Slavery fall.

The forests shall know it, and lift up their
voice,
To bid the green prairies and valleys rejoice;

And the "Father of Waters," join Mexico's sea,
In the anthem of Nature for millions set free.
Then huzza, then huzza!
Truth's glittering falchion for freedom we
draw.

Liberty, pp. 164-166; and Freedom, pp. 258-260.

Free Soil, pp. 26-28, as "Free Soil Gathering," to the same
tune.

197. FREE SOIL SONG

Author: unspecified
Tune: Indian Chief

Ye sons of the soil, where for freedom your
sires
Struck the sparks from the flint to enkindle
its fires,
Shall the demon of Slavery now rule with a
rod,
The soil that was wet with your forefathers'
blood?
From the shores of Atlantic e'en to the far
West,
Where'er beats a heart in a true freeman's
breast,
From hill-top and mountain to valley below,
Let the answer be echoed in thunder-tones -
"No!"

Then, freemen, arouse and go forth in your
might,
United and firm for the truth and the right;
With the right on our side and the power in
our hand,
Shall oppression be suffered to stalk through
the land?
From the shores of Atlantic, etc.

In the conflict with slavery, shall freedom
succumb,
And the priests of her altar be silent and
dumb?
Shall the sons of the pilgrim bow down with
dismay,
And cravenly cower beneath slaveholding sway?
From the shores of Atlantic, etc.

Huzza for Free Soil! Free Soil evermore,
Till its boundaries embrace on our land every shore;
And should traitors essay the foul curse to extend,
Shall it any less speedily come to its end?
From the shores of Atlantic, etc.

Free Soil, pp. 222-223.

Freedom, p. 308, as "Ye Sons of the Soil!" to the tune, "The Campbells are Coming."

198. SONG

For Jenny Lind to sing to the American People.

Author: L. N. Y.
Tune: unspecified

Republic of the setting sun!
My heart has often turned to thee;
Thy praise, streams and forests dun,
Shore, lake, and waterfall, and lea
Have of my being formed a part;
And now I'm welcomed to thy heart.

Republic of the setting sun!
What mean those notes that quench my lay?
A wail I hear of hearts undone;
It fills my soul with sore dismay.
You gladly shelter Europe's brave,
And make your home-born man a slave.

I've sung beneath the iron reign
Of Muscovite, whose will is law;
But O, my soul! so foul a stain
In other land I never saw.
My heart grows sick! God's form divine
You sell for CASH with herds of swine.

Republic of the setting sun!
Wipe out at once this foul disgrace;
Then shalt thou make all peoples one,
And Freedom guard for every race.
O give the world this deed sublime,
And man's one heart I pledge thee thine.

Liberator, October 11, 1850, p. 164.

199. ORIGINAL HYMN
For August 1st, 1851

The following excellent original Hymn was sung at
the recent celebration of West Indian Emancipation
at Worcester.

Author: Rev. E. Davis
Tune: Scots Wha Hae

Hail again the glorious day,
When the despot's bloody sway
Passed forevermore away,
In the Western Main!
When, upon the bondman's night,
Broke old Freedom's joyful light, -
And against the conquering RIGHT,
Strove the WRONG in vain.

Sing the triumph, when, at last -
Years of fiery trial passed -
Slavery's hated form was cast
To a loathsome grave;
And the friends, who, for his good,
Watching through the night, had stood
To their holy brotherhood,
Took the ransomed Slave.

Sing, that, in their unchained flight,
With convincing power and might,
Freedom's growing years unite,
This great truth to swell;
Laid to RIGHT'S unbending line,
Where God's living counsels shine,
FREEDOM is of birth divine,
BONDAGE is of hell!

Let the shouts of freemen ring!
On her white, far-flashing wing,
God's free angel comes to bring,
To our own fair shore,
Freedom, peace, and righteousness;
Comes the plundered to redress;
Comes the Fugitive to bless,
Fugitive no more!

Strong, then, be each heart and hand
Of the brave, true-hearted band,
Who, to save a guilty land,
Strike for Liberty!

Be they feeble, faint or few,
They shall smite Oppression through;
They shall conquer - GOD IS TRUE -
And the Slave go free!

Liberator, August 15, 1851, p. 132.

200. THE SLAVE-CATCHER

Recited, by Mr. Garrison, at the West Indian
Emancipation Celebration at Framingham.

Author: Rev. John Pierpont
Tune: Scots Wha Hae

Children of the Pilgrim flock!
Off shoots from the Pilgrim stock,
Planted first on Plymouth rock,
By the surging main!
When upon that shore they dwelt,
When upon that rock they knelt,
Would those men have lived, and felt
Slavery's galling chain?

When they all were kneeling there,
When the incense of their prayer
Rose upon the frosty air -
From a wigwam's shade
Had they heard the savage call,
"Hunt us down yon fleeing thrall!
Seize and hold him, each and all!"
Would they have obeyed?

Had they done it, would they dare
Kneel again, and breathe a prayer
To the God they worshipped there?
Had they prayed, would HE,
Who their steps had thither led,
Who his guardian wing had spread
Over their defenceless head,
On the wintery sea -

His all-gracious ear have bowed?
Had they called on him aloud,
Would the column and the cloud,
Once to Israel given,

Have descended, as their guide
Through those forests, dark and wide,
Where to thee, O God, they cried,
And were heard of Heaven?

Hark! that savage call we hear!
Now 'tis ringing in our ear!
See! the panting thrall is near!
Shall we play the hound?
Shall we join the unleashed pack,
Yelping on a brother's track?
Shall we seize and drag him back,
Fainting, bleeding, bound?

Yes; - when we're in love with chains!
Yes; - when, in our dastard veins,
Not a drop of blood remains
From those Pilgrim men!
Yes; - when we our backs shall strip,
That what blood we have may drip
For the lordlings of the whip -
Then, and not till then!

Liberator, August 6, 1852, p. 126.

201. FREEDOM'S CALL

Author: Joshua Simpson
Tune: unspecified

Come come to freedom's call -
Old and young come one and all,
Join now to celebrate
Eighteen hundred and thirty eight.
Sing freemen sing, O sing freemen sing,
Sing a Song
For it won't be long
'Till the slaves are all set free.

In old Jamaica's Isles
See the Sun of freedom smiles,
Chains are now no longer worn
Despots from their Thrones are torn.
Praise freemen praise, O praise freemen praise
Praise the Lord
For it was his word
That set the Captive free.

Hark! what is this I hear!
A dismal sound salutes my ear.
Groans from the living graves
Of thirty hundred thousand slaves.
Pray christians pray; pray christians pray
Weep and pray.
For the glorious day
When the slaves shall all go free.

Go! go! with one accord -
Preach my Gospel saith the Lord.
Cry on the Land and Sea,
"God created all men free,"
Preach ye heralds preach, preach ye heralds
preach,
Preach and pray
For the glorious day
When the slaves shall all go free.

Now in the eastern skies
See that brilliant light arise.
Darkness is fleeing fast
Slavery's die will soon be cast
Plead freemen plead, plead freemen plead,
Plead and Pray
Till the glorious day
When the slaves shall all go free.

Blow! blow! the trumpet blow
Round the walls of Jerico -
Loud let the echo sound.
Slavery's wall's are tumbling down.
Blow christians blow, blow the trumpet blow;
Blow and pray
Till the glorious day
When the slaves shall all go free.

Original, pp. 10-11; and Car, pp. 45-46.

202. FREE AMERICANS - A NEW SONG

Author: W. Milne
Tune: Scots Wha Hae

Free Americans! how long,
Calmly, will ye suffer wrong -
See the feeble by the strong
Held in chains and slavery?

Ye to whom a freeman's lot
Is so dear, have ye forgot
How your sable brother fought,
By your side, for liberty?

Every moment he remains,
Held by you in servile chains,
Deeper, darker makes the stains
Of your guilt and knavery.

Rise! and with a giant's might,
Freedom's moral battles fight;
Lest the sword of Justice smite
Down your Eagle, suddenly!

Sable cheeks are wet with tears,
And a wailing fills His ears,
Who in mercy ever hears
The faintest cry of misery.

Heavy burdens haste undo,
Lest in wrath He visit you,
And the vengeance justly due,
Be requited fearfully.

Helpless infancy invokes,
Hoary age with snowy locks,
Woman, too, for justice knocks
At your doors beseechingly.

Shall their tears to pity move,
Tears observed by God above,
God, whose justice, truth and love,
Never sides with tyranny?

Blush, Americans! for shame;
There's a blot upon your fame -
Wipe it out, and get a name
For justice, truth and equity.

Then the Union, all around,
Songs of Jubilee shall sound,
And a State no more be found,
Stained with human slavery.

Liberator, September 24, 1852, p. 156.

203. THE FIRST OF AUGUST IN JAMAICA

Author: Joshua Simpson
Tune: Hail Columbia

Hail thou sweet and welcome day;
Let the Angels join the lay,
And help us swell the anthems high.
Tune all your golden harps once more,
And strike to notes ne'er struck before,
Yea let the morning's zephyr-breeze
Bear the echo o'er the seas;
Let all the islands bond and free
Proclaim Jamaica's liberty,
And while we praise the God most high
Who rules the heavens, the earth and sky,
Let Queen Victoria honored be
As mother of our liberty.

Today we gladly congregate,
A happy band to celebrate,
The day we rose from slavery's tomb.
Our clanking chains no more are heard;
Our limbs no more by fetters scared;
Our backs no more are drenched with blood;
Our tears have ceased our cheeks to flood;
Our wives and children, all so dear
Are bowed around the altar here.
May Haiti gladly catch the gale;
And Portorico tell the tale;
Let the Atlantics dancing spray
Salute this new-born happy day.

The knee with sacred awe we bend,
With melting hearts once more to spend
This day in free, unfettered praise,
Our thanks belong to God alone,
For he this mighty work has done.
He saw the Tyrant wield the lash;
He counted every bleeding gash;
He heard our children beg for bread
Which o'er our master's table spread.
He it was who heard our groans
Which rose before the Eternal Throne;
Our scalding tears in silence shed
Were coals of fire upon his head,

Wake the psaltry, lute and lyre,
And let us set the world on fire.
And may Jehovah blow the flame
Till all mankind shall see the light
Of knowledge; liberty and right!
Our hands are clear of human blood;
We bought our liberty from God,
Love, joy and peace are now combined
With freedom's golden chain entwined,

Firm united may we stand
A happy free and social band;
Each brother feel his brother's care,
And each his brothers' burthen bear.

Original, pp. 13-15; and Car, pp. 53-54.

204. CELEBRATION ADIEU

Author: Joshua Simpson
Tune: Lindon Waltz

Low in the west, see the sun now declining -
Closing the day with its seasons of glee:
Low in the west, through the hill-tops he's
smiling,
And silently bids a good night to the free.
Glory, and honor; both power and salvation
Be given to God who this day has been kind.
In his own hand is the faith of all nations
And he shall accomplish his will and designs.
O! let it be to our great consolation
That God, to the poor and oppressed is kind.

Days must depart, and seasons must wither;
Time as a thought is but here and is gone:
Years doth unite, what moments must sever,
For Time is a monarch, and Earth is his
throne.
Now we must part, and perhaps part forever;
The place that now knows us may know us no
more.
Waters and mountains our bodies may sever;
But love, and affection will last ever more.
Though on this spot we'll meet again never,
God grant us a meeting on Canaan's blest
shore.

While we have spent this day celebrating;
While we have spent it in feasting and glee;
Three million slaves in our own land are
waiting
To hail as a Nation this grand Jubilee.
O! hear ye not those chains that are clanking,
While low to the earth the poor bondmen are
bound -
Low to the earth which their own blood is
drenching -
The "Land of the free" and the home of the
proud.

Burdened and bruised, and tortured, and
mangled -
Their chains are their mantle - their tears
are their shroud.

O! weary bondman weep thou no longer:
God is thy refuge he'll soon give thee aid; -
Blest freedom's host, grows stronger and
stronger;
The hand of the Despot will ere long be
stayed.
We're coming! We're coming! We're coming!
We're coming!
Our <u>weapons</u> <u>of</u> <u>warfare</u> we hold in our hands.
We come not to greet you with fifing and
drumming -
The clashing of steel is not heard in our
band.
O! weary bondmen weep thou no longer,
For soon Ethiopia shall stretch forth her
hands.

<u>Original</u>, pp. 27-28.

205. ORIGINAL HYMN

Written for and sung at the celebration of
Independence Day, at Abington, July 5, 1852.

Author: D. S. Whitney
Tune: [America?]

The theme, the place, the hour,
Inspire, as by Thy power,
God of the free!
O fill each mind with light,
And arm each soul with might,
As here our hearts unite
To worship Thee.

Children of Pilgrim stock,
Firm as your granite rock,
Now stand for Right!
It's your good destiny
To help Men to be free,
Wherever they may be
Beneath God's light.

First purify the soil,
Hallowed by Pilgrim's toil,
From slavery's brand;
Then break the dark man's chain
On every Southern plain,
And Liberty proclaim
Through all this land.

Passing beyond the sea,
Help Europe to be free
From Priest and Czar -
To farthest Asia's plains,
And Afric's wild domains -
Wherever man's in chains,
Urge Freedom's ear.

Liberator, July 16, 1852, p. 110.

206. SONG OF FREEDOM

Author: A Nantucket Lady
Tune: Hail, Columbia

Hail! for Freedom's sacred cause!
Hail! for Freedom's righteous laws,
Which shall around the wide world ring,
Which shall around the wide world ring,
Till heaven and earth, and sky and sea,
Send back the sound, our soil is free;
Though deepest shadows veil the sky,
And though night dews around us lie,
Let us shrink not from the task,
While life and hope and truth shall last.
Sound the trump from shore to shore,
Slavery's curse shall be no more;
And the anthem of the free
Raise aloud for Liberty!

Strike for violated rights!
Shrink not till each heart unties,
And kneels around our God-built shrine,
And kneels around our God-built shrine,
Which, based upon the broadest plan,
Shall bind the brotherhood of man;
What though the world dance madly on,
The victory shall yet be won,
And peal on peal our shout shall be,
Columbia, land of liberty!

Sound the trump from shore to shore,
Slavery's curse shall be no more;
And the anthem of the free
Raise aloud for Liberty!

Liberator, March 4, 1853, p. 36.

207. A JUST COMMAND

Author: Joshua Simpson
Tune: any C. P. metre

Ho! white man, hear the great command,
It echoes loud throughout the land,
To you it loudly calls.
God wrote it with his own right hand,
In living characters it stands
Upon your Government's walls.

Go free the slave, go break the bands
That bind the captive's feet and hands,
Subdue the tyrant's power.
Go, tell the despot, make him see
That God created all men free,
And none are made to cower.

Go, free the slave, ye men of God;
Who say you're washed by pardoning blood,
No longer sleep and dream.
Go, break those stubborn hearts of steel,
And make the base slave-holder feel
That God is judge supreme.

Go, free the slave, ye valiant sons
Of brave, heroic Washington,
Who bless your father's graves.
Your father's deeds were justified
For "Equal rights" they bled and died,
And why should we be slaves?

Go, free the slave, the time has come
When men no longer must be dumb;
All men are now involved.
If legislations do not change
The law that binds all men in chains,
"The Union must dissolve."

Go, free the slave, before the cloud
Which gathers thick and thunders loud,
Shall shower its missiles down.
E'er blood for blood shall be the cry,
And slave and slave shall bleed and die
Upon the battle ground.

Car, pp. 51-52.

208. THE FREEMEN'S SONG

Author: unspecified
Tune: Scots Wha Hae

Men, who bear the Pilgrims' name,
Men, who love your country's fame,
Can you brook your country's shame,
Chains and slavery?

Traitors, shaped in Southern mould,
Have our honest birthright sold;
Wolves are set to guard our fold;
Shame! Democracy!

Hunted in his native lair,
Furious fights the Northern bear;
Woe to those who rouse his ire;
Let them turn and flee.

From our mountains in the North,
Freedom's legions silly forth,
Shouting o'er the trembling earth,
Death to slavery!

Raise the standard in the van,
Sacred to the Rights of Man;
Tyrants! meet us, if you can!
We are ready, now.

Ere a score of years be past,
Slavery shall breathe her last;
Spike the colors to the mast;
Hurrah for Liberty!

Liberator, September 22, 1854, p. 152.

209. ANNIVERSARY

Author: Joshua Simpson
Tune: Sweet Birds Are Singing

The morning is breaking,
And daylight appears -
And daylight appears;
And Freemen are waking
With many loud cheers -
With many loud cheers.
Come, freemen, sing with me,
Merrily - merrily -
Come, freemen, sing with me,
Happy, happy day.

Sweet music is swelling,
It floats on the breeze -
It floats on the breeze,
As daylight is smiling
O'er land and the seas -
O'er land and the seas:
Come, freemen, join with me,
Merrily - merrily -
Come, freemen, join with me,
Merry, merry day.

The sons of Jamaica,
Are now on their way -
Are now on their way,
While daylight is breaking,
To join in the lay -
To join in the lay;
Come, freemen, join with me,
Cheerily - cheerily,
Come, freemen, join with me,
Sing a merry lay.

Sound ye the trumpet
From mountain to sea -
From daylight 'till sunset
We'll keep up the glee -
We'll keep up the glee.
Sing, freemen, sing with me,
Cheerily - cheerily,
Sing, freemen, sing with me,
Happy, happy day.

Car, pp. 18-19.

210. SONG OF THE "ALIENED AMERICAN"

Author: Joshua Simpson
Tune: America

My country, 'tis of thee,
Dark land of Slavery,
In thee we groan.
Long have our chains been worn -
Long has our grief been borne -
Our flesh has long been torn,
E'en from our bones.

The white man rules the day -
He bears despotic sway,
O'er all the land.
He wields the Tyrant's rod,
Fearless of man or God,
And at his impious nod,
We "fall or stand."

O! shall we longer bleed?
Is there no one to plead
The black man's cause?
Does justice thus demand
That we shall wear the brand,
And raise not voice nor hand
Against such laws?

No! no! the time has come,
When we must not be dumb,
We must awake.
We now "Eight Millions Strong,"
Must strike sweet freedom's song
And plead ourselves, our wrong -
Our chains must break.

Car, pp. 17-18.

211. FOURTH OF JULY IN ALABAMA

Author: Joshua Simpson
Tune: America

O, thou unwelcome day,
Why hast thou come this way?
Why lingered not?

I watch with restless eye,
Thy moments slowly fly -
Each seems to stop and die -
And leave a "blot."

Though cannon's loudly roar,
And banners highly soar -
To me 'tis gloom.
Though "lads" and "lasses" white,
With face and spirits bright -
Hail thee with such delight,
With sword and plumes.

I hear the loud huzzas,
Mingled with high applause,
To Washington.
The youth in every street,
Their votes of joy repeat;
While Patriots' names they greet,
For victory won.

Brass bands of music play
Their sweet and thrilling lay,
Which rend the skies;
Old Fathers seem to feel
New animating zeal,
While tones of thunder peal
On every side.

Yet we have got no song.
Where is the happy throng
Of Africa's sons?
Are we among the great
And noble of the State,
This day to celebrate?
Are we the ones?

No! we must sing our songs
Among the Negro Gongs
That pass our doors.
How can we strike the strains,
While o'er those dismal plains,
We're bleeding, bound in chains,
Dying by scores?

While e'er four million slaves
Remain in living graves,
Can I rejoice,
And join the jubilee
Which set the white man free,
And fetters brought to me?
'Tis not my choice.

O, no! while a slave remains
Bound in infernal chains
Subject to man,
My heart shall solemn be -
There is no song for me,
'Till all mankind are free
From lash and brand.

Car, pp. 40-42, with the introduction: "The following
piece is the meditation and feelings of the Poor Slave, as he
toils and sweats over the hoe and cotton hook, while his
master, neighbors, and neighbors' children are commemorating
that day, which brought life to the whites and death to the
African."

212. FOR FREEDOM, HONOR, AND NATIVE LAND

Author: unspecified
Tune: unidentified

For freedom, honor, and native land,
Each liberty's sons shall for ever stand,
The host of the foe he will never fear,
When ruin shall threaten a land so dear.
All united, unaffrighted,
March we on in freedom's cause,
All united, unaffrighted,
Bound in love to freedom's laws;
Freedom's sacred band,
True to freedom's land,
True to freedom's land.

Abuse of power will the free repel,
The flame of sedition they'll strive to quell;
Alike are they friendly to equal rights,
And hostile to anarchy's deadly blights.
All united, etc.

For equal laws and for Heaven's pure word,
The hosts of the free have their life's blood
poured;
And never shall freedom's pure spirit die,
Till earth, under bondage, shall cease to die.
All united, etc.

Freedom, pp. 51-52.

213. SONS OF THE NORTH LAND

Author: unspecified
Tune: Scots Wha Hae

Men who breathe New England air,
Men with souls to do and dare,
Will ye tamely, calmly bear
The yokes of Slavery?

Hear ye not its clanking chains?
They are forged on Kansas' plains!
Now the blood of freemen stains
The green turf of the West.

Fear ye now to act or speak?
Is your faith in truth so weak?
Dare ye not the chains to break?
Will ye too be slaves?

Shall the soil to Freedom given,
From her sons again be riven?
Shall the brave men who have striven,
Be left alone to die?

Now's the day, and now's the hour;
If ye bow to Slavery's power,
Infamy will be your dower,
In all coming time!

Sure ye will not basely cower,
Now when storm-clouds thickly lower;
For strongest in the trial hour
The true heart e'er will be.

Remember how in days of old,
A birth-right was for pottage sold:
Shall ours be bought with Southern gold?
Or changed for cotton bales?

Sons of Pilgrim fathers brave,
Shall th' oppressor's banner wave
O'er your martyred heroes graves?
Will ye basely yield?

On old Bunker's heights of fame
Shall the slave-mart tell your shame?
Shall it to the world proclaim
The reign of Tyranny!

Shall the bloody scourge and chain
E'er heard on Concord's plain?
And the Mystic's soft refrain
For Freedom chant the dirge?

By each memory that endears;
By the love your home that cheers;
By the suffering bondman's tears,
Strike ye for liberty!

Liberator, April 4, 1856, p. 56.

214. ROUSE, BROTHERS, AROUSE!

Author: Jenny Marsh Parker
Tune: Flag of Our Union

Rouse, brothers, arouse! and arm for the
fight!
A darkness broods over our land -
Wrong crushes the right, - arm, arm for the
fight!
For freedom lift up a strong hand.
For freedom! for freedom! hark! old Bunker
Hill
Echoes lack the wild shout that you raise;
There our brave fathers sleep, and shall we
not keep
The banner their valor did praise?

Rouse, brothers, arouse! look now at our flag,
The flag of the free and the brave,
And see the black stain - say, shall it remain
To shadow the land of the slave?
That flag is the crown of liberty's height,
But mark where 'tis trailing today!
Rouse brothers, arouse! and hoist it once more
Where its stars with the eagle may play.

Rouse, brothers, arouse! the good God above
Will lend his strong arm to the right,
As he did in the days when Washington prayed,
Ere trusting his sword in the fight.
The God of the right will watch o'er the
fight!

Rouse! brothers, arouse and go forth,
And believe that at night the conqueror's
might
Will be with the sons of the North!

Freedom, p. 83.

215. THE DAY OF JUBILEE

Author: Daniel S. Whitney
Tune: [America?]

A song of jubilee
Comes swelling o'er the sea
From Indian isles;
Each heart beats quick and strong -
Just rights to all belong -
Each face, in all the throng,
Is wreathed in smiles.

We celebrate the day
When Freedom found her way
To that fair land;
With them that do rejoice
We join, with heart and voice;
Through weal or wo our choice
With right to stand.

But, while we join the song
Which gladdens now the throng
Of hearts made free;
Upon the Southern gale
There comes a stifled wail: -
How does the cheek turn pale
The sight to see!

Millions of hearts are crushed;
Yea, every voice is hushed
By mortal fear!
Prostrate and mute they lie,
Appointed there to die -
Though speechless, yet they cry,
"Send Freedom here!"

They shall not cry in vain!
Be sundered every chain,
Let all decree!

Christ's love commands the deed -
And though with him we bleed,
No UNION will we heed
Till all are free!

Liberator, August 1, 1856, p. 122.

216. WAKE, COLUMBIA!

Author: unspecified
Tune: Hail, Columbia

Wake, Columbia! wake once more!
Strike for freedom as of yore!
See on the tombstones of our sires,
Heart-sick Liberty expires -
Drenched in SUMNER'S patriot blood,
Where her WASHINGTON once stood!
Awake, oh North, 'tis time to say
If she shall live or die today!
'Tis time the question to decide,
If thus for nought our sires have died!
Firm, united, let us be,
Rallying round our Liberty!
Truth our motto, Right our cause -
God our Judge - from him our laws!

No evil did our fathers flee,
But we today are forced to see;
No shriek of butchered Hungary
More wild than outraged Kansas' cry;
No crowned and sceptred tyranny
More desperate than Slavery!
Then wake, oh North! we look to thee
To say this must not, shall not be!
To rise before the expectant world,
And end this scorn on manhood hurled!
Firm, united, let us be,
Glorying in our Liberty;
In the God of Freedom's might,
Strong to work for Freedom's right!

Heart of our great WASHINGTON,
Beat today in ours as one!
Then shall we need no trumpet-call,
No bloody breach, no cannon-ball,
For Freedom's eagle eye alone
Hath power her coward foes to stun!
Awake, then, every honest heart!
To brothers act a brother's part!

By all that Crime would wrest away,
Oh, North! put forth thy strength today!
Firm, united, let us be,
Heart and hand for Liberty!
We are strong above all powers -
Our fathers' strength is joined with ours!

Liberator, June 20, 1856, p. 100.

217. [UNTITLED]

At a July 4 celebration at Framingham,
the whole audience sang [the following],
from a printed sheet.

Author: unspecified
Tune: unspecified

From British yoke and galling chain,
Our fathers loosed the land;
But other yokes and bonds remain,
Their sons with shame to brand.

Liberator, July 10, 1857, p. 110.

218. THE NATION MUST BE FREE

An Original Song, sung (oddly enough!) at the
Banks's Young Men's Convention at Worcester,
Sept. 7, 1857, by the Waltham Glee Club.

Author: unspecified
Tune: Auld Lang Syne

In Freedom's cause we meet today,
A young, but Spartan band,
With BANKS to point the shining way
Where FREE MEN love to stand!
From every hill-top, vale and plane,
O'er land - from sea to sea -
Ring forth the paean, shout the strain,
"THE NATION MUST BE FREE!"

In Freedom's cause our sires fought,
In days lang syne -
For boon like this we well may shout,
Hurrah! for auld lang syne!

From Berkshire's green and rugged hills,
To Cape Cod's glittering sand,
The joyous clamor, echoing, thrills -
"Freedom throughout the land!"
From hill-top, valley, river, plain -
O'er land - from sea to sea -
Proclaim our motto - ring the strain -
"THE NATION MUST BE FREE!"
In Freedom's cause our sires fought, etc.

Then - up, boys, up! Gird on the sword,
And mount your ready steeds!
The "iron man" will give the word -
We'll follow where HE leads.
Fling out the banner! Spread the sail!
Our watchword - "VICTORY!"
With BANKS, "there's no such work as FAIL" -
"The Nation MUST be FREE!"
In Freedom's cause our sires fought, etc.

Liberator, September 18, 1857, p. 151.

219. THE PATRIOT'S HYMN
A PARODY

Author: S. G. C.
Tune: [America]

My country! 'tis for thee,
Sad land of slavery!
For thee I sigh:
Land! where my fathers died,
Land! once the pilgrims' pride,
I hear on every side
Oppression's cry.

Dear country! I love thee,
Debased by Slavery,
With tarnished name;
I love thy rocks and rills,
Thy woods and airy hills,
While grief my spirit fills
To see thy shame.

Let mourning swell each breeze
That murmurs mid the trees,
Let prayers ascend
From every mortal breast,
That in thee hopes for rest,
Till Heaven remove each pest
That doth thee rend.

Our fathers' God! to Thee,
Fountain of liberty,
To Thee we pray;
May our dark land be bright,
Once more, with Freedom's light;
Dispel the fearful night,
And send us day.

Liberator, December 25, 1857, p. 208.

220. FREEDOM'S BATTLE

Prepared for and sung at the Commemorative
Festival of the Boston Massacre, Faneuil Hall.

Author: Miss Francis Ellen Watkins
Tune: unspecified

Onward, O ye sons of Freedom,
In the great and glorious strife;
You've a high and holy mission
On the battle-fields of life.

See, Oppression's heel of iron
Grinds a brother to the ground,
And from bleeding heart and bosom
Gapeth many a fearful wound.

On my blighted people's bosom
Mountain loads of sorrow lay;
Stop not, then, to ask the question,
Who shall roll the stone away.

O, be faithful! O, be valiant!
Trusting not in human might;
Know that in the darkest conflict
God is on the side of right.

Liberator, March 26, 1858, p 52.

221. THE COLORED AMERICAN HEROES OF 1776

Prepared for and sung at the Commemorative
Festival of the Boston Massacre, Faneuil Hall.

Author: unspecified
Tune: Our Flag is There

They fought, their country to redeem
From stern Oppression's iron hand,
And braved the tyrant's brutal power,
To purchase freedom for this land.
They, side by side with WASHINGTON,
For equal blessings did contend,
And with great WARREN bled and died,
Their country's honor to defend.

In conflict with the foe, their blood
Has reddened many a tented field;
The trophies of the fight they won
Are blazoned on our country's shield.
They, side by side, etc.

They shrank not in that fearful hour,
When sternest patriotism quailed;
They smote Oppression's hateful form,
And Freedom smiled, and Right prevailed.
They, side by side, etc.

Yet now that British rule has ceased,
And Independence has been gained,
Judicial tryants have decreed
Such have no rights to be maintained!
They, side by side, etc.

Their children's children all are doomed!
Their rank is with the brutes assigned!
No matter what their woes or wrongs,
Protection they may never find!
They, side by side, etc.

In vain they show their bleeding wounds,
"Our native land!" in vain they cry:
The government derides their claims,
The courts their heaven-born rights deny!
They, side by side, etc.

Oh, perfidy beyond compare!
Oh, base requital - cruel wrong!
When shall this vile oppression end?
Answer - "How long, O Lord, how long!"
They, side by side, etc.

Liberator, March 26, 1858, p. 52.

222. THE PATRIOT'S BANNER
A Parody.

Author: S. G. C.
Tune: [The Star-Spangled Banner?]

What is it we see, in Oppression's dark night,
Which so dearly was bought when the daylight
was beaming,
By the hearts true and brave that for Freedom
did fight,
While it ever waved as the life-blood was
streaming?
And the cannon's swift glare, "the bombs
bursting in air,"
Gave proof to the foe it was guarded with
care?
'Tis the star-spangled banner, while it doth
wave
O'er the land no more free - 'tis the land of
the slave!

"On shore dimly seen through the mists of the
deep,"
When the ships, from afar, near the land it
discloses,
What doth wave in the breeze, o'er the
towering steep,
While the nation it marks in pride's slumber
reposes?
What is seen in the gleam of the morning's
bright beam,
And smiles in sad lustre beneath the clear
stream?
'Tis the star-spangled banner! while it doth
wave
O'er a land no more free, the dark land of the
slave!

Where now are the foes, who so fiercely did
fight
'Gainst the patriot band that so bravely
contended
For their home, and their friends, and their
nation's just rights,
And, mid hardships and danger, their country
defended?
They have gone from the earth, but their
children remain
To witness the shame, and to see the foul
stain
On the star-spangled banner; while it doth
wave
O'er the land no more free, the sad land of
the slave!

Call now upon Him, in Oppression's dread
night,
While the darkness is deep, and full many are
falling.
Whose just rod and firm staff are encircled
with light,
And whose voice mid the storms of affliction
is calling,
"Come, with haste, unto me, and my power ye
shall see,
And my healing wings a sure refuge will be;
I will lift my own banner against each dark
foe,
And, with glory, the star-spangled banner
shall glow."

Liberator, April 2, 1858, p 56.

223. FIRST OF AUGUST, 1858

Author: Justitia
Tune: Lucy Neal

We love thee, native land,
Where "all men are born free," -
But mourn the lot of those who pine
In abject slavery.
We feel our country's shame,
And to her some appeal;
Till freedom is enjoyed by all,
We happy ne'er shall feel;

We happy ne'er shall feel,
We happy ne'er shall feel.
Till freedom is enjoyed by all,
We happy ne'er shall feel.

When a long time ago,
Our fathers did agree
To form a "Union" with the South,
It was to make us free;
But she has proved untrue,
And placed on us her heel!
Till freedom is enjoyed by all,
We happy ne'er can feel, etc.

To her we've long appealed
To act the manly part,
But she has bid us quit her soil,
And from her coasts depart.
Wipe out this burning shame,
Sons of the boasted free!
Till freedom is enjoyed by all,
We happy ne'er can be, etc.

Let us no more succumb
To her despotic power,
But fling our banners to the breeze,
And make her tyrants cower;
Show her we've some back bone,
To meet her "chivalry,"
And ne'er will suffer her to rule
The children of the free, etc.

Let's emulate the deed
We celebrate today,
By which eight hundred thousand slaves
Cast all their chains away;
Break here the tyrant's power,
Like that across the sea,
And God shall blessings on us pour,
Through those we thus make free, etc.

With panoply and song,
We'll hasten to the fray,
Where, if we in the right are strong,
We're sure to win the day;
We'll break the tyrant's chain,
And set the captive free -
And Justice on our standard perch,
Sure sign of victory, etc.

Liberator, July 30, 1858, p. 124.

224. FREE THE BONDMAN FROM HIS CHAIN

Author: James H. Dean
Tune: Scots Wha Hae

Sons of sires who Freedom bought,
Nourish now each glowing thought,
Gather round the hallowed spot,
Sacred to their name;
Let not shouts of Liberty,
Let not tears your offering be;
Rather bring a soul that's free -
Free, and knows no shame.

What's the Freedom they have won,
Though bequeathed from sire to son?
Freedom's battle is not done
With the triumph cry:
Victory's field the hero reaps -
Valor conquers - Virtue keeps;
'Tis the craven soul that creeps
Back to slavery.

Oh, ye sons of patriot sires,
Light again the battle fires;
Freedom's sacred life requires
Heart, and soul, and hand;
There's nobler strife for you,
Foes, more subtle, to subdue;
There's grander triumph too!
Stand! like freemen, stand!

Strike! for those who pine in pain,
Free the bondman from his chain,
Cleanse your land from every stain, -
Bid her rise and shine:
Then, with truest freedom free,
Fixed stars our States shall be,
Beaming still, o'er land and sea,
With a light divine.

Liberator, August 6, 1858, p 28.

Mentioned in Liberator, August 19, 1859, p. 132, as having
been sung twice at the New England Colored Citizens'
Convention.

225. SONG TO FREEDOM

Author: unspecified
Tune: Suoni la Tromba

Freedom! thou fount for all races!
How, with the greed of a tiger,
Men decoy men on the Niger!
Who hears if they repine?
Hurled from their homes and their places!
Art thou of men, or from heaven?
Say, Freedom! scatter thy leaven,
And Nature's face will shine.
Hurrah!
Say, Freedom! Scatter thy leaven,
And Nature's face will shine.

Why does one take from another
All that he earns by his labor?
Wherefore withhold from your neighbor
A richer gain than gold?
Look at this African brother!
Throne of iniquity tries him,
Rights of white men it denies him,
And so the man is sold!
Hurrah!
Rights of white men it denies him,
And so the man is sold!

Sold! and his future employment
Ruled at the robber's intention!
Sold! and without intervention
Of Law to be his guard!
But by Law, Freedom's enjoyment
Ever proscribed from possessing!
Speak, Freedom! Say, from this blessing
If MEN shall be debarred?
Hurrah!
Speak, Freedom! Say, from this blessing
If MAN shall be debarred:

Freedom! can tyrants expel thee?
No! thy dominions are spacious;
No! for thy hands are tenacious;
No! by the Earth and the Sea!
Well! if there's no one to quell thee,
No flood of mischief to drown thee,
Say, if Philanthropy crown thee,
If MEN for sale shall be?
Hurrah!
Say, if Philanthropy crown thee,
If MEN for sale shall be?

Oh! love of power and of money!
Man a mere chattel thou makest,
Life for thy pleasure thou takest,
And to the sordid mind
Sweeter thou seemest than honey! -
When will Love, broad as the ocean,
Set the wide world in commotion,
And every bond unbind?
Hurrah!
Set the wide world in commotion,
And every bond unbind!

Liberator, December 10, 1858, p 200.

226. AN APPEAL TO AMERICAN FREEMEN
Fourth of July, 1859.

Author: Justitia
Tune: America

Sons of the boasted free,
Who prize your liberty
'Bove Southern trade;
Look to your fathers' graves,
Filled by your country's braves; -
Be ruled no more by knaves,
You've masters made.

Light up again the fires
Once kindled by your sires
In Freedom's cause;
Where has that spirit fled
Which moved those heroes deas,
Before which tyrants sped,
'Mid loud huzzas?

Let all who would be men,
By deed, and tongue, and pen,
Join hand in hand;
Swear that on Pilgrim's soil,
Where hardy freemen toil,
The tyrant's power to spoil,
They'll firmly band.

Let all who join in the prayer -
Here, Lord, a place prepare
For Freedom's home:

Where sleep our honored dead,
Ne'er may a despot tread,
No traitor lift his head -
The good time come!

Liberator, July 1, 1859, p. 104.

227. [UNTITLED]

Sung by children at Milford for a July 4 celebration.

Author: unspecified
Tune: unspecified

From the pine of the North to the Southern savannah,
From these dark sounding shores to the bright Western tide,
How glorious the sweep of the star-spangled banner!
How vast thy dominion, O land of our pride!

Liberator, July 8, 1859, p. 107.

228. [UNTITLED]

Sung by children at Milford for a July 4 celebration.

Author: unspecified
Tune: unspecified

That freedom the fathers from heaven receiving,
Preserved unpolluted by Tyranny's breath,
And bequeathed to their children the birthright, believing
It hallowed the morn by their lives and their death.

Liberator, July 8, 1859, p. 107.

229. HYMN

Sung at a celebration of Aug. 1 at Abington.

Author: unspecified
Tune: Missionary Hymn

Blest day of Britain's freedom,
We hail thy brilliant light;
Our vision is extended
To see the joyful sight.

Liberator, August 9, 1861, p. 126.

GET OFF
THE TRACK!

Ho! the car Emancipation
Rides majestic thro' our nation,
Bearing on its train the story,
LIBERTY! a nation's glory.
Roll it along, thro' the nation,
Freedom's car, Emancipation.

"Get Off the Track" (song 255) possibly was the most popular of the antislavery "rallying" songs which constitute this section, and is one of the few antislavery songs to appear consistently in modern collections of various kinds. Set to the tune, "Old Dan Tucker," it was written by Jesse Hutchinson in 1844 and printed that year in Garrison's Liberator (April 19, p. 63) with eleven verses, one of which was adapted continually to the political fluctuations of the era. The notoriety it soon gained seems to validate the prediction of the publication notice preceding it in the Liberator, which reads in part:

> This Song, with the music accompanying it, is one of those happy devices to operate on public sentiment, which never fail to accomplish a mighty work. It will obtain an immense circulation, and be sung by thousands of voices, and heard by multitudes, that no other form of anti-slavery "agitation" can reach.

First sung by the Hutchinson Family at the Broadway Tabernacle in New York on March 21, 1844, the song capitalized upon two objects of nineteenth-century fascination: the railroad and, in the tune, the minstrel show. An earlier use of railroad imagery can be found in "Hymn 15" (252), while songs that may have been influenced by "Get Off the Track"

include "Freedom's Glorious Day" (268) and "Clear the Way"
(292). An even more direct connection can be seen between
this song and those of black poet Joshua Simpson, particularly
in his use of "Emancipation Car" as a title of both a song
(365, in the next section) and one of his collections. In
addition, one of his few non-antislavery works, "The Car of
Education," is set to "Old Dan Tucker" and begins:

> Ho! the Car of Education
> Loudly thunders through the nation;
> Come, ye little lads and lasses,
> Jump on board before she passes.
> Jump on the cars all are singing,
> Education's bell is ringing.

Although all antislavery songs were intended to some
degree to convert new "believers" and edify those already
committed, these, like "Get Off the Track," are more expressly
for those purposes. A variety of techniques of encouragement
can be found here, all reminiscent of revivalism: calls to
awaken and join (231, 241, 256, etc.); the cry to "Never Give
Up" (270); and predictions of ultimate victory (233, 244, 275,
etc.) Interestingly, a dozen of these are directed to slaves
rather than to abolitionists, as in the first song, "O, Poor
Afric!" (230). Finally, interspersed throughout the section
are lyrics either welcoming leaders of the movement, like
those for British abolitionist George Thompson (280, 281), or
commemorating their deaths, such as the elegies to Elijah P.
Lovejoy (235, 236). These too, it seems, would serve to rally
the reformers and unite them in their cause.

230. O, POOR AFRIC!

Author: Charles W. Dennison
Tune: Greenville

Once poor Afric's day was shining;
Once her night flashed many a star:
But that day saw a declining,
O'er her sky spread clouds afar.
O, poor Afric! O, poor Afric!
O'er her sky spread darkness far.

Once she had her halls of learning;
Once possessed her sacred groves:
But her halls long since were burning,
Mid her walls the slaver roves.
O, poor Afric! O, poor Afric!
Mid her walls the slaver roves.

Once her hills proclaimed her power;
Once her fountains gushed with wealth:
But in treach'ry's darkling hour,
Wolf-like, came the white in stealth!
O, poor Afric! O, poor Afric!
To thy folds crept whites in stealth.

Sires of Afric! Once ye wandered
O'er your soil, all happy - free!
Here behold your offspring squandered -
Chains and stripes their liberty!
O, poor Afric! O, poor Afric!
Chains and stripes their liberty!

Ah! that slavers should have brought ye
From your land - your bodies sold!
Ah, that CHRISTIANS should have bought ye
Should oppress ye still for gold!
O, poor Afric! O, poor Afric!
Ye are still oppressed for gold.

But tonight must follow morning;
Darkness must give place to day.
Yea, awake! - the light is dawning!
Soon your clouds shall flee away!
O, poor Afric! O, poor Afric!
Soon your clouds shall flee away!

God is still your friend! Look to Him:
Lift to Him your suppliant prayer!
None distrust who ever knew Him;
None who know Him need despair!
O, poor Afric! O, poor Afric!
None who know Him need despair!

Liberator, October 5, 1833, p. 160.

231. FREEDOM'S SUMMONS

Author: Alonzo Lewis
Tune: Strike the Cymbal

STROPHE
Wake, ye Numbers! from your slumbers!
Hear the song of Freedom pour!
By its shaking, fiercely breaking
Every chain upon our shore!
Flags are waving! all tyrants braving!
Proudly, freely, o'er our plains!
Let no minions check our pinions,
While a single grief remains!

ANTISTROPHE
Proud oblations! Thou Queen of Nations!
Have been poured upon thy waters!
Afric's bleeding sons and daughters,
Now before us, loud implore us!
Looking to Jehovah's throne!
Chains are wearing! Hearts despairing!
Will ye hear a nation's moan?
Soothe their sorrow, ere the morrow
Change their aching hearts to stone!

EPODE
Then the light of Nature's smile,
Freedom's realm shall bless the while!
And the pleasance Mercy brings,
Flow from all her latent springs!
Delight shall spread her shining wings,
Rejoicing!

SECOND STROPHE
Daily, nightly! burning brightly!
Glory's pillar fills the air!
Hearts are waking! Chains are breaking!
Freedom bids her sons prepare!

O'er the ocean, in proud devotion,
Incense rises to the skies!
From our mountains, o'er our fountains,
See, our Eagle proudly flies!

SECOND ANTISTROPHE
What deploring impedes her soaring?
Million souls in bondage sighing!
Long in deep oppression lying!
Shall their story mar our glory?
Must their life in sorrow flow?
Tears are falling! fetters galling!
Listen to the cry of wo!
Still oppressing! never blessing!
Shall their grief no ending know?

SECOND EPODE
Yes! our nation yet shall feel!
Time shall break the chain of steel!
Then the slave shall nobly stand!
Peace shall smile with lustre bland!
Glory shall crown our happy land,
Forever!

Liberator, July 26, 1834, p. 120.

Hymns, pp 36-37, under no title, to the same tune.

Collection, pp. 25-26; Free Soil, pp. 139-142; and Freedom,
pp. 139-142, as "Wake Ye Numbers!" to the same tune.

Mentioned in Liberator, August 26, 1852, p. 126, as having
been sung at a West Indian Emancipation Celebration at
Framingham.

232. ORIGINAL HYMN

Sung at the late Annual Meeting of the
Vermont Anti-Slavery Society.

Author: Oliver Johnson
Tune: unspecified

Hark! a voice from heaven proclaiming,
Comfort to the bleeding slave;
God has heard him long complaining,
And extends his arm to save:
Proud Oppression
Soon shall find an endless grave.

See! the light of truth is breaking,
Full and clear on every hand;
And the voice of Mercy, speaking,
Now is heard through all the land!
Firm and fearless,
See the sons of Freedom stand.

Lo! the nation is arousing,
From its slumbers, long and deep;
And the church of God is waking,
Never, never more to sleep,
While a bondman,
In his chains remains to weep.

Long, too long, have we been dreaming,
O'er our country's sin and shame;
Let us now, the time redeeming,
Press the helpless captive's claim,
Till exulting,
He shall cast aside his chain.

Liberator, May 28, 1836, p. 88.

Picknick, pp. 110-111, as "Progress of the Cause," to the
tune, "Zion."

Melodies, pp. 22-23, as "Hymn 14," to the tune, "Zion."

Free Soil, p. 174; Harp, pp. 46-47; and Freedom, p. 174,
as "Light of Truth"; no tune specified.

Free Soil, pp. 145-146; and Freedom, pp. 145-146, as "Hark!
A Voice from Heaven," to the tune, "Zion."

Mentioned in Liberator, July 7, 1837, p. 111, as having
been sung at the beginning of a meeting of the Massachusetts Anti-Slavery Society celebrating July 4; and in
Liberator, February 3, 1860, p. 18, as being sung at that
same organization's annual meeting.

The following two verses appear in Anniversary, p. 4, as "The
Nation Rousing," to music by Lowell Mason:

Hark! a voice from heaven proclaiming
Comfort to the mourning slave;
God has heard him long complaining,
And extends his arm to save;
Proud oppression
Soon shall find a shameful grave.

Even now the word is spoken!
"Lo! the tyrant's power must cease!
From the slave the chain is broken";
Captives, hail the kind release;
Then in splendor,
Christ shall reign, the Prince of Peace.

233. THE DAY IS AT HAND

Author: Montgomery
Tune: unspecified

Let mammon hold while mammon can,
The bones and blood of living man;
Let tyrants scorn while tyrants dare,
The shrieks and writhings of despair.

The end must come, it will not wait,
Bonds, yokes and scourges have their date;
Slavery itself must pass away,
And be a tale of yesterday.

Songs, pp. 98-99.

Liberator, July 7, 1837, p. 111, as "Hymn"; no tune
specified. An introduction indicates that it was sung at the
meeting of the Massachusetts Anti-Slavery Society celebrating
July 4.

Picknick, p. 134, as "Slavery Must Pass Away," to an
unidentified tune.

Mentioned in Liberator, August 26, 1859, p. 136, as having
been sung at the New England Colored Citizens' Convention, to
the tune, "Old Hundred."

234. ANTI-SLAVERY HYMN

Author: unspecified
Tune: Missionary Hymn

A beacon has been lighted,
Bright as the noon-day sun,
On worlds of <u>mind</u> benighted,
Its rays are pouring down.
Full many a shrine of error,
And many a deed of shame,

Dismayed, has shrunk in terror
Before the lighted flame.
Victorious on, victorious!
Proud beacon, onward haste,
Till floods of light all glorious,
Illume the moral waste.

Oppression, stern, has foundered,
The demon gasps for breath,
His rapid march is downward
To everlasting death.
Old age and youth united,
His works have prostrate hurl'd;
And soon himself affrighted,
Shall hurry from this world.
Victorious on, etc.

Bold LIBERTY untiring,
Strikes at the monster's heart;
Beneath her blows expiring,
He dreads her well-aimed dart.
Her blows, we'll pray "God speed" them,
The darkness to dispel;
And how we fought for freedom,
Let future ages tell.
Victorious on, etc.

<u>Liberator</u>, March 24, 1837, p. 52.

<u>Collection</u>, pp. 14-15; and <u>Free Soil</u>, pp. 115-116, as
"A Beacon Has Been Lighted," to the tune, "Blue-Eyed Mary."

235. HYMN

Sung at a meeting in Lowell,
to commemorate the death of E. P. Lovejoy.

Author: Miss P. P. Morse
Tune: unspecified

Now "rouse ye" - for the "storm hath come,"
The wise have presag'd long;
Ye men of iron hearts and nerves
Be firm, for truth, and strong.
The banner's folds are stained with gore,
The stars are drench'd in blood,
The eagle's crest is colored with
The crimson of that flood.

And must the stern New Englander,
Upon his sterile sod,
Bow with his forehead to the south,
In worship to his God?
And must he speak no more for truth,
And stand no more for right -
But when the storm of malice comes,
A refuge seek in flight?

Never - 'tis written on the earth,
His feet have always trod,
And deeply on his inmost soul,
'Tis graven by his God.
Never - there's life within the land;
The forest oak shall bow
Beneath the summer breeze, as soon
As thou, New England, thou.

Liberator, January 12, 1838, p. 8.

236. HYMN

Sung at a meeting in Taunton, in
commemoration of the death of Lovejoy.

Author: unspecified
Tune: unspecified

Ho! ye who bind your fellow men,
And proudly mock at Freedom's God -
Knew ye, a dying martyr's groan
Would break oppression's iron rod?

Ho! bondmen, slaves on freedom's soil,
Who long have toil'd and pray'd in vain -
Knew ye, a drop of martyr's blood
Had power to break your cruel chain?

'Tis done! ye haughty tyrants, hear -
A martyr's groan is on the breeze:
In tones of thunder it demands
The bleeding captive's quick release.

'Tis done! A martyr's blood has flow'd -
Quick let the joyful tidings fly:
Look up, ye captives and rejoice -
The day of your redemption's nigh.

Liberator, February 2, 1838, p. 20.

237. ODE

Composed for the visit of J. Q. Adams
to Hingham, and sung with fine effect.

Author: unspecified
Tune: unspecified

Thrice welcome, hoary sage,
To this our tranquil Wood;
New England's daughters raise the song,
'Gainst whom was aimed the burning wrong,
Which Adams had withstood.

May not a woman plead
That evils be redressed?
Has God spurned woman from his throne?
Has He refused to hear the groan
Which bursts from woman's breast?

Thrice, welcome, champion true
Of woman's heaven-born right;
Thy generous aid, thy fearless stand
For the injured daughters of the land,
We hail with pure delight.

Thrice welcome, freedom's friend,
Oppression's dreadful foe;
The tyrant's threat thou laught'st to scorn,
From thy lips his gag is torn,
Thou deal'st him blow for blow.

Still fill the fearful breach
Till the tyrant is o'er thrown;
Till speech is free, petitions heard,
Oppression a forgotten word,
And justice mounts her throne.

What chorus rolls along
From the Caribbean sea?
Four-hundred-thousand voices swell,
Four-hundred-thousand captives tell,
That they, two days are free.

Oh, night wind, waft the sound
O'er all our Southern skies;
And let it soothe the captive's pain,
Till God shall break his galling chain,
And songs of freedom rise.

Farewell, thou honored guest,
Farewell, our noblest friend;
Thy name shall stand on history's page,
And brighter glow, from age to age,
Till time itself shall end.

Liberator, August 17, 1838, p. 132.

238. HYMN

Sung at the Marlboro' Chapel, on the 17th ult.
as a part of the public services in commemoration of
the life and character of the lamented FOLLEN.*

Author: Maria W. Chapman
Tune: unspecified

Oh, Father! from the happy spheres
Wherein thou dwellest, hear the hymn
So faintly uttered through these tears,
That make the eyes that shed them dim.

Oh, let thy comfort from above,
To every grief-worn heart appear,
Till this dark mystery remove,
And eyes and faith alike are clear!

Oh, Jesus! through our stricken souls,
Thy free, o'ermastering spirit pour,
To bear us onward, though there rolls
The oppressor's wrath our steps before:

That when our work on earth is done,
This true soul, taken from our need,
May welcome us before thy throne,
With the glad myriads of the Freed!

Liberator, May 1, 1840, p. 72.

*Abolitionist Karl, or Charles, Follen was killed on the
steamboat Lexington in 1840.

239. HYMN

Sung at the Marlboro' Chapel, on the 17th ult.
as a part of the public services in commemoration of
the life and character of the lamented FOLLEN.

Author: John Pierpont
Tune: unspecified

O, not for thee we weep: - we weep
For, her, whose lone and long caress,
And widow's tears, from fountains deep,
Fall on the early fatherless.

'Tis for ourselves we mourn: - we mourn
Our blighted hopes, our wishes crossed,
Thy strength, that hath our burdens borne,
Thy love, thy smiles, thy counsels lost.

'Tis for the slave we sigh: - we sigh
To think thou sleepest on a shore
Where thy calm voice and beaming eye
Shall plead the bondman's cause no more.

'Tis for our land we grieve: - we grieve
That Freedom's fane, Devotion's shrine,
And Faith's fresh altar, thou shouldst leave,
And they all lose a soul like thine.

A soul like thine - so pure a soul,
Wife, friends, our land, the world must miss:
The waters o'er thy corse may roll -
But thy pure spirit is in bliss.

Liberator, May 1, 1840, p. 72.

240. SONG OF THE ABOLITIONIST

Author: Wm. Lloyd Garrison
Tune: Auld Lang Syne

I am an Abolitionist!
I glory in the name;
Though now by SLAVERY'S minions hissed,
And covered o'er with shame:
It is a spell of light and power -
The watchword of the free: -
Who spurns it in the trial-hour,
A craven soul is he!

I am an Abolitionist!
Then urge me not to pause;
For joyfully do I enlist
In FREEDOM'S sacred cause:
A nobler strife the world ne'er saw,
Th' enslaved to disenthral;
I am a soldier for the war,
Whatever may befall!

I am an Abolitionist -
Oppression's deadly foe;
In God's great strength will I resist,
And lay the monster low;
In God's great name do I demand,
To all be freedom given,
That peace and joy may fill the land,
And songs go up to heaven!

I am an Abolitionist!
No threats shall awe my soul,
No perils cause me to desist,
No bribes my acts control;
A freeman will I live and die,
In sunshine and in shade,
And raise my voice for liberty,
Of nought on earth afraid.

I am an abolitionist -
The tyrant's bate and dread -
The friend of all who are oppressed -
A price is on my head!
My country is the wide, wide world,
My countrymen mankind: -
Down to the dust be Slavery hurled!
All servile chains unbind!

Liberator, December 31, 1841, p. 212, with this note to verse
five, line four: "Although it is not literally true that a

price has been set upon the head of every abolitionist, yet it is undeniably true that all abolitionists are outlawed by the South, and not one of them can travel in that part of the country, except at the peril of his life." This version appears also in Liberty Bell, 1842, pp. 64-66; Picknick, pp. 141-142 (first four verses); and Melodies, pp. 70-71 (first four verses).

Hymns, pp. 4-5, under no title, to the same tune.

Harp, P. 18; and Liberator, February 7, 1851, p. 23, as "I am an Abolitionist," to the same tune.

241. THE ANTI-SLAVERY CALL

Author: unspecified
Tune: When I Can Read My Title Clear

Come join the Abolitionists,
Ye young men bold and strong,
And with a warm and cheerful zeal,
Come help the cause along.
Come help the cause along,
Come help the cause along,
And with a warm and cheerful zeal,
Come help the cause along.
O that will be joyful, joyful, joyful,
O that will be joyful,
When slavery is no more,
When slavery is no more;
When slavery is no more,
'Tis then we'll sing and offerings bring,
When slavery is no more.

Come join the Abolitionists,
Ye men of riper years,
And save your wives and children dear,
From grief and bitter tears.
From grief and bitter tears,
From grief and bitter tears,
And save your wives and children dear,
From grief and bitter tears.
O that will be joyful, etc.

Come join the Abolitionists,
Ye men of hoary heads,
And end your days where Liberty,
Its peaceful influence sheds,

Its peaceful influence sheds,
Its peaceful influence sheds,
And end your days where Liberty,
Its peaceful influence sheds.
O that will be joyful, etc.

Come join the Abolitionists,
Ye dames and maidens fair,
And breathe around us in our path,
Affection's hallowed air.
Affection's hallowed air,
Affection's hallowed air,
And breathe around us in our path,
Affection's hallowed air.
O that will be joyful, joyful, joyful,
O that will be joyful,
When woman cheers us on,
When woman cheers us on,
To conquests not yet won,
'Tis then we'll sing and offerings bring,
When woman cheers us on.

Come join the Abolitionists,
Ye who the weak enslave,
Who sell the father, mother, child,
Whom Christ has died to save,
Whom Christ has died to save,
Whom Christ has died to save,
Who sell the father, mother, child,
Whom Christ has died to save!
O that will be joyful, joyful, joyful,
O that will be joyful,
When chains are forged no more,
When Slavery is no more,
Our happy land all o'er,
'Tis then we'll sing and offerings bring,
When Slavery is no more.

Come join the Abolitionists,
Ye sons and daughters all,
Of this our own America,
Come at the friendly call.
Come at the friendly call,
Come at the friendly call,
Of this our own America,
Come at the friendly call.
O that will be joyful, joyful, joyful,
O that will be joyful,
When all shall proudly say,

This, this is Freedom's day,
Oppression flee away!
'Tis then we'll sing and offerings bring,
When Freedom wins the day!

Picknick, pp. 118-121; Melodies, pp. 60-63 (verses three
and five o•itted); and Harp, pp. 40-41.

Liberty, pp. 96-98, as "Come Join the Abolitionists"; Free
Soil, pp. 131-133, as "Come Join the Free Soilers"; and
Freedom, pp. 131-133, as "Come Join the Friends of Liberty,"
all to the same tune but with verses three and five omitted.

242. THE DAWN OF LIBERTY

Author: Dunbarton
Tune: Watchman, Tell Us of the Night

Treble Voice.
Freeman, tell us of the night,
What its signs of promise are:
Tenor Voice.
Bondman - Lo! Britannia's light!
Freedom's glory beaming star!
Treble Voice.
Freeman! do its blessed rays
Promise good to slaves like me?
Tenor Voice.
Bondman! yes, its glorious blaze
Lights your path to liberty.
Chorus.
Bondman! yes, its glorious blaze
Lights your path to liberty.

Treble Voice.
Freeman, tell us of the night,
Does its star approach our land?
Tenor Voice.
Bondman - mark yon dawning light!
Lo! the breaking day's at hand;
Treble Voice.
Freeman! can these beams alone
Bid our dreadful bondage cease?
Tenor Voice.
Bondman! GOD is on the throne,
He will bring thee quick release.
Chorus.
Bondman! GOD is on the throne,
He will bring thee quick release.

Treble Voice.
Freeman, shall our fetter'd race
Cease to wear the galling chain?
Tenor Voice.
Bondman - lo! the God of grace
Comes to end thy tyrant's reign.
Treble Voice.
Freeman! can it, can it be?
Shall we share the glorious name?
Tenor Voice.
Bondman! yes, thou shalt be free -
Spread thy great Deliv'rer's fame.
Chorus.
Bondman! yes, thou shalt be free -
Spread thy great Deliv'rer's fame,
Spread thy great Deliv'rer's fame.

Picknick, pp. 92-93.

Free Soil, pp. 197-199; and Freedom, pp. 197-199, as
"Freeman! Tell Us of the Night," to the same tune.

243. [UNTITLED]

Author: unspecified
Tune: Flower When Evening Gathers Round Thee

He that goeth forth with weeping;
Bearing still the precious seed,
Never tiring, never sleeping,
Soon shall see his toil succeed:
Show'rs of rain will fall from heaven,
Then the cheering sun will shine,
So shall plenteous fruit be given,
Through an influence all divine.

Sow the seed, be never weary,
Let not fear thy mind employ;
Though the prospect be most dreary,
Thou may'st reap the fruits of joy:
Lo! the scene of verdure bright'ning,
See the rising grain appear;
Look again! the fields are whit'ning,
Harvest-time is surely near.

Hymns, p. 27.

244. THE DAY OF JUBILEE

Author: A. J. Duncan
Tune: unidentified

It comes! the joyful day,
When tyranny's proud sway,
Stern as the grave,
Shall to the ground be hurl'd;
And Freedom's flag, unfurl'd,
Shall wave throughout the world,
O'er ev'ry slave.

Trump of glad Jubilee!
Echo o'er land and sea,
Freedom for all!
Let the glad tidings fly,
And ev'ry tribe reply,
"Glory to God on high!"
At Slavery's fall.

Picknick, p. 96.

245. ODE

Sung by the constituents of John Quincy Adams
on his return from Congress, September 17, 1842.

Author: unspecified
Tune: [America?]

Not from the bloody field,
Borne on the battered shield,
By foes o'ercome,
But, from a sterner fight,
In the defence of Right,
Clothed in a conqueror's might,
We hail him home.

Where Slavery's minion's cower,
Before the servile power,
He bore their ban;
And, like an aged oak,
That braved the lightning's stroke,
When thunders round it broke,
Stood up, A MAN.

Nay when they stormed aloud,
And round him, like a cloud,
Came, thick and black,
He, single-handed, strove,
And, like Olympian Jove,
With his own thunder, drove
The phalanx back.

No leafy wreath we twine,
Of oak or Isthmian pine,
To grace his brow;
Like his own lockes of gray,
Such leaves would fall away,
As will the grateful lay
We weave him now.

But Time shall touch the page
That tells how Quincy's sage
Has dared to live,
Save as he touches wine,
Or Shakespeare's glowing line,
Or Raphael's forms divine,
New life to give.

Liberator, September 23, 1842, p. 151.

246. UNCHAIN THE LABORER

Author: John Pierpont
Tune: unidentified, by G. A. Hewes

Strike from that laborer's limbs his chain!
In the fierce sun the iron burns;
By night, it fills his dreams with pain;
By day, it galls him as he turns.

Yes! and your dreams it visits too,
When Fear stands o'er your restless bed,
And shakes it in your ears, till you
Tremble, as at an earthquake's tread.

The chain, that binds you to your slave,
Binds you to him, with links so strong
That you must wear it to your grave,
If, all your days, you do him wrong.

Then break his chain, and let him go,
And, with the spirit of a man,
Earn your own bread; and you shall know
Peace, that you know not now, nor can.

Yes, from his body, and your soul,
Throw off the load, while yet you may;
Thus strive, in faith, for heaven's high goal,
And wait, in hope, the Judgment Day.

Picknick, pp. 130-131.

Hymns, p. 8, under no title, to the tune, "Uxbridge."

Melodies, p. 8, four verses only, as "Hymn 2," to an
unidentified tune.

247. [UNTITLED]

Author: unspecified
Tune: Wake Isles of the South

WAKE, States of the South! your redemption
draws near,
No longer repose in the borders of gloom;
The strength of his chosen in love will
appear,
And light shall arise on the verge of the
tomb.

The billows that girt you - the wild waves
that roar -
The zephyrs that play when the ocean-storms
cease -
Shall bear the rich freight to the
tempest-toss'd shore,
Shall waft the glad tidings of freedom and
peace.

On regions that sit in the darkness of night,
The lands of despair to oppression a prey,
The morning will open with healing and light,
The glad star of Bethle'em will brighten
today.

Hymns, pp. 35-36.

248. NOW'S THE DAY AND NOW'S THE HOUR

Author: Harriet Martineau
Tune: [Scots What Hae?]

Now's the day and now's the hour!
Freedom is our nation's dower,
Put we forth a nation's power
Struggling to be free!
Raise your front the foe to daunt!
Bide no more the snare, the taunt!
Peal to highest heaven the chant, -
"Law and Liberty."

Gather like the muttering storm!
Wake your thunders for reform!
Bear not, like the trodden worm,
Scorn and mockery!
Waking from their guilty trance,
Shrink the foes as storms advance
Scathed beneath a nation's glance,
Where's their bravery?

Waves on waves compose the main,
Mountains rise by grain on grain,
Men an empire's might sustain
Knit in unity!
Who shall check the ocean tide?
Who o'erthrow the mountain's pride?
Who a nation's strength deride,
Spurning slavery?

Hearts in mutual faith secure,
Hands from spoil and treachery pure,
Tongues that meaner oaths abjure,
These shall make us free!
Bend the knee, and bare the brow!
God, our guide, will hear us now!
Peal to highest heaven the vow,
"Law and Liberty."

Melodies, pp. 50-51.

249. THE WORLD FROM ITS TRANCE IS AWAKING

Author: unspecified
Tune: unidentified

Oh the world from its trance is awaking,
With the spring of regenerate youth,
And the error-freed people are slaking
Their thirst at the fountain of truth.

Oh! the canker-worm, custom, was eating
Its way through the vein of the age,
Till man like the wild-bird, seemed beating
His breast on the bars of the cage.

Hark! a voice to the nations hath spoken,
In tones that have startled the world,
Let the dark chain of error be broken,
Let Liberty's flag be unfurled.
For time and progressive opinion,
Shall conquer where cohorts shall fail,
And freedom assert her dominion;
Hail Freedom, Hail Freedom, all hail.

Melodies, pp. 68-69.

250. HYMN 12

Author: unspecified
Tune: unidentified

Oh, who shall see that joyful day,
When, high on glory's throne,
Freedom shall rule, with sov'reign sway,
And call the world her own?

When man no more shall dread the frown,
That gloom'd the tyrant's brow,
And sorrow's cheerless night hath flown
To climes unpeopled now.

See, see, already 'tis begun;
Or is it but a dream?
The nations hail the rising sun,
And catch the thrilling beam.

God speed, God speed the Heav'n-born cause,
O'er ev'ry land and sea,
Till all the world, with loud applause,
Proclaims the Man is free.

Melodies, p. 20.

251. OPPRESSION SHALL NOT ALWAYS REIGN

Author: Henry Ware, Jr.
Tune: unspecified

Oppression shall not always reign;
There comes a brighter day,
When freedom, burst from every chain,
Shall have triumphant way.
Then right shall over might prevail,
And truth, like hero armed in mail,
The hosts of tyrant wrong assail,
And hold eternal sway.

E'en now that glorious day draws near,
Its coming is not far;
In earth and heaven its signs appear;
We see its morning star;
Its dawn has flushed the Eastern sky;
The Western hills reflect it high;
The Southern clouds before it fly;
Hurra, hurra, hurra!

It flashes on the Indian Isles,
So long to bondage given;
Their faded plains are decked in smiles,
Their blood-stained fetters riven.
Eight hundred thousand newly free
Pour out their songs of Jubilee,
That shake the globe from sea to sea,
As with a shout from heaven.

That shout, which every bosom thrills,
Has crossed the wondering main;
It rings in thunder from our hills,
And rolls o'er every plain.
The waves reply on every shore;
Old Faneuil echoes to the roar,
And rocks as ne'er it rocked before,
And never rocks in vain.

What voice shall bid the progress stay
Of Truth's victorious car?
What arm arrest the growing day,
Or quench the solar star?
What dastard soul, though stout and strong,
Shall dare bring back the ancient wrong,
Or Slavery's guilty night prolong,
And Freedom's morning bar?

The hour of triumph comes apace,
The fated, promised, hour,
When earth upon a ransomed race
Her bounteous gifts shall shower.
Ring, Liberty, thy glorious bell!
Bid high thy sacred Banner swell!
Let trump on trump the triumph tell
Of Heaven's avenging power!

The Day has come! the Hour draws nigh!
We hear the coming car!
Send forth the glad exulting cry!
Hurra, hurra, hurra!
From every hill, by every sea,
In shouts proclaim the Great Decree,
"All chains are broke, all men are free!"
Hurra, hurra, hurra!

Melodies, pp. 86-87.

Liberator, March 15, 1844, p. 44.

Two verses appear in Liberator, December 21, 1860, p. 202,
read by Wendell Phillips and sung by the choir at the Twenty-
Eighth Congregational Society's "usual Sunday meeting" at the
Boston Music Hall.

252. HYMN 15

Author: unspecified
Tune: Zion

See the car of freedom speeding
Onward with resistless force;
Clear the way whate'er's impeding,
Onward, speed it in its course:
Speed it onward,
Speed it onward,
In its circle round the earth.
In its circle round the earth.

Lo, a brighter day is dawning
On our country, on the world;
Hearts long-riven cease their mourning,
Where thy banners are unfurl'd.
Wave thy banners,
Wave thy banners,
Where oppression's darts are hurl'd.
Where oppression's darts are hurl'd.

Rise N.' England's sons and daughters,
Put your shoulder to the wheel;
Jesus by example taught us
For our neighbor's woes to feel:
Let his spirit,
Let his spirit,
Prompt us all their wounds to heal.
Prompt us all their wounds to heal.

Soon shall ev'ry earth-bound nation
See the sun .of freedom rise;
Vale and mount shall be its station,
Whither all shall turn their eyes.
Haste the era, Haste the era,
When shall cease the bondman's sighs.
When shall cease the bondman's sighs.

Melodies, pp. 24-25.

Mentioned in Liberator, August 5, 1859, p. 122, as having
been sung at a celebration of August 1 at Abington.

253. WELCOME TO JOHN QUINCY ADAMS

Written for and sung at an address of John Quincy Adams
to his constituents at Dedham, October 24, 1843.

Author: unspecified
Tune: [Auld Lang Syne?]

We come, no warrior to meet,
No chief with sword and shield
Returning home with blood-stained feet,
From some great battle field;
We come, the FRIEND OF MAN to greet,
The Hero who hath stood
Undaunted - scorning to retreat -
When Slavery threatened blood.

We come, to render homage due
From freemen to that ONE,
Who, foremost of the brave and true,
Is Freedom's champion.
We come to hear the fearless voice,
Long raised in Freedom's cause,
And from the statesman of our choice
Learn how to guard her laws.

Thou more that Hero - Patriot, Sage,
Shield of the rights of man -
Thy name shall shine on History's page,
A light to guide and warn;
And when our sons to future days
Shall meet round Freedom's shrine,
Thy name shall mingle with their lays
Of love for "AULD LANG SYNE."

Liberator, November 11, 1843, p. 174.

254. HYMN

Author: D. S. W.
Tune: Old Church Yard

Here we've had a cordial greeting,
And we've had a thrilling meeting,
And our labour here completing
We'll seek the next town,
From town to town we'll battle,
From town to town we'll battle,
From town to town we'll battle,
Until slavery's beat down.

But we leave here faithful legions,
To defend these conquer'd regions,
And to keep the battle raging,
In all the towns about,
Here you'll guard the fortress,
Here you'll guard the fortress,
Here you'll guard the fortress,
And put the foe to rest.

Now the churches must awaken,
The state [must] now be shaken,
And a mighty stride be taken,
Toward the truth and the light;
And all must fear and tremble,
And all must fear and tremble,
And all must fear and tremble,
Who refuse to do the right.

Now we'll give the foe no quarter,
At the ballot-box or altar, -
She is Babylon's foul daughter,
And our work, it must not pause,
And we'll fight for freedom,
And we'll fight for freedom,
And we'll fight for freedom,
True religion and just laws.

Liberator, March 1, 1844, p. 35.

Liberty, p. 214, as "Liberty Meetings," to the same tune (except titled here "Old Granite State").

Freedom, p. 305, as "We've Had a Cordial Greeting," to the same tune ("Old Granite State").

255. GET OFF THE TRACK!

Author: Jesse Hutchinson
Tune: Old Dan Tucker

Ho! the car Emancipation
Rides majestic thro' our nation,
Bearing on its train the story,
LIBERTY! a nation's glory.
Roll it along, thro' the nation,
Freedom's car, Emancipation.

First of all the train, and greater,
Speeds the dauntless LIBERATOR
Onward cheered amid hosannas,
And the waving of free banners.
Roll it along! Spread your banners,
While the people shout hosannas.

Men of various predilections,
Frightened, run in all directions;
Merchants, editors, physicians,
Lawyers, priests, and politicians.
Get out of the way! every station!
Clear the track of 'mancipation!

Let the ministers and churches
Leave behind sectarian lurches;
Jump on board the Car of Freedom,
Ere it be too late to need them.
Sound the alarm! Pulpits thunder!
Ere too late you see your blunder!

Politicians gazed, astounded,
When, at first, our bell resounded:
Freight trains are coming, tell these foxes,
With our votes and ballot boxes.
Jump for your lives! politicians,
From your dangerous, false positions.

Railroads to Emancipation
Cannot rest on Clay foundation;
And the tracks of "The Magician"
Are but railroads to perdition!
Pull up the rails! Emancipation
Cannot rest on such foundation.

(Railroads to Emancipation
Cannot rest on <u>Clay</u> foundation.
And the road that Polk erects us,
Leads to Slavery, and to Texas!
Pull up the rails! Emancipation
Cannot rest on such foundation. <u>Collection</u>)

(Railroads to emancipation
Cannot rest on Whig foundation.
And the Baltimore Convention,
Leads direct to slave extension.
Pull up the rails! Emancipation
Cannot rest on such foundation.
                    <u>Free</u> <u>Soil</u> and <u>Liberty</u>)

(Railroads to emancipation
Cannot rest on false foundation.
And the road of Hunkerdomation
Leads direct to slave extension.
Pull up the rails! Emancipation
Cannot rest on such foundation. <u>Freedom</u>)

All true friends of Emancipation,
Haste to Freedom's railroad station;
Quick into the cars get seated,
All is ready, and completed.
Put on the steam! all are crying,
And the liberty flags are flying.

Now again the bell is tolling,
Soon you'll see the car-wheels rolling;
Hinder not their destination,
Chartered for Emancipation.
Wood up the fire! keep it flashing,
While the train goes onward dashing.

Hear the mighty car-wheels humming!
Now look out! <u>The</u> <u>Engine's</u> <u>coming</u>!
Church and statesmen! hear the thunder!
Clear the track! or you'll fall under.
Get off the track! all are singing,
While the <u>Liberty</u> <u>Bell</u> is ringing.

On triumphant see them bearing,
Through sectarian rubbish tearing;
The bell and whistle and the steaming,
Startle thousands from their dreaming.
Look out for the cars, while the bell rings!
Ere the sound your funeral knell rings.

See the people run to meet us;
At the depots thousands greet us;
All take seats with exultation,
In the Car Emancipation.
HUZZA! HUZZA! Emancipation
Soon will bless our happy nation.
HUZZA! HUZZA! HUZZA!!!

Liberator, April 19, 1844, p. 63.

Collection, pp. 35-36, under the same title, to the same
tune, with verse six indicated above.

Harp, pp. 25-26, under the same title, to the same tune,
with verse six omitted.

Free Soil, pp. 169-170; Liberty, p. 144; and Freedom,
pp. 169-170, under the same title, to the same tune,
but with verses two, eight, and nine omitted and verse
six as indicated above.

256. THE CALL

Author: F. M. Adlington
Tune: Oh! 'Tis My Delight in a Shiny Night

Come, all you philanthropic souls,
Who love the human face,
And seek, like Sol, where'er he rolls,
To bless the human race.
CHORUS:
Come, Freedom's kindling watch-fires fan,
Till every despot quake;
Come, vindicate the rights of man,
Till every fetter break!

To drive the clouds of ignorance
Before the light of Truth, -
To plead the cause of innocence,
Of age and helpless youth; -
CHORUS

Where Freedom's altars dimly blaze,
Your faithful hearts unite
To scatter wide the golden rays
That gem her brow of light; -
CHORUS

To advocate man's inborn right
To think, to act, to know,
Unshackled by superior might,
Whate'er a man should do; -
CHORUS

To nerve the timid heart with power,
Expand the human brain,
And teach them in the trial-hour
To spurn a tyrant's chain; -
CHORUS

To purge the long dishonor'd seat,
That Justice used to own,
Till nations underneath their feet
Shall trample Slavery's throne; -
CHORUS

Your great reward, if slow, is sure;
The nations will awake,
To honor those whose aims are pure,
Who strive for Virtue's sake.

Liberator, December 20, 1844, p. 204.

257. BE FREE, O MAN, BE FREE

Author: Mary H. Maxwell
Tune: unspecified

The storm-winds wildly blowing,
The bursting billows mock,
As, with their foam-crests glowing,
They dash the sea-girt rock;
Amid the wild commotion,
The revel of the sea,
A voice is on the ocean,
Be free, O man, be free.

Behold the sea-brine leaping
High in the murky air;
List to the tempest sweeping
In chainless fury there.
What moves the mighty torrent,
And bids it flow abroad?
Or turns the rapid current?
What, but the voice of God?

> Then, answer, is the spirit
> Less noble or less free?
> From does it inherit
> The doom of slavery?
> When man can bind the waters,
> That they no longer roll,
> Then let him forge the fetters
> To clog the human soul.
>
> Till then a voice is stealing
> From earth and sea, and sky,
> And to the soul revealing
> Its immortality.
> The swift wind chants the numbers
> Careering o'er the sea,
> And earth aroused from slumbers,
> Re-echoes, "Man, be free."

Collection, pp 40-41; and Harp, p. 27.

Free Soil, pp. 163-164; and Freedom, pp. 163-164, under
the same title, to original music by G. W. C.

258. WE ARE COME, ALL COME

Author: G. W. C.
Tune: unidentified

> We are come, all come, with the crowded
> throng,
> To join our notes in a plaintive song;
> For the bond man sighs, and the scalding tear
> Runs down his cheek while we mingle here.
>
> We are come, all come, with a hallowed vow,
> At the shrine of slavery never to bow,
> For the despots reign o'er hill and plain,
> Spreads grief and woe in his horrid train.
>
> We are come, all come, a determined band,
> To rescue the slave from the tyrant's hand;
> And our prayers shall ascend with our songs to
> Him
> Who sits in the midst of the cherubim.

We are come, all come, in the strength of
youth,
In the light of hope and the power of truth;
And we joy to see in our ranks today,
The honored locks of the good and grey.

We are come, all come, in our holy might,
And freedom's foes shall be put to flight;
Oh God! with favoring smiles from thee,
Our songs shall soon chant the victory.

Collection, p. 6; Free Soil, p. 134; and Freedom, p. 134.

259. WE'LL FREE THE SLAVE

Sung at the Anti-Slavery League Soiree, held in the
Music Hall, [Newcastle, England], December 28, 1846.

Author: E. P. Hood
Tune: Ye Banks and Braes of Bonny Doon

How bright the sun of freedom burns,
From mount to mount, from shore to shore!
"The slave departs, the man returns,"
The reign of force and fraud is o'er:
'Tis Truth's own beam, from sea to sea,
From vale to vale, from wave to wave;
Her ministers this night are we,
To free, to free, to free the slave!

We'll free the slave of every clime,
Whate'er the chain that binds his soul;
And publish forth this truth sublime,
From farthest Indus to the Pole,
That man, how proud soe'er he be,
Is but a poor and paltry knave,
Who joins not now with you and me,
To free, to free, to free the slave!

We'll free the slave, the poisoned bow!
Has fettered to low crime and care;
We'll bid him burst its harsh control,
And break its fetters of despair.
We'll free the slave of Mammon's power;
And War's poor darling, called the brave;
And, Tyrants! yes, from this blest hour,
We'll free, we'll free, we'll free the slave!

Poor Afric's sons, though slaves they be,
Shall spring to freedom and to light;
And what they shall be, you may see, -
One of those sons is here to-night!
And ASIA from her sleep supine,
and EUROPE from her feudal grave,
Yes, e'en AMERICA shall join,
To free, to free, to free the slave!

You laugh! but, ah! you do not know
How great a power the truth can wield;
Though always aims the surest blow,
And wisdom is the safest shield.
The spirits of six thousand years
Are round us, and they make us brave;
Come, brother, quell ignoble fears,
And free, and free, and free the slave!

Liberator, February 5, 1847, p. 24.

260. THE COMING DAYS

Author: W. J. Linton
Tune: The Days When We Went Gypsying

O, the days when we are freemen all, whenever
that shall be,
Will surely be the worthiest that earth can
ever see;
When man unto his fellow-man, whatever may
befall,
Holds out the palm of fellowship, and Love is
lord of all;
When man and woman, hand in hand, along life's
pathway go,
And the days of youthful joy eclipse and
sorrow long ago.

O, the days when we are freemen all; when
equal rights and laws
Shall rule the commonwealth of earth, amid a
world's applause;
When equal rights and duties claim the equal
care of all,
And man, as man, beneath high heaven, assumes
his coronal;
When the day of Pentecost is come, when the
poor man's hearth shall be
An altar for the beacon fire of Peace and
Liberty!

O, the days when we are freemen all, the days
when thoughts are free
To travel as the winds of heaven towards their
destiny;
When man is sovereign of himself, and himself
the priest,
And crowned Wisdoms recognize the manhood of
the least.
Then God shall walk again with man, and
fruitful converse grow,
As in the noon of Paradise, a long time ago.

But holier still shall be the day when human
hearts shall dare
To kneel before one common Hope, the common
toil to share;
When Love shall throw his armor off, to
wrestle with the fear,
The selfishness, which is the seal upon the
sepulchre
Hark to the Voices of the Years! the
spring-tide of their glee -
Love hath o'ercome the prophecy: Humanity is
free!

Liberator, February 5, 1847, p. 24.

261. ODE ON THE RECEPTION OF FREDERICK
DOUGLASS, THE EMANCIPATED SLAVE

Sung by the Barker family at a Ladies' Meeting in Lynn
for the reception of Frederick Douglass, May 1, 1847.

Author: Alonzo Lewis
Tune: unspecified

We hail thy return from the realms of the
East,
Where the soul of the slave is from bondage
released;
We welcome thee home to the land that should
be,
In truth, as in title, the land of the free!
From regions afar, o'er the blue ocean's foam,
We welcome thee home! yes, we welcome thee
home!

O, Douglass! brave Douglass! the "tender and
true!"
'Twas the motto of Douglass, when Scotch
arrows flew;
He stood for his rights with the free and the
brave,
Their homes and their loved ones from tyrants
to save!
From regions afar, o'er the blue ocean's foam,
We welcome thee home! yes, we welcome thee
home!

We welcome thee home to the hall and the cot:
The North shall be free, if the South land be
not!
Our climate is cold, but our spirits are warm,
With scorn for the tyrant, in mind and in
form!
From regime afar, o'er the blue ocean's foam,
We welcome thee home! yes, we welcome thee
home!

On the hills of New England our eagle is free!
No chains on his thunder-scarred pinions has
he!
Here our brethren may dwell free from bondage
and thrall,
And we say unto thee, as we say unto all,
From regions afar, o'er the blue ocean's foam,
We welcome thee home! yes, we welcome thee
home!

Liberator, May 7, 1847, p. 75.

262. WELCOME TO [WILLIAM LLOYD] GARRISON, [FREDERICK] DOUGLASS, [ARNOLD] BUFFUM AND [STEPHEN S.] FOSTER

Sung at the late Annual Meeting of the Western
Anti-Slavery Society, held at New Lyme, Ohio.

Author: Benjamin S. Jones
Tune: unspecified

Welcome, thrice welcome, ye friends of the
slave,
To our hearts and our homes in the
wide-spreading West!
Your spirits are free as the waters that lave
The shores of our Erie and whiten its breast

Oh, not as to victors from battle-fields red
With the blood of the slaughtered in hatred
cut down.
Where the steed of the foeman has trampled the
dead,
And the beautiful earth with destruction is
strown;

But as men who are fearlessly battling for
Right
With the sword of the Spirit, and breast-plate
of Love,
Whose watchwords of Freedom, and Justice, and
Light,
Are watchwords of glorified spirits above.

Then welcome, thrice welcome! Age, manhood,
and youth,
All unite in their welcome to heart and to
home,
For they honor untiring devotion to truth,
And are friends to the friends of the crushed
and the Dumb.

We rejoice to have with us the man who has
been
The bold pioneer in Humanity's cause,
Who attacked single handed our national sin,
Entrenched in its strong hold of pulpit and
laws.

Right bravely he bore him. With standard
unfurled,
He demanded full freedom for body and mind,
His motto, "My Country, God's beautiful world
My countrymen all who belong to mankind."

And our hearts are made glad by the presence
of one
Who was chattelized, beaten, and sold in our
land;
Who is guilty of naught, save that Africa's
sun
Pressed his ancestors' brow with too heavy a
hand.

He can tell of the woes that have gnawed at
his heart;
Of the lash that has left its deep scar on his
back;
How the tenderest ties are torn rudely apart,
And the soul and the body both doomed to the
rack.

And we welcome him too, who, with knowledge
and zeal,
Piles facts upon facts at Humanity's call,
And is making the cowardly oppressor to feel
Tis by facts that his system is destined to
fall.

And he who returns unto us as a friend
Who has scattered the truth where the field is
now white,
Will not doubt of a welcome, but joyfully lend
His labor to gather the Harvest of Right.

Then welcome, thrice welcome, ye friends of
the slave,
To our hearts and our homes in the
wide-spreading West!
Your spirits are free as the waters that lave
The shores of our Erie and whiten its breast.

Liberator, October 29, 1847, p. 176.

263. COMFORT FOR THE BONDMAN

Author: unspecified
Tune: Indian Philosopher

Come on, my partners in distress,
My comrades in this wilderness,
Who groan beneath your chains;
A while forget your griefs and fears,
And look beyond this vale of tears,
To yon celestial plains.

Beyond the bounds of time and space,
Look forward to that heavenly place,
Which mortals never trod;
On faith's strong eagle pinions rise,
Work out your passage to the skies,
And scale the mount of God.

If, like our Lord, we suffer here,
We shall before his face appear,
And at his side sit down;
To patient faith the prize is sure,
For all who to the end endure
Shall wear a glorious crown.

Thrice blessed, exalted, blissful hope!
It lifts our fainting spirits up,
It brings to life the dead;
Our bondage here will soon be past,
Then we shall rise and reign at last,
Triumphant with our Head.

Free Soil, pp. 143-144; and Freedom, pp. 143-144.

264. FLING OUT THE ANTI-SLAVERY FLAG

Author: William Wells Brown
Tune: Auld Lang Syne

Fling out the Anti-slavery flag
On every swelling breeze;
And let its folds wave o'er the land,
And o'er the raging seas,
Till all beneath the standard sheet,
With new allegiance bow;
And pledge themselves to onward bear
The emblem of their vow.

Fling out the Anti-Slavery flag,
And let it onward wave
Till it shall float o'er every clime,
And liberate the slave;
Till, like a meteor flashing far,
It bursts with glorious light,
And with its Heaven-born rays dispels
The gloom of sorrow's night.

Fling out the Anti-Slavery flag,
And let it not be furled,
Till like a planet of the skies,
It sweeps around the world.
And when each poor degraded slave,
Is gathered near and far;
O, fix it on the azure arch,
As hope's eternal star.

Fling out the Anti-Slavery flag,
Forever let it be
The emblem to a holy cause,
The banner of the free.

And never from its guardian height,
Let it by man be driven,
But let it float forever there,
Beneath the smiles of heaven.

Harp, p. 21.

Mentioned in Liberator, August 26, 1859, p. 136, as having
been sung at the New England Colored Citizens' Convention.

265. I DREAM OF ALL THINGS FREE!

Author: Mrs. Hemans
Tune: original, by G. W. C.

I dream of all things free!
Of a gallant, gallant bark,
That sweeps thro' the storm at sea,
Like an arrow to its mark!
Of a stag that o'er the hills
Goes bounding in his glee;
Of a thousand flashing rills -
Of all things glad and free.
Of all things glad and free.

I dream of some proud bird,
A bright-eyed mountain king;
In my visions I have heard
The rustling of its wing.
I follow some wild river,
On whose breast no sail may be;
Dark woods around it shiver -
I dream of all things free.
I dream of all things free.

Of a happy forest child,
With the fawns and flowers at play;
Of an Indian 'midst the wild,
With the stars to guide his way:
Of a chief his warriors leading,
Of an archer's green wood tree -
My heart in chains is bleeding,
And I dream of all things free,
And I dream of all things free.

Free Soil, pp. 208-210; and Freedom, pp. 209-211.

266. THE SWEETS OF LIBERTY

Author: unspecified
Tune: Is There a Heart

Is there a man that never sighed
To set the prisoner free?
Is there a man that never prized
The sweets of liberty?
Then let him, let him breathe unseen,
Or in a dungeon live;
Nor never, never know the sweets
That liberty can give.

Is there a heart so cold in man,
Can galling fetters crave?
Is there a wretch so truly low,
Can stoop to be a slave?
O, let him, then, in chains be bound,
In chains and bondage live;
Nor never, never know the sweets
That liberty can give.

Is there a breast so chilled in life,
Can nurse the coward's sigh?
Is there a creature so debased,
Would not for freedom die?
O, let him then be doomed to crawl
Where only reptiles live;
Nor never, never know the sweets
That liberty can give.

Harp, p. 15.

267. MANHOOD

Author: Robert Burns
Tune: Our Warriors' Hearts

Is there for honest poverty,
That hangs his head, and a' that;
The coward slave, we pass him by,
We dare be poor, for a' that;
For a' that and a' that;
Our toils obscure, and a' that,
The rank is but the guinea's stamp,
The man's the gowd for a' that.

What though on homely fare we dine,
Wear hodden gray and a' that;
Gie fools their silks, and knaves their wine,
A man's a man for a' that;
The honest man tho' e'er so poor,
Is king o' men for a' that;
The rank is but the guinea's stamp,
The man's the gowd for a' that.

Then let us pray that come it may,
As come it will for a' that,
That sense and worth o'er a' the earth,
May bear the gree and a' that;
For a' that and a' that,
It's coming yet, for a' that,
That man to man, the world all o'er,
Shall brothers be, for a' that.

Liberty, p. 178; and Freedom, pp. 298-299.

Free Soil, p. 211, as "A Man's a Man," to the same tune.

268. FREEDOM'S GLORIOUS DAY

Author: unspecified
Tune: Crambambule

Let waiting throngs now lift their voices,
As Freedom's glorious day draws near,
While every gentle rejoices,
And each bold heart is filled with cheer,
The slave has seen the Northern star,
He'll soon be free, hurrah, hurrah!
Hurrah, hurrah, hurrah, hurrah!

Though many still are writhing under
The cruel whips of "chevaliers,"
Who mothers from their children sunder,
And scourge them for their helpless tears -
Their safe deliv'rance is not far!
The day draws nigh! - hurrah, hurrah!
Hurrah, hurrah, hurrah, hurrah!

Just ere the dawn the darkness deepest
Surrounds the earth as with a pall;
Dry up thy tears, O thou that weepest,
That on thy sight the rays may fall!
No doubt let now thy bosom mar:
Send up the shout - hurrah, hurrah!
Hurrah, hurrah, hurrah, hurrah!

No more again shall it be granted
To southern overseers to rule -
No more will pilgrims' sons be taunted
With cringing low in slavery's school.
So clear the way for Freedom's car -
The free shall rule! - hurrah, hurrah!
Hurrah, hurrah, hurrah, hurrah!

Send up the shout Emancipation -
From heaven let the echoes bound -
Soon will it bless this franchised nation,
Come raise again the stirring sound:
Emancipation near and far -
Swell up the shout - hurrah! hurrah!
Hurrah, hurrah, hurrah, hurrah!

Free Soil, pp. 171-172; Harp, pp. 45-46; and Freedom,
pp. 171-172.

Liberty, pp. 146-147, as "Emancipation Song," to the same
tune.

269. LIBERTY GLEE

Author: unspecified
Tune: The Pirate's Glee

March on! march on! we love the Liberty flag,
That's waving o'er our land;
As fearless as the eagle soaring
O'er the cloud-capped mountain crag.
Slavery in terror flies before us;
We fling our banner to the blast;
It there shall float triumphant o'er us,
We will defend it to the last.
March on! march on, etc.

Vote on! vote on, we hail the Liberty flag,
That leads us on our way;
We'll boldly vote, our country saving,
And bravely conquer while we may.
The world is up - for freedom moving,
The thunders' distant roar we hear -
From land to land the free are calling,
And slave with joy and rapture hear.
Vote on! vote on, etc.

Free Soil, p. 217. This song also appears in Freedom,
p. 306, as "March On! March On!" to the same tune. Although

the verses following are significantly different from those above, it is considered here to be the same song:

March on! march on, ye friends of freedom for all,
For truth and right contend;
Be ever ready at humanity's call,
Till tyrants' power shall end.
The proud slaveholders rule the nation,
The people's groans are loud and long;
Arouse, ye men, in every station,
And join to crush the power of wrong.
March on! march on, etc.

Fight on! fight on, ye brave, till victory's won
And justice shall prevail;
Till all shall feel the rays of liberty's sun,
Streaming o'er hill and dale.
The tyrants know their guilt and tremble,
The glowing light of truth they fear;
Then let them all their hosts assemble,
And slavery's dreadful sentence hear.
Fight on! fight on, etc.

Roll on! roll on, ye brave, the liberty car,
Our country's name to save;
Soon shall our land be known to nations afar,
As the home of the free and brave.
The voice of free men loud hath spoken,
A brighter day we soon shall see;
When Slavery's chains shall all be broken,
And all the captive millions free.
Roll on! roll on, etc.

270. NEVER GIVE UP

Author: Tupper
Tune: original, by G. W. C.

Never! never give up! it is wiser and better,
Always to hope than once to despair;
Fling off the load of doubt's cankering fetter,
And break the dark spell of tyrannical care:

Never! never give up! or the burden may sink
you.
Providence kindly has mingled the cup,
And in all trials or troubles bethink you,
The watchword of life must be never! never
give up!

Never! never give up! there are chances and
changes,
Helping the hopeful a hundred to one,
And thro' the chaos, high Wisdom arranges
Ever success - if you'll only hope on:
Never! never give up! for the wisest is
boldest,
Knowing that Providence mingles the cup,
And of all maxims the best as the oldest,
Is the true watchword of never! never give up!

Never! never give up! tho' the grapeshot may
rattle,
Or the full thundercloud over you burst,
Stand like a rock, and the storm or the battle
Little shall harm you, tho' doing their worst:
Never! never give up! if adversity presses
Providence wisely has mingled the cup,
And the best counsel in all your distresses
Is the stout watchword of never! never give
up!

Free Soil, pp. 92-94.

271. THE MAN FOR ME

Author: unspecified
Tune: The Rose That All Are Praising

Oh, he is not the man for me,
Who buys or sells a slave,
Nor he who will not set him free,
But sends him to his grave;
But he whose noble heart beats warm
For all men's life and liberty;
Who loves alike each human form -
Oh that's the man for me,
Oh that's the man for me,
Oh that's the man for me.

He's not at all the man for me,
Who sells a man for gain,
Who bends the pliant servile knee,
To Slavery's God of shame!
But he whose God-like form erect
Proclaims that all alike are free
To think, and speak, and vote, and act,
Oh that's the man for me,
Oh that's the man for me,
Oh that's the man for me.

He sure is not the man for me
Whose spirit will succumb,
When men endowed with Liberty
Lie bleeding, bound and dumb;
But he whose faithful words of might
Ring through the land from shore to sea,
For man's eternal equal right,
Oh that's the man for me,
Oh that's the man for me,
Oh that's the man for me.

No, no, he's not the man for me
Whose voice o'er hill and plain,
Breaks forth for glorious liberty,
But binds himself, the chain!
The mightiest of the noble band
Who prays and toils the world to free,
With head, and heart, and voice, and vote -
Oh that's the man for me,
Oh that's the man for me,
Oh that's the man for me.

Free Soil, pp. 121-122; Harp, pp. 33-34; and Freedom,
pp. 121-122.

272. A TRIBUTE TO DEPARTED WORTH

As sung by G. W. C. at the erection of the monument
to the memory of Myron Holley, Mount Hope, Rochester.
It may be sung as a Dirge.*

Author: unspecified
Tune: unidentified

Oh, it is not the tear at this moment shed,
When the cold turf has just been laid o'er
him,
That can tell how beloved was the soul that's
fled,

Or how deep in our hearts we deplore him.
'Tis the tear through many a long day wept,
Through a life by his loss all shaded,
'Tis the sad remembrance fondly kept,
When all other griefs have faded.

Oh! thus shall we mourn, and his memory's
light
While it shines through our hearts will
improve them;
For worth shall look fairer, and truth more
bright,
When we think how he lived but to love them.
And as buried saints the grave perfume,
Where fadeless they've long been lying; -
So our hearts shall borrow a sweetening bloom
From the image he left there in dying.

Liberty, pp. 152-153.

*Holley was instrumental in encouraging the formation of an
abolitionist political party, the Liberty Party, in 1840.

273. THE CHASE

Author: unspecified
Tune: Sweet Afton

Quick, fly to the covert, thou hunted of men!
For the bloodhounds are baying o'er mountain
and glen;
The riders are mounted, the loose rein is
given,
And curses of wrath are ascending to heaven.
0, speed to thy footsteps! for ruin and death,
Like the hurricane's rage, gather thick round
thy path;
And the deep muttered curses grow loud and
more loud,
As horse after horse swells the thundering
crown.

Speed, speed, to thy footsteps! thy track has
been found;
Now, sport for the rider, and blood for the
hound!
Through brake and through forest the man-prey
is driven;
0, help for the hopeless, thou merciful
Heaven!

On! on to the mountain! they're baffled again,
And hope for the woe-stricken still may remain;
The fast-flagging steeds are all white with their foam,
The bloodhounds have turned from the chase to their home.

Joy! joy to the wronged one! the haven he gains,
Escaped from his thraldom, and freed from his chains!
The heaven-stamped image - the God-given soul
No more shall the spoiler at pleasure control.
O, shame to Columbia, that on her bright plains,
Man pines in his fetters, and curses his chains!
Shame! shame! that her star-spangled banner should wave
Where the lash is made red in the blood of the slave.

Sons of old Pilgrim Fathers! and are ye thus dumb?
Shall tyranny triumph, and freedom succumb?
While mothers are torn from their children apart,
And agony sunders the cords of the heart?
Shall the sons of those sires that once spurned the chain,
Turn bloodhounds to hunt and make captive again?
O, shame to your honor, and shame to your pride,
And shame on your memory every abide!

Will not your old sires start up from the ground,
At the crack of the whip, and bay of the hound,
And shaking their skeleton hands in your face,
Curse the germs that produced such a miscreant race?
O, rouse ye for freedom, before on your path
Heaven pours without mixture the vials of wrath!
Loose every hard burden - break off every chain -
Restore to the bondman his freedom again.

Harp, pp. 20-21.

274. WE ARE ALL CHILDREN OF ONE PARENT

Author: unspecified
Tune: unidentified, by L. Mason

Sister, thou art worn and weary,
Toiling for another's gain;
Life with thee is dark and dreary,
Filled with wretchedness and pain.
Thou must rise at dawn of light,
And thy daily task pursue,
Till the darkness of the night
Hide thy labors from thy view.

Oft, alas! thou hast to bear
Sufferings more than tongue can tell;
Thy oppressor will not spare,
But delights thy grief to swell;
Oft thy back the scourge has felt,
Then to God thou'st raised the cry
That the tyrant's heart he'd melt
Ere thou should'st in tortures die.

Injured sister, well we know
That thy lot in life is hard;
Sad thy state of toil and wo,
From all blessedness debarred;
While each sympathizing heart
Pities thy forlorn distress;
We would sweet relief impart,
And delight thy soul to bless.

And what lies within our power
We most cheerfully will do,
That will haste the blissful hour
Fraught with news of joy to you;
And when comes the happy day
That shall free our captive friend,
When Jehovah's mighty sway
Shall to slavery put an end:

Then, dear sister, we with thee
Will to heaven direct our voice;
Joyfully with voices free
We'll in lofty strains rejoice;
Gracious God! thy name we'll bless,
Hallelujah evermore,
Thou hast heard in righteousness,
And our sister's griefs are o'er.

Free Soil, p. 190; and Freedom, p. 190.

275. THERE'S A GOOD TIME COMING

Author: Charles Mackay
Tune: [There's a Good Time Coming]

There's a good time coming boys,
A good time coming,
There's a good time coming boys,
Wait a little longer.
We may not live to see the day,
But earth shall glisten in the ray,
Of the good time coming.
Cannon balls may aid the truth,
But thought's a weapon stronger;
We'll win our battle by its aid -
Wait a little longer. Oh!
There's a good time coming, boys,
A good time coming,
There's a good time coming boys,
Wait a little longer.

There's a good time coming boys,
A good time coming,
There's a good time coming boys,
Wait a little longer.
The pen shall supersede the sword,
And right not might shall be the lord,
In the good time coming.
Worth, not birth, shall rule mankind,
And be acknowledged stronger;
The proper impulse has been given -
Wait a little longer. Oh!
There's a good time, etc.

There's a good time coming boys,
A good time coming,
There's a good time coming boys,
Wait a little longer.
Hateful rivalries of creed,
Shall not make their martyrs bleed,
In the good time coming.
Religion shall be shorn of pride,
And flourish all the stronger;
And charity shall trim her lamp -
Wait a little longer. Oh!
There's a good time, etc.

There's a good time coming boys,
A good time coming,
There's a good time coming boys,
Wait a little longer.

War in all men's eyes shall be
A monster of iniquity,
In the good time coming.
Nations shall not quarrel, then,
To prove which is the stronger;
Nor slaughter men for glory's sake -
Wait a little longer. Oh!
There's a good time, etc.

Harp, pp. 41-42; and Freedom, pp. 72-75.

276. VOICE OF NEW ENGLAND

Author: Whittier
Tune: original, by G. W. C.

Up the hill side, down the glen,
Rouse the sleeping citizen;
Summon out the might of men!
Like a lion growling low,
Like a nightstorm rising slow,
Like the tread of unseen foe.

It is coming - it is nigh!
Stand your homes and altars by;
On your own free threshholds die.
Clang the bells in all your spires;
On the gray hills of your sires
Fling to heaven your signal fires.

Whoso shrinks or falters now,
Whoso to the yoke would bow,
Brand the craven on his brow.
Freedom's soil hath only place
For a free and fearless race -
None for traitors false and base.

Take your land of sun and bloom;
Only leave to Freedom room
For her plough, and forge, and loom.
Take your slavery-blackened vales;
Leave us but our own free gales,
Blowing on our thousand sails.

Onward with your fell design;
Dig the gulf and draw the line;
Fire beneath your feet the mine:
Deeply, when the wide abyss
Yawns between your land and this,
Shall ye feel your helplessness.

By the hearth, and in the bed,
Shaken by a look or tread,
Ye shall own a guilty dread.
And the curse of unpaid toil,
Downward through your generous soil,
Like a fire shall burn and spoil.

Our bleak hills shall bud and blow,
Vines our rocks shall overgrow,
Plenty in our valley flow; -
And when vengeance clouds your skies,
Hither shall ye turn your eyes,
As the damned on Paradise!

We but ask our rocky strand,
Freedom's true and brother band,
Freedom's strong and honest hand,
Valleys by the slave untrod,
And the Pilgrim's mountain sod,
Blessed of our fathers' God!

Free Soil, pp. 117-118; and Freedom, pp. 117-118.

277. WAKE, WAKE, YE FREEMEN ALL!

Author: unspecified
Tune: Lucy Long

Wake, wake, ye freemen all,
'Tis past the breaking dawn;
Rouse ye at freedom's call;
Up with the risen morn;
Come on, come on amain,
Ye stout hearts and ye free,
From mountain, vale, and plain,
From lake, and stream, and sea!
Wake, wake, ye freemen all,
'Tis past the breaking dawn;
Rouse ye at freedom's call;
Up with the risen morn.

Redeem, redeem the land,
Accurs'd with slavery's chain;
Be strong in his right hand,
Whose strength is never vain.
Grasp, grasp with all your might,
The freeman's holy sword,
And let its blade of light,
Leap forth at freedom's word.
Redeem, etc. [repeat first four lines]

Down, down, that banner black,
Polluting freedom's air,
And drive the minions back,
Who come to plant it here!
Lift, lift the ensign white,
In heaven's broad canopy,
And spread its folds of light,
To flash from sea to sea!
Down, etc.

Strike, strike your manhood blow;
Strike sure, and strike it home!
Nor let earth's darkest foe,
Up from the grave-dust come.
Shout, shout the victory!
Earth's joyous realms around;
Till the loud pealing cry,
Back from the skies resound!
Strike, etc.

Free Soil, pp. 71-72; and Freedom, pp. 268-269.

278. THE BRANDED HAND

Author: Whittier
Tune: original, by G. W. C.

Welcome home again, brave seaman!
With thy thoughtful brow and gray,
And the old heroic spirit,
Of our earlier, better day -
With that brow of calm endurance,
On whose steady nerve in vain
Pressed the iron of the prison,
Smote the fiery shafts of pain!

Why, that brand is brightest honor! -
Than its traces never yet
Upon old armorial hatchments
Was a prouder blazon set;
And thy unborn generations,
As they crowd our rocky strand,
Shall tell with pride the story
Of their FATHER'S BRANDED HAND!

As the templar home was welcomed,
Back again from Syrian wars,
The scars of Arab lances,
And of Paynim scimetars,

The pallor of the prison,
And the shackle's crimson span,
So we meet thee, so we greet thee,
Truest friend of God and man!

He suffered for the ransom
Of the dear Redeemer's grave,
Thou for his living presence
In the bound and bleeding slave;
He for a soil no longer
By the feet of angels trod;
Thou for the true Shechina,
The present home of God!

In thy lone and long night watches,
Sky above and wave below,
Thou didst learn a higher wisdom
Than the babbling school men know;
God's stars and silence taught thee,
As his angels only can,
That the one sole, sacred thing
Beneath the cope of heaven is man!

That he, who treads profanely
On the scrolls of law and creed,
In the depths of God's great goodness
May find mercy in his need:
But woe to him that crushes
The soul with chain and rod,
And herds with lower nature,
The awful form of God!

Then lift thy manly right hand,
Bold ploughman of the wave!
Its branded palm shall prophecy
"Salvation to the slave!"
Hold up its fire-wrought language,
That whoso reads may feel
His heart swell strong within him,
His sinews change to steel.

Hold it up before our sunshine,
Up against our Northern air -
Ho! men of Massachusetts,
For the love of God look there!
Take it henceforth for your standard -
Like Bruce's heart of yore,
In the dark strife closing round ye,
Let that hand be seen before!

Free Soil, pp. 200-202; and Freedom, pp. 200-202, with
this note: "Jonathan Walker, a citizen of Massachusetts,
returning from Florida, on the high seas, took on board his
ship, and befriended some poor fugitives escaping from the

horrors of slavery. For this humane act he was imprisoned at
Pensacola, Florida, made to pay a fine, put in the stocks,
pelted with eggs, and at last the letters 'S. S.' branded
into the living flesh of his right hand, with a hot iron.
These lines were addressed to him by Whittier, on his return
home."

279. RIGHT ONWARD WE GO!

Author: unspecified
Tune: original, by G. W. C.

We're afloat! we're afloat! on a fierce
rolling tide,
Freedom is our bark and the Truth is our
guide;
No rest for the sluggard, no peace for the
foe,
But thro' all opposition right onward we go.

The storm gathers round us, the thunder is
heard;
What matter? our bark rideth on like a bird;
With the flag of the Union above our free men,
She has brav'd it before, and will brave it
again.

Far above the dark storm-cloud the clear
sunbeams rest,
And the bright bow of promise gleams forth on
its breast;
Before us a future of labor and love -
Free brethren around us - a just God above.

A future of labor, brave, honest and free -
No monarch, no slaves, but a brotherhood we;
A future of love, when the just and the true
Shall rule in the place of the strong and the
few.

Throw out the broad canvass to catch the free
wind -
Leave old party issues, like rubbish, behind;
With Justice and Love to lead on our van,
Live and die we, for Freedom, for Truth, and
for Man.

Free Soil, pp. 15-16; and Freedom, pp. 280-281.

280. SONG OF WELCOME

Sung at a Welcome Meeting for George Thompson,
Tendered by the Colored Citizens of Boston,
at the Belknap Street Church on November 18.

Author: William Lloyd Garrison
Tune: Auld Lang Syne

Our noble advocate and friend,
Thy presence here we hail!
But, oh! our feelings to express,
The strongest words must fail!
Yet still accept a grateful song -
Our blessings on thee rest -
For thou has pleaded well the cause
Of all who are oppressed.

Thy love of liberty extends
To every race and clime;
Thy hatred of oppression burns
To the remotest time:
In thee the slave a champion finds,
Intrepid, faithful, strong,
Though scorn and wrath assail thy course,
And perils round thee throng.

While traffickers in human flesh
Their teeth upon thee gnash;
While for thy precious life they hunt
Who wield the gory lash;
While thine abettors here conspire
To howl and mob thee down;
Thou need'st no higher meed of praise -
Can'st wear no brighter crown!

All noble spirits of the past -
Saints, martyrs, heroes true -
All of the present, loving God
And man, the wide earth through -
Are with thee in this trial-hour,
To strengthen and applaud -
And angel-voices cheer thee on,
In th' name of Christ, our Lord!

The ransomed bondmen of the isles
Thy name shall shout with pride;
And India's plundered millions bless
Their champion true and tried;

And England's crushed and toiling poor, -
Columbia's fettered race, -
Thy memory ever shall revere,
Thy brow with laurels grace.

Once more we greet thee with delight,
Remembering "auld lang syne,"
And pray kind Heaven may richly smile,
Through life, on thee and thine!
We offer thee a grateful song -
Our blessings on thee rest -
For thou hast pleaded well the cause
Of all who are oppressed!

Liberator, November 29, 1850, p. 189.

281. SONG OF WELCOME

Written for and sung at the appearance of
George Thompson at Hopedale Community.

Author: Mrs. A. H. Price
Tune: unspecified

From our Fatherland afar,
O'er the deep and foamy sea,
Welcome Freedom's radiant star,
Thou of heart and spirit free.
Joyfully! joyfully!
Friends of Freedom all are we;
Heart and hand we give to thee,
Welcome, welcome, joyfully!

From the proud and gilded halls,
Where the titled great do stand,
Welcome to these humble walls,
From a glad and happy band.
Joyfully, etc.

We've no pearls to deck thy brow,
Laurels none so green as thine;
But our love shall crown thee now,
Meekly with thy gems to shine.
Joyfully, etc.

Brothers both we gladly meet;
From this time new hopes shall spring;
We will hold communion sweet,
While our songs of welcome ring.
Joyfully, etc.

May devotion now revive,
Zeal grow brighter from this hour;
We new hope and faith derive
From your presence and your power.
Joyfully! joyfully!
Friends of Freedom all are we;
Heart and hand we give to you,
Friends of Freedom ever true.

Liberator, February 14, 1851, p. 26.

282. A WELCOME TO GEORGE THOMPSON

Sung at a meeting held in Hopedale on
Sunday last - Mr. T. being present.

Author: E. D. Draper
Tune: unspecified

We joyfully welcome our brother so dear,
Him with a spirit so free,
A friend to the poor, be they distant or near
Thanks for his company!
This wide world hath some who will toil for
the right,
Whose pathway is gilt with a halo of light;
Long may they live,
Blessings to give,
Joy to the darkness of night!

We heard the deep tone of his clarion voice
Come o'er the broad ocean wave;
Its silvery notes made the bondmen rejoice,
And the minions of tyranny rave;
Affrighted they fled as he came to our shore,
And uttered their yells with a terrible roar:
Faneuil Hall
Gathered them all,
And yielded to demons her floor.

O shame! that the Cradle young Liberty loved
Did nurture that serpent-like brood,
That the shadows of brave men whom trial had
proved,
To witness such revelry stood!
Poor Freedom! the stars on her banner grow
dim,
And fainter, and fainter, her rich swelling
hymn;

Then summoned her band
To holier land,
And Worcester gave welcome to him.

Glad anthems now peal from her glorious lyre,
To welcome this Champion brave;
They rise o'er the mountain tops, higher and
higher,
All full of the joy of the slave.
She crowns with new trophies her weather-beat
son,
The blessings and laurels his valor hath won;
Mighty his power
To hasten the hour
Of the good time that now hath begun.

Liberator, February 14, 1851, p. 28.

283. THE DAY OF PROMISE COMES

Sung by the Hutchinson Family at a
Woman's [Rights] Convention in Akron.

Author: unspecified
Tune: unidentified

Behold the day of promise comes full of
inspiration,
The glorious day by prophets sung for the
healing of the nations.
Old midnight errors flee away, they son will
all be gone,
While heavenly voices seem to say the Good
Time's coming on.
The good time, the good time, the good time's
coming on.
The good time, the good time, the good time's
coming on.

Already in the golden east the glorious light
is dawning,
And watchmen from the mountain tops can see
the blessed morning,
O'er all the land their voices ring, while yet
the world is slumb'ring,
And e'en the sluggard begins to spring, as he
hears the thunders rumbling.
The good time, etc.

The captive now begins to rise and burst his
chains asunder.
While politicians stand aghast in anxious fear
and wonder,
No longer shall the bondman sigh beneath the
galling fetters,
He sees the dawn of freedom nigh, and reads
the golden letters.
The good time, etc.

And all the old distilleries shall perish and
burn together.
The brandy, rum, and gin, and wine, and all
such whatsoever.
The world begins to feel the fire, and e'en
the poor besotter,
To save himself from burning up, jumps in the
cooling water.
The good time, etc.

Liberator, June 13, 1851, p. 96; Freedom, pp. 14-16.

284. ALL THINGS SPEAK

Author: Joshua Simpson
Tune: All is Well

Hark! Hark! A voice! A voice is loudly
sounding -
Free the slave - Free the slave!
Sweet freedom's voice - O'er hill and dale
resounding -
Free the slave - Free the slave!
All nature shrinks the lash to hear -
The crimson dye - the groans and tears
All speak in accents loud and clear
Free the slave - Free the slave!

Slack! slack your hands! ye tyrants cease your
folly;
Free the slave - free the slave!
Your brother's blood cries to the Lord Most
holy
Free the slave - free the slave!
Your land is smitten with disgrace -
Your laws are rigid, vile and base,
And conscience speaks from every breast
Free the slave - free the slave!

Call back those hounds! O! let their beys no
longer
Grieve the slave - grieve the slave!
Let not your horns in dismal tones of thunder
Grieve the slave - grieve the slave!
Your fetters break - your bondman free;
And let the song of "Liberty"
Re-echo o'er the land and sea;
Free the slave - free the slave!

Behold your banner gently, gently floating
O'er the slave - o'er the slave!
Your Eagle spreads his golden wings exulting
O'er the slave - o'er the slave!
Three million slaves are in his grasp,
And millions more he longs to clasp
But God forbid his power shall last.
Free the slave - free the slave!

Heralds go forth. And may success attend you.
Free the slave - free the slave!
And may the God of Righteousness defend you.
Free the slave - free the slave!
Put on your Armor - make it bright,
And draw the bow with holy might
And speed the arrows in their flight.
Free the slave! free the slave!

Original, pp. 8-9; and Car, pp. 22-23.

285. FREEDOM'S CAUSE

Author: Joshua Simpson
Tune: We Won't Give Up the Bible

Our cause is just and holy -
To it we'll ever stand:
Our right to life and liberty -
Is all that we demand.
Our sword is truth - our shield is love -
Our best plea faith and prayer -
Our armour is the fear of God,
And we the foe will dare:
Our cause is just and holy,
To it we'll ever stand.

Our cause is just and holy;
And backed by power divine;
To trust in God's own sacred word
Our hearts are well inclined,

And it shall be our pride and boast
To sink the gospel truth
Into the hearts of all our foes -
The aged and the youth,
Our cause is just and holy,
To it we'll ever stand.

Our cause is just and holy -
Our country's good at stake:
We wish to pull down Tyranny
And laws of justice make:
And this we fancy not to do
By shedding human blood;
Our veins shall never drain to make
A mighty crimson flood,
Our cause is just and holy;
To it we'll ever stand.

Our cause is just and holy -
We feel it in our veins;
For Jesus came all men to save
From misery, sin, and chains:
His blood ran free on Calvary
For every human soul
From Palestine to Africa -
It saves from poll to poll.
Our cause is just and holy
To it we'll ever stand.

Our cause is just and holy,
And we are not ashamed
To sing it on the Mountain tops,
And sound it o'er the main,
That we are friends of Liberty
That attribute of love -
As God created all men free,
We freedom's cause, will move.
Our cause is just and holy
To it we'll ever stand.

Our cause is just and holy,
For it we'll ever pray,
Although we may not see the good
We do till Judgment day.
We'll plead our cause where e'er we go;
Till all mankind shall see;
And Slavery's friends shall feel and own
That God made all men free.
Our cause is just and holy
To it we'll ever stand.

Original, pp. 5-6; and Car, pp. 11-13.

286. THE CAUSE OF LIBERTY

Author: unspecified
Tune: I See Them on Their Winding Way

Tell us no more of Slavery's power,
'Tis weakness when compared with ours!
'Tis Satan's power condemned to die -
Freedom is strengthened from on high.
Tyrants now quail, their courage fails,
But ours, inspired by Heaven, prevails;
Thrice armed are we in righteousness,
And this our foes themselves confess.
The onward, onward, onward still!
See how our ranks with freemen fill!
Soon o'er the world will all men see
Triumphant, glorious Liberty.

For years have freemen bravely stood,
And breasted Persecution's flood;
With justice armed, they've kept the field,
No threats or flattery made them yield.
Their flag so fair, still floats in air,
And, mark! next year 'twill still be there,
Inscribed in letters bold and free,
With one great idea - LIBERTY!
Then sound it, sound it, sound it strong!
That FREEDOM'S RIGHT - that SLAVERY'S WRONG!
And soon this truth will all men see,
And shout for GLORIOUS LIBERTY!

Liberator, August 5, 1853, p. 124.

287. THE TRUE SPIRIT

Author: Joshua Simpson
Tune: Roll on the Liberty Bell [Ball]
[Rosin the Bow; see song 166]

Come all ye true friends of your Nation,
Awake from stupidity's grave,
Come join in your country's salvation,
And free the American slave.

Come all of you half hearted freemen,
Your honesty now is at stake,
While over the slave you are dreaming,
Your government's standard will break.

We wish not to sever the Union,
But rather in love to unite;
We hold not from our communion,
No man who will strive to do right.

We loathe the bare name of man-stealing,
And all who will aid in its cause,
And we are intent on repealing
That outrageous Fugitive Law.

We'll sacrifice time and our money,
And life, too, if it is required,
While the blood of our brethren is running
We'll flinch not nor ever grow tired.

Car, pp. 86-87.

288. THE VOICE OF SIX HUNDRED THOUSAND,
           NOMINALLY FREE

Author: Joshua Simpson
Tune: Marseilles Hymn

Come, friends, awake! The day is dawning,
'Tis time that we were in the field;
Shake off your fears and cease your yawning,
And buckle on your sword and shield,
And buckle on your sword and shield,
The enemy is now advancing.
The Tyrant-Host is great and strong;
But ah, their reign will not be long,
We shrink not at their war-steeds prancing.
Stand up, stand up my boys,
The battle field is ours;
Fight on! Fight on! all hearts resolved,
To break the Tyrant's power.

The men of God have quite deserted
The battle-field and gone their way;
The world will never be converted,
While tyrants bear despotic sway;
While tyrants bear despotic sway;
The infidels are quite astounded,
And Atheists do speechless stand,
To see God's image wear the brand,
While with God's word, they thus surrounded.
Stand up! Stand up! my braves,
The army ne'er forsake;
March on! March on! all hearts resolved,
The tyrant's power to break.

We boast not of our might in number;
Our weapons are not carnal steel;
The weight of arms does not encumber
Our progress in the battle field;
Our progress in the battle field;
But truth, the mighty arm of power,
Shall smite the great Goliath down,
And pluck from Monarch's head the crown
Which o'er our race has long been towering.
Be brave! Be brave my boys!
The battle ne'er give o'er.
March on! March on! all hearts resolved,
To leave the ranks no more.

'Tis true that we are few in number,
And yet, those few are brave and strong,
Like Athens' mighty sons of thunder,
Upon the plains of Marathon;
Upon the plains of Marathon.
With courage bold, we'll take our station,
Against the mighty host of whites,
And plead like men for equal rights,
And thus exalt our fallen Nation.
"To arms! To arms! my braves,"
The sword of truth unsheath.
March on! March on! all hearts resolved,
On Liberty or death.

Car, pp. 27-29.

289. AND THE DAYS OF THY MOURNING SHALL BE ENDED

Author: [E. L. Follen?]
Tune: Missionary Hymn

Lift up a voice of gladness,
Ye lowly waiting throng!
O, dry your tears of sadness,
And raise a cheerful song!

Hope on! A glorious morrow
Your aching hearts shall see;
And quench their burning sorrow
In freedom's jubilee.

The word of doom is spoken.
Your chains are loosening fast.
Ere long, they shall be broken;
And Justice reign at last.

Nation to nation calling,
Cries - liberty for all!
The tyrant's power is falling,
Is quailing at that call.

From mountain back to mountain,
Its echoes shall be heard;
And maidens at the fountain
Shall pass the holy word.

O'er mighty lake and river
Shall go the great decree,
The tyrant's chain to sever,
And set the captive free.

O'er many a flowery prairie,
Like breath from Heaven, it sighs;
And bids the sad and weary
Lift up their tearful eyes.

Ocean and ocean swelling,
With loud exulting waves,
The joyful word is telling -
There shall be no more slaves.

Tracts, pp. 5-6.

290. HYMN

To be sung at the erection of the
Monument on the grave of Asa R. Wing.

Author: Rev. John Pierpont
Tune: [America?]

Over thy grassy grave,
Friend of the hunted slave,
This pile we rear;
In an unfaltering trust,
That future time, more just,
Will reverence the dust
Reposing here.

Thy cross was bravely borne,
The martyr-crown was worn
Without a sigh;
Thy pitying tears have gushed
For the enslaved sand crushed,
And when thy voice was hushed,
Calm could'st thou die.

Peace to thy resting-place,
Friend of a hated race,
Hated and wronged;
Thy praise, here little known,
By angel trumpets blown
Round the Eternal throne,
Shall be prolonged.

<u>Liberator</u>, August 24, 1855, p. 136.

291. THE GATHERING

Author: unspecified
Tune: Hunter's Chorus

From hill and from valley
They eagerly sally,
Like billows of Ocean,
The MASS is in motion -
The lines are extending
O'er mountain and plain;
Like torrents descending,
They hurry amain.
The Gathering! The Gathering!
We'll be there! we'll be there!
The Gathering! The Gathering!
We'll be there! we'll be there!
There! there! there!

Each eye flashes brightly,
Each bosom beats lightly -
The banners are glancing,
And merrily dancing,
While proudly the standard
Of Liberty floats,
And the music is swelling
Inspiring notes.
The Victory! The Victory!
That we'll gain! that we'll gain!
The Victory! The Victory!
That we'll gain! that we'll gain!
Gain! gain! gain!

Again we assemble -
The traitor shall tremble!
For strong as the ocean,
A people in motion!
THE IDES OF NOVEMBER,
The day of his doom,

He long shall remember
In silence and gloom.
He long shall remember
In silence and gloom.
The Traitor! The Traitor!
He shall fall! he shall fall!
The Traitor! The Traitor!
He shall fall! he shall fall!
FALL! FALL! FALL!

Freedom, pp. 309-310.

292. CLEAR THE WAY

Author: Charles Mackay
Tune: original, by G. W. C.

Men of thought be up and stirring,
Night and day, night and day!
Sow the seed, withdraw the curtain -
Clear the way, clear the way!
Men of action, aid and cheer them,
As ye may, as ye may!
There's a fount about to stream,
There's a light about to beam,
There's a warmth about to glow,
There's a flower about to blow;
There's a midnight blackness changing
Into gray, into gray!
Men of thought, and men of action
CLEAR THE WAY, CLEAR THE WAY.

Once the welcome light has broken,
Who shall say, who shall say,
What the unimagined glories -
Of the day? Of the day?
What the evil that shall perish
In its ray? In its ray!
Aid the dawning tongue and pen,
Aid it hopes of honest men;
Aid it paper, aid it type -
Aid it for the hour is ripe,
And our earnest must not slacken,
Into play, into play;
Men of thought, and men of action
CLEAR THE WAY, CLEAR THE WAY.

Lo! a cloud's about to vanish,
From the day, from the day;
And a brazen wrong to crumble,
Into clay, into clay.
Lo! the right's about to conquer,
CLEAR THE WAY, CLEAR THE WAY.
With that right shall many more
Enter, smiling, at the door;
With the giant wrong shall fall
Many others great and small,
That for ages long have held us
For their prey, for their prey;
Men of thought, and men of action
CLEAR THE WAY, CLEAR THE WAY.

Freedom, pp. 6-9.

293. THE JOYS OF FREEDOM

Author: unspecified
Tune: unidentified

Merrily every bosom boundeth,
Merrily O! merrily O!
Where the song of freedom soundeth,
Merrily O! merrily O!
There the parents' smile hath more brightness,
There the youthful heart hath more lightness,
Every joy the home surroundeth,
Merrily O! merrily O!
Merrily, merrily, merrily O!
Merrily O! merrily O!

Wearily every bosom pineth,
Wearily O! wearily O!
Where the chains of slavery bindeth,
Wearily O! wearily O!
There the parents' smile yields to sadness,
There the youthful heart hath no gladness,
Every flower of life declineth,
Wearily O! wearily O!
Wearily, wearily, wearily O!
Wearily O! wearily O!

Cheerily then awake the chorus,
Cheerily O! cheerily O!
Liberty and peace before us,
Cheerily O! cheerily O!
Now the parents' smile beams the dearest,
Now the parents' hopes are the clearest,

Every joy is now before us,
Cheerily O! cheerily O!
Cheerily, cheerily, cheerily O!
Cheerily O! cheerily O!

Freedom, pp. 57-59.

294. THE DAY BREAKETH

Author: Horatio
Tune: Bavaria

On the earth the day is dawning;
Lovely beams a rising star;
Prisoner, greet a glorious morning -
Hail the day-spring from afar!

Tyrants now are seized with trembling,
While they madly urge the war;
Dark and serried hosts assembling,
Blindly drag their bloody car.

'Tis their last, their fated hour,
For their reign of blood shall cease;
Sinks and dies their waving power -
Soon shall reign the King of peace.
[See end of this section.]

Freedom, p. 313.

295. ONE HUNDRED YEARS HENCE

Author: [G. W. C.?]
("Words altered and adapted from the Hutchinsons")
Tune: original, by G. W. C.

One hundred years hence what a change will be
made,
In politics, morals, religion and trade,
In statesmen who wrangle and ride on the
fence,
These things shall be altered one hundred
years hence,
One hundred years hence -
These things shall be altered one hundred
years hence.

Our laws then will be just and equitous rules,
Our prisons, converted to national schools;
The pleasures of sinning - 'tis all a
pretence,
And the people will find it so a hundred years
hence,
A hundred years hence -
The people will find it so a hundred years
hence.

Oppression and war shall be heard of no more,
Nor the foot of a slave, leave its print on
our shore;
Conventions will then be a needless expense,
For mankind shall be brothers a hundred years
hence,
A hundred years hence -
For mankind shall be brothers a hundred years
hence.

Instead of speech making to justify wrong,
All shall join in the chorus swelling
freedom's glad song;
The Maine Law shall then be a temperance
defense,
We'll keep time to that music a hundred years
hence,
A hundred years hence -
We'll keep time to that music a hundred years
hence.

Lying, cheating and fraud, shall be laid on
the shelf,
Men will neither get drunk or be wrapt up in
self;
But all live together as neighbors and
friends,
Just as good people ought to one hundred years
hence,
One hundred years hence -
Just as good people ought to one hundred years
hence.

Then Woman man's equal a partner shall stand,
And beauty and harmony govern the land;
To think for one's self shall not be an
offence,
For the world will be thinking a hundred years
hence,
A hundred years hence -
For the world will be thinking a hundred years
hence.

Freedom, pp. 31-32.

296. TILL THE LAST CHAIN IS BROKEN

Author: unspecified
Tune: The Last Link is Broken

Till the last chain is broken
That galls the poor slave,
Let us ne'er boast of freedom,
And the "land of the brave;"
For where is our justice?
And our bravery?
If the slave we ne'er pity,
And render him free.
CHORUS:
May each fellow being
Be free as the wave,
And the fair rays of freedom
Enlighten the slave;
Then shall the glad story
Be borne o'er the sea,
And tell - to our glory -
COLUMBIA IS FREE,
Then shall the glad story
Be borne o'er the sea,
And tell - to our glory -
COLUMBIA IS FREE!

The slave's cry is unheeded,
His deep groans are spurned,
But a lesson of vengeance
May shortly be learned;
For God, who views justly
Each deed we have done,
May ne'er spurn with contempt,
The poor, injured one.
CHORUS

Then up to the effort!
Endeavor to save,
From soul-galling bondage,
The down-trodden slave;
Afford him the pleasures
Designed by his Lord,
And the richest of treasures
Shall be thy reward.
CHORUS

When the last chain is broken
That galls the poor slave,
Then the words shall be spoken,
"The land of the brave";

For then we'll have freedom,
And <u>true</u> bravery,
When the poor slave we've pitied
And rendered him free.

<u>Freedom</u>, pp. 20-23.

297. WE LONG TO SEE THAT HAPPY TIME

Author: unspecified
Tune: Hebron

We long to see that happy time,
That dear, expected, blissful day,
When countless myriads of our race
The glorious gospel shall obey.

The prophecies must be fulfilled,
Though earth and hell should dare oppose:
The stone cut from the mountain's side,
Though unobserv'd, to empire grows.

Afric's emancipated sons
Shall shout to Asia's rapturing song -
Europe resound her Saviour's fame,
And Western climes the notes prolong.

From east to west, from north to south,
Immanuel's kingdom must extend;
And every man, in every face,
SHALL MEET A BROTHER AND A FRIEND!

<u>Freedom</u>, pp. 313-314.

298. UP, LAGGARDS OF FREEDOM

Author: Whittier
Tune: Campbells are Coming

Whoso loves not his kind, and fears not the
Lord,
Let him join that foe's service, accurs'd and
abhorr'd!

Let him do his base will, as the slave only
can -
Let him put on the bloodhound, and put off the
Man!

Let him go where the cold blood that creeps in
his veins
Shall stiffen the slave-whip, and rust on his
chains -
Where the black slave shall laugh in his
bonds, to behold
The white slave beside him, self-fettered and
sold!

But ye, who still boast of hearts beating and
warm,
Rise, from lake, shore, and ocean, like waves
in a storm!
Come, throng round our banner in Liberty's
name,
Like winds from your mountains, like prairies
a-flame!

Our foe, hidden long in his ambush of night,
Now, forced from his covert, stands black in
the light.
Oh, the cruel to Man, and the hateful to God,
Smite him down to the earth, that is curs'd
where he trod!

For deeper than thunder of Summer's loud
shower,
On the dome of the sky God is striking the
hour!
Shall we falter before what we've prayed for
so long,
When the Wrong is so weak, and the Right is so
strong?

Come forth, altogether! - come old and come
young -
Freedom's vote in each hand, and her song on
each tongue;
Truth naked is stronger than Falsehood in mail
The Wrong cannot prosper, the Right cannot
fail!

Like leaves of the Summer once numbered the
foe,
But the hoar-frost is falling, the Northern
winds blow;
Like leaves of November, ere long shall they
fall,
For Earth wearies of them, and God's over all!

Freedom, p. 309.

299. THE BREAKING DAWN

Author: [J. H. Hidley?]
Tune: [original?], by C. M. Traver

With joy we see the breaking morn
Now glimm'ring thro' the misty gloom
Whose bright unclouded sun shall light
Earth's haughty tyrants to their doom.
CHORUS:
Then hail the dawn so bright and clear,
The dawn of the good time coming! coming!
coming!
When Freedom's foes shall quake with fear
At the dawn of the good time coming,
Then hail to the glorious dawn,
Then hail to the glorious dawn,
Then hail to the dawn of the good time coming,
coming, coming,
The dawn of the good time coming.

O! 'twas a glorious morning when
O'er this fair land shone Freedom's sun;
But brighter far will be the day
Whose breaking morn is now begun.
CHORUS

For then shall Freedom's banner wave,
Beyond Columbia's blood-bought shore;
And Freedom's Star, with brilliant ray,
Undimm'd shine on for evermore.
CHORUS

Then sound the tocsin loud and long,
Through ev'ry land, o'er isle and sea;
And let its echoing strains proclaim
The Earth is only for the Free.
CHORUS

Freedom, pp. 9-12.

300. FREEDOM'S CALL

Author: C. C. Burleigh
Tune: Hail to the Chief

Hark to the trumpet-call, bidding us rally,
Friends of humanity, lovers of right,
Down from the mountain come, up from the
valley,
Clad in the harness of Liberty's fight;
Come from the prairie wide,
Lake-shore and river-side,
Clearings that lie in the dim forest shade,
Inland and ocean-strand
Come, joining heart and hand,
Freedom, imperilled, is calling for aid.

Not with the weapons of murderous battle,
Squadrons arrayed for the death-dealing
strife,
Thunder of cannon, and musketry's rattle,
Mangling of bodies and wasting of life;
Not with such enginery
Fight we for Liberty,
But with the power of the heart-swaying WORD;
Right is our panoply,
Love our artillery,
Soul-piercing Truth is our two-edged sword.

Vainly the tyrant shall frown his defiance,
Vainly redouble the chains of his slave,
God and his Truth are our steadfast reliance,
Press we right onward, the bondman to save.
Long hath his bitter wail
Loaded the Southern gale,
Long hath his blood cried for vengeance to
God;
Light of his spirit dim,
Fetters on soul and limb,
Long hath he bowed under Tyranny's rod.

On to his rescue! the day-star has risen,
Morning is dawning on Slavery's night,
Burst we asunder the bars of his prison,
Lead him abroad into Liberty's light;
Then in the fulness of
Gratitude, joy and love,

Bend we to Him who the victory gave,
Vowing that, never more,
All our wide country o'er,
Room shall be found for a tyrant or slave.

Liberator, July 9, 1858, p. 112.

301. THE IRREPRESSIBLE CONFLICT

Sung by the Hutchinson Family at an
Anti-Slavery Convention in Cummington.

Author: George W. Putnam
Tune: unspecified

Ridden by the Slave Power,
Crushed beneath the chain,
Now is come our rising hour,
Lo! we're up again.
And voices from the mountain height,
Voices from the vale,
Say to Freedom's fearless host,
There's no such word as fail!

Aye! we are up to hurl the fiend
From off the tyrant throne;
To strike for man a mightier blow
Than earth hath ever known;
To drag your code of whips and gyves
Up to the light of day,
And wash from our escutcheon's front
The bloody stain away.

Free to speak the burning truth,
All fetterless the hand,
Never shall the Yankee's brow
Bear the cursed brand.
Send the gathering freemen's shout
Booming on the gale;
Omnipotence is for us, -
There's no such word as fail!

They're gathering on the mountain,
They're gathering on the plain;
And 'neath the tramp of Freedom's host,
The broad earth shakes again.

And this their glorious rallying-cry,
Whose firm hearts never quail:
God and the people! on for right, -
There's no such word as fail!

Liberator, December 9, 1859, p. 196.

302. THE PROSPECT

Author: Justitia
Tune: What Fairy Like Music

Weep no longer, ye captives, your redemption
is near!
Every day brings some tidings your spirits to
cheer;
While men's hearts are full of the spirit of
fight,
Out of all this gross darkness God will bring
to you light.

Ye who've toiled long as bondmen, in sorrow
and pain,
Trodden down by your masters - made vassals
for gain -
Shall ere long be delivered, for God doth
decree
That the black and the white shall be all
alike free.

Though the great men of earth may unite all
their skill
To cover up Justice, and Truth's voice to
still,
In a moment unlooked for shall a voice come
from heaven,
Saying, "Strike off the fetters - let freedom
be given."

How cheering the prospect which breaks on the
view,
When our country no more shall be ruled by the
few;
When all men as brothers acknowledged shall
be,
And our land be "the home of the brave and the
free!"

Dry your tears, then, ye captives, and lift up
your head,
Freedom's hosts are uprising, filling tyrants
with dread;
Soon your chains shall be riven, your shouts
rend the air,
And God be acknowledged the hearer of prayer.

A "good time is coming" - have patience to
wait -
God shall raise up the fallen, and humble the
great;
His will shall on earth as in heaven be done,
And slavery no more shall be known 'neath the
sun.

Liberator, September 20, 1861, p. 152.

303. [UNTITLED]

Author: unspecified
Tune: Marseilles Hymn

Ye fettered slaves! awake to glory!
Hark! hark! what myriads bid you rise!
Your children, wives, and grandsires hoary,
Behold their tears and hear their cries!
To arms, to arms, ye brave!
The patriot sword unsheath!
March on, march on, all hearts resolved
On liberty or death!

Liberator, January 24, 1862, p. 15.

304. [UNTITLED]

Sung at a celebration of August 1 at Abington.

Author: unspecified
Tune: unspecified

Strike grandly, in this hour sublime,
A blow to ring through endless time!
Strike! for the listening ages wait!
Emancipate! Emancipate!

Liberator, August 8, 1862, p. 127.

305. LINES IN HONOR OF GEORGE THOMPSON

Author: Caroline A. Robbins
Tune: Hail to the Chief

Press forward to hear him, the eloquent
stranger
Who comes from the shores of Old England
tonight;
Through life he has been holy Freedom's
avenger,
For God and the slave ever ready to fight.
Come, then, brave pioneers,
Freedom's true warriors!
Listen and learn from the lips that you love,
What this brave man has done,
How he has fought and won
The battle of Truth, led by powers above.

He heard the base slanders by rebel chiefs
spoken
Against Northern freemen, this land to
enslave;
He roused like a lion; the chains he has
broken
Around the true hearts of his countrymen
brave.
Come, all ye Northern men,
From every mount and glen,
Make the air ring with your shouts of delight;
Each heart be true as steel.
For your loved country's weal
Thompson has fought; go, and hear him
to-night!

Come, Women, Great Britain has sent us a
champion
As bold and as kind as a chivalry knight;
You could not select from the old Roman
Pantheon
A hero more grand or more true to the right.
Come, daughters of freedom, then,
Welcome him back again,
To the land where he suffered in Freedom's
dark hour;
The joy which you manifest
Shall erase from his noble breast
The deeds that were done by despots in power.

Twine a garland of olive, of bay, and of
myrtle,
The symbols of Peace, highest Honor and Love!
Round this patriot's brows you then may
encircle
A tribute he'll prize many honors above.
Come, hear our brother brave!
Our land he's tried to save;
Flinging behind him the favor and frown
Of wealth, birth and station, he
On the altar of liberty
All that self values has nobly laid down.

<u>Liberator</u>, April 22, 1864, p. 68.

Three additional verses to song 294 were discovered in the
final stages of editing. They are:

Ho! ye royal hosts of Freedom -
Strong of heart, and truly brave;
See your brethren, chained and bleeding -
Fly on lightning's wing to save!

Grasp the bolt of slavery's thunder -
Hurl them [sic] back along the sky:
Break their bars and bolts asunder -
Boldly do, or bravely die!

On the earth the light is dawning;
Lovely beams the rising sun;
Prisoner, greet the glorious morning -
Soon we'll shout, "The day is won!"

GONE, SOLD AND GONE

> Gone, gone - sold and gone,
> To the rice-swamp dank and lone,
> From Virginia's hills and waters, -
> Woe is me my stolen daughters!

Although there are in these lyrics hints of all the arguments against slavery examined thus far, they are distinguishable for one central premise: the humanity of the slaves. Here the abolitionists are at their most empathetic as well as sympathetic with the plight of the slaves, and here too is seen the influence of black abolitionists operating alongside the imagination of the white, for these songs describe the inhumane aspects of slavery from not only the observer's perspective but also that of slaves themselves. While occasional references to slavery as an abstract sin against both Christian and American ideals remain, then, these retreat into the background against the reality of the auction, the division of families, and the general atmosphere of prejudice and racism faced by black Americans, free or slave (for the latter, an interesting example is song 308, written from the point of view of the black children at Prudence Crandall's controversial school).

Several sets of lyrics, for example, refer to the inconsistency perceived between Christianity and slavery, as in the cry of "The Fugitive Slave to the Christian": "O Christian will you send me back?" (325; see also 310, 328, 338, 356, and 359). Similarly, there occasionally appear the now typical allusions to American liberty (340, 349, 363). Most prominent, however, is the message that blacks, because they are human, suffer under slavery (the songs that ask "Am I Not a Man and Brother?" [337] and "Am I Not a Sister?" [338] are typically direct in their approach).

These lyrics are all the more significant in that it is less the obvious brutality possible under the system - beatings, whippings, and harsh and unremitting labor - than the actual and always imminent separation of families that forms the basis of their appeal. Listeners are told not just to look upon scenes of family members being sold away from one another (as in 320, 322, or the title song, 343), but to place themselves in the scene, with their own emotions, and imagine their responses as those of the slaves ("Was ever infant from thee torn and sold before thine eyes?" asks song 334 of mothers). Thus it is that the contemporaty "cult" of family and children, and the attendant sentimentality, intersect so nicely with antislavery purposes, to the possible advantage and further development of all three simultaneously. Thus it is too that the "Appeal to Woman" (354) is as often implicit as it is that explicit (and it is notable that nearly half of all such appeals are in this section), reminding us of the important roles of women in abolition and, conversely, of abolition in American women's ultimate demands for equality.

Finally, this group is of special interest due to the attention given fugitives generally and the "underground railroad" specifically, again often from the point of view of the slaves. In this case, there seems to be a progression from the relatively disinterested accounts of "The Flying Slave" (321) and "The Fugitive" (327) as early as 1844 and 1845, respectively, to increasingly more personalized and vivid descriptions by 1848 (341, 342). Once the Fugitive Slave Law passed Congress in 1850, the poets, it seems, saw no reason to restrain either the outrage they shared with many Northerners or the impulse to "advertise" the fact that many were willing to help escapees in direct defiance of the federal government. In this context, the twenty-three songs of Joshua Simpson in this section, eleven of which concern fugitives and/or the underground railroad (364-368, 373, 375-377, 382, 383) are potentially important primary sources, as he most likely was one of the many "conductors" of the railroad in Ohio.

306. NEGRO'S COMPLAINT

Author: unspecified
Tune: Isle of Beauty

Forced from home and all its pleasures,
Afric's coast I left forlorn;
To increase a stranger's treasures,
O'er the raging billows borne.
Christian people bought and sold me,
Paid my price in paltry gold:
But though slave they have enrolled me,
Minds are never to be sold.

Still in thought as free as ever,
What are Freedom's rights, I ask,
Me from my delights to sever,
Me to torture, me to task?
Fleecy locks and dark complexion,
Cannot forfeit Nature's claim;
Skins may differ, but affection
Dwells in white and black the same.

Deem our nation brutes no longer,
Till some reason ye shall find,
Worthier of regard and stronger
Than the color of our kind.
Slaves of gold! whose sordid dealings
Tarnish all tour boasted powers;
Prove that you have human feelings,
Ere you proudly question ours.

Liberator, March 19, 1831, p. 46.

Free Soil, pp. 46-47; and Freedom, pp. 246-247, as "The
Negro's Appeal," to the same tune, with these additional
verses in place of verse two:

Is there, as ye sometimes tell me,
Is there one who reigns on high?
Has he bid you buy and sell me,
Speaking from his throne - the sky?
Ask him, if your knotted scourges,
Matches, blood-extorting screws,
Are the means that duty urges
Agents of his will to use.

Hark! he answers - wild tornadoes,
Strewing yonder sea with wrecks,
Wasting towns, plantations, meadows,
Are the voice with which he speaks.

He, forseeing what vexations
Afric's sons should undergo,
Fixed their tyrant's habitations,
Where his whirlwinds answer - No!

By our blood in Afric' wasted,
Ere our necks received the chain;
By the miseries that we tasted,
Crossing in your barks the main:
By our sufferings, since ye brought us
To the man-degrading mart,
All sustained by patience, taught us
Only by a broken heart -

307. SONG, SUPPOSED TO BE SUNG BY SLAVES
       IN INSURRECTION

       Author: William J. Snelling
          Tune: unspecified

See, tyrants, see; your empire shakes;
Your flaming roofs the wild winds fan;
Stung to the soul, the negro wakes:
He slept, a brute - he wakes, a man!
His shackles fall;
Erect and tall,
He glories in his new found might,
And wins with bloody hand his right.

Just Heaven, and can it be, - the strong,
With mind to think and heart to feel,
Has borne upon his neck so long
A weak as cruel tyrant's heel;
When one brave stroke
Had burst his yoke!
Day dawns at last on mental night,
And Sampson girds him for the fight.

The land is ours - our fathers' blood
Free spilled, our own, manures the soil,
Who gave us evil for our good,
And paid with stripes our sweat and toil.
'Twas he, the foe -
Now, blow for blow:
Remember that the heavy debt
Of ages is to cancel yet.

Where's he, who in a cause like this
Would turn him from the coming fight,
Again a master's hand to kiss?
Who shuns to combat for the right?
Hence, hence away,
No longer stay:
Go, wretch, in soul and body slave,
And fill a coward's shameful grave.

Up, Afric, up; the land is free,
It sees no slave to despot bow:
Our battle cry is LIBERTY -
On; strike for God and vengeance now.
Fly, tyrants, fly,
Or stay - to die.
No chains we bear, no scourge we fear,
We conquer, or we perish here!

Liberator, July 23, 1831, p. 117; Liberator, January 19,
1849, p. 12; and Liberator, November 4, 1859, p. 176.

308. PERSECUTED CHILDREN'S COMPLAINT

Author: unspecified
Tune: unspecified

Four little children here you see,
In modest dress appear;
Come listen to our songs so sweet,
And our complaints you'll hear.

'Tis here we come to learn to read,
And write and cypher too;
But some, in this enlightened land,
Declare 'twill never do.

The morals of this favorite town
Shall be corrupted soon;
Therefore they strive, with all their might,
To drive us to our home.

Sometimes when we have walk'd the street,
Saluted we have been,
By guns and drums, and cow-bells too,
And horns of polished tin.

With warnings, threats, and words severe,
They visit us at times;
And gladly would they send us off
To Afric's burning clime.

Our teachers, too, they put in jail,
Fast held by bars and locks;
Did e'er such persecution reign
Since Paul was in the stocks?

But we forgive, forgive the men,
Who persecute us so;
May God in mercy save their souls
From everlasting woe.

You see, kind friends, with simple tone,
We've offered up our boon;
We thank you for attention paid,
So now, good afternoon.

Liberator, January 11, 1834, p. 8, with this introduction:
"The following ballad is sung by the colored pupils at Miss
Crandall's School in Canterbury, Ct. It is a brief but
graphic description of the brutal outrages which have been
perpetrated upon them by the Goths of that never-to-be forgotten place, and contains an excellent rebuke given in the true
spirit of forgiveness."

309. ODE

Sung at the celebration of the first of August,
in Belknap-Street meeting-house, Boston.

Author: S. R. Alexander
Tune: unspecified

On Afric's land our fathers roamed;
A free, but savage race;
No word of light their mind informed
Of God's recovering grace.

Dark as the color of their skin,
Their state, by nature, stood;
Through damps and mists of cherished sin,
And passion's roaring flood.

Yet color is no mark that shows
The inward state of mind;
Through white and black, corruption flows,
Infecting all mankind.

Though man is cruel, God is good, -
He turns our wrath to praise;
To lead us o'er Atlantic's flood,
That we might learn his ways.

The children of that very race,
That gave our fathers pain,
Are striving in the strength of grace,
To wipe away the stain.

Who knows but in Americ's wild,
A Christian black may sow
The word of God - pure, undefiled,
And a rich harvest grow.

Liberator, August 16, 1839, p. 132.

310. [UNTITLED]

Author: unspecified
Tune: O, No, We Never Mention Her

O! how can we forget the slave,
Since Christ for him hath died?
Yes, 'twas his captive soul to save,
Our Lord was crucified.

O! how can we forget the slave,
Robbed of the Book of God?
While brutal tyrants o'er him wave,
Oppression's bloody rod.

O! how can we forget the slave,
Dying in fettered toil,
And sinking to a heathen grave,
Beneath a Christian soil!

No, we will not forget the slave!
We'll free him if we can!
Though Power at him and us may rave,
He yet shall be A MAN!

Hymns, pp. 13-14.

311. THE SLAVE'S LAST APPEAL

Author: unspecified
Tune: unspecified

They say there is joy in the earth,
That spring-time has come with its flowers;
I hear the gay breathing of mirth
From freemen's luxurious bowers.
I hear this - but never can feel,
For callous and sore is my heart,
And must be till freedom shall heal
And bid grief with slavery depart.

Ah! what are the blessings of life
To one who claims death for his friend?
With curses the spring-time is rife,
And gladly I look to its end.
The sun brings no warmth to my heart -
O would that it shone on my grave;
I then should no more feel life's smart,
I then should no more be a slave.

O white man! - oppressor! - I've plead
With tears from my heart's fountain warm,
For freedom from that which all dread,
But pleading thus met with thy scorn;
For years I have groaned to be free -
For years you my groaning have heard,
On the land and the raging sea,
But pity has scarcely been stirred.

I have plead with the young and gay,
I have plead with the aged too;
But they all have turned away,
And mercy refused to show.
Quite hopeless I turned to the fair,
Still bleeding beneath the harsh rod:
E'en woman refused my prayer,
Lo now I appeal unto God!

Eternal JEHOVAH! I cry
'Gainst the steel-hearted tyrant's chains;
O hear my weak voice up on high;
Of oppression a poor slave complains.
Come Israel's Deliverer, come!
And cast down the proud white man's might,
Restore me some low humble home,
O give me my freedom - my right!

O God of compassion! regard
A poor fault'ring African's prayer:
O do not deliverance retard,
But lay thy Almighty arm bare!
Thou, Lord, art my last but sure hope,
Come quickly and let me be free;
In servitude darkly I grope,
For freedom I now look to Thee.

Hymns, pp. 9-11.

312. WHO IS MY NEIGHBOR?

Author: unspecified
Tune: Auld Lang Syne

Thy neighbor? It is he whom thou
Hast power to aid and bless,
Whose aching heart or burning brow
Thy soothing hand may press.

Thy neighbor? 'Tis the fainting poor,
Whose eye with want is dim,
Whom hunger sends from door to door,
Go thou and succor him.

Thy neighbor? 'Tis the weary men
Whose years are at their brim
Bent low with sickness, cares and pain,
Go thou, and comfort him.

Thy neighbor? 'Tis the heart bereft
Of every earthly gem;
Widow and orphan helpless left
Go thou, and shelter them.

Thy neighbor? Yonder toiling slave
Fettered in thought and limb,
Whose hopes are all beyond the grave,
Go thou and ransom him.

When'er thou meet'st a human form
Less favored than thine own,
Remember 'tis thy neighbor worn,
Thy brother or thy son.

Oh pass not, pass not heedless by,
Perhaps thou canst redeem
The breaking heart from misery:
Go share thy lot with him.

Hymns, pp. 18-19.

313. THE SLAVE'S CONDITION AND PROSPECT

Author: R. R.
Tune: Sweet Home

The black man in slavery, I hear him complain,
While tears from his eyes are flowing like
rain;
He goes to his labor with sadness and gloom,
And sighs for the joys of his free brother's
home.
Home, home, sweet, sweet home,
No joys there await him; he sighs for a home.

His wife and children are taken away;
In sorrow and sadness he passes the day;
He's like one forsaken, and left all alone,
No comforts are taken like those of a home.
Home, home, sweet, sweet home,
Disconsolate and gloomy, he sighs for a home.

Compell'd by his master to toil night and day,
And stripes from his slave-whip received for
his pay.
Then left to his toil, his fate to bemoan,
He groans in his bondage, and sighs for a
home.
Home, home, sweet, sweet home,
That blessing's denied him, he has not a home.

But, glory to Jesus! he'll not always be
Confined in his bondage, he soon shall be
free.
Awake, then, ye Christians, for you're not
alone,
Our God will assist us to find him a home.
Home, home, sweet, sweet home,
He then will enjoy in his freedom a home.

Liberator, October 13, 1843, p. 164.

314. THE BONDMAN

Author: H. W. H.
Tune: The Troubadour

Feebly the bondman toiled,
Sadly he wept -
Then to his wretched cot
Mournfully crept;
How doth his free-born soul
Pine 'neath his chain!
Slavery! slavery!
Dark is thy reign.

Long ere the break of day,
Roused from repose,
Wearily toiling
Till after its close -
Praying for freedom,
He spends his last breath:
Liberty! Liberty!
Give me or death.

When, when, O Lord! will right
Triumph o'er wrong?
Tyrants oppress the weak,
O Lord! how long?
Hark! Hark! a peal resounds
From shore to shore -
Tyranny! Tyranny!
Thy reign is o'er.

E'en now the morning
Gleams from the East -
Despots are feeling
Their triumph is past -
Strong hearts are answering
To freedom's loud call -
Liberty! Liberty!
Full and for all.

Liberator, April 7, 1843, p. 56; Liberator, August 4, 1848,
p. 124; Free Soil, p. 124; Harp, pp. 34-35; and Freedom,
p. 124.

315. THE SLAVE-MOTHER

Author: Abby H. Price
Tune: Araby's Daughter

I pity the slave-mother, care-worn and weary,
Who sighs, as she presses her babe to her
breast;
I lament her sad fate, all so hopeless and
dreary -
I lament for her woes, and her wrongs
unredressed.

O, who can imagine her heart's deep emotion,
As she thinks of her children about to be
sold!
You may picture the bounds of the rock-girdled
Ocean,
But the grief of that mother can never be
told!

The mildew of slavery has blighted each
blossom,
That ever has bloomed in her path-way below;
It has froze every fountain that has gushed in
her bosom,
And chilled her heart's verdure with pitiless
wo.

Her parents, her kindred, all crushed by
oppression;
Her husband still doomed in its desert to
stay;
No arm to protect from the tyrant's aggression
She must weep as she treads on her desolate
way.

O, who will pour balm o'er her cup-full of
sorrow?
Where, where is the hand that is stretched out
to save?
Dawns not for that mother one happy to-morrow,
Ere she lays herself down in a merciless
grave?

O, slave-mother! is there no vision of
gladness,
In the far-coming future, to light up the sky?
Is there nothing for thee but hard-toiling and
sadness -
No repose for thy form, but to lie down and
die?

O, slave-mother, hope! See - the nation is
shaking!
The arm of the Lord is awake to thy wrong!
The slaveholder's heart now with terror is
quaking -
Salvation and Mercy to Heaven belong!

Rejoice, O rejoice! for the child thou art
rearing,
May one day lift up its unmanacled form,
While hope, to thy heart, like the rainbow so
cheering,
Is born, like the rainbow, 'mid tempest and
storm.

Liberator, February 10, 1843, p. 22

Collection, pp. 4-5; Free Soil, pp. 66-67; Harp, p. 6;
and Freedom, pp. 228-229, three verses only, as "O Pity the
Slave Mother," to the same tune.

316. I WOULD NOT LIVE ALWAYS

Author: John Pierpont
Tune: unspecified

I would not live always; I ask not to stay
Where I must bear the burden and heat of the
day;
Where my body is cut with the lash or the
cord,
And a hovel and hunger are all my reward.

I would not live always, where life is a load
To the flesh and the spirit; since there's an
abode
For the soul disenthralled, let me breathe my
last breath,
And repose in thine arms, my deliverer death.

I would not live always, to toil as a slave;
O no; let me rest, though I rest in my grave;
For there, from their troubling the wicked
shall cease,
And, free from his master, the slave be at
peace.

Melodies, p. 50; Free Soil, p. 100; and Freedom, p. 100.

317. THE SLAVE AT MIDNIGHT

Author: Professor Longfellow
Tune: unidentified

Loud he sang the psalm of David,
He a negro and enslaved,
Sang of Israel's victory,
Sang of Zion bright and free.

And the voice of his devotion,
Filled my soul with strange emotion,
For its tones by turns were glad,
Sweetly solemn, wildly sad.

Paul and Silas, in their prison,
Sang of Christ, the Lord arisen,
And the earthquake's arm of might
Broke their dungeon gates at night.

But, alas, what holy angel,
Brings the slave this glad evangel,
And what earthquake's arm of might
Breaks his dungeon gates at night?

Melodies, p. 77.

Free Soil, p. 195; and Freedom, p. 196, as "The Slave
Singing at Midnight," to the tune, "Bavaria."

318. OFT IN THE CHILLY NIGHT

Author: John Pierpont
Tune: Oft in the Stilly Night

Oft in the chilly night,
Ere slumber's chain has bound me,
When all her silvery light
The moon is pouring round me,
Beneath the ray,
I kneel and pray
That God would give some token,
That slavery's chains,
On Southern Plains,
Shall all ere long be broken.
Yes, in the chilly night,
Though slavery's chain has bound me,
Kneel I, and feel the might
Of God's right arm around me.

When at the driver's call,
In cold or sultry weather,
We slaves, both great and small,
Turn out to toil together,

I feel like one,
From whom the sun
Of hope has long departed;
And morning's light,
And weary night
Still find me broken-hearted.
Thus, when the chilly breath
Of night is sighing round me,
Kneel I, and wish that death
In his cold chain had bound me.

Melodies, pp. 88-90.

Free Soil, p. 152; Harp, pp. 43-44; and Freedom, p. 152,
under the same title; no tune specified.

319. SONG

Sung at the late Nantucket Anti-Slavery Fair.

Author: Mrs. A. H.
Tune: A Man's a Man for a' That

Though stripped of all the dearest rights
Which nature claims, and a' that,
There's that which in the slave unites
To make the man for a' that:
For a' that and a' that,
Though dark his skin, and a' that,
We cannot rob him of his kind,
The slave's a man for a' that.

Though by his brother bought and sold,
And beat, and scourged, and a' that,
His wrongs can ne'er be felt or told,
Yet he's a man for a' that:
For a' that and a' that,
His body chained, and a' that,
The image of his God remains,
The slave's a man for a' that.

How dark the spirit that enslaves;
Yet darker still than a' that,
He, who amid the light, still craves
Apologies, and a' that:
For a' that and a' that,
Small evil finds, and a' that,
In crimes which are of darkest hue,
And foulest deeds, and a' that.

If those who now in bondage groan
Were white, and fair, and a' that,
O should we not their fate bemoan,
And plead their cause, and a' that?
For a' that and a' that,
Would any say, in a' that
We've nought to do, they are not here,
We'll mind our own, and a' that?

O tell us not they're clothed and fed,
'Tis insult, stuff, and a' that:
With freedom gone, all joy is fled,
For Heaven's best gift is a' that:
For a' that and a' that,
Free agency, and a' that,
We get from Him who rules on high,
The slave we rob of a' that.

Then think not to escape his wrath,
Who's equal, just, and a' that;
His warning voice is sounded forth,
We heed it not, for a' that:
For a' that and ' that,
'Tis not less sure, for a' that;
His vengeance, though 'tis long delayed,
Will come at last, for a' that.

Liberator, January 13, 1843, p. 8.

320. THE BEREAVED MOTHER

Author: Jesse Hutchinson
Tune: Kathleen O'Moore

O deep was the anguish of the slave mother's
heart,
When called from her darling for ever to part;
So grieved that lone mother, that heart broken
mother,
In sorrow and woe.

The lash of the master her deep sorrows mock,
While the child of her bosom is sold on the
block;
Yet loud shrieked that mother, poor heart
broken mother,
In sorrow and woe.

The babe in return, for its fond mother cries,
While the sound of their wailings together
arise;
They shriek for each other, the child and the
mother,
In sorrow and woe.

The harsh auctioneer to sympathy cold,
Tears the babe from its mother and sells it
for gold;
While the infant and mother, loud shriek for
each other,
In sorrow and woe.

At last came the parting of mother and child,
Her brain reeled with madness, that mother was
wild;
Then the lash could not smother the shrieks of
that mother,
Of sorrow and woe.

The child was borne off to a far distant
clime,
While the mother was left in anguish to pine;
But reason departed, and she sank broken
hearted,
In sorrow and woe.

That poor mourning mother, of reason bereft,
Soon ended her sorrows and sank clod in death:
Thus died that slave mother, poor heart broken
mother,
In sorrow and woe.

Oh! list ye kind mothers to the cries of the
slave;
The parents and children implore you to save;
Go! rescue the mothers, the sisters and
brothers,
From sorrow and woe.

Liberator, May 24, 1844, p. 84; Collection, pp. 27-28;
Free Soil, pp. 84-85; Harp, p. 19; and Freedom, pp. 84-85.

321. THE FLYING SLAVE

Author: unspecified
Tune: To Greece We Give Our Shining Blades

The night is dark, and keen the air,
And the Slave is flying to be free;
His parting word is one short prayer;
O God, but give me Liberty!
Farewell - farewell;
Behind I leave the whips and chains,
Before me spreads sweet Freedom's plains.

One star shines in the heavens above,
That guides him on his lonely way; -
Star of the North - how deep his love
For thee, thou star of Liberty!
Farewell - farewell;
Behind he leaves the whips and chains,
Before him spreads sweet Freedom's plains.

Liberator, June 7, 1844, p. 96; Free Soil, p. 212; Harp,
p. 47; and Liberty, p. 179.

322. THE PLANTATION SONG

The following song is said to be sung by the slaves
as they are chained in gangs when about to start to
the far off South - children taken from parents,
husbands from wives, and brothers from sisters.

Author: unspecified
Tune: unspecified

See these poor souls from Africa,
Transported to America;
We are stolen, and sold to Georgia, will you
go along with me?
We are stolen and sold to Georgia, go sound
the jubilee.

See wives and husbands sold apart,
The children's screams! - it breaks my heart;
There's a better day a coming - will you go
along with me?
There's a better day a coming, go sound the
jubilee.

O gracious Lord! when shall it be,
That we poor souls shall all be free?
Lord, break them Slavery powers - will you go
along with me?
Lord, break them Slavery powers, go sound the
jubilee.

Dear Lord! dear Lord! when Slavery'll cease,
Then we poor souls can have our peace;
There's a better day a coming, will you go
along with me?
There's a better day a coming, go sound the
jubilee.

Liberator, November 1, 1844, p. 176.

Collection, p. 26; Harp, p. 30; and Liberty, pp. 22-23, as
"Song of the Coffle Gang"; no tune specified in the former
two and original music by G. W. C. in the latter.

323. THE BEREFT SLAVE

Author: G.
Tune: Pilot of the Deep

"Ah me! how slowly wears the day;
How lags the burning sun;
Still, faint and wretched, I must stay
Until this task be done.
This hoe my hand can hardly raise;
My limbs have lost their power;
Oh, gracious God! grant that my days
Be numbered with this hour.

"Last night, toil-worn, I hied me home,
My wife and child to meet;
But to the door they did not come,
As erst, my step to greet!
What could it mean? I hurried in -
No wife, no child was there!
I called, and called, and called again; -
Alas, they would not hear!

"The frightful thought flashed on my mind,
They were to me no more;
That some cursed dealer in his kind
Had torn them from my door!
The thought is awful truth, I'm told;
Oh, God! and is it so?
That my poor heart is reft for gold?
Take, take the spirit too!"

Thus groaned the slave. His heart was full;
His task went sadly on;
The driver's whip, that moved the dull,
Fell as upon a stone.

He heeded not the threats or blows -
All that he loved was fled;
His hopes were crushed - his spirit froze -
The mind - the mind was dead!

Liberator, May 16, 1845, p. 80.

324. THE BLIND SLAVE-BOY

Author: Mrs. Dr. Bailey
Tune: unspecified

Come back to me, mother! why linger away
From thy poor little blind boy, the long weary
day!
I mark every footstep, I list to each tone,
And wonder my mother should leave me alone!
There are voices of sorrow, and voices of
glee,
But there's no one to joy or to sorrow with
me;
For each hath of pleasure and trouble his
share,
And none for the poor little blind boy will
care.

My mother, come back to me! close to thy
breast
Once more let thy poor little blind one be
pressed;
Once more let me feel thy warm breath on my
cheek,
And hear thee in accents of tenderness speak!
O mother! I've no one to love me - no heart
Can bear like thine own in my sorrows a part,
No hand is so gentle, no voice is so kind,
Oh! none like a mother can cherish the blind!

Poor blind one! No mother thy wailing can
hear,
No mother can hasten to banish thy fear;
For the slave-owner drives her, o'er mountain
and wild,
And for one paltry dollar hath sold thee, poor
child!
Ah! who can in language of mortals reveal
The anguish that none but a mother can feel,
When man in his vile lust of mammon hath trod
On her child, who is stricken and smitten of
God!

Blind, helpless, forsaken, with strangers
alone,
She hears in her anguish his piteous moan;
As he eagerly listens - but listens in vain,
To catch the loved tones of his mother again!
The curse of the broken in spirit shall fall
On the wretch who hath mingled this wormwood
and gall,
And his gain like a mildew shall blight and
destroy,
Who hath torn from his mother the little blind
boy!

Collection, p. 5.

Free Soil, pp. 73-75; Harp, p. 7; and Freedom, pp. 222-224,
under the same title, to the tune, "Sweet Afton."

325. THE FUGITIVE SLAVE TO THE CHRISTIAN

Author: Elizur Wright, Jr.
Tune: unspecified

The fetters galled my weary soul, -
A soul that seemed but thrown away;
I spurned the tyrants base control,
Resolved at last the man to play: -
The hounds are baying on my track;
O Christian! will you send me back?
The hounds are baying on my track;
O Christian will you send me back?

I felt the stripes, the lash I saw,
Red, dripping with a father's gore;
And, worst of all their lawless law,
The insults that my mother bore!
The hounds, etc.

Where human law o'errules Divine,
Beneath the sheriff's hammer fell
My wife and babes, - I call them mine, -
And where they suffer, who can tell?
The hounds, etc.

I seek a home where man is man,
If such there be upon this earth,
To draw my kindred, if I can,
Around its free, though humble hearth.
The hounds, etc.

Collection, p. 44; Harp, pp. 27-28; and Liberator, April 5, 1850, p. 56.

Free Soil, pp. 68-70; and Freedom, pp. 225-227, under the same title, to the tune, "Cracovienne."

326. BROTHERS BE BRAVE FOR THE PINING SLAVE

Author: E. D.
Tune: Sparkling and Bright

Heavy and cold in his dungeon hold,
Is the yoke of the oppressor;
Dark o'er the soul is the fell control
Of the stern and dread transgressor.
Oh then come all to bring the thrall
Up from his deep despairing,
And out of the jaw of the bandit's law,
Retake the prey he's tearing:
Oh then come all to bring the thrall
Up from his deep despairing,
And out of the jaw of the bandit's law,
Retake the prey he's tearing.

Brothers be brave for the pining slave,
From his wife and children riven;
From every vale their bitter wail
Goes sounding up to Heaven.
Then for the life of that poor wife,
And for those children pining;
O ne'er give o'er till the chains no more
Around their limbs are twining.
Then for the life, etc. [repeat last four lines]

Gloomy and damp is the low rice swamp,
Where their meagre bands are wasting;
All worn and weak, in vain they seek
For rest, to the cool shade hasting;
For drivers fell, like fiends from hell,
Cease not their savage shouting;
And the scourge's crack, from quivering back,
Sends up the red blood spouting.
For drivers fell, etc.

Into the grave looks only the slave,
For rest to his limbs aweary;
His spirit's light comes from that night,
To us so dark and dreary.
That soul shall nurse its heavy curse
Against a day of terror,
When the lightning gleam of his wrath shall
stream
Like fire, on the hosts of error.
That soul shall nurse, etc.

Heavy and stern are the bolts which burn
In the right hand of Jehovah;
To smite the strong red arm of wrong,
And dash his temples over;
Then on a main to rend the chain,
Ere bursts the vallied thunder;
Right onward speed till the slave is freed -
His manacles torn asunder.
Then on a main, etc.

Collection, pp. 3-4; Liberator, January 21, 1848, p. 12;
Free Soil, pp. 58-60; and Freedom, pp. 233-235.

327. THE FUGITIVE

Author: L. M. C.
Tune: Bonny Doon

A noble man of sable brow
Came to my humble cottage door,
With cautious, weary step and slow,
And asked if I could feed the poor;
He begged if I had ought to give,
To help the panting fugitive.
He begged if I had ought to give,
To help the panting fugitive.

I told him he had fled away
From his kind master, friends, and home;
That he was black - a slave astray,
And should return as he had come;
That I would to his master give
The straying villain fugitive.
That I would to his master give
The straying villain fugitive.

He fell upon his trembling knee
And claimed he was a brother man,
That I was bound to set him free,
According to the gospel plan;
And if I would God's grace receive,
That I must help the fugitive.
And if I would God's grace receive,
That I must help the fugitive.

He showed the stripes his master gave,
The festering wound - the sightless eye,
The common badges of the slave,
And said he would be free, or die;
And if I nothing had to give,
I should not stop the fugitive.
And if I nothing had to give,
I should not stop the fugitive.

He owned his was a sable skin,
That which his Maker first had given;
But mine would be a darker sin,
That would exclude my soul from heaven;
And if I would God's grace receive,
I should receive the fugitive.
And if I would God's grace receive,
I should receive the fugitive.

I bowed and took the stranger in,
And gave him meat, and drink, and rest,
I hope that God forgave my sin,
And made me with that brother blest;
I am resolved, long as I live,
To help the panting fugitive.
I am resolved, long as I live,
To help the panting fugitive.

Collection, p. 16; Free Soil, pp. 95-96; and Freedom, pp.
95-96.

328. THE SLAVE AND HER BABE

Author: Charlotte Elizabeth
Tune: unspecified

O, massa, let me stay, to catch
My baby's sobbing breath;
His little glassy eye to watch,
And smooth his limbs in death,

And cover him with grass and leaf,
beneath the plantain tree!
It is not sullenness, but grief -
O, massa, pity me!

God gave me babe - a precious boon,
To cheer my lonely heart,
But massa called to work too soon,
And I must needs depart.
The morn was chill - I spoke no word,
But feared my babe might die,
And heard all day, or thought I heard,
My little baby cry.

At noon - O, how I ran! and took
My baby to my breast!
I lingered - and the long lash broke
My sleeping infant's rest.
I worked till night! - till darkest night,
In torture and disgrace;
Went home, and watched till morning light,
To see my baby's face.

The fulness from its cheek was gone,
The sparkle from its eye;
Now hot, like fire, now cold, like stone,
I knew my babe must die.
I worked upon plantation ground,
Though faint with woe and dread,
Then ran, or flew, and here I found -
See massa, almost dead.

Then give me but one little hour -
O! do not lash me so!
One little hour - one little hour -
And gratefully I'll go.
Ah me! the whip has cut my boy,
I heard his feeble scream;
No more - farewell my only joy,
My life's first gladsome dream.

I lay thee on the lonely sod,
The heaven is bright above:
These christians boast they have a God,
And say his name is Love:
O gentle, loving God, look down!
My dying baby see;
The mercy that from earth is flown,
Perhaps may dwell with THEE!

Collection, pp. 38-40.

Free Soil, p. 45; and Freedom, p 249, under the same title,
to the tune, "Slave Girl Mourning Her Father" (see song 333).

329. THE POOR LITTLE SLAVE

Author: unspecified
Tune: The Charter Oak

O pity the poor little slave,
Who labors hard through all the day -
And has no one,
When day is done,
To teach his youthful heart to pray.

No words of love - no fond embrace -
No smiles from parents kind and dear;
No tears are shed
Around his bed,
When fevers rage, and death is near.

None feel for him when heavy chains
Are fastened to his tender limb;
No pitying eyes,
No sympathies,
No prayers are raised to heaven for him.

Yes I will pity the poor slave,
And pray that he may soon be free
That he at last,
When days are past,
In heaven may have his liberty.

Collection, p. 19; Free Soil, p. 83; and Freedom, p. 211.

330. THE STRANGER AND HIS FRIEND

Author: Montgomery and Dennison
Tune: Duane Street

A poor wayfaring man of grief,
Hath often crossed me on my way,
Who sued so humbly for relief,
That I could never answer nay;
I had not power to ask his name,
Whither he went or whence he came;
Yet there was something in his eye,
Which won my love, I knew not why.

Once, when my scanty meal was spread,
He entered - not a word he spake -
Just perishing for want of bread,
I gave him all; he blessed it, brake,
And ate, but gave me part again:
Mine was an angel's portion then,
For while I fed with eager haste,
The crust was manna to my taste.

'Twas night. The floods were out, it blew
A winter hurricane aloof:
I heard his voice abroad, and flew
To bid him welcome to my roof;
I warmed, I clothed, I cheered my guest,
I laid him on my couch to rest:
Then made the ground my bed and seemed
In Eden's garden while I dreamed.

I saw him bleeding in his chains,
And tortured 'neath the driver's lash,
His sweat fell fast along the plains,
Deep dyed from many a fearful gash:
But I in bonds remembered him,
And strove to free each fettered limb,
As with my tears I washed his blood,
Me he baptized with mercy's flood.

I saw him in the negro pew,
His head hung low upon his breast,
His locks were wet with drops of dew,
Gathered while he for entrance pressed.
Within those aisles, whose courts are given
That black and white may reach one heaven;
And as I meekly sought his feet,
He smiled, and made a throne my seat.

In prison I saw him next condemned
To meet a traitor's doom at morn;
The tide of lying tongues I stemmed,
And honored him midst shame and scorn.
My friendship's utmost zeal to try,
He asked if I for him would die;
The flesh was weak, my blood ran chill,
But the free spirit cried, "I will."

Then in a moment to my view,
The stranger darted from disguise;
The tokens in his hands I knew,
My Saviour stood before my eyes!

He spoke, and my poor name he named -
"Of me thou hast not been ashamed,
These deeds shall thy memorial be;
Fear not, thou didst them unto me."

Collection, pp. 8-10; Free Soil, pp. 182-184; and Freedom,
pp. 182-184.

331. [UNTITLED]

Author: Rev. J. Blanchard
Tune: Araby's Daughter

The slave-mother leaned on her mattock full
weary,
At the grey of the dawn, in that home of the
dead:
Where the tall city's shade made each green
grave look dreary,
Though spangled with tears which kind nature
had shed.
But she recked not that cold dews were falling
around her,
Though weary with toil, and though fainting
for food,
For the last tie was broke which to feeling
had bound her,
And froze e'en the fondness for life in her
blood.

Her children, as mothers love, once she had
loved them;
But sold were they all save the corpse by her
side:
God saw all her fears for her child, and
removed them,
And her last pulse of hope with her last babe
had died,
O, then, though she knew when its young eyes
first met her,
In language of smiles which the lips could not
speak,
She thought that its safety in death was far
better,
Than the joy she had felt when it breathed on
her cheek.

And she prayed, as she turned to her strange
task, preparing
The shroudless and coffinless rest for her
child,
That soon her torn breast might her babe's
sleep be sharing,
Her heart no more rung, and her brain no more
wild;
For she said, while around her damp vapors
aspirant
Rose chill from the moist turf which covered
the grave.
That earth was less cold than the heart of a
tyrant,
And death far less drear than the life of a
slave.

Liberator, August 15, 1845, p. 132, with this introduction:
"In the year 1844, near the city of Louisville, Ky., as the
sexton went to open a grave-yard, he found there a slave
mother digging a grave for her own infant, which, without
shroud or coffin, was lying be her on the earth. Her mistress
had sent her thus to bury her infant, to save the expense of
grave-clothes and coffin!"

332. STOLEN WE WERE

Author: A Colored Man
Tune: unidentified

Stolen we were from Africa,
Transported to America;
It's work all day and half the night,
And rise before the morning light;
Sinner! man! why don't you repent?
For the judgment is rolling around!
For the judgment is rolling around!

Like the brute beast in public street,
Endure the cold and stand the heat;
King Jesus told you once before
[To] go your way and sin no more;
Sinner! man! etc.

If e'er I reach the Northern shore,
I'll ne'er go back, no, never more;
I think I hear these ladies say,
We'll sing for Freedom night and day;
Sinner! man! etc.

Now let us all, yes, every man,
Vote for the Slave, for now we can;
Break every yoke and every chain,
And make the slave a man again;
Sinner! man! etc.

Come let us go for James G. Birney,
Who sells not flesh and blood for money;
He is the man you all can see,
Who gave his slaves their liberty;
Sinner! man! etc.

We hail thee as an honest Man,
God made thee on his noblest plan;
To stand for freedom in that hour,
To thrust a blow at Slavery's power;
Sinner! man! etc.

Collection, p. 41; and Liberty, pp. 140-141.

333. SLAVE GIRL MOURNING HER FATHER

Author: G. W. C.
("Parodied from Mrs. Sigourney")
Tune: unspecified

They say I was but four years old
When father was sold away;
Yet I have never seen his face
Since that sad parting day.
He went where brighter flowrets grow
Beneath the Southern skies;
Oh who will show me on the map
Where that far country lies?

I begged him, "father, do not go!
For, since my mother died,
I love no one so well as you;"
And, clinging to his side,
The tears came gushing down my cheeks
Until my eyes were dim;
Some were in sorrow for the dead,
And some in love for him.

He knelt and prayed of God above,
"My little daughter spare,
And let us both here meet again,
O keep her in thy care."

He does not come! - I watch for him
At evening twilight grey,
Till every shadow wears his shape,
Along the grassy way.

I muse and listen all alone,
When stormy winds are high,
And think I hear his tender tone,
And call, but no reply;
And so I've done these four long years,
Without a friend or home,
Yet every dream of hope is vain, -
Why don't my father come?

Father - dear father, are you sick,
Upon a stranger shore? -
The people say it must be so -
O send to me once more,
And let your little daughter come,
To soothe your restless bed,
And hold the cordial to your lips,
And press your aching head.

Alas! - I fear me he is dead! -
Who will my trouble share?
Or tell me where his form is laid,
And let me travel there?
By mother's tomb I love to sit,
Where the green branches wave;
Good people! help a friendless child
To find her father's grave.

Collection, pp. 37-38.

Free Soil, pp. 44-45; and Freedom, pp. 248-249, under the
same title, to an unidentified tune.

334. WHAT MEANS THAT SAD AND DISMAL LOOK?

Author: Geo. Russell
Tune: unspecified

What means that sad and dismal look,
And why those falling tears?
No voice is heard, no word is spoke,
Yet nought but grief appears.

Ah! Mother, hast thou ever known
The pain of parting ties?
Was ever infant from thee torn
And sold before thine eyes?

Say, would not grief thy bosom swell?
Thy tears like rivers flow?
Should some rude ruffian seize and sell
The child thou lovest so?

There's a feeling in a Mother's breast,
Though colored be her skin!
And though at Slavery's foul behest,
She must not weep for kin.

I had a lovely, smiling child,
It sat upon my knee;
And oft a tedious hour beguiled,
With merry heart of glee.

That child was from my bosom torn,
And sold before my eyes;
With outstretched arms, and looks forlorn,
It uttered piteous cries.

Mother! dear Mother! - take, O take
Thy helpless little one!
Ah! then I thought my heart would break;
My child - my child was gone.

Long, long ago, my child they stole,
But yet my grief remains;
These tears flow freely - and my soul
In bitterness complains.

Then ask not why "my dismal look,"
Nor why my "falling tears,"
Such wrongs, what human heart can brook?
No hope for me appears.

Collection, pp. 44-46.

Free Soil, pp. 40-41; and Freedom, pp. 252-253, under the
same title, to the tune, "Near the Lake."

335. THE SLAVE'S LAMENTATION

Author: unspecified
Tune: Long, Long Ago

Where are the friends that to me were so dear,
Long, long ago, long, long ago!
Where are the hopes that my heart used to
cheer?
Long, long ago, long, long ago!
Friends that I loved in the grave are laid
low,
All hope of freedom hath fled from me now.
I am degraded, for man was my foe,
Long, long ago, long, long ago!

Sadly my wife bowed her beautiful head -
Long, long ago, long, long ago!
Oh, how I wept when I found she was dead!
Long, long ago, long, long ago!
She was my angel, my love and my pride -
Vainly to save her from torture I tried,
Poor broken heart! She rejoiced as she died,
Long, long ago, long, long ago!

Let me look back on the days of my youth -
Long, long ago, long, long ago!
Master withheld from me knowledge and truth -
Long. long ago, long, long ago!
Crushed all the hopes of my earliest day,
Sent me from father and mother away -
Forbade me to read, nor allowed me to pray -
Long, long ago, long, long ago!

Collection, pp. 26-27; Free Soil, pp. 180-181; Harp,
pp. 13-14; and Freedom, pp. 180-181.

336. THE BEREAVED FATHER

Author: Miss Chandler
Tune: unspecified

Ye've gone from me, my gentle ones!
With all your shouts of mirth;
A silence is within my walls,
A darkness round my hearth,
A darkness round my hearth.

Woe to the hearts that heard, unmoved,
The mother's anguish'd shriek!
And mock'd, with taunting scorn, the tears
That bathed a father's cheek,
That bathed a father's cheek.

Woe to the hands that tore you hance,
My innocent and good!
Not e'en the tigress of the wild,
Thus tears her fellow's brood,
Thus tears her fellow's brood.

I list to hear your soft sweet tones,
Upon the morning air;
I gaze amidst the twilight's gloom,
As if to find you there,
As if to find you there.

But you no more come bounding [forth]
To meet me in your glee;
And when the evening shadows fall,
Ye are not at my knee,
Ye are not at my knee.

Your forms are aye before my eyes,
Your voices on my ear,
And all things wear a thought of you,
But you no more are here,
But you no more are here.

You were the glory of my life,
My blessing and my pride!
I half forgot the name of slave,
When you were by my side,
When you were by my side!

Woe for your lot, ye doom'd ones! woe
A seal is on your fate!
And shame, and toil, and wretchedness,
On all your steps await,
On all your steps await!

Collection, p. 33.

Free Soil, pp. 42-43; and Freedom, pp. 250-251, under the
same title, to original music by G. W. C.

337. AM I NOT A MAN AND BROTHER?

Author: A. C. L.
Tune: Bride's Farewell

Am I not a man and brother?
Ought I not, then, to be free?
Sell me not one to another,
Take not thus my liberty.

Christ our Saviour, Christ our Saviour,
Died for me as well as thee.
Christ our Saviour, Christ our Saviour,
Died for me as well as thee.

Am I not a man and brother?
Have I not a soul to save?
Oh, do not my spirit smother,
Making me a wretched slave:
God of mercy, God of mercy,
Let me fill a freeman's grave!
God of mercy, God of mercy,
Let me fill a freeman's grave!

Yes, thou art a man and brother,
Though thou long hast groaned a slave,
Bound with cruel cords and tether
From the cradle to the grave!
Yet the Saviour, yet the Saviour,
Bled and died all souls to save.
Yet the Saviour, yet the Saviour,
Bled and died all souls to save.

Yes, thou art a man and brother,
Though we long have told thee nay:
And are bound to aid each other,
All along our pilgrim way.
Come and welcome, come and welcome,
Join with us to praise and pray!
Come and welcome, come and welcome,
Join with us to praise and pray!

Free Soil, pp. 97-98; Harp, pp. 5-6; and Freedom, pp. 97-98.

338. AM I NOT A SISTER?

Author: A. C. L.
Tune: unspecified

Am I not a sister, say?
Shall I then be bought and sold
In the mart and by the way,
For the white man's lust and gold?
Save me then from his foul snare,
Leave me not to perish there!

Am I not a sister say,
Though I have a sable hue!
Lo! I have been dragged away,

From my friends and kindred true,
And have toiled in yonder field,
There have long been bruised and peeled.

Am I not a sister, say?
Have I an immortal soul?
Will you, sisters, tell me nay?
Shall I live in lust's control,
To be chattled like a beast,
By the Christian church and priest?

Am I not a sister, say?
Though I have been made a slave?
Will you not then for me pray,
To the God whose power can save,
High and low, and bond and free?
Toil and pray and vote for me!

Free Soil, p. 98; and Freedom, p. 98.

339. FREEDOM'S STAR

Author: unspecified
Tune: Silver Moon

As I strayed from my cot at the close of the
day,
I turned my fond gaze to the sky;
I beheld all the stars as so sweetly they lay,
And but one fixed my heart or my eye.
Shine on, northern star, thou'rt beautiful and
bright
To the slave on his journey afar;
For he speeds from his foes in the darkness of
night,
Guided on by thy light, freedom's star.

On thee he depends when he threads the dark
woods
Ere the bloodhounds have hunted him back;
Thou leadest him on over mountains and floods,
With thy beams shining full on his track.
Shine on, etc.

Unwelcome to him is the bright orb of day,
As it glides o'er the earth and the sea;
He seeks then to hide like a wild beast of
pray,
But with hope, rests his heart upon thee.
Shine on, etc.

May never a cloud overshadow thy face,
While the slave flies before his pursuer;
Gleam steadily on to the end of his race,
Till his body and soul are secure.
Shine on, etc.

Harp, p. 9.

340. A SONG FOR FREEDOM

Author: unspecified
Tune: Dandy Jim

Come all ye bondmen far and near,
Let's put a song in massa's ear,
It is a song for our poor race,
Who're whipped and trampled with disgrace.
My old massa tells me, O,
This is a land of freedom O;
Let's look about and see if it's so,
Just as massa tells me, O!

He tells us of that glorious one,
I think his name was Washington;
How he did fight for liberty,
To save a threepence tax on tea.
My old massa, etc.

And he informs us that there was
A Constitution, with this clause,
That all men equal were created,
How often have we heard it stated.
My old massa, etc.

But now we look about and see,
That we poor blacks are not so free;
We're whipped and thrashed about like fools,
And have no chance at common schools.
Still my old massa tells me, O,
This is a land of freedom O;
Let's look about and see if 'tis so,
Just as massa tells us O.

They take our wives, insult and mock,
And sell our children on the block,
They choke us if we say a word,
And say that niggers shant be heard.
Still my old massa, etc.

Our preachers, too, with whip and cord,
Command obedience to the Lord;
They say they learn it from the book.
But for ourselves we dare not look.
My old massa tells me, O,
This is a Christian country O,
Let's look about and see if 'tis so,
Just as massa tells me O.

There is a country far away -
Friend Hopper says 'tis Canada,
And if we reach Victoria's shore,
He says that we are slaves no more.
Now hasten bondsmen, let us go,
And leave this Christian country O;
Haste to the land of the British Queen
Where whips for negroes are not seen.

Now if we go we must take the night -
We're sure to die if we come in sight -
The bloodhounds will be on our track,
And wo to us if they bring us back.
Now hasten bondsmen, let us go,
And leave this Christian country O;
God help us to Victoria's shore,
Where we are free and slaves no more.

Harp, pp. 37-38.

Freedom, pp. 33-35, as "My Old Massa Tells Me So," to the
same tune.

^41. FLIGHT OF THE BONDMAN

Dedicated to William W. Brown,
and sung by the Hutchinsons.

Author: Elias Smith
Tune: Silver Moon

From the crack of the rifle and baying of
hound,
Takes the poor panting bondman his flight;
His couch through the day is the cold damp
ground,
But northward he runs through the night.
O, God speed the flight of the desolate slave;
Let his heart never yield to despair;

There is room 'mong our hills for the true and
the brave,
Let his lungs breathe our free northern air!

O, sweet to the storm-driven sailor the light,
Streaming far o'er the dark swelling wave;
But sweeter by far 'mong the lights of the
night,
Is the star of the north to the slave.
O, God speed, etc.

Cold and bleak are our mountains and chilling
our winds,
But warm as the soft southern gales
Be the hands and the hearts which the hunted
one finds,
'Mong our hills and our own winter vales.
O, God speed, etc.

Then list to the 'plaint of the heart-broken
thrall,
Ye blood-hounds, go back to your lair;
May a free northern soil soon give freedom to
all,
Who shall breathe in its pure mountain air.
O, God speed, etc.

Harp, pp. 14-15.

342. FUGITIVE'S TRIUMPH

Author: unspecified
Tune: unidentified, by Pax

Go, go, thou that enslav'st me,
Now, now thy power is o'er;
Long, long have I obeyed thee,
I'm not a slave any more -
No, no - oh, no!
I'm a free man evermore!

Thou, thou, brought'st me ever,
Deep, deep sorrow and pain;
But I have left thee forever,
Nor will I serve thee again -
No, no - oh, no!
No, I'll not serve thee again.

Tyrant! thou hast bereft me
Home, friends, pleasures so sweet,
Now, forever I've left thee,
Thou and I never shall meet -
No, no - oh, no!
Thou and I never shall meet.

Joys, joys, bright as the morning,
Now, now, on me will pour,
Hope, hope, on me is dawning.
I'm not a slave any more!
No, no - oh, no,
I'm a FREE MAN evermore!

Free Soil, p. 191; and Freedom, p. 191.

Harp, pp. 36-37, under the same title; no tune specified.

343. GONE, SOLD AND GONE

Author: Whittier
Tune: original, by G. W. Clark

Gone, gone - sold and gone,
To the rice-swamp dank and lone,
Where the slave-whip ceaseless swings,
Where the noisome insect stings,
Where the fever demon strews
Poison with the falling dews,
Where the sickly sunbeams glare
Through the hot and misty air, -
Gone, gone - sold and gone,
To the rice-swamp dank and lone,
From Virginia's hills and waters, -
Woe is me my stolen daughters!

Gone, gone - sold and gone,
To the rice-swamp dank and lone,
There no mother's eye is near them,
There no mother's ear can hear them;
Never when the torturing lash
Seams their back with many a gash,
Shall a mother's kindness bless them,
Or a mother's arms caress them.
Gone, etc.

Gone, gone - sold and gone,
To the rice-swamp dank and lone,
Oh, when weary, sad, and slow,
From the fields at night they go,

Faint with toil, and rack'd with pain,
To their cheerless homes again -
There no brother's voice shall greet them -
There no father's welcome meet them.
Gone, etc.

Gone, gone - sold and gone,
To the rice-swamp dank and lone,
From the tree whose shadow lay
On their childhood's place of play -
From the cool spring where they drank -
Rock, and hill, and rivulet bank -
From the solemn house of prayer,
And the holy counsels there.
Gone, etc.

Gone, gone - sold and gone,
To the rice-swamp dank and lone,
Toiling through the weary day,
And at night the Spoiler's prey;
Oh, that they had earlier died,
Sleeping calmly, side by side,
Where the tyrant's power is o'er,
And the fetter galls no more!
Gone, etc.

Gone, gone - sold and gone,
To the rice-swamp dank and lone,
By the holy love He beareth -
By the bruised reed He spareth -
Oh, may He, to whom alone
All their cruel wrongs are known,
Still their hope and refuge prove,
With a more than mother's love.
Gone, etc.

Free Soil, pp. 35-37; and Freedom, pp. 254-256.

344. MY CHILD IS GONE

Author: unspecified
Tune: original, by G. W. C.

Hark! from the winds a voice of woe,
The wild Atlantic in its flow,
Bears on is breast the murmur low,
My child is gone!

Like savage tigers o'er their prey,
They tore him from my heart away;
And now I cry, by night and day -
My child is gone!

How many a free-born babe is press'd
With fondness to its mother's breast,
And rocked upon her arms to rest,
While mine is gone!

No longer now, at eve I see,
Beneath the sheltering plantain tree,
My baby cradled on my knee,
For he is gone!

And when I seek my cot at night,
There's not a thing that meets my sight,
But tells me that my soul's delight,
My child is gone!

I sink to sleep, and then I seem
To hear again his parting scream
I start and wake - 'tis but a dream -
My child _is_ gone!

Gone - till my toils and griefs are o'er,
And I shall reach that happy shore,
Where negro mothers cry no more -
My child is gone!

Free Soil, p. 81; and Freedom, p. 221.

345. HEARD YE THAT CRY

Author: unspecified
Tune: Wind of the Winter Night

Heard ye that cry! Twas the wail of a slave,
As he sank in despair, to the rest of the
grave;
Behold him where bleeding and prostrate he
lies,
Unfriended he lived, and unpitied he died.

The white man oppressed him - the white man
for gold,
Made him toil amidst tortures that cannot be
told;

He robbed him, and spoiled him, of all that
was dear,
And made him the prey of affliction and fear.

But his anguish was seen, and his wailings
were heard,
By the Lord God of Hosts; whose vengeance
deferred,
Gathers force by delay, and with fury will
burst,
On his impious oppressor - the tyrant
accursed!

Arouse ye, arouse ye! ye generous and brave,
Plead the rights of the poor - plead the cause
of the slave;
Nor cease your exertions till broken shall be
The fetters that bind him, and the slave shall
be free.

Free Soil, pp. 86-87; and Freedom, pp. 86-87.

346. HELP! O HELP!

Author: unspecified
Tune: original, by G. W. C.

Help! O help! thou God of Christians!
Save a mother from despair;
Cruel white men steal my children,
God of Christians! hear my prayer.

From my arms by force they're rended,
Sailors drag them to the sea -
Yonder ship at anchor riding,
Swift will carry them away.

There my son lies pale and bleeding;
Fast with cords his hands are bound;
See the tyrants, how they scourge him;
See his sides a reeking wound.

See his little sister by him,
Quaking, trembling, how she lies!
Drops of blood her face besprinkle -
Tears of anguish fill her eyes.

Hear the little daughter begging -
Take me, white men, for your own;
Spare! O spare my darling brother!
He's my mother's only son.

Christians, who's the God you worship?
Is he cruel, fierce, or good?
Does he take delight in mercy,
Or in spilling human blood?

"Ah! my poor distracted mother!
Hear her scream upon the shore!"
Down the savage captain struck her
Lifeless on the vessel's floor.

Up his sails he quickly hoisted,
To the ocean bent his way:
Head long plunged the raving mother
From a rock into the sea.

Free Soil, p. 192; Liberty, p. 188; and Freedom, p. 192.

347. I AM MONARCH OF NOUGHT I SURVEY

Author: unspecified
Tune: Old De-Fleury

I am monarch of nought I survey,
My wrongs there are none to dispute;
My master conveys me away,
His whims or caprices to suit.
O slavery, where are the charms
That "patriarchs" have seen in thy face;
I dwell in the midst of alarms,
And serve in a horrible place.

I am out of humanity's reach,
And must finish my life with a groan;
Never hear the sweet music of speech
That tells me my body's my own.
Society, friendship, and love,
Divinely bestowed upon some,
Are blessings I never can prove,
If slavery's my portion to come.

Religion! what treasures untold,
Reside in that heavenly word!
More precious than silver or gold,
Or all that this earth can afford.

But I am excluded the light
That leads to this heavenly grace;
The Bible is clos'd to my sight,
Its beauties I never can trace.

Ye winds, that have made me your sport,
Convey to this sorrowful land,
Some cordial endearing report,
Of freedom from tyranny's hand.
My friends, do they not often send,
A wish or a thought after me?
O, tell me I yet have a friend,
A friend I am anxious to see.

How fleet is a glance of the mind!
Compared with the speed of its flight;
The tempest itself lags behind,
And the swift-winged arrows of light.
When I think of Victoria's domain,
In a moment I seem to be there,
But the fear of being taken again,
Soon hurries me back to despair.

The wood-fowl has gone to her nest,
The beast has lain down in his lair;
To me, there's no season of rest,
Though I to my quarter repair.
If mercy, O Lord, is in store,
For those who in slavery pine;
Grant me when life's troubles are o'er,
A place in thy kingdom divine.

Free Soil, pp. 52-53; and Freedom, pp. 240-241.

348. THE SLAVE BOY'S WISH

Author: Eliza Lee Follen
Tune: [Near the Lake?]

I wish I was that little bird,
Up in the bright blue sky;
That sings and flies just where he will,
And no one asks him why.

I wish I was that little brook,
That runs so swift along;
Through pretty flowers and shining stones,
Singing a merry song.

I wish I was that butterfly,
Without a thought or care;
Sporting my pretty, brilliant wings,
Like a flower in the air.

I wish I was that wild, wild deer,
I saw the other day;
Who swifter than an arrow flew,
Through the forest far away.

I wish I was that little cloud,
By the gentle south wind driven;
Floating along, so free and bright
Far, far up into heaven.

I'd rather be a cunning fox,
And hide me in a cave;
I'd rather be a savage wolf,
Than what I am - a slave.

My mother calls me her good boy,
My father calls me brave;
What wicked action have I done,
That I should be a slave.

I saw my little sister sold,
So will they do to me;
My Heavenly Father, let me die,
For then I shall be free.

Free Soil, p. 41; and Freedom, p. 253.

349. THE SLAVE'S ADDRESS

Author: unspecified
Tune: [original, by G. W. C.]

Natives of a land of glory,
Daughters of the good and brave!
Hear the injured Negro's story; -
Hear and help the kneeling Slave.

Think how nought but death can sever
Your lov'd children from your hold; -
Still alive, but lost forever -
Ours are parted, bought and sold!

Seize, oh! seize the favoring season -
Scorning censure or applause;
Justice, Truth, Religion, Reason
Are your leaders in the cause!

Follow! - faithful, firm, confiding; -
Spread our wrongs from shore to shore;
Mercy's God your efforts guiding,
Slavery shall be known no more.

Liberty, p. 189.

350. ZAZA - THE FEMALE SLAVE

Author: Miss Ball
Tune: original, by G. W. C.

O my country, my country! how long I for thee,
Far over the mountain, far over the sea.

Where the sweet Joliba
Kisses the shore,
Say, shall I wander by
Thee never more?
Where the sweet Joliba
Kisses the shore,
Say, shall I wander by
Thee never more?
O my country, etc.

Say, O fond Zurima,
Where dost thou stay?
Say, doth another
List to thy sweet lay?
Say, doth the orange still
Bloom near our cot?
Zurima, Zurima,
Am I forgot?
O my country, etc.

Under the baobab
Oft have I slept,
Fanned by sweet breezes
That over me swept.
Often in dreams
Do my weary limbs lay
'Neath the same baobab,
Far, far away.
O my country, etc.

O for the breath
Of our own waving palm,
Here, as I languish,
My spirit to calm -
O for a draught
From our own cooling lake,
Brought by sweet mother,
My spirit to wake.
O my country, etc.

Free Soil, pp. 88-89; and Freedom, pp. 88-89.

Harp, pp. 30-31, under the same title; no tune specified.

351. TO THOSE I LOVE

Author: Miss E. M. Chandler
Tune: from an old air

Oh, turn ye not displeased away   though I
should sometimes seem
Too much to press upon your ear, an oft
repeated theme;
The story of the negro's wrongs is heavy at my
heart,
And can I choose but wish from you a
sympathizing part?

I turn to you to share my joy, - to soothe me
in my grief -
In wayward sadness from your smiles, I seek a
sweet relief:
And shall I keep this burning wish to see the
slave set free,
Locked darkly in my secret heart, unshared and
silently?

If I had been a friendless thing - if I had
never known,
How swell the fountains of the heart beneath
affection's tone,
I might have, careless, seen the leaf torn
rudely from its stem,
But clinging as I do to you, can I but feel
for them?

I could not brook to list the sad sweet music
of a bird,
Though it were sweeter melody than ever ear
hath heard,

If cruel hands had quenched its light, that in
the plaintive song,
It might the breathing memory of other days
prolong.

And can I give my lip to taste the life-bought
luxuries, wrung
From those on whom a darker night of anguish
has been flung -
Or silently and selfishly enjoy my better lot,
While those whom God hath bade me love, are
wretched and forgot?

Oh no! - so blame me not, sweet friends,
though I should sometimes seem
Too much to press upon your ear an oft
repeated theme;
The story of the negro's wrongs hath won me
from my rest, -
And I must strive to wake for him an interest
in your breast!

Free Soil, pp. 109-110; and Freedom, pp. 109-110.

352. THE SLAVE'S WAIL

Author: Jesse Hutchinson
Tune: Over the Mountain

Over the mountain and over the moor,
Comes the sad wailing of many a poor slave;
The father - the mother - the children, are
poor,
And they sigh for the day they their freedom
shall have.
Pity, oh pity, ye friends of Humanity,
Cold is the world to the cries of God's Poor.
Give us our freedom - ye friends of Equality,
Give us our Rights - for we ask nothing more.

Call us not ignorant, vile and degraded,
White men have robbed us of all we hold dear,
Parents and children - the young and the aged,
Are scourg'd by the lash of the rough
Overseer.
Pity, oh pity, ye friends of Humanity,
Cold is the world to the cries of God's Poor.
Give us our freedom - ye friends of Equality,
Give us our Rights - for we ask nothing more.

God in His mercy will crown your endeavor,
The blessings of Heaven shall be your reward,
The promise of Jesus to you shall be given,
Enter, ye faithful, the joy of your Lord.
Pity, oh pity, ye friends of Christianity,
Cold is the world to the cries of God's Poor.
Give us our freedom - ye friends of Humanity,
Give us our Rights - for we ask nothing more.

Free Soil, pp. 107-108; Liberty, pp. 186-187; and Freedom,
pp. 107-108.

353. OVER THE MOUNTAIN

Author: unspecified
Tune: [Over the Mountain?]

Over the mountain, and over the moor,
Hungry and weary I wander forlorn;
My father is dead, and my mother is poor,
And she grieves for the days that will never
return;
Give me some food for my mother in charity;
Give me some food and then I will be gone.
Pity, kind gentlemen, friends of humanity,
Cold blows the wind and the night's coming on.

Call me not indolent beggar and bold enough,
Fain would I learn both to knit and to sew;
I've two little brothers at home, when they're
old enough,
They will work hard for the gifts you bestow;
Pity, kind gentlemen, friends of humanity.
Cold blows the wind, and the night's coming
on;
Give me some food for my mother in charity,
Give me some food, and then I will be gone.

Harp, p. 11.

354. APPEAL TO WOMAN

Author: unspecified
Tune: Bavaria

Sister! were thy brother bleeding,
Shedding slavery's scalding tear,
If for him we now came pleading,
Should we meet the cruel sneer?
Daughter! were thy parent weeping,
Clanking now the iron chain,
Should we come and find thee sleeping, -
Rouse thee, but to plead in vain!

Mother! were thy nursling taken
From thee by a ruffian hand,
Should we find thee now unshaken,
Hear thee say, - "'Tis God's command!"
Should thou see thy loved and chosen -
Thy fond husband sold for gain,
Thou wouldst deem that bosom frozen,
That should heedless know thy pain.

Why then loiter, freedom's daughter!
Hear ye not the plaintive tone
Wafted from the field of slaughter!
'Tis a sister's dying moan!
Sisters! Mothers! lift your voices,
Join, the cursed chain to break;
Onward, till the slave rejoices,
Freed from bondage: wake - oh! wake.

Free Soil, p. 196; and Freedom, p. 199.

355. THE QUADROON MAIDEN

Author: Longfellow
Tune: Theme from the Indian Maid

The Slaver in the broad lagoon,
Lay moored with idle sail;
He waited for the rising moon,
And for the evening gale.

The Planter under his roof of thatch,
Smoked thoughtfully and slow;
The Slaver's thumb was on the latch,
He seemed in haste to go.

He said, "My ship at anchor rides
In yonder broad lagoon;
I only wait the evening tides,
And the rising of the moon."

Before them, with her face upraised,
In timid attitude,
Like one half curious, half amazed,
A Quadroon maiden stood.

And on her lips there played a smile
As holy, meek, and faint,
As lights, in some cathedral aisle,
The features of a saint.

"The soil is barren, the farm is old,"
The thoughtful Planter said,
Then looked upon the Slaver's gold,
And then upon the maid.

His heart within him was at strife,
With such accursed gains;
For he knew whose passions gave her life,
Whose blood ran in her veins.

But the voice of nature was too weak:
He took the glittering gold!
Then pale as death grew the maiden's cheek,
Her hands as icy cold.

The Slaver led her from the door,
He led her by the hand,
To be his slave and paramour
In a far and distant land.

Free Soil, pp. 63-65; and Freedom, pp. 230-232.

356. NEGRO BOY SOLD FOR A WATCH

Author: Cowper
Tune: from an old theme

When avarice enslaves the mind,
And selfish views alone bear sway
Man turns a savage to his kind,
And blood and rapine mark his way.
Alas! for this poor simple toy,
I sold the hapless Negro Boy.

His father's hope, his mother's pride,
Though black, yet comely to the view
I tore him helpless from their side,
And gave him to a ruffian crew -
To fiends that Afric's coast annoy,
I sold the hapless Negro Boy.

From country, friends, and parents torn,
His tender limbs in chains confined,
I saw him o'er the billows borne,
And marked his agony of mind;
But still to gain this simple toy,
I gave the weeping Negro Boy.

In isles that deck the western wave
I doomed the hapless youth to dwell,
A poor, forlorn, insulted slave!
A BEAST THAT CHRISTIANS BUY AND SELL!
And in their cruel tasks employ
The much-enduring Negro Boy.

His wretched parents long shall mourn,
Shall long explore the distant main
In hope to see the youth return;
But all their hopes and sighs are vain:
They never shall the sight enjoy,
Of their lamented Negro Boy.

Beneath a tyrant's harsh command,
He wears away his youthful prime;
Far distant from his native land,
A stranger in a foreign clime.
No pleasing thoughts his mind employ,
A poor, dejected Negro Boy.

But He who walks upon the wind,
Whose voice in thunder's heard on high,
Who doth the raging tempest bind,
And hurl the lightning through the sky,
In his own time will sure destroy
The oppressor of the Negro Boy.

Free Soil, pp. 50-51; and Freedom, pp. 242-243, with this
note: "An African prince having arrived in England, and having
been asked what he had given for his watch, answered, 'What I
will never give again - I gave a fine boy for it.'"

357. THE LITTLE SLAVE GIRL

Author: A Lady
Tune: Morgiana in Ireland

When bright morning lights the hills,
Where free children sing most cheerily,
My young breast with sorrow fills,
While here I plod my way so wearily:
Sad my face, more sad my heart,

From home, from all I had to part,
A loving mother, my sister, my brother,
For chains and lash in hopeless misery,
Children try it, could you try it;
But one day to live in slavery,
Children try it, try it, try it;
Come, come, give me liberty.

Ere I close my eyes to sleep,
Thoughts of home keep coming over me;
All alone I wake and weep -
Yet mother hears not - no one pities me -
Never smiling, sick, forlorn,
Oh that I had ne'er been born!
I should not sorrow to die tomorrow,
Then mother earth would kindly shelter me;
Children try it, could you try it!
Give me freedom, yes, from misery!
Children try it, try it, try it!
Come, come, give me Liberty!

Free Soil, pp. 167-168; and Freedom, pp. 167-168.

358. THE AFRIC'S DREAM

Author: Miss Chandler
Tune: Emigrant's Lament

Why did ye wake me from my sleep? It was a
dream of bliss,
And ye have torn me from that land, to pine
again in this;
Methought, beneath yon whispering tree, that I
was laid to rest,
The turf, with all its with'ring flowers, upon
my cold heart pressed.

My chains, these hateful chains, were gone -
oh, would that I might die,
So from my swelling pulse I could forever cast
them by!
And on, away, o'er land and sea, my joyful
spirit passed,
Till, 'neath my own banana tree, I lighted
down at last.

My cabin door, with all its flowers, was still
profusely gay,
As when I lightly sported there, in
childhood's careless day!

But trees that were as sapling twigs, with broad and shadowing bough,
Around the well-known threshhold spread a freshening coolness now.

The birds whose notes I used to hear, were shouting on the earth,
As if to greet me back again with their wild strains of mirth;
My own bright stream was at my feet, and how I laughed to lave
My burning lip, and cheek, and brow, in that delicious wave!

My boy, my first-born babe, had died amid his early hours,
And there we laid him to his sleep among the clustering flowers;
Yet lo! without my cottage-door he sported in his glee,
With her whose grave is far from his, beneath yon linden tree.

I sprang to snatch them to my soul; when breathing out my name,
To grasp my hand, and press my lip, a crowd of loved ones came!
Wife, parents, children, kinsmen, friends! the dear and lost ones all,
With blessed words of welcome came, to greet me from my thrall.

Forms long unseen were by my side; and thrilling on my ear,
Came cadences from gentle tones, unheard for many a year;
And on my cheeks fond lips were pressed, with true affection's kiss -
And so ye waked me from my sleep - but 'twas a dream of bliss!

Free Soil, pp. 54-55; and Freedom, pp. 238-239.

359. THE SLAVE-AUCTION - A FACT

Author: unspecified
Tune: unspecified

Why stands she near the auction stand,
That girl so young and fair;
What brings her to this dismal place,
Why stands she weeping there?

Why does she raise that bitter cry?
Why hangs her head with shame,
As now the auctioneer's rough voice,
So rudely calls her name?

But see! she grasps a manly hand,
And in a voice so low,
As scarcely to be heard, she says,
"My brother, must I go?"

A moment's pause: then midst a wail
Of agonizing woe,
His answer falls upon the ear,
"Yes, sister, you must go!"

"No longer can my arm defend,
No longer can I save
My sister from the horrid fate
That waits her as a SLAVE!"

Ah! now I know why she is there, -
She came there to be sold!
That lovely form, that noble mind,
Must be exchanged for gold!

O God! my every heart-string cries,
Dost thou these scenes behold
In this our boasted Christian land,
And must the truth be told?

Blush, Christian, blush! for e'en the dark
Untutored heathen see
Thy inconsistency, and lo!
They scorn thy God, and thee!

Harp, pp. 24-25.

360. SLAVE'S WRONGS

Author: Miss Chandler
Tune: Rose of Allandale

With aching brow and wearied limb,
The slave his toil pursued;
And oft I saw the cruel scourge
Deep in his blood imbrued;
He tilled oppression's soil where men
For liberty had bled,
And the eagle wing of Freedom waved
In mockery, o'er his head.

The earth was filled with the triumph shout
Of men who had burst their chains;
But his, the heaviest of them all,
Still lay on his burning veins;
In his master's hall there was luxury,
And wealth, and mental light;
But the very book of the Christian law,
Was hidden from his sight.

In his master's halls there was wine and
mirth,
And songs for the newly free;
But his own low cabin was desolate
Of all but misery.
He felt it all - and to bitterness
His heart within him turned;
While the panting wish for liberty,
Like a fire in his bosom burned.

The haunting thought of his wrongs grew
changed
To a darker and fiercer hue,
Till the horrible shape it sometimes wore
At last familiar grew;
There was darkness all within his heart,
And madness in his soul;
And the demon spark, in his bosom nursed,
Blazed up beyond control.

Then came a scene! oh! such a scene!
I would I might forget
The ringing sound of the midnight scream,
And the hearth-stone redly wet!
The mother slain while she shrieked in vain
For her infant's threatened life;
And the flying form of the frightened child,
Struck down by the bloody knife.

There's many a heart that yet will start
From its troubled sleep, at night,
As the horrid form of the vengeful slave
Comes in dreams before the sight.

The slave was crushed, and his fetters' link
Drawn tighter than before;
And the bloody earth again was drenched
With the streams of his flowing gore.

Ah! know they not, that the tightest band
Must burst with the wildest power? -
That the more the slave is oppressed and
wronged,
Will be fiercer his rising hour?
They may thrust him back with the arm of
might,
They may drench the earth with his blood -
But the best and purest of their own,
Will blend with the sanguine flood.

I could tell thee more - but my strength is
gone,
And my breath is wasting fast;
Long ere the darkness to-night has fled,
Will my life from the earth have passed:
But this, the sum of all I have learned,
Ere I go I will to thee; -
If tyrants would hope for tranquil hearts,
They must let the oppressed go free.

Free Soil, pp. 76-78; Liberty, pp. 40-42; and Freedom,
pp. 218-220.

361. THE FREED SLAVE

Author: unspecified
Tune: [Carrier Dove?]

Yet once again, once more again,
My bark bounds o'er the wave;
They know not, who ne'er clanked the chain,
What 'tis to be a slave:
To sit alone, beside the wood,
And gaze upon the sky:
This may, indeed, be solitude,
But 'tis not slavery.

Fatigued with labor's noontide task,
To sigh in vain for sleep;
Or faintly smile, our griefs to mask,
When 't would be joy to weep;

To court the shade of leafy bower,
Thirst for the freeborn wave,
But to obtain denied the power -
This is to be a slave!

Son of the sword! on honor's field
'Tis thine to find a grave;
Yet, when from life's worst ill 'twould
shield,
It comes not to the slave.
The lightsome to the heavy heart,
The laugh changed to the sigh;
To live from all we love apart -
Oh! this is slavery.

Free Soil, p. 149; Liberty, p. 114; and Freedom, p. 149.

362. THE SLAVEHOLDER'S REST

Author: Joshua Simpson
Tune: Uncle Ned

SERVANT
Come all my brethren, let us take a rest,
While the moon shines so brightly and clear;
Old master has died and left us all at last,
And has gone at the bar to appear.
Old master is dead, and lying in his grave;
And our blood will awhile cease to flow,
He will no more trample on the neck of the
slave,
For he's gone where the slaveholders go.
BRETHREN
Hang up the shovel and the hoe;
Take down the fiddle and the bow,
Old master has gone to the slaveholder's rest,
He has gone where they all ought to go.

SERVANT
I heard the old doctor say the other night,
As he pass'd by the dining room door.
"Perhaps the old gentleman may live through
the night,
But I think that he will die about four."
The old mistress sent me at the peril of my
life,
For the parson to come down to pray;
"For," said she, "your old master is now about
to die,"
And said I, "God speed him on his way!"

BRETHREN
Hang up the shovel and the hoe,
Take down the fiddle and the bow, etc.

SERVANT
At four o'clock this morning, the family was
called
Around the old man's dying bed,
And I tell you now I laughed to myself, when I
was told
That the old man's spirit had fled.
The children all grieved, and so I did
pretend;
The old mistress very near went mad;
And the old Parson's groans, did the heavens
fairly rend;
But I tell you now I felt mighty glad.
BRETHREN
Hang up the shovel and the hoe,
Take down the fiddle and the bow, etc.

ALL JOIN TOGETHER
We will no more be roused by the blowing of
his horn,
Our backs no longer he will score;
He will no more feed us on cotton seeds and
corn,
For his reign of oppression now is o'er;
He will no more hand our children on the tree,
To be eat by the carrion crow;
He will no more sell our wives to Tennessee,
For he's gone where the slaveholders go.
Hang up the shovel and the hoe,
Take down the fiddle and the bow,
We'll dance and sing,
And make the forest ring
With the fiddle and the old banjo.

Liberator, November 23, 1849, p. 188; Original, pp. 15-17;
and Car, pp. 57-59, with this introduction in the latter
two: "A Song, illustrative of the true feelings of the Slave,
when a tyrant master dies, sung by the body-servant, and his
field brethren, in a retired Negro quarter."

363. THE AMERICAN SLAVE'S ADDRESS
TO THE AMERICAN EAGLE

Author: A. B. C.
Tune: Carrier Dove

Fly away from thy native hills, proud bird,
Thou emblem of the free;
For a deep-drawn sigh in the land is heard,
It crosses the waves of the sea;
'Tis the sigh of the slave who pines in his chain,
As he bends 'neath the despot's yoke,
Where the scorn, and the lash, and the tyrant's rein,
Have his spirit subdued and broke.

As he goes to his toil at early morn,
The bloodhounds are watching his track
And the pay for his work when his labor is done,
Can be known by the scars on his back!
His wife, she is torn from his bosom away,
No more shall her form greet his sight,
And, helpless, he no word can say
'Gainst this power that tramples on right.

The children that played round his cabin door,
To gladden his heart by their glee,
Are torn from his arms, and he no more
Their cherished forms shall see;
He himself hath no home or abiding place,
Like a beast he is forced by the rod
To the auction-block, oh! deep disgrace,
To be endured by the image of God!

Oh, fly from this land, from scenes like these,
As dark and as drear as the grave!
Where the songs of the free, as they float on the breeze,
Are drowned by the cry of the slave!
Go to the haughty tyrant's throne;
Leave this, thy native land,
Where the rulers may buy, or sell, or own,
The life of a brother man.

Liberator, March 8, 1850, p. 40.

Freedom, p. 297, as "The Slave's Address to the Eagle," to the same tune.

364. THE FUGITIVE IN MONTREAL

Author: Joshua Simpson
Tune: Dandy Jim

Come all my brethren, now draw near;
I have a tale to tell to you;
I have escaped the Auctioneers,
Though hard the blood-hounds did pursue.
Far in the south I was a slave
Where Sugar-cane, and cotton grows;
My Master was a cruel knave,
As every body may suppose.
My old master don't like me;
I begged him so to set me free -
He swore before he'd let me go
He'd feed me to the carrion crow.

One day as I was grinding cane,
My Master passed me too, and fro;
Says I what can old master mean?
It's nothing good for me I know.
I caught his eye - he [dropped] his head,
And stuck his cigar in his mouth.
Ha! Ha! says I. Old master Ned;
You're going to sell me farther south!
My old master don't like me, etc.

I soon beheld a hard old case -
He was a stranger too, to me;
He come and stared me in the face,
And says "my boy I'll set you free."
That night I lay me on my bed,
But there was no repose for me -
Ten-thousand thoughts ran through my head,
But all was about old Tennessee.
My old master don't like me, etc.

I Heard old master plainly say
"Well mother I have sold old Sam;
He leaves about the break of day -
I've got one thousand in my hand."
Thinks I, this is my only chance,
For life and death are now at stake;
I gathered up my coat, and pants,
And for the North I made a break.
My old master don't like me, etc.

It was dark, and dreary night,
'Bout one o'clock, when all was still;
No stars, nor moon to give me light;
And nought to be heard but the whippoorwill.
I wandered not to the left nor right,
(Though hard it was to find the way)
And just six weeks from that dark night
I landed safe in Canada.
My old master don't like me, etc.

I have a wife, I know not where;
(At least sometimes I call her mine)
When last I saw her countenance fair,
She was on her way to <u>Caroline</u>.
I have a son both young and brave,
Who broke the ice some time ago,
And now with me (though not a slave)
He's safe beneath the LION'S paw
My old master don't like me, etc.

<u>Original</u>, pp. 11-13; and <u>Car</u>, pp. 46-49.

365. EMANCIPATION CAR

Author: Joshua Simpson
Tune: unspecified

HERE comes Emancipation's Car,
I hear the bell resound;
Her hand's towards the Northern Star,
For Canada she's bound;
Her steam is up, - she's rightly manned -
Her engine new and bright;
And I am bound to leave the land
Of slavery to-night.
So hie me away to Canada,
That cold and dreary shore -
Oh! carry me back to Alabama,
To Alabama no more -
Oh! carry be back to Alabama,
To Alabama no more.

The laws against the Fugitive
Are very hard they say
But I must venture die or live
I will not be a slave
She bribes the Martial with a TEN
If I'm, returned alive
But should I prove myself a MAN
He only gets a Five;
So hie me away, etc.

I oft have heard old master tell,
Of freedom's land before;
And why should I in slavery dwell,
On Alabama's shore?

When I am dead and gone to rest,
I want my bones to lie
Beneath the soil which God has bles't,
With life and Liberty.
So hie me away, etc.

I've served my master all my days,
Without a dime's reward;
And now I'm forced to run away,
To flee the lash, abhorr'd.
The hounds are baying on my track,
The master's just behind,
Resolved, that he will bring me back,
Before I cross the line.
So hie me away, etc.

There, something speaks within my breast;
The voice can not be hushed!
Though this poor body is oppressed,
The spirit can't be crushed.
It speaks and tells me, "rise and live,
And show myself a man.
The soul which God to me has given,
The tyrant ne'er can brand.
So hie me away, etc.

Farewell to Alabama's shore,
Farewell to the galling yoke,
I ne'er expect to wear thee more;
Thou art forever broke.
Farewell to master, friends, and foes,
Your face, no more I'll see:
Put on the steam - and off she goes:
Huzzah for Liberty.
So hie me away to Canada,
That cold and dreary shore,
Oh! carry me back to Alabama,
To Alabama no more -
Oh! carry me back to Alabama,
To Alabama no more.

Original, pp. 29-31; and Car, pp. 7-9.

366. AWAY TO CANADA

Adapted to the case of Mr. S.,
fugitive from Tennessee.

Author: Joshua Simpson
Tune: [O, Susannah!]

I'm on my way to Canada,
That cold and dreary land;
The dire effects of slavery,
I can no longer stand.
My soul is vexed within me so,
To think that I'm a slave;
I'm now resolved to strike the blow
For freedom or the grave.
O righteous Father,
Wilt thou not pity me?
And aid me on to Canada,
Where colored men are free.

I heard old Queen Victoria say,
If we would all forsake
Our native land of slavery,
And come across the Lake,
That she was standing on the shore,
With arms extended wide,
To give us all a peaceful home,
Beyond the rolling tide.
Farewell, Old Master!
That's enough for me -
I'm going straight to Canada,
Where colored men are free.

I heard the old soul driver say,
As he was passing by,
That Darkey's bound to run away.
I see it in his eye.
My heart responded to the charge
And thought it was no crime,
And something seemed my mind to urge,
That now's the very time.
O! old Driver,
Don't you cry for me -
I'm going up to Canada,
Where colored men are free.

Grieve not, my wife - grieve not for me,
O! do not break my heart,
For nought but cruel slavery
Would cause me to depart.
If I should stay to quell your grief,
Your grief I would augment;
For no one knows the day that we
Asunder might me rent.
O! Susannah,
Don't you cry for me -
I'm going up to Canada,
Where colored men are free.

I heard old Master pray last night -
I heard him pray for me;
That God would come, and in his might
From Satan set me free;
So I from Satan would escape,
And flee the wrath to come -
If there's a fiend in human shape,
Old Master must be one.
O! Old Master!
While you pray for me,
I'm doing all I can to reach
The land of Liberty.

Ohio's not the place for me;
For I was much surprised,
So many of her sons to see,
In garments of disguise.
Her name has gone out through the world
Free Labor - Soil - and Men; -
But slaves had better far be hurled
Into the Lion's Den.
Farewell Ohio!
I am not safe in thee;
I'll travel on to Canada,
Where colored men are free.

I've now embarked for yonder shore,
Where Man's a man by Law,
The vessel soon will bear me o'er,
To shake the Lion's paw.
I no more dread the Auctioneer;
Nor fear the Master's frowns; -
I no more tremble when I hear
The baying Negro-hounds.
O, Old Master!
Don't think hard of me -
I'm just in sight of Canada,
Where colored men are free.

I've landed safe upon the shore,
Both soul and body free;
My blood and brain, and tears no more
Will drench old Tennessee,
But I behold the scalding tear,
Now stealing from my eye,
To think my wife - my only dear,
A slave must live and die.
O, Susannah!
Don't grieve after me -
For ever at a throne of Grace
I will remember thee.

Original, pp. 21-24; Liberator, December 10, 1852, p. 200;
and Car, pp. 63-67. The first two verses are quoted in

an article, "Good News from Slavery," in <u>Liberator</u>, May 20, 1853, p. 88, with this third verse and chorus (author unspecified):

> I've served my master all my days,
> Without a dime's reward;
> And I am forced to run away,
> To flee the lash abhorred;
> The hounds are baying on my track -
> The master's just behind,
> Resolved that he will bring us back,
> Before we cross the Line.
> O, old master!
> Don't come after me;
> I'm going up to Canada,
> Where colored men are free.

367. QUEEN VICTORIA CONVERSING
WITH HER SLAVE CHILDREN

Author: Joshua Simpson
Tune: Come Come Away

QUEEN
O come! come away, my sable sons and daughters
Why linger there
In dark despair?
O come! come away!
On Erie's northern banks I stand,
With open arms, and stretched out hands;
From tyrant Columbia's land
O come! come away!

SLAVES
O, mother Victoria,
Why do you thus torment us?
Do you not see
That we'er not free,
And can't come away?
We'er watched by day and chained by night;
Both robbed of liberty and right;
While crushed by the oppressors might
<u>We</u> <u>can't</u> <u>come</u> <u>away</u>.

QUEEN
O come! come away, my sable sons and
daughters.
Your galling chains
Now rend in twain
And come, come away.

Here in my province still is room,
And I will give you if you come
A long, free, and happy home.
O come! come away!

SLAVES
The bloodhounds (our guards)
Surround our whole plantation;
The patrols too
Will us pursue,
We can't come away.
Also our master and their wives
Sleep on their swords and <u>Bowieknives</u>,
And swear they will take our lives;
<u>We can't come away.</u>

QUEEN
O come! come away, my sable sons and
daughters,
Fear not those hounds
Nor master's frowns,
But come! come away!
While dogs and masters are asleep,
Then slily from your cabins creep,
And no more in slavery weep:
O come! come away!

SLAVES
The journey is long,
And great the undertaking:
We'll have to go
Through frost and snow;
We can't come away.
The cane brake and the cotton field
Must be our shelter and our shield,
And wild beasts are there concealed;
<u>We can't come away.</u>

QUEEN
O come! come away, my sable sons and daughters
Dry up your tears
Dismiss your fears
And come! come away!
The Lord will take you by the hand,
And lead you through the forest land;
The beasts are at his command;
O come! come away!

SLAVES
Our masters we fear will blight our
undertaking;
Our very eyes
They'll advertise -
We can't come away.

The northern states though free by name
Have negro dogs in every range
Who linger there for pocket change;
We can't come away.

QUEEN
O come! come away, why will you longer tarry?
The Lord will stand
At your right hand
O come, come away!
You'll meet with many a northern friend
Who will his best endeavors lend
To speed you on to freedom's land;
O Come, come away!

SLAVES
O! mother Victoria should we be overtaken;
Our grief untold
Will be ten fold;
We can't come away.
They'll either hang us on a tree,
Or sell us down to Tennessee
Into endless slavery;
We can't come away.

QUEEN
O come, come away! I cannot tease you longer;
You need not fear
John Bull is here -
O come, come away!
The Lyon's paw shall guard thy head,
His shaggy mane shall be thy bed,
And none upon thy rights shall tread,
O come, come away.

SLAVES' RESPONSE
The Lyon's paw shall guard our heads!
His shaggy mane shall be our beds!
And none upon our rights shall tread!
We'll all come away!

Original, pp. 17-21; and Car, pp. 59-63.

368. THE LITTLE MAID ON HER WAY

Author: Joshua Simpson
Tune: Buy a Broom

O! say little maid, whither now are you going
Whether now are you going this cold winter
day?
I'm bound for the North where the cold winds
are blowing
For I was a slave, and am running away.

O! say little maiden how far have you traveled
How far have you traveled this cold winter
day?
I have come full ten miles, over mountains and
valley,
And I must be making quick speed on my way.

O! say little maid - fear ye not you will
perish -
Fear ye not you will perish this cold winter
day?
I'm cold it is true - but a hope I do cherish,
That I shall soon warm me in old Canada.

O! say little maid will you not have some
biscuits,
To keep you from starving this cold winter
day?
I have some old crust which I stole from my
mistress,
And this will support me awhile on the way.

O! say little maid, have you no one to guard
you?
And how can you travel this cold winter day?
The Lord is my pilot, he's always beside me
And this makes me happy, and blithe on the
way,

O! say little maid, can you no longer tarry -
Can you no longer tarry this cold winter day,
O no! I'm afraid, that some wretch will betray
me;
I'll bid you farewell, and will haste on my
way.

Original, pp. 31-32; and Car, pp. 9-11.

369. WHERE CAN THE SLAVE FIND REST?

Author: B. S. J.
Tune: Where Can the Soul Find Rest?

Tell me, thou Northern wind that cools my
fevered blood,
Dost thou not know some spot sacred to
Freedom's God,
Some dark and lonesome dell, some cave or
mountain breast,
Where, free from galling chains, the weary
slave many rest?
The North wind dwindled to a whisper low,
And moaned in sadness as it answered, No!

Ye mighty Oceans tell, whose waves around me
roar,
Know ye some favored spot upon Columbia's
shore,
Where pining captives find the bliss of which
they dream,
Where Slavery dare not come, and Freedom
reigns supreme?
The far Pacific paused not in its flow,
But echoed back the near Atlantic's No!

And ye, bright stars that shine with steadfast
light,
Creation's gems upon the brow of night,
See ye within my country's bounds no spot
Which Slavery's blighting presence curseth
not?
And from the stars a voice, distinct and low,
In soft and saddened tone responded, No!

Tell me, my longing soul, oh tell me, Truth
and Right,
Is there no day of joy to follow slavery's
night?
Is there no future hour when sin and wrong
shall cease,
And all God's children live in brotherhood and
peace?
Truth, Right, and Love, man's angel helpers
given,
Whispered, "Be strong, toil on, and trust in
Heaven."

Liberator, January 9, 1852, p. 8.

370. THE AFRICAN GIRL

Author: Joshua Simpson
Tune: Long Long Ago

This world to me at the best is but base -
Here is no rest - here is no rest!
Here I am sunk in the deepest disgrace -
Here is no rest - here is no rest!
Here I'm forsaken and left all alone;
Far from my country, my friends and my home;
Far o'er the billows from all have been borne;
Here is no rest; here's no rest.

Here I must rise at the sound of the horn!
Here is no rest! here is no rest!
Go to the field e'en before day is dawned!
Here is no rest! here's no rest!
Here I must labor, and toil as a beast
And when I murmer my task is increased;
No one to pity; no arm to release;
Here is no rest, here's no rest.

Here I must toil at the end of the lash;
Here is no rest, here is no rest!
And dare not shrink from its deep painful
gash;
Here is no rest; here is no rest!
Heart broken daughter of grief and despair;
No one to help me my burthen to bear -
No one on earth for my soul who will care.
Here is no rest, here's no rest.

Here I'm a slave, and a slave must remain;
Here is no rest; here is no rest!
Winter and summer to me are the same;
Here is no rest; here is no rest!
Here I must labor though tempests may blow;
Toil without mantle through frost and through
snow;
O tell me when shall my tears cease to flow?
Here is no rest, here's no rest!

Could I but soar to those mansions on high!
There there is rest; there there is rest!
There in the arms of my Savior to lie;
There there is rest; there there is rest!
Speed fleeting moments and bear me away!
Free my sad soul from this prison of clay,
Far from this wilderness bear me away!
There, there is rest; There is rest.

Original, pp. 7-8.

Car, pp. 23-25, as "The Slave Girl," to the same tune.

371. THE TASKMASTER'S HOME

Author: P. A. H.
Tune: Old Folks at Home

Away off upon the stormy ocean,
Far, far away,
Or where the British hold dominion,
There, there alone can I stray.
All up and down the States of freedom
I may not roam,
For they'll send me to the old plantation,
And to my taskmaster's home.
All my lot is sad and dreary,
Everywhere I roam,
I for freedom long till weary,
Far from my taskmaster's home.

Oh, for a home far away on the billow,
With all I love,
Where, with my wife and children precious,
I may in freedom rove!
What is life worth without such blessings,
Freedom and home,
Where none my loved ones can from me sever,
Where none can make me roam!
All my lot is sad and dreary,
Everywhere I roam,
I for freedom long till weary,
Far from my taskmaster's home.

White men, who love your friends and freedom,
Give such to me;
Oh, 'twill not rob you, but add to your
blessings,
If all the slaves are free!
All through life will my wife and children,
And, too, will I,
Pray that the friends of freedom prosper,
Pray to the Lord on high.
All my lot is sad and dreary,
Everywhere I roam;
Give me freedom! take, oh! take me,
Far from my taskmaster's home!

Liberator, February 4, 1853, p. 20.

372. A SABBATH MORNING EXERCISE

Author: Joshua Simpson
Tune: unspecified

Behold that wretch with haggard look,
With bloated face and swollen eyes,
His raging brow, his curling lip,
World almost cause one's hair to rise.

See by his side a cowhide hangs;
He grasps a club and bowieknife -
In meditation see him stand
As though intent on human life.

His eyes with vengeance seem to flash;
Loud oaths escape in every breath;
He hungers now for human flesh,
He'll soon commit the deed of death.

Hark! now I think I hear him speak
With lifted hand and language brave,
I'll go to hell if I don't break
The neck of that rebellious slave.

The cabin he at length has reached,
He enters quick, and slams the door,
And Oh! what wild terrific shrieks!
Such cries I never heard before.

Now muttering to himself he comes
"I've gratified my aching heart,
I've sent one rebel nigger home,
There to receive his just desserts.["]

Poor faithful slave what has he done
To have his skull in pieces broke?
Naught but the dangerous risk to run,
To attempt to break the slavish yoke.

But hasten on! he goes again,
To perpetrate some dreadful deed,
His haughty spirit seems inflamed
As quick he mounts the prancing steed.

Hark now! o'er hill and dale resounds
The bugle's piercing notes to tell
The fugitive, that greedy hounds
Will shortly bey her funeral knell.

Away they bolt, on track of what?
A bounding stag? I fancy not
For what do they so fiercely -
A human being is the prey.

O'er cotton fields and sugar farms
In hot pursuit he winds his way,
Sworn by his God, and his right arm
To bring her back without delay.

And now the victim he has found
A mangled body, nearly dead;
No friend is there to dress the wound,
No one to bathe her aching head.

Her dying bed is tangled grass,
Her pillow is a rugged stone;
In misery here she breathes her last,
Far, far away from friends, alone.

The savage wretch sheds not a tear
He leaves her lying on the ground,
And hastens home God's word to hear,
And feigns to weep beneath the sound.

Car, pp. 87-89.

373. THE FINAL ADIEU

Author: Joshua Simpson
Tune: I'm Bound to Run All Night [Camptown Races?]

Come all my brethren now draw near -
Good-bye, Good-bye.
My resolution you shall hear,
I'll soon be on my way.
Last night I heard some spirit say,
Good-bye, Good-bye,
'Tis time to go to Canada,
I'll soon be on my way.
[CHORUS:]
FIRST VOICE
I'm bound to run all night,
SECOND VOICE
I'm bound to sleep all day,
Let the wind blow high,
Come wet or dry,
I'm bound for Canada.

I've served my time, my cup is full,
Good-bye, Good-bye;
Now I must see old Johnny Bull,
I'll soon be on my way.
When master blows his negro horn,
Good-bye, Good-bye,
He'll find this "darkie" out and gone,
I'll soon be on my way.
CHORUS (no first and second voice)

When I get on the other shore,
Good-bye, Good-bye,
I'll be a man for evermore,
I'll soon be on my way.
When master comes to look for me,
Good-bye, Good-bye,
He'll find me where "all men are free,"
I'll soon be on my way.
CHORUS

(A voice is heard in a low but distinct tone
from
the kitchen cellar, uttered by an old house
servant.)

If you get there before I do,
Good-bye, Good-bye.
Look out for me I'm coming too,
I'll soon be on my way.
I have a son that's gone before;
Good-bye, Good-bye,
And I will meet him on that shore,
I'll soon be on my way.
CHORUS

Car, pp. 49-51.

374. THE VOICE ON THE BREEZE

Author: Joshua Simpson
Tune: Alabama Again

Far, far from the South, where the sugar-cane
growing,
And rice-swamps are spreading through valleys
and plains,
On every dull breeze, which from that region's
blowing,
I hear the sad wail of the slave in his
chains.

Here I am a slave and am destined to labor,
And bear all the burthen and heat of the day -
Get food to sustain both myself and my
neighbor,
Let what may befall me, I must not say nay.

We're led like the innocent lamb to the
slaughter,
Like sheep in the hands of the shearers we're
mute;
The white man will see both our sons and our
daughters,
And his sovereign right there's none to
dispute.

The white man is driving his base legislation,
And putting in force all his impious plans,
Which tend to degrade our poor sable nation,
And why he thus treats us, we dare not demand.

The morning is dawning, the day-star is
rising,
And Africa's sons are beginning to wake;
Our progress to the white man is now quite
surprising,
For God is intending our fetters to break.

Car, pp. 39-40.

375. THE FUGITIVE'S DREAM

Author: Joshua Simpson
Tune: My Old Kentucky Home

I dreamed last night of my old Kentucky home,
Of my old Kentucky home far away;
I thought old master and I were all alone
In the parlor about the break of day.
I thought old master was weeping like a child,
Said I, O, master, what is wrong?
He heard my voice, and he then began to smile,
Why, said he, what made you stay so long?
Weep no more, old master -
Weep no more, I pray;
I will sing one song at my old Kentucky home,
And return again to old Canada.

He says, my boy come let us take a walk;
Thinks I, there's something yet behind;
And the first think I know I'll be standing on
the block,
Or be writhing 'neath a sweet "ninety nine."
Says I, O master, I pray don't punish me!
I'm weary, my journey has been long;
I have been up North where the colored man is
free,
Now I'll sing to you a sweet little song.
Weep no more, old master, etc.

I have been up North to that "free and happy
land;"
My brothers are all doing well.
They are free from chains, and they do not
wear the brand;
And I've something better yet quite to tell;
There we are <u>men</u> by the <u>power</u> <u>of</u> <u>the</u> <u>law</u>,
Our rights none dare to take away,
When once we get <u>there</u>, 'neath the <u>British</u>
<u>Lion's</u> <u>paw</u>,
We can sing sweet music all the day.
Weep no more, old master, etc.

I have served my time at my old Kentucky home;
My wages were <u>nothing</u> every day;
My bread was <u>doubtful</u>, and better I had <u>none</u>,
And you never gave me time e'en to pray.
By and by, one day, as a Trader came along,
He gave me a mighty pleasant look;
Thinks I, "old coon," I had better now be
gone,
For your motive I can read like a book.
Weep no more, old master, etc.

Now the moon shone bright, and the day began
to break!
It was time for the Negro Horn to blow;
The old master says you shall never see the
Lake,
You are <u>mine</u>, I shall never let you go;
Then he gave one yell and the hounds began to
bey;
He bolted the West parlor door -
I awoke from sleep just as we commenced the
fray,
And beheld, '<u>twas</u> <u>a</u> <u>dream</u> and nothing more.
Weep no more, old master,
Weep no more, I pray;
I will sing one song of my old Kentucky home,
Of my old Kentucky home, far away.

<u>Car</u>, pp. 55-57.

376. THE FUGITIVE AT HOME

Author: Joshua Simpson
Tune: Sweet Alice Ben Bolt

I stand as a freeman upon the Northern bank
Of old Erie, this fresh water Sea,
And it cheers my very soul
To behold the billows roll,
And to think, like these waves, I am free.

Old master, I pray thee, do not come after me,
For I can't be a slave any more;
I'm beyond the tyrant's law -
Safe beneath the Lion's paw,
And he'll growl if you come near the shore.

I am free as the waters that roll at my feet
Or the sea-gull that glides slowly by,
And no hammer do I hear,
Nor dread the Auctioneer,
And the driver and lash I defy.

Old master and mistress, pray don't grieve
after me
Though the waters between us are wide,
Here the atmosphere is pure,
And my freedom secure,
For old JOHNNY is close by my side.

O, don't you remember that tall towering oak,
Where you put on my last "fourty-four?"
When he bows his lofty head,
To behold where I bled -
O, remember, I'll bleed there no more.

O, don't you remember the promise that you
made,
To my old mother's dying request?
That I never should be sold,
Not for silver nor gold,
While the sun rolled from the East to the
West.

O! don't you remember as soon as she was dead,
E'en the grass had not grown on her grave?
I was advertised for sale,
And would now be in jail,
Had I not crossed the old dancing waves.

And now while I'm standing upon the water's
brink,
I can raise both my hands free from chains.
I disdain the tyrant's power,
From this very hour,
or the land where the bold tyrant reigns.

<u>Car</u>, pp. 72-73.

377. ALBERT MORRIS

Author: Joshua Simpson
Tune: We're Traveling Home to Heaven Above

I'm going to see the old North Star,
Will you go, will you go?
They tell me "freedom" reigns up there
Will you go, will you go?
I've long resolved with all my heart,
This very night to make a start,
From chains forever to depart;
Will you go, will you go?

I'm going to see Victoria's face;
Will you go, will you go?
At her right hand I'll find a place;
Will you go, will you go?
Her arms of love extend to me,
She says, "My son, I'll set you free,"
"A slave no more, you e'er shall be,"
Come away, come away!

I'm going to see Old Johnny Bull;
Will you come, will you come?
And drink a draught at Freedom's pool;
Will you come, will you come?
And Johnny long has been our friend,
And will be until time shall end;
To black men, aid he'll always lend,
Will you come, will you come?

I'm going to hear the cannon roar,
Will you come, will you come?
Upon Lake Erie's northern shore,
Will you come, will you come?
I cannot stay - I must be gone;
I hear the rolling fife and drum,
And Queen Victoria bids me come;
Let me go, let me go.

I'm going to see my friends once more,
Will you come, will you come?
Who long ago have gone before;
Will you come, will you come?
O, what a shouting there will be,
When we each other's face shall see,
In that blest "Land of Liberty,"
I must go, I must go.

Old tyrant Master, fare you well;
I must go, I must go.
In chains no longer I can dwell;
I must go, I must go.
I've been your servant many a day,
I've served without one cent of pay;
And now I'm bound to run away;
I must go, I must go.

I hope the time will not be long,
I must go, I must go.
When I shall join that happy throng,
I must go, I must go.
I've many friends to Chatham gone,
And many more will follow on -
To master, lash and "Negro Gong,"
Fare you well, fare you well.

Car, pp. 25-27.

378. THE DYING SLAVE

Author: Joshua Simpson
Tune: The Man for Me

I've heard them talk of a happy home,
A land where all are free;
A land where slavery is unknown -
"Of Life and Liberty."
I've often thought if I should live,
That happy land I soon would see;
But now I'm going to Heaven
And there I shall be free;
And there I shall be free;
And there I shall be free.

O! what a joyous sight appears:
Far, far beyond the skies!
What heavenly sounds salute my ears;
A song that never dies.

I see ten thousand spirits bright,
Sweet angels clothed in garments white,
And none are fetters wearing:
O! there is Liberty;
O! there is Liberty;
O! there is Liberty.

My father dwells in Georgia State,
My mother dwells up there;
I see her on the pearly gates,
A crown of life she wears.
I saw her die beneath the lash:
I counted every bleeding gash,
But now no scars she's wearing.
She's happy and she's free;
She's happy and she's free;
She's happy and she's free.

A few more fleeting moments here,
And then my toils are o'er;
The hammer of the Auctioneer
Will grieve my soul no more.
I'm going to join that happy throng,
Beyond the sound of "Negro Gongs";
O! sweet emancipation.
My soul will then be free;
My soul will then be free;
My soul will then be free.

I'm going where Christ, my Saviour lives,
Where friends will part no more;
A seat at his right hand he gives
To all his suffering poor.
There, souls by color are not known,
Around God's bright eternal throne;
There, all are "free and equal."
O! that's the place for me;
O! that's the place for me;
O! that's the place for me.

I've suffered long enough below!
I would no longer stay;
My Saviour calls, and I must go,
And leave this mortal clay;
My yoke and fetters, chains and all,
With this poor body here must fall,
And I'll say Hallelujah!
For grace has made me free;
For grace has made me free;
For grace has made me free.

Car, pp. 31-33.

379. THE CHILD'S INQUIRY

Author: Joshua Simpson
Tune: unspecified

CHILD
O, where has mother gone, papa?
What makes you look so sad?
Why sit you here alone, papa?
Has any one made you mad?
O, tell me, tell me, dear papa,
Has master punished you again?
Shall I go bring the salt papa,
To rub your back and cure the pain?

FATHER
Go 'way my child, you are too bad;
You notice things too soon;
Did you not see that I was sad
When I came home at noon?
Go to the gate and call mamma,
And see if she's in sight.
The hour is late - I fear your ma
Will not be home to-night.

CHILD
O, no, papa, I am afraid
To go to the gate alone:
I fear there's men in the high-grass laid,
To catch little Mary Jones.
But what makes mother stay so long?
'Tis getting very late,
Pa-pa, go bring my mother home,
And I'll stay at the gate.

When mother left me early this morn,
She kissed me and she wept;
I saw the tears come trickling down
Upon the pillow where I slept.
She pressed me up to her bosom hard,
As though it was the last embrace,
She sobbed, but did not say a word,
Nor would she let me see her face.

FATHER
Pull off your shoes my dearest child,
And say your evening prayer;
And go to your bed and after a while
Perhaps your mother will be there.

Go hush those little eyes to sleep,
And dream some pretty dream to-night;
Perhaps in the morning when you wake
You'll find all things are right.

CHILD
O! tell me, papa! don't drive me away -
'Tis dark! the stars are thick and bright
Is mother sold? O, tell me I pray!
I fear she'll not be home, to-night.
O, come, papa, come, go with me,
Perhaps we'll meet her in the lane,
And then she'll sing a song to me,
And take me in her arms again.

FATHER
Come here, my daughter, come to me,
I find that I must tell you true,
Come now and sit upon my knee -
The dismal tale I'll tell to you.
Your mother's "sold" - she's sold, my dear;
Her face you'll see no more;
Her cheering voice no more you'll hear
On this side Canaan's peaceful shore.

CHILD
O, tell me, papa, when mother dies,
Will she come home again?
Or will we meet above the skies,
Where Christ the Savior reigns?
Would you not like to die to-night,
If mother too would die?
And with sweet angels dressed in white,
Meet her above the sky?

FATHER
O yes, my child, my life is dear,
And you I love full well;
But I no longer can tarry here,
I soon will bid this world farewell.
I cannot live, my heart is broke,
My grief is more than I can bear;
This very strap and that great oak
Will end my life in deep despair.

Car, pp. 76-78.

380. A JOURNEY THROUGH THE WILDERNESS

Author: Joshua Simpson
Tune: Go to Dark Gethsemane

Sons and daughters of the free,
You who love the Tyrant's power,
Take a view of slavery,
Go with me one bitter hour;
Turn not from the scene away -
Come along without delay.

Follow to the throne of Grace,
There behold a kneeling pair;
Mark the difference in the face -
One is dark, the other fair.
Now they rise their joys to tell,
"Jesus has done all things well."

But we must not tarry here;
Follow to the cotton field;
There behold those brothers dear,
Who were at the altar kneeled;
Here the white man tyrant reigns -
Binds his brother down with chains.

See him ply the bloody lash
To his sable brother's frame;
Every stroke he leaves a gash,
Bringing blood from every vein.
None for him can intercede;
Learn like this poor slave to bleed.

Follow to the auction block,
There this sable brother's wife
Writhes in chains that's firmly locked,
Now she's sold a slave for life!
O! ye men with hearts of steel,
Learn like this poor slave to feel.

Follow on to yonder shed,
There's a fair young female tied
To the beam that's overhead,
While the lash is well applied,
By the minister of God!
Learn like her to bear the rod.

Listen to these doleful sounds!
Let us hasten to the spot!
'Tis the beying negro hounds!
There, their victims they have caught.
See him mangled! hear him cry!
Learn like the poor slave to die.

Car, pp. 36-38.

381. AN EVERY DAY SCENE

Author: Joshua Simpson
Tune: One Hundred Years Ago

A vision passed before my mind -
A daily Southern scene.
But he who travels South will find
'Tis more than a fancied dream.
A boy stood on the Auction Block,
He was beautiful and mild;
He had a sweet angelic look -
He was an only child.

I saw the mother of that lad,
Come pressing through the crowd;
Her gentle form was neatly clad,
Her cries were keen and loud.
She clung around her master's feet;
I thought she would go wild,
And every breath she would repeat,
O, master, where's my child?

The auctioneer paid no regard
To weeping, wails nor cries;
His heart like adamant was hard,
And glassy was his eyes;
He loudly cried the child is sound,
And worth his weight in gold!
Come, Speculators, come around;
This negro must be sold.

I saw the hammer lifted up,
To drive the final dart.
Which pointed like a thunderbolt,
To that fond mother's heart.
Nine hundred dollars then was bid;
The master turned and smiled;
Although the mother constant plead,
O, master, where's my child?

Nine hundred! cried the Auctioneer;
Can I not hear the ten?
This bid is quite inferior
Among so many men!
Nine hundred, there's a bargain here,
To him who gives fifteen,
And if you think the child is dear,
Just bring him back again.

The mother, overcome with grief,
Lay senseless on the ground;
The master to her groans was deaf,
No favor could be found.
The sound like tones of thunder fell
Upon the mighty throng -
One thousand's bid, I cannot dwell,
He's going! going!! gone!!!

The mother started from her sleep,
With shrieks and piercing yells,
Which would have made a demon weep
In his infernal cell.
The master of his gold was proud,
Which had his soul beguiled,
Although the mother cried aloud
O, master, where's my child?

I heard that mother's last appeal -
But could not take her part,
I thought before that man could feel,
While he retained a heart.
She died a raving maniac,
Her master only smiled;
She cried with her expiring breath,
O, master, where's my child?

Car, pp. 82-84, with this introduction: "Many who have escaped the yoke of the taskmasters, have no doubt witnessed, and perhaps experienced the full spirit of the following lines."

382. THE SON'S REFLECTIONS

Author: Joshua Simpson
Tune: Old Folks at Home

'Way down upon the Mobile river,
Close to Mobile Bay,
There's where my thoughts are running ever,
All through the live-long day.
There I've a good and kind old mother,
Though she is a slave,
There I've a sister and a brother,
Lying in their peaceful graves.
[CHORUS:]
Oh! could I some how or other,
Drive these tears away;
When I think about my poor old mother,
Down upon the Mobile Bay.

O! could I see that old fence corner,
Where she used to pray,
Though master laid the lash upon her,
Driving her abruptly away.
There often while we all were sleeping,
Free from every care,
You can find my poor old mother weeping,
Sending up her anxious prayer.
CHORUS

No one had she to soothe her sorrow -
None on earth but me;
And where I might be sent to-morrow,
To her was in eternity.
One day, she says, I'm old and feeble,
Naught can do but pray,
Now, my son, while you're young and able,
Try to get to Canada.
CHORUS

Oh! how my heart did fail and falter,
Oh! how bad I felt,
When before that sacred family altar,
I was for the last time knelt.
There to leave my mother old and weary,
Her sad fate to share,
There to spend her days so lone and dreary,
Filled my heart with deep despair.
CHORUS

But when I viewed my sad condition,
Young and in my prime,
I resolved to change my situation,
For a free and healthy clime.
My mother wept for joy when I told her,
I should run away -
That I never would be three days older,
Ere I left for Canada.
CHORUS

I never can forget that morning,
When my chains I broke,
Just about the time that day was dawning,
I threw off the tyrant's yoke.
Two thousand miles or more to freedom,
And a road unknown!
Was it not for mother's constant pleading,
Never would I left my home.
CHORUS

Car, pp. 79-81.

383. THEY ARE STILL TRAVELING NORTH

Author: Joshua Simpson
Tune: We Are All Noddin'

We are like a band of pilgrims,
In a strange and foreign land;
With our knapsacks on our shoulders,
And our "cudgels" in our hands,
We have many miles before us,
But it lessens not our joys,
We will sing a merry chorus,
For we are the "tramping boys."
[CHORUS:]
And we're all jogging,
Jog, jog, jogging,
And we're all jogging -
We are going to the North.

We have left our friends behind us,
Where the bloody tyrant reigns,
And our chains no more shall bind us,
On the burning southern plains.
We defy the master's power,
We have robbed him of his might,
We were freemen from that hour,
That we took our Northern flight.
CHORUS

When we lived in old Kentucky,
We were slaves and nothing more,
But we felt ourselves quite lucky,
When we reached Ohio's shore,
We all stuck our heads together,
And resolved to fight like men,
And to brook all kinds of weather,
And to ne'er return again.
CHORUS

Car, pp. 85-86, with this introduction: "This remark was
made by an Anti-Slavery friend in Putnam, the other day, after
reading the intelligence of forty slaves escaping at one communication. 'Yes,' responded another, 'the Fugitive Slave Law
seems to help them along.' 'Yes,' says I, 'they are all jogging,' at which it seemed as though the muse caught the echo
from them as it came revibrating [sic] over the hills."

384. THE BONDMAN'S HOME

Author: Joshua Simpson
Tune: There is a Happy Land

We have a happy home,
Far, far away;
Where slavery is not known
In Canada.
Here men have equal rights,
As the blacks, so are the whites,
There like a band of knights,
"All men are free."

There men protected are
By the Lion's paw;
All equal rights do share,
By a righteous law.
John Bull is the man for me,
He doth set the captive free,
Both on the land and sea,
Free one and all.

There mid the tempests cold,
On that blessed shore;
Are all both young and old,
Who have gone before,
Crying with loudest strains,
Cast your yoke on break your chains,
And from old Georgia's plains,
Come, come away.

Car, pp. 38-39.

385. THE BONDMAN'S CRY

Author: Joshua Simpson
Tune: Herdman's Flute

When the first faint morning's ray
O'er the hill is breaking,
Loudly thrills the bondman's cry;
Mournful echoes waking.
O! Lord; O! Lord; O! Lord!
O! Lord; O! Lord; O! Lord!

Lo they scamper at the call;
For the slaves are bounding;
Now for mercy hear them call
While the lash is sounding.
O! Lord; O! Lord; O! Lord!
O! Lord; O! Lord; O! Lord!

Now behold the crimson flow
From the gory fountain,
While the slaves with axe and hoe
Climb the rugged mountain.
O! Lord; O! Lord; O! Lord!
O! Lord; O! Lord; O! Lord!

When the silvery evening star
Sees them homeward stealing,
Listening peasants from afar
Hear their cries still pealing.
O! Lord; O! Lord; O! Lord!
O! Lord; O! Lord; O! Lord!

Car, p. 43.

386. SOBER REFLECTIONS

Author: Joshua Simpson
Tune: Lilly Dale

When the sun goes down, and the rosy light
'Gins to fade over the western hills;
Then the slave returns to a dreary night,
While deep sorrow his bosom fills.
O, Freedom! Sweet Freedom!
Hear his mid-night cry;
I would give this world,
Could I once be free;
But a slave I must live and die.

I must now lie down on my cabin floor,
There to rest my weary bones,
With not e'en a mantle to spread me o'er,
And my pillow a cold rough stone.
O, Freedom! Sweet Freedom!
How I weep for thee;
I must now lie down
On the cold, damp ground,
But there's no repose for me.

My wife and children have all been sold,
And their faces no more I'll see;
The Auctioneer, for the shining gold,
Sold them down to old Tennessee.
O, Freedom! Sweet Freedom!
How thine echoes swell -
For thee I pray,
Both night and day,
My deep sorrow no tongue can tell.

They can find no crime that I've ever done,
That I thus am bound in chains;
For to have my daughters, wife and sons,
Borne away to the southern plains.
O, Freedom! Sweet Freedom!
How I long for thee;
I would give this world,
Was it all my own,
If the bondmen could all go free.

See the eagle poised on his golden wings,
'Mid the thirteen darling Stars;
How he soars on high, and so sweetly sings
Of the joys that we all ought to share,
Sweet Freedom! O, Freedom!
Sweet Freedom dear;
While the white man sings
'Neath thy balmy wings,
I must die here in deep despair.

Car, pp. 29-30.

387. THE BAND OF THIEVES

Author: Joshua Simpson
Tune: In the Sabbath School [Scots Wha Hae?]

Who are those who loud declare
All mankind their rights should share;
But the slaves their chains should wear?
'Tis the band of thieves.

Who are those who rule and reign -
Bind the black man down with chain -
Then his prayer and groans disdain?
'Tis the band of thieves.

Who are those who preach and pray
On the Holy Sabbath day;
Yet for slaves have naught to say?
'Tis the band of thieves.

Who are those who whine and sing
Praises to their Heavenly King;
Yet, will call the slave a "thing?"
'Tis the band of thieves.

Who so gentle meek and mild,
Say that they are undefiled;
Yet will steal their brother's child?
'Tis the band of thieves.

Who are those that's free from strife
Would not quarrel for their life,
Yet will sell their brother's wife?
'Tis the band of thieves.

Car, p. 44.

388. OH, CARRY ME BACK!

Author: unspecified
Tune: Carry Me Back to Old Virginny

The burning sun from day to day,
Looks down on toil and pain,
Where drivers hold their heartless sway
With whip and clanking chain;
With cracking whip and clanking chain,
Our woes will soon be o'er -
Oh, carry me back to old Virginia,
To old Virginia's shore!

Where broad Potomac rolls away,
A snow-white cabin gleams,
A mother with her child at play -
Oh, God, they mock my dreams.
The crackling whip and clanking chain,
In dreams are heard no more.
Oh, carry me back to old Virginia,
To old Virginia's shore.

They coin our very heart for gold,
Our sweat makes rich their soil,
Where cotton fields are wide unrolled
We drop and die in toil;

The cracking whip and clanking chain
In death are heard no more.
Oh, carry me back to old Virginia,
To old Virginia's shore.

Freedom, pp. 295-296.

389. THEY WORKED ME ALL THE DAY
     WITHOUT A BIT OF PAY

Author: unspecified
Tune: Dearest May

Come, freemen, listen to my song, a story I'll
relate,
It happened in the valley of the old Carlina
State.
They marched me to the cotton field at early
dawn of day,
And worked me there from morn till night
without a bit of pay.
They worked me all the day without a bit of
pay,
So I took my flight in the middle of the night
When the moon am gone away.

Old massa give me a holler day and say he'd
give me more,
I thank'd him very kindly, and shoved my boat
from shore:
I drifted down the river, my heart was light
and free,
I had my eye on the bright North star, and
thought of liberty.
They worked me all the day, etc.

I jumped out of my good old boat, and pushed
it from the shore
And travelled faster on that night than ever
I'd done before;
I came up to a farmer's house just at the
break of day,
And saw a white man standing there - says he,
You're a runaway
Yes, but they worked me all the day, etc.

I told him I had left the whips, and the
baying of the hound,
To find a place where man is man, if such
there could be found

That I had heard in Canada that all mankind
were free,
That I was going northward now in search of
liberty; -
For they worked me all the day, etc.

Freedom, p. 296.

390. THE MINSTREL BOY

Author: unspecified
Tune: [original, by G. W. C.?]

The Minstrel Boy to the war has gone,
In the ranks of death you'll find him;
His Father's sword he has girded on,
And his wild harp hung behind him: -
"Land of song," said the warrior bard -
"Tho' all the world betrays thee;
One sword at least thy right shall guard -
One faithful harp shall praise thee."

The Minstrel fell, but the foeman's chain
Could not bring his proud soul under:
The harp he loved ne'er spoke again,
For he tore its cords asunder,
And said, "No chains shall sully thee,
Thou son of love and bravery,
Thy songs were made for the pure and free,
They shall never sound in SLAVERY!"

Freedom, pp. 302-303.

391. THE STOLEN BOY

Author: unspecified
Tune: unidentified, from S. Lover

A mother came, when stars were paling,
Wailing out in accents wild;
Thus she cried, while tears were falling,
Calling for her stolen child;
"Why with spell my boy caressing,
Courting him with fairy joy?
Why destroy a mother's blessing?
Wherefore steal my baby boy?

Why with spell my child decoying,
Luring him with gaudy toys?
Why destroy a mother's blessing?
Wherefore steal my baby boy?"

"O'er the mountain, thro' the wild wood,
Where his childhood loved to play;
Where the flowers are freshly springing,
There I wander day by day;
There I wander, growing fonder
Of the child that made my joy;
On the echoes wildly calling
To restore my darling boy;
There I wander, growing fonder
Of the child that made my joy;
On the echoes wildly calling
To restore my stolen boy."

"But in vain my plaintive calling,
Tears are falling all in vain;
He is gone for ever from me,
I no more my boy shall see;
Fare thee well, my child, for ever!
In this world I've lost my joy;
But in heaven we ne'er shall sever,
There I'll find my angel boy.
[Fare thee well, etc.]"

Freedom, pp. 69-71.

392. O WHEN WE GO BACK DAR

Author: G. W. C.
Tune: from a Negro Melody

O whar is de spot what we were born on,
Whar is de spot what we were born on,
Whar, O whar is de spot we were born on,
Way down in de Carlina state.
O when we go back where we were born,
We'll sing our songs both night and morn,
Case de day of slavery's gone,
Way down in de Carlina state.
CHORUS:
O den by and by we do hope to meet um,
By and by we do hope to meet um,
By and by we do hope to meet um,
Way down in de Carlina state.

O thar lives father, and thar lives mother,
Thar lives sister, and thar lives brother,
When shall we all meet each other,
Way down in de Carlina state.
O when we do back where we were born,
We'll sing our songs both night and morn,
Case de day of slavery's gone,
Way down in de Carlina state.
CHORUS

We'll have de grand times, de best we ever had
dere,
We'll work no more for de tyrant lords dere,
We'll work no more for de tyrant lords dere,
Way down in de Carlina state.
O, father verry glad when he know dat it be
us,
Mother verry glad too, case she can see us,
All de Massas goine for to free us,
Wat down in de Carlina state.
CHORUS

Freedom, pp. 54-56, with this note: "Slaves anticipating the
day of deliverance from slavery, and their return to the loved
ones, and loved spot where they were born."

393. PRAISE TO GOD WHO EVER REIGNS

Author: unspecified
Tune: [by] Pleyel

Praise to God who ever reigns -
Praise to Him who burst our chains;
For the priceless blessing giv'n,
Thanks, our grateful thanks, to Heaven!

Here no more the bloody scourge
Afric's fainting sons shall urge;
Here no more shall galling chains
Wear our flesh with fest'ring pains.

Here no more the frantic slave
Fly for refuge to the grave:
Freedom comes to banish fear -
Hallelujah! God is here.

Long and loud with praises fill
Deepest glen and highest hill;
Mountain peak and sea-girt shore
Echo slavery's reign is o'er.

Kindred - country now we claim,
Praise to God's beloved name;
Father, for this jubilee,
Thanks, eternal thanks, to Thee!

Freedom, p. 314.

394. THE NEGRO FATHER'S LAMENT

Author: unspecified
Tune: unidentified, by Wurzel*

They've sold me down the river,
And I must parted be,
From all I loved most dearly,
And all who care for me;
My heart is filled with sorrow,
There's naught for me but woe,
They've sold me down the river,
And I, alas! must go!
CHORUS:
Farewell! my peaceful cabin,
Beside the old oak tree,
Farewell, my wife and children,
And all that's dear to me.

My little ones are mourning,
I know 'tis for my sake,
My poor lone wife is weeping,
As tho' her heart would break,
O, Massa, do not grieve them,
When I am far from thee,
But ever treat them kindly,
As thou hast treated me.
CHORUS

But I will cease my mourning,
My sorrows meekly bear,
For there is One above us,
Who listens to our prayer;
An eye that looks upon us,
And when our toils are o'er,
He'll take us up to Heaven,
To dwell for ever more.
CHORUS

Freedom, pp. 212-213.

*"Wurzel" was the German pseudonym of American composer George
Frederick Root.

395. THE POOR UNHAPPY SLAVE

Author: G. W. H. Griffin
Tune: [The Poor Old Slave Has Gone to Rest]

'Tis just one year ago today,
That I remember well,
I sat down by poor Nelly's side,
And a story she did tell:
'Twas 'bout a poor unhappy slave,
That lived for many a year;
But now he's dead, and in his grave,
No master does he fear.
The poor old slave has gone to rest;
We know that he is free:
Disturb him not, but let him rest,
Way down in Tennessee.

She took my arm, we walked along
Into an open field,
And there she paused to breathe a while,
Then to his grave did steal.
She sat down by that little mound,
And softly whispered there:
"Come to me, father, 'tis thy child!"
Then gently dropped a tear.
The poor old slave, etc.

But since that time how things have changed!
Poor Nelly, that was my bride,
Is laid beneath the cold grave sod,
With her father by her side.
I planted there, upon her grave,
The weeping willow-tree;
I bathed its roots with many a tear,
That it might shelter me.
The poor old slave, etc.

Freedom, pp. 66-68.

396. SWANEE RIVER

Author: unspecified
Tune: Old Folks at Home

Way down upon de Swanee River, far, far away,
Thar's whar my heart is turning ever,
That's whar de loved ones stay; -
All up and down de whole creation, sadly I
roam,
Still longing for de old plantation,
And for de loved ones at home.
All de world am sad and dreary
Every where I roam,
When will de day of Mancipation
Bring all de darkies home?

All round de little farm I wandered when I was
young,
Den many happy days I squandered,
Many de songs I sung.
When I was playing wid my brother, happy was
I,
But when dey sold me down de River,
Den seemed my heart would die.
All de world, etc.

One little hut among de bushes, one dat I
love,
Still sadly to my memory rushes,
No matter where I rove; -
When shall I hear de bees a humming all round
de comb?
When shall I hear de sound of Freedom
Down in my dear old home?
All de world, etc

Freedom, p. 295.

397. BRIGHT ORIANIA

Author: Carrie
Tune: Blue Juniata

Sad wept the maiden lone,
Bright Oriania.
Where sweeps the waters of
The blue Alabama.

Lightly through the cornfields, now,
Her step no more is bounding;
Sadly now her song at eve
Is through the cabin sounding: -

"Bold was my Henri brave,
The love of Oriania,
But no more with me he'll rove
By the Alabama;

For the love of freedom burned
In his soul too brightly,
And the chains he would have spurned,
Now are bound more tightly.

Where the red Missouri's tide
The prairies green is laving;
Where, beneath the Southern sun,
The cotton-fields are waving:

There my Henri, brave and bonnie,
There in grief he's pining;
And no more upon his way
Love's bright star is shining."

So sang the maiden lone,
Bright Oriania;
But there's many an aching heart
By the Alabama.

Liberator, November 27, 1857, p. 192.

398. FUGITIVE SLAVE'S SONG

Author: Charles C. Burleigh
Tune: unspecified

A moonless night! - the sky is clear,
And the North Star holds his lamp for me;
I cast behind me doubt and fear,
For the hope before is liberty;
I go, I go;
In Slavery's land I will not stay,
I will not stay,
For the North Star beacons me away,
And I obey,
For the North Star beacons me away.

The darkness veils my Northward flight,
And by day the greenwood covers me;
My Guiding Star shines, all the night,
On the path which leads to liberty.
I go, I go;

I'm on my way to liberty,
To liberty,
For the North Star thither beacons me
To liberty,
Where the North Star shines to beacon me.

The dogs are howling on my track,
But the forded stream will foil their scent,
And turn their baffled fury back,
While I onward press, with soul intent,
To go, to go
Where shines the Star, my way to show,
My way to show,
My way to show;
For the North Star points where I may go,
May safely go,
For the North Star shines my way to show
And on I go.

Though hunger wastes my failing strength,
And the North wind blusters fierce and strong,
And, toil-worn with the journey's length,
I can scarcely drag my limbs along,
Yet on I go,
On toward the land where slaves are free,
Where slaves are free,
For the North Star thither beacons me,
Still beacons me
To the happy land where slaves are free.

Now on yon lake the star-beams glance;
How gaily its ripples flash and dance!
For yonder, on that Northern shore,
My toil and peril will all be o'er;
Hurrah! hurrah!
The Star shines now to welcome me,
To welcome me!
How gladly it shines to welcome me
To the land of the free,
To the land where slaves henceforth are free!

Liberator, July 30, 1858, p. 124.

399. WHY A FATHER WAS IMPRISONED!

A father is imprisoned in Washington
for harboring his own child!

Author: H.
Tune: On No, I Never Mention Her

Oh, must we ever mention it?
Oh, might it be concealed!
With boiling blood, and brain on fire,
We hear the truth revealed:
The father now must spurn his child,
And say, "My son, depart!
I cannot feed or shelter you,
Or press you to my heart!"

"You must away, unwarmed, unfed;
Nor must it e'er be known,
That you, my child, sought shelter here,
In your paternal home."
The father's heart was not of stone;
He could not turn aside,
But bade come in his much loved boy,
And placed him by his side -

And warmed and fed the wandering one: -
Would ye not do the same,
Ye fathers? - if ye can say nay,
Then man is not your name.
A jail for this, the father's doom!
Is this a land of slaves?
The Christian name henceforth blot out,
And write, "A land of knaves!"

His Maker's voice has sent him forth
As lord of land and sea;
"His soul was made to walk the skies" -
The child of Deity!
Wo to the nation that shall dare
To stifle in its breast
The voice of conscience in the soul,
Which pleads for the oppressed!

We call on all with souls not dead,
To join the moral fight;
Consider well your mission here,
And vindicate the right.
This you can do - will you be dumb
When deeds like these abound?
Your victims now for mercy call -
Will you be recreant found?

Liberator, March 25, 1859, p. 48.

400. THE SLAVE

Sung at a celebration of August 1 at Abington.

Author: unspecified
Tune: Scots Wha Hae

Lo! in Southern skies afar,
Mounted on Oppression's ear,
Rides a pale and sickly star -
God of Slavery!
Misery, with ghastly train,
Dealing horror, woe and pain,
Sweeps along his fell domain,
Like the troubled sea.

Liberator, August 16, 1861, p. 130.

AMERICAN
UNION

There's not a slave within the land
But has the wit to understand
It is the Northern people's hand
That rivets fast oppression's band,
And thus preserves the Union.

The narrator of the title song, "American Union" (435), is a fugitive who tells a dramatic story of being captured in Africa and transported to America, witnessing the separation of his family through death and sale, and fleeing after murdering his master. This content would seem to place the song in the previous section, but because the verses contain also a concise summary of themes present throughout this volume - especially the combination of Christianity and nationalism - and specifically the idea of the "Union," it serves well in introducing the ninety-two "political" songs of this last section.

Generally, these lyrics reflect the entrance of antislavery into politics, and politics into antislavery. Included are campaign songs written in support of presidential candidates, whether of a major party or an antislavery "third" party (e.g., 429 and 450 for the former, 425 and 426 for the latter). Here also are lyrics expressing faith in "The vote, the vote, the mighty vote" (from song 424; see also 411-413) and praising the resistance of its abuse through bribery (421), and those quoting the catchwords of the 1840s and 1850s: "free soil" (e.g., 409, 414, 428).

But, defined more broadly, "politics" refers also to events and persons which gained national attention at the time or in retrospect could be regarded as important or influential to an understanding of the ultimate political and military crisis. Thus the first song (401), written about the Boston

anti-abolition riot of October, 1835, is appropriate here, as
are those referring to _Uncle Tom's Cabin_ (438, 446), the
Kansas-Nebraska Act (441, 448, for example), the Sumner-Brooks
affair (445, 451, and 456; mentioned in 447 also), and the
martyrdom of John Brown (458-460, 462, 476, 480). Fugitive
slaves are subjects, as in the last section, but in these
cases the songs describe not the experience or necessity of
flight but instead the legal issue through specific cases (the
controversy surrounding the imprisonment in Boston of fugitive
George Latimer in 1842 [402-405 and 417], and the rescue of
fugitive Jerry McHenry from a Syracuse jail in 1851 [436,
437]).

Given the attention to events now less familiar, it is
not surprising that the dissolution of the union and the war
that followed did not escape being set to music (467-470).
Nor, of course, did the assassination of Abraham Lincoln (490,
491). Despite these tragedies, though, the singers of
antislavery were able to rejoice at last in achieving their
goal of more than three decades as they proclaimed, in the
last song, "Our nation's free! our nation's free!"

401. THERE WERE SOME LITTLE SOULS

Author: unspecified
Tune: There Was A Little Man, and He Woo'd a Little Maid

There were some little souls, with the optics
of moles;
And they said to one another, let us try, try,
try,
If we cannot get judge LYNCH, to serve at a
pinch,
The ends of little you and little I, I, I.

He'll allow us to seize whomsoever we please,
And stretch them, if we will, on the rack,
rack, rack:
Then forward let us trudge in pursuit of the
judge,
Who sits upon the cotton woolsack, sack, sack.

He's prompt and he's bold, and he's sure, when
he's told,
To bid Northern blood to be shed, shed, shed:
We need but tell him when, and 5000 Northern
men
Will hang be their necks till they're dead,
dead, dead.

There are certain at the North, who
shamelessly set forth,
That to buy and sell men is a sin, sin, sin!
We must drum about their town, for a MOB to
put them down;
Or the people to believe them will begin,
'gin, 'gin.

The cotton-trading clan will join, to a man:
And the holders of our mortgages, in scores,
scores, scores;
And of this sort if we a majority should see,
The clergymen will follow them, of course,
course, course.

'Twas but the other day, a portly rector did
say,
That, though sin "in the abstract" might lurk
in a plantation,
He would labor day and night, to prove to ears
polite,
That to say so, was an insult to a Christian
congregation.

Then be very, very merry - we have taken
sanctuary,
For as long as we choose, in the church,
church, church.
And whenever we've applied, they throw the
door so wide,
That intemperance need not stand in the porch,
porch, porch.

Like Pilate and Herod, their differences
buried,
Dame Harvard and Dame Andover agree in
calculation,
That their children shall bow down to our
idols as their own,
And pass through fire to Moloch for their
matriculation.

Then the men of "moral worth," who're so rife
at the North,
To strengthen our executive, are emulating
Haman:
They'll gratify their wish to feast upon our
dish,
If our "Cook" will but call himself a "Layman,
Layman, Layman."

Nor in marshalling their powers for a contest
like ours,
Will the "old respectability" fail, fail,
fail.
Whenever we're in doubt, they'll be sure to
bear us out;
So, shout to their corporal, "Hale! Hale!
Hale!"

The Whigs, young and old, in our cause will be
bold -
The "American Society to urge expatriation" -
The "Union," too will creep from the den of
its sleep,
"Recorded" and "Registered" against
emancipation.

When our myrmi-dons fall short, we can always
resort
To those who boast of cousins at the South,
South, South;
And those who there have been as strangers
taken in,
Against us will not open their mouth, mouth,
mouth.

We do not count them foes, who but abstractly
oppose,
Though about their lofty sentiments they
tattle, tattle, tattle;
Such trumpeters are found so uncertain in
their sound,
That no one can prepare himself for battle,
battle, battle.

The LADIES of our party, in their efforts will
be hearty;
They may plan at tar-and-feathering with very
great propriety.
For once we will permit, that their "sphere"
they should quit,
To aid in flinging mud at this most pestilent
society.

They will throng one and all, as they did to
Faneuil Hall,
That plot to keep "nonentities" out of men's
notices:
Then be vigorous and bold, - we are always
sure to hold
The hearts of noble fellows like the
Fletchers, Spragues and Otises.

Then beat the base drum, in concert they'll
come,
With liar notes low, and the voice of soft
"Recorders."
This jury of Judge LYNCH, come what may, will
never flinch
In aiding us of righteousness to purge all our
borders.

With the rich and the great, in the State,
State, State,
And a priest to preside over every
city-steeple,
We surely can contrive, if stoutly we strive,
To blindfold and handcuff the whole New
England people.

Liberator, February 13, 1836, p. 28, with this introduction:
"The following lines were written shortly after the riot in
Boston, in October last; but they have been delayed to give
'gentlemen of wealth and respectability,' who were somewhat
excited at that time in the Literary Emporium, an opportunity
to become cool; for it is desirable they should read and
commit them to memory, so that whenever they shall make
another gallant attack upon a meeting of ladies, they may be
animated by repeating these truly patriotic stanzas."

402. THE SLAVEHOLDER

Author: unspecified
Tune: Good Old Colony Times

In our good old Bay State,
When we lived under king Knave,
Three roguish chaps, they laid their traps,
All for to catch a slave,
Three roguish chaps, etc.

The first he was a lawyer,
The second he was a jailor,
And the third he was a slaveholder,
Three roguish chaps together,
Three roguish chaps together, etc.

Now the lawyer he made laws,
And the jailor found huge paws,
And the slaveholder found a lash for
To help the righteous cause,
And the slaveholder, etc.

But the lawyer's tricks did fail,
And the jailor was jugged in his jail,
And the devil cried hurrah at the slaveholder,
As he lashed him about with his tail,
And the devil cried hurrah, etc.

Liberator, November 25, 1842, p. 188.

403. THE SLAVE ATTORNEY

Author: unspecified
Tune: The King and Countryman

There once was a man, smart as ever you see,
When the British came over, he flourished and
frowned;
Would not hear of their laying a tax upon tea,
Or of having his grandchildren's faces ground.
Ri tu di nu di nu di nu
Ri tu di nu di nu di nah!

So he signed a paper which went to declare
That all of right ought to be equal and free;
That freedom and justice, and all of that 'ere
Should settle on him and his posteritie.
Ri tu di nu, etc.

But see how unlucky! one sunshiny day,
A rogue of a slaveholder came from the South;
The name of the fellow was J.__ B.__ G.__,
And he wanted the use of a Northerner's mouth;
Ri tu di nu, etc.

So he seized on the grandson of that good man,
(In spite of his grandfather's noble intents,)
And ground his face till he joined in a plan
To sell justice and freedom for dollars and
cents!
Ri tu di nu, etc.

Oh! fortunate slaveholder! - since it was his
To win on the chances fate offers to few;
For 'tis rare in the land of the pilgrim, I
wis,
While hunting for one slave, to light upon
two.
Ri tu di nu, etc.

Yet, grandson of G****, though low in yon
cell,
At the word of thy lips may poor Latimer be,
Loaded down with the chains from thy fingers
that fell,
'Tis degrading to him to compare him with
thee!
Ri tu di nu, etc.

Liberator, November 25, 1842, p. 188.

404. SONG OF THE PEOPLE
During Latimer's Trial

Author: unspecified
Tune: Auld Lang Syne

Come, gather round the spot, dear friends,
And breathlessly await
The single word whereon depends
The Freedom of our State!

Come, gentlemen of SUFFOLK now!
And bend the steady knee,
That never bends but when ye vow
Forever to be free!

Look - Judges of our Commonwealth!
How thick the grand array,
That gathers not by trick or stealth,
But openly as day!
The law is with us in its might!
Bold ESSEX comes to see
If her true children have the right
To gather peacefully!

Next, noble NORFOLK takes her stand
For Liberty and Law!
Her offspring are a stalwart band,
Her faith without a flaw!
"Ready, aye ready" - 'mid the roll
Of musketry are we!
We bear no armor - so each soul
From fear and doubt is free!

Hark! "BRISTOL now for LATIMER!"
That brother-voice of cheer
Shall bid a slumbering nation stir
The flame it kindles here!
Now BERKSHIRE! to the soul of Gray!
Ye need not strike him down -
His slavish spirit shrinks away,
Beneath a Freeman's frown.

Old PLYMOUTH of the Puritans,
Has sent her children here
To mark how strong their brother stands;
So raise for SPRAGUE a cheer!
Oh, judge a righteous judgment now! -
Let Massachusetts see
Thou never will to slavery bow -
She'll give thee three times three!

But if thou judge unrighteously,
Hear countless thousands swear
To scoff the shameful memory
Of guilt they will not share.
Now God do so to him, and more,
If ever from this day,
A son that Massachusetts bore
The fugitive betray!

Liberator, December 2, 1842, p. 192.

405. RESCUE THE SLAVE!

Author: A. B. C.
Tune: The Troubadour

Sadly the fugitive weeps in his cell,
Listen awhile to the story we tell;
Listen ye gentle ones, listen ye brave,
Lady fair! Lady fair! weep for the slave.

Praying for liberty, dearer than life,
Torn from his little one, torn from his wife,
Flying from slavery, hear him and save,
Christian men! Christian men! help the poor
slave.

Think of his agony, feel for his pain,
Should his hard master e'er hold him again;
Spirit of liberty, rise from your grave,
Make him free, make him free, rescue the
slave.

Freely the slave master goes where he will;
Freemen, stand ready, his wishes to fulfill,
Helping the tyrant, or honest or knave,
Thinking not, caring not, for the poor slave.

Talk not of liberty, liberty is dead;
See the slave master's whip over our head;
Stooping beneath it, we ask what he craves,
Boston boys! Boston boys! catch me my slaves.

Freemen, arouse ye, before it's too late;
Slavery is knocking, at every gate,
Make good the promise, your early days gave,
Boston boys! Boston boys! rescue the slave.

Liberator, December 2, 1842, p. 192; and Tracts, p. 6.

Harp, pp. 28-29, with this introduction: "This song was
composed while George Latimer, the fugitive slave, was confined in Leverett Street Jail, Boston, expecting to be carried
back to Virginia by James B. Gray, his claimant."

406. LIBERTY SONG

Author: Village Bard
Tune: And To Begging I Will Go

O! don't you hear the buckeye boys
Huzza for liberty!
No longer will they stand
In the ranks of slavery.
But for Birney they will go,
But for Birney they will go, will go, will go,
But for Birney they will go.

Huzza, huzza, for Liberty!
There's Birney just in sight!
And freemen of Ohio,
We'll have a freeman's right.
And for Birney, etc.

The Whigs they try to win us, by
Log cabins and by coons:
The locos try that game
With their gold and silver spoons.
But for Birney, etc.

And there is Johnny Tyler, too;
A Captain great was he,
He hoped to be a MAJOR,
But missed it mightily.
And a sneaking home he'll go, etc.

And there was little Matty Van,
The nomination sought;
He said he'd win the day,
By his "sober second thought."
But the Locos said no, no, etc.

For when the Loco Focos, sir,
At Baltimore did meet,
This cunning little Matty
Met with a sad defeat.
And for Kinderhook he'll go, etc.

Cass, Stewart, and Buchanan too,
Under the two-thirds rule -
Just followed in the footsteps,
And took it very cool.
And for Salt River did go, etc.

Then freemen of America,
You'll surely vote for Clay:
O no indeed we can't,
For Missouri's in the way.
But for Birney we will go, etc.

No, no, we cannot vote for him,
Who shot at ROANOKE: -
Why, in this matter, sir,
He is not as good as POLK.
So for Birney, etc.

And Marshall says to Harry Clay,
You tried to murder me;
You are a man of blood,
As the people plainly see.
So for Birney they, etc.

Well, then, you'll "jim along" for Polk,
He's surely not a fool:
No, sir, we cannot swallow
His slaves, and the gag rule.
But for Birney, etc.

No! freemen cannot vote for Polk,
That foe to right and peace;
Why, he'll get beat so bad,
That he'll wish he was a geese.
When for Birney, etc.

There's Clay of old Kentucky, sir,
He'll never do you see:
And neither will we vote
For that Polk of Tennessee.
But for Birney, etc.

Liberator, September 27, 1844, p. 156.

407. THE LAMENT OF "THAT SAME OLD COON"

Author: unspecified
Tune: Lament of the Irish Emigrant

I'm sitting on the rail, Harry,
Where we sat that fine day,
When all the Whigs at Baltimore,
Threw up their hats for Clay;
The election then went gloriously,
And the coons sang loud and high,
And you thought you'd be elected, Harry,
I saw it in your eye.

The world is little changed, Harry,
It stands as firm as then;
The Yankee boys have thrown their votes,
And gone to work again.

And they've left you still at Ashland, Harry,
With your negroes fat and sleek,
And the words of hope are words, Harry,
That you no more will speak.

'Tis not unto the capitol;
And the white house stands quite near,
Where you thought to find snug quarters, Hal,
With your twenty-five a year.
But Salt River rolls between us, Harry,
And just now 'tis very high;
Alas! we've neither bridge nor boat,
And can't get over dry.

I'm in a pack of trouble, Harry,
For the party's running down;
And we've little left to brag of now,
But our old days of renown.
You were our life and soul, Harry,
Of all the men the man;
If you could not be chosen, Harry,
Where is the Whig that can?

You played your part right well, Harry,
And still kept boasting on,
Amidst disasters and defeats,
When the party's hope was gone;
You ne'er a duel better fought,
When your overseer eye
Glanced back defiance on the foe
Whom you had doomed to die.

But we're mostly sadly beaten, Harry,
And my heart is fit to break,
When I think of those who electioneered
For the loaves and fishes' sake;
And when I think of you, Harry,
I'm filled with woe and pain;
Alas! you are so old a man,
You can't be run again.

I can't stand this another day,
I've served you eight long years,
Till the fur is all clipped off my hide,
By the Locofoco shears;
And through my skin my bones stick out,
I am a woeful sight;
No honest coon that steals his corn,
Was e'er in such a plight.

Good by, I'm off - but in the woods
I'll sit, and shut my eyes,
And think of all the tricks we used,
The forgeries and lies;

And I'll think I see the self-same rail
Where we sat that fine day,
Before you were a used up man,
Poor fallen Harry Clay.

Liberator, December 6, 1844, p. 196.

408. THE YANKEE GIRL

Author: Whittier
Tune: unspecified

She sings by her wheel at that low cottage
door,
Which the long evening shadow is stretching
before;
With a music as sweet as the music which seems
Breathed softly and faint in the ear of our
dreams!

How brilliant and mirthful the light of her
eye,
Like a star glancing out from the blue of the
sky!
And lightly and freely her dark tresses play
O'er a brow and a bosom as lovely as they!

Who comes in his pride to that low
cottage-door -
The haughty and rich to the humble and poor?
'Tis the great Southern planter - the master
who waves
His whip of dominion o'er hundreds of slaves.

"Nay, Ellen - for shame! Let those Yankee
fools spin,
Who would pass for our slaves with a change of
their skin;
Let them toil as they will at the loom or the
wheel,
Too stupid for shame, and too vulgar to feel!

But thou art too lovely and precious a gem
To be bound to their burdens and sullied by
them -
For Shame, Ellen, shame! - cast thy bondage
aside,
And away to the South, as my blessing and
pride.

Oh, come where no winter thy footsteps can
wrong,
But where flowers are blossoming all the year
long,
Where the shade of the palm tree is over my
home,
And the lemon and orange are white in their
bloom!

Oh, come to my home, where my servants shall
all
Depart at thy bidding and come at thy call;
They shall heed thee as mistress with
trembling and awe,
And each wish of thy heart shall be felt as a
law."

Oh, could ye have seen her - that pride of our
girls
Arise and cast back the dark wealth of her
curls,
With a scorn in her eye which the gazer could
feel,
And a glance like the sunshine that flashes on
steel!

"Go back, haughty Southron! thy treasures of
gold
Are dim with the blood of the hearts thou hast
sold!
Thy home may be lovely, but round it I hear
The crack of the whip and the footsteps of
fear!

And the sky of thy South may be brighter than
ours,
And greener thy landscapes, and fairer thy
flowers;
But, dearer the blast round our mountains
which raves,
Than the sweet summer zephyr which breathes
over slaves!

Full low at thy bidding thy negroes may kneel,
With the iron of bondage on spirit and heel;
Yet know that the Yankee girl sooner would be
In fetters with them, than in freedom with
thee!"

Collection, pp. 30-31; and Harp, pp. 22-23.

Free Soil, pp. 176-179; and Freedom, pp. 176-179, under the
same title, to original music by G. W. C.

409. FREE SOIL CHORUS

Author: unspecified
Tune: Auld Lang Syne

All hail! ye friends of liberty,
Ye honest sons of toil,
Come, let us raise a shout today,
For freedom and free soil.
For freedom and free soil, my boys,
For freedom and free soil;
Ring out the shout to all about,
For freedom and free soil.

We wage no bloody warfare here,
But gladly would we toil,
To show the South the matchless worth
Of freedom and free soil.
For freedom, etc.

Nor care we aught for party names,
We ask not for the spoils;
But what we'll have is liberty,
For freemen and free soil.
For freedom, etc.

Too long we've dwelt in party strife,
'Tis time to pour in oil;
So here's a dose for Uncle Sam,
Of freedom and free soil.
For freedom, etc.

Our southern neighbors feel our power,
And gladly would recoil;
But 'tis "too late," the cry's gone forth,
For freemen and free soil.
For freemen, etc.

Then let opponents do their best
Our spirits to embroil;
No feuds shall e'er divide our ranks
Till victory crowns free soil.
For freemen, etc.

They've called us Sisslers long enough,
We now begin to boil,
And ere November shall come round,
We'll cook them up free soil.
For freedom, etc.

Then let us sing <u>God bless</u> <u>the</u> <u>free</u>,
The noble sons of <u>toil</u>;
And let the shout ring all about,
Of freedom and free soil.
For freedom, etc.

<u>Free Soil</u>, pp. 38-39; and <u>Freedom</u>, pp. 293-294.

410. A VISION

Author: Crary
Tune: original, by G. W. C.

At dead of night, when others sleep,
Near Hell I took my station;
And from that dungeon, dark and deep,
O'erheard this conversation:
"Hail, Prince of Darkness, ever hail,
Adored by each infernal,
I come among your gang to wail,
And taste of death eternal."

"Where are you from?" the fiend demands,
"What makes you look so frantic?
Are you from Carolina's strand,
Just west of the Atlantic?
Are you that man of blood and birth,
Devoid of human feeling?
The wretch I saw, when last on earth,
In human cattle dealing?"

"Whose soul, with blood and rapine stain'd,
With deeds of crime to dark it;
Who drove God's image, starved and chained,
To sell like beasts in market?
Who tore the infant from the breast,
That you might sell its mother?
Whose craving mind could never rest,
Till you had sold a brother?"

"Who gave the sacrament to those
Whose chains and handcuffs rattle?
Whose backs soon after felt the blows,
More heavy than thy cattle?"
"I'm from the South," the ghost replies,
"And I was there a teacher;
Saw men in chains, with laughing eyes:
I was a Southern Preacher!"

"In tasselled pulpits, gay and fine,
I strove to please the tyrants,
To prove that slavery is divine,
And what the Scripture warrants.
And when I saw the horrid sight,
Of slaves by tortures dying,
And told their masters all was right,
I knew that I was lying."

"I knew all this, and who can doubt,
I felt a sad misgiving?
But still, I knew, if I spoke out,
That I should lose my living.
They made me fat, they paid me well,
To preach down abolition,
I slept - I died - I woke in Hell,
How altered my condition!"

"I now am in a sea of fire,
Whose fury ever rages;
I am a slave, and can't get free,
Through everlasting ages.
Yes! when the sun and moon shall fade,
And fire the rocks dissever,
I must sink down beneath the shade,
And feel God's wrath for ever."

Our Ghost stood trembling all the while -
He saw the scene transpiring;
With soul aghast and visage sad,
All hope was now retiring.
The Demon cried, on vengeance bent,
"I say, in haste, retire!
And you shall have a negro sent
To attend and punch the fire."

Liberty, pp. 142-143, with this note: "Scene in the nether
world - purporting to be a conversation between the departed
ghost of a Southern slaveholding clergyman, and the devil."

411. COME, VOTERS, COME

Author: unspecified
Tune: original, by G. W. C.

Come, voters, come!
Trumpet and drum!
Morning is breaking!
Freedom awaking!

Hark! hark! the sound!
Echoes around!
Come, come away,
And give your vote for liberty.
O'er the land the peal is ringing!
And hope is bright, and hearts are gay!
Every lip a welcome singing,
Come, and help the cause today.

Rise! voters, rise!
Lift to the skies!
O'er, o'er earthly sadness!
Songs of your gladness!
Then as they roll!
Quick to the poll!
Haste, haste away,
And give your vote for liberty.
Young and old in one combining!
And fair or withered, sad or gay;
All as with one soul uniting -
Come, and help the cause today.

Free Soil, pp. 218-220; and Freedom, pp. 206-208.

Liberty, pp. 197-199, as "Come and Help the Cause Today," to the same tune.

412. THE BALLOT

Author: J. E. Dow
Tune: Bonnie Doon

Dread sovereign, thou! the chainless WILL -
Thy source the nation's mighty heart -
The ballot box thy cradle sill -
Thou speak'st, and nineteen millions start;
Thy subjects, sons of noble sires,
Descendants of a patriot band -
Thy lights a million's household fires -
Thy daily walk, my native land.

And shall the safeguard of the free,
By valor won on gory plains,
Become a solemn mockery
While freemen breathe and virtue reigns?
Shall liberty be bought and sold
By guilty creatures clothed with power?
Is HONOR but a name for GOLD,
And PRINCIPLE A WITHERED FLOWER?

The parricide's accursed steel
Has pierced thy sacred sovereignty;
And all who think, and all who feel,
Must act or never more be free.
No party chains shall bind us here;
No mighty name shall turn the blow:
Then, wounded sovereignty, appear,
And lay the base apostates low.

The wretch, with hands by murder red,
May hope for mercy at the last;
And he who steals a nation's bread,
May have oblivion's statute passed.
But he who steals a sacred right,
And brings his native land to scorn,
Shall die a traitor in her sight,
With none to pity or to mourn.

Free Soil, pp. 213-214; and Liberty, p. 181.

Freedom, p. 299, without the first verse.

413. THE BALLOT-BOX

Author: unspecified
Tune: Lincoln

Freedom's consecrated dower,
Casket of a priceless gem!
Nobler heritage of power,
Than imperial diadem!
Cornerstone, on which was reared,
Liberty's triumphal dome,
When her glorious form appeared,
'Midst our own Green Mountain home.

Guard it, Freemen! guard it well,
Spotless as your maiden's fame!
Never let your children tell
Of your weakness, of your shame;
That their fathers basely sold,
What was bought with blood and toil,
That you bartered right for gold,
Here, on Freedom's sacred soil.

Let your eagle's quenchless eye,
Fixed, unerring, sleepless, bright,
Watch, when danger hovers nigh,
From his lofty mountain height;

While the stripes and stars shall wave
O'er this treasure, pure and free -
The land's Palladium, it shall save
The home and shrine of liberty.

Free Soil, pp. 79-80; and Freedom, pp. 216-217.

414. THE FREE SOIL VOTER'S SONG

Author: A. Warren Stearns
Tune: Old Granite State

Hark! the sound is swelling louder,
Hear it booming o'er the plain,
Like the rush of mighty waters -
Hark! the echo rings again!
Through the valley, o'er the mountain,
By the river-side and sea,
From Penobscot's farthest fountain,
And from every northern lea.
CHORUS:
We are all free soilers,
We are all free soilers,
We are all free soilers,
And we'll sound it through the land.

List, again! the sound approaches,
Nearer yet, and nearer still -
Lo, they come! the marshalled forces,
Streaming over yonder hill!
'Tis the mighty hosts of freemen,
And the hardy sons of toil,
They are girding on their armor,
And their cry is heard - "FREE SOIL!"
CHORUS

Freemen, up! let's join the chorus,
Let us swell the increasing throng;
All around us, and before us,
See the tide that rolls along;
They rally from the northern lake,
And from the eastern hill,
While from their western prairie homes,
Behold them, coming still!
CHORUS

Who would tarry now, or linger?
Coward! let him stay behind!
Freedom's cause must not be periled,
We a better man can find!

On, with speed! our eagle soaring,
Waves his pinions once again,
Slavery's chains shall break asunder,
Ere it reach the western main.
CHORUS

Sing aloud the songs that gladden
Each free soil voter's heart;
Foes are spreading, hopes may wither,
One more cheer and then we part.
Huzza! huzza! for freedom's cause,
Nor yield it but with life -
We've enlisted for the battle,
We are ready for the strife.
CHORUS

Free Soil, p. 11; and Freedom, p. 288. It appears again in
Free Soil, pp. 223-224, under the same title, to the tune,
"Sweet Home," with the choruses omitted.

415. HURRAH! FOR OUR CAUSE

Author: unspecified
Tune: The Campbells are Coming

Hurrah! for our cause: we now bid you all
welcome,
Come join in the song we are singing for
Martin;
Free soil is our pledge - its success we are
sure in,
And we work, hand in hand, for Martin Van
Buren.
Free Soilers are coming, oh! ho! oh! ho!
Free Soilers are coming, oh! ho! oh! ho!
From mountain and valley,
They meet and they rally,
They never will dally, oh! ho! oh! ho!

The North and the South shall no longer be
kneeling,
For chang'd are the purpose, the will, and the
feeling;
The path we have chosen is wiser and better,
Than with party to cling to the ironbound
fetter.
Free Soilers are coming, etc.

Free Soil we will have - work without
melancholy,
For Toil to the Freeman is pleasant and holy;
We'll bow to no power but the Spirit who gave
us
Such hearts - that Tyrants shall never enslave
us.
Free Soilers are coming, etc.

One effort, my brother - one pull all
together,
And the balance of party is light as a
feather;
One party is trembling - hurrah! for our
thunder,
And the other - believe me - goes tumbling
under.
Free Soilers are coming, etc.

Then Freedom and Labor shall hold sweet
communion;
The Rich and the Poor find a brotherly union;
The record of Time tell of Liberty's story,
And "Our Country" again be the watchword of
glory.
Free Soilers are coming, etc.

Free Soil, pp. 5-7.

Freedom, pp. 282-284, under the same title, to the same tune,
but with "States" and "Statesmen" replacing "Soil" and "Soilers," and minor changes in verse one to accomodate "Dayton and
Fremont" replacing "Martin Van Buren."

416. BIRNEY AND LIBERTY

Author: unspecified
Tune: [Our Warrior's Heart?]

Hurrah! the ball is rolling on,
Hurrah! hurrah! hurrah!
In spite of whig or loco don,
Hurrah! hurrah! hurrah!
Our country still has hope to rise,
The bravest efforts win the prize,
Hurrah! hurrah! hurrah! hurrah!
Hurrah! hurrah! hurrah!

With joy elate our friends appear,
Hurrah! hurrah! hurrah!
Our vaunting foes are filled with fear,
Hurrah! hurrah! hurrah!
Ten thousand slaves have run away
From Georgia to Canada;
Hurrah! hurrah! hurrah! hurrah!
Hurrah! hurrah! hurrah!

Lo! all the world for Birney now,
Hurrah! hurrah! hurrah!
See! as he comes the parties bow,
Hurrah! hurrah! hurrah!
No iron mixed with miry clay,
Will ever do, the people say,
Hurrah! hurrah! hurrah! hurrah!
Hurrah! hurrah! hurrah!

Then up, ye hearties, one and all!
Hurrah! hurrah! hurrah!
Be faithful to your country's call;
Hurrah! hurrah! hurrah!
Let none the vote of freedom shun,
Run to the meeting - run, run, run!
Hurrah! hurrah! hurrah! hurrah!
Hurrah! hurrah! hurrah!

Be Birney's name the one you choose,
Hurrah! hurrah! hurrah!
Let not a soul his ballot lose,
Hurrah! hurrah! hurrah!
No other man in this our day
Will ever do, the people say:
Hurrah! hurrah! hurrah! hurrah!
Hurrah! hurrah! hurrah!

Liberty, p. 129.

417. THE BIGOT FIRE

Written on the occasion of George Latimer's
Imprisonment in Leverett Street Jail, Boston.

Author: unspecified
Tune: unspecified

O, kindle not that bigot fire,
'T will bring disunion, fear and pain;
'T will rouse at last the souther's ire,
And burst our starry land in twain.

Theirs is the high, the noble worth,
The very soul of chivalry;
Rend not our blood-bought land apart,
For such a thing as slavery.

This is the language of the North,
I shame to say it but 't is true;
And anti-slavery calls it forth,
From some proud priests and laymen too.

What! bend forsooth to southern rule?
What! cringe and crawl to souther's clay,
And be the base, the supple tool,
Of hell-begotten slavery?

No! never, while the free air plays
O'er our rough hills and sunny fountains,
Shall proud New England's sons be <u>free</u>,
And clank their fetters round her mountains.

Go if ye will and grind in dust,
Dark Afric's poor, degraded child;
Wring from his sinews gold accursed,
And boast your gospel warm and mild.

While on our mountain tops the pine
In freedom her green branches wave,
Her sons shall never stop to bind
The galling shackle of the slave.

Ye dare demand with haughty tone,
For us to pander to your shame,
To give our brother up alone,
To feel the lash and wear the chain.

Our brother never shall go back,
When once he presses our free shore;
Though souther's power with hell to back,
Comes thundering at our northern door.

No! rather be our starry land,
Into a thousand fragments riven;
Upon our own free hills we'll stand,
And pour upon the breeze of heaven,
A curse so loud, so stern, so deep,
Shall start ye in your guilty sleep.

<u>Harp</u>, pp. 42-43.

418. THE EMBLEM OF THE FREE

Author: unspecified
Tune: 'Tis Dawn, the Lark is Singing

Our emblem is the Cedar,
That knoweth not decay;
Its growth shall bless the mountains
Till mountains pass away.

Its top shall greet the sunshine -
Its leaves shall drink the rain;
And on its lower branches,
The slave shall hang his chain.

God bless the people's party -
The party of the free,
And give it faith and courage
To strike for Liberty.

This party - we will name it
THE PARTY OF THE WHOLE! -
Hath for its firm foundation,
The substance of the Soul.

It groweth out of reason,
The strongest soil on earth;
How glorious is the promise
Of Him who gave it birth!

Of what is true and living
God makes himself the nurse;
While "ONWARD!" cry the voices
Of all His Universe.

Free Soil, p. 222; and Freedom, pp. 306-307.

419. THE SLAVE-HOLDER'S ADDRESS TO THE NORTH STAR

Author: unspecified
Tune: unspecified

Star of the North! Thou art not bigger
Than is the diamond in my ring;
Yet, every black, star-gazing nigger
Looks at thee, as at some great thing!
Yes, gazes at thee, till the lazy
And thankless rascal is half crazy.

Some Abolitionist has told them,
That, if they take their flight toward thee,
They'll get where "massa" cannot hold them,
And therefore to the North they flee.
Fools to be led off, where they can't earn
Their living, by thy lying lantern.

We will to New England write,
And tell them not to let thee shine
(Excepting of a cloudy night)
Anywhere south of Dixon's line;
If beyond that thou shine an inch,
We'll have thee up before Judge Lynch.

And when, thou Abolition star,
Who preachest Freedom in all weathers,
Thou hast got on thy coat of tar,
And over that, a cloak of feathers,
Thou art "fixed" none will deny,
If there's a fixed star in the sky.

Harp, p. 29.

420. THE BUFFALO CONVENTION

Author: unspecified
Tune: Rory O'More

They come from the mountain, they come from
the glen,
Their motto - "Free Labor, Free Soil, and Free
Men;"
They sweep to the rally like clouds to the
storm,
From hill-top and valley they gather and form.

They cry, "To the rescue!" their march is
begun,
Their number is legion - their hearts are but
one;
Their cause is their country, they war for the
right,
And the minions of slavery turn pale at the
sight.

At the voice of Jehovah the ocean waves stayed
Its billows rolled back, and the mandate
obeyed;

Thus the tyrant is checked - he beholds with
surprise,
The slave power recoil when stern freemen
arise.

They speak - and that voice shall awaken
mankind
From the sleep that has rested so long on the
mind;
"No party shall bind us - we are free from
this hour;
We bow not in meekness to slaveholding power."

Thou monster Oppression, shrink back to thy
den,
For the shackles have burst from the spirits
of men;
They spread their broad pinions, all proudly
they soar;
Thy efforts are vain - thou canst bind them no
more.

Where slavery now rears its broad front to the
day,
Let them hug the foul fiend to their hearts as
they may;
But there they must stop, for we sternly
proclaim,
No slave shall pollute our free soil with his
chain.

Free Soil, p. 224.

Freedom, p. 317, without the last two verses, as "To the
Rescue!" to the same tune.

421. THE POOR VOTER'S SONG

Author: unspecified
Tune: Lucy Long

They knew that I was poor,
And they thought I was base;
They thought that I'd endure
To be covered with disgrace;
They thought me of their tribe,
Who on filthy lucre doat,
So they offered me a bribe
For my vote, boys! my vote!

O shame upon my betters,
Who would my conscience buy!
But I'll not wear their fetters,
Not I, indeed, not I!

My vote? it is not mine
To do with as I will;
To cast, like pearls, to swine,
To these wallowers in ill.
It is my country's due,
And I'll give it, while I can,
To the honest and the true,
Like a man, like a man!
O shame, etc.

No no, I'll hold my vote,
As a treasure and a trust,
My dishonor none shall quote,
When I'm mingled with the dust;
And my children, when I'm gone,
Shall be strengthened by the thought,
That their father was not one
To be bought, to be bought!
O shame, etc.

Free Soil, pp. 211-212; Liberty, pp. 178-179; and Freedom, pp. 297-298.

422. 'TIS A GLORIOUS YEAR

Author: Jesse Hutchinson, Jr.
Tune: [Our Warrior's Heart?]

'Tis a glorious year in which we live,
Hurrah! hurrah! hurrah!
And now three hearty cheers we'll give,
Hurrah! hurrah! hurrah!
From all the honest sons of toil,
The cry is heard - "free soil! free soil!"
Hurrah! hurrah! hurrah! hurrah!
Hurrah! hurrah! hurrah!

On every breeze glad tidings roll,
Hurrah! hurrah! hurrah!
And echoes bound from pole to pole,
Hurrah! hurrah! hurrah!
All parties are rallying to the test,
From the north and east and glorious west,
Hurrah! hurrah! hurrah! hurrah!
Hurrah! hurrah! hurrah!

We pledge to free soil the eastern States,
Hurrah! hurrah! hurrah!
And the west will go for our candidates,
Hurrah! hurrah! hurrah!
Whigs, democrats will all unite,
And liberty boys - for our cause is right,
Hurrah! hurrah! hurrah! hurrah!
Hurrah! hurrah! hurrah!

The good time boys, is coming near,
Hurrah! hurrah! hurrah!
And myriad hearts shall bless this year,
Hurrah! hurrah! hurrah!
The orator's tongue and poet's pen,
All tell us where, and how, and when,
Hurrah! hurrah! hurrah! hurrah!
Hurrah! hurrah! hurrah!

Then let us give three cheers once more,
Hurrah! hurrah! hurrah!
With a voice as loud as "Niagara's roar,"
Hurrah! hurrah! hurrah!
This shall inspire us as we toil;
Free men, free speech, and God's free soil,
Hurrah! hurrah! hurrah! hurrah!
Hurrah! hurrah! hurrah!

Free Soil, p. 34.

Freedom, p. 273, under the same title, to the same tune, with this third verse:

We pledge to freedom the eastern States,
Hurrah! hurrah! hurrah!
And the west will go for our candidates,
Hurrah! hurrah! hurrah!
Whigs, democrats, and nativites,
Will yet unite - for our cause is right,
Hurrah! hurrah! hurrah! hurrah!
Hurrah! hurrah! hurrah!

423. THE VOICE OF THE PEOPLE

Author: T. E. T.
Tune: Rory O'Moore

The voice of the people, like thunder's deep
roar,
Or the rush of the sea when it breaks on the
shore,

Speaks forth to the world with omnipotent
might
In defense of humanity, of freedom and right;
From river to river, from mountain to vale
Floats lightly the grand, patriotic appeal;
"'Tis heard in the cottage, 'tis heard in the
hall,"
And thousands respond to the glorious call.

But why this commotion - say, why this display
This rush of the people in adverse array?
Are the masses before us in fight to engage?
Are we invaded - this the battle's fierce
rage?
No, nought of all this, the invasion we scorn;
Long since, of its magic the sceptre was
shorn.
Not England's proud kingdom does liberty
dread;
Her vials were poured on our infantile head:
But despots at home, the legalized lord
Our fears and our sad apprehensions afford.

He now aspires to the mantle of state,
Who holds the poor slave in his down-trodden
state,
E'en now, at his gate the wan menial stands,
Awaiting, with fear, his grin lordling's
commands;
E'en now, at his door, the sobs and the sighs
Of thousands on thousands, commingling arise;
Thus Africa's sons in terror must cower
In the land of the free to a fallen man's
power.

But the days of the despot are numbered, thank
God!
Not long shall the weak be enchained by his
nod;
Not long shall pale fear and dejected despair
Send forth the wild shriek on the nocturnal
air;
For the voice of the freemen, that terrible
roll,
Will tear with convulsions the slave-holder's
soul;
The chains of the menial will fall to the
ground,
And he stand redeemed at the wonderful sound.

Arouse, then, O freemen, speak forth in your
might,
In defense of humanity, of freedom and right;

"Free labor, free soil," be your watch-word
and cry,
Let it burst o'er the earth - resound through
the sky;
"Free labor, free soil," let the oligarch
hear,
Till his shelterless soul shall tremble with
fear.
Arouse to the conflict and charge on our foes.
We've a God to battle, who can oppose?

Free Soil, p. 216.

424. THE VOTER'S SONG

Author: E. Wright, Jr.
Tune: Niel Gow's Farewel'

The vote, the vote, the mighty vote,
Though once we used a humbler note,
And prayed our servants to be just,
We tell them now they must, they must.
The tyrant's grapple, by our vote,
We'll loosen from our brother's throat;
With Washington we here agree,
The vote's the weapon of the free.

We'll scatter not the precious power
On parties that to slavery cower;
But make it one against the wrong,
Till down it comes, a million strong.
The tyrant's grapple, etc.

We'll bake the dough-face with our vote,
Who stood the scorching when we wrote;
And though they spurned our earnest prayers,
The ballot bids them now, beware.
The tyrant's grapple, etc.

Our vote shall teach all statesmen law,
Who in the Southern harness draw;
So well contented to be slaves,
They fain would prove their fathers knaves!
The tyrant's grapple, etc.

We'll not provoke our wives to use
A power that we through fear abuse;
His mother shall not blush to own
One voter of us for a son.

The tyrant's grapple, by our vote,
We'll loosen from our brother's throat;
With Washington we here agree,
Whose MOTHER taught him to be free!

Free Soil, pp. 61-62; and Freedom, pp. 270-271.

425. WE ASK NOT MARTIAL GLORY

Author: unspecified
Tune: [Missionary Hymn?]

We ask not "martial glory,"
Nor "battles bravely won";
We tell no boastful story
To laud our "favorite son";
We do not seek to gather
From glory's field of blood,
The laurels of the warrior,
Steeped in the crimson flood -

But we can boast that Birney
Holds not the tyrant's rod,
Nor binds in chains and fetters,
The image of his God;
No vassal, at his bidding,
Is doomed the lash to feel;
No menial crouches near him,
No Charleys at his heel.

His heart is free from murder,
His hand without its stain;
His head and heart united,
To loose the bondman's chain:
His deeds of noble daring,
Shall make the tyrant cower;
Oppression flees before him,
With all its boasted power.

Soon shall the voice of freedom,
O'er earth its echoes roll -
And earth's rejoicing millions
Be free, from pole to pole.
Then rally round your leader,
Ye friends of liberty;
And let the shout for Birney,
Ring out o'er land and sea.

Liberty, p. 95.

426. ODE TO JAMES G. BIRNEY

Author: Elizur Wright
Tune: original, by G. W. C.

We hail thee, Birney, just and true,
The calm and fearless, staunch and tried,
The bravest of the valiant few,
Our country's hope, our country's pride!
In Freedom's battle take the van;
We hail thee as an honest man.

Thy country, in her darkest hour,
When heroes bend at Mammon's shrine,
And virtue sells herself to Power,
Lights up in smiles at deeds like thine!
Then welcome to the battle's van -
We hail thee as an HONEST MAN!

Thy own example leads the way
From Egypt's gloom to Canaan's light;
Thy justice is the breaking day
Of Slavery's long and guilty night;
Then welcome to the battle's van -
We hail the as an honest man.

Thine is the eagle eye to see,
And thine a human heart to feel;
A worthy leader of the free,
We'll trust thee with a Nation's weal;
We'll trust thee in the battle's van -
We hail thee as an honest man.

An honest man - an honest man -
God made thee on his noblest plan,
To do the right and brave the scorn;
To stand in Freedom's "hope forlorn";
Then welcome to the triumph's van -
WE HAIL THEE AS OUR CHOSEN MAN!

Liberty, pp. 150-151.

427. THE FREE SOIL DEBATE

Author: unspecified
Tune: Old Granite State

We have come to our meeting, each other kindly
greeting,
Resolved to have no cheating, in the free soil
debate.
O, the mischief is a brewing, for Cass and
Taylor's ruin,
For the folks are up and doing, in the free
soil debate.
Then hurrah for freedom, then hurrah for
freedom,
Then hurrah for freedom, in the old Empire
State.

O, the Slavocrats are quaking, at the move we
are making,
They make a dreadful shaking, at the free soil
debate:
By the men whom they have cheated, they are
sure to be defeated,
Measure for measure meted, in the free soil
debate.
Then hurrah for freedom, then hurrah for
freedom,
Then hurrah for freedom, in the Green Mountain
State.

We'll have in our delegation honest men of
every station,
Who're resolved to save the nation, in the
Congress debate;
For our faith we have plighted, that Dough
faces shall be righted,
And we'll all be united in the National
debate.
Then hurrah for freedom, then hurrah for
freedom,
Then hurrah for freedom, in the Keystone
State.

Free Soil, pp. 8-10.

Freedom, pp. 285-287, under the same title, to the same tune,
with "State" replacing "soil," "Slavery's utter ruin" replacing
"Cass and Taylor's ruin," "as a true brother band" replacing
"in the National debate," and "Throughout our native land" as
the final phrase of every chorus.

428. THE FREE SOILER'S SONG

Author: unspecified
Tune: [Missionary Hymn?]

We hoist fair Freedom's standard,
On hill and dale it stands;
From broad Atlantic's borders,
To Oregon's far lands.
Where e'er the winds may wander,
Where e'er the waters roll,
Its wide-spread folds extending,
Shall spread from pole to pole.

Tho' slavery's frightened forces
May sound their loud alarms,
And call their flying squadrons
To muster up their arms.
Tho' Whig and Loco falter,
And knees of Doughface shake,
No "free soil" soul shall tremble
Nor for slave thunder quake.

Tho' Taylorites and Cassites
May jibe, and jeer, and flout,
With "free soil" on our banner,
We'll whip the cravens out.
"free soil, free speech" for ever,
Shall on our "free flag" fly,
Till mountain and till valley
Shall echo back the cry.

Free Soil, p. 49.

Freedom, p. 245, with "Fillmoreites and Buckites" replacing
"Taylorites and Cassites."

429. SALT RIVER CHORUS

Author: unspecified
Tune: Cheer Up, My Lively Lads

We've all turn'd out this glorious day,
To join the convocation -
To cheer the friends of liberty,
And stop the slave extension.

Then, cheer up, my lively lads,
In spite of Cass or Taylor,
Cheer up, we'll stop their craft,
And up Salt River sail her.

The beacon lights of th' Empire State,
Are spreading thro' the nation,
North, east and west are all on fire,
In one great conflagration.
Then, cheer up, etc.

Our Southern friends are coming on -
Fraternity's our motto;
We welcome them with all our heart,
As every freeman ought to.
Then, cheer up, etc.

We'll sing "free soil, free soil," my boys,
Nor sing for Cass or Taylor;
For Taylor rhymes are growing stale,
And hunker songs grow staler.
Then, cheer up, etc.

Now Slavery's craft is floating by,
Containing Cass and Taylor,
Aboard, my boys, and seize the helm,
And up Salt River sail her.
Then, cheer up, etc.

For conscience whigs, and liberty men,
And every true barnburner,
Here join to stay proud Slavery's curse,
And from free soil to spurn her.
Then, cheer up, etc.

Our flag is floating on the breeze,
Though not for Cass or Taylor,
'Tis for FREE SOIL, FREE SOIL, my boys,
And to the MAST we'll nail her.
Then, cheer up, etc.

Free Soil, pp. 19-20.

Freedom, pp. 278-279, under the same title, to the same tune,
with these verses:

We've all turn'd out this glorious day,
To join the convocation -
To cheer the friends of liberty,
And stop the slave extension.
Then, cheer up, my lively lads,
In spite of Slavery's power,
Cheer up, we'll stop their craft,
And up Salt River sail her.

The beacon lights of Liberty,
Are spreading thro' the nation,
North, east and west are all on fire,
In one great conflagration.
Then, cheer up, etc.

Our Southern friends are coming on -
Fraternity's our motto;
We welcome them with all our heart,
As every freeman ought to.
Then, cheer up, etc.

We'll sing "free speech, free men," my boys,
Nor sing for Buck and Fillmore;
For Hunker rhymes are growing stale,
And Hindoo songs grow staler.
Then, cheer up, etc.

Now Slavery's craft is floating by,
Containing Buck and Fillmore -
Aboard, my boys, and seize the helm,
And up Salt River sail her.
Then, cheer up, etc.

For conscience and your Country's sake,
Come every true reformer -
Here join to stay proud Slavery's curse,
And from free soil to spurn her.
Then, cheer up, etc.

Our flag is floating on the breeze,
Though not for the Pirate Slaver -
'Tis for Free Speech, Free Soil, Free Men,
And to the MAST we'll nail her.
Then, cheer up, etc.

430. SLAVEHOLDER'S LAMENT

Author: L. P. Judson
Tune: from Lucy Neal

What shall we do? slaveholders cry,
O'erwhelmed with dreadful grief,
Slavery, we fear must quickly die,
Unless we find relief;
Fanatics labor night and day,
The North is in a blaze,
While in the South there's many a man
Fears not his voice to raise.

We preach and print in every mood,
And rob the "negro-pen,"
Railroads and stages throng the wood,
Take "things" and make them men;
But worst of all, the Free soil crew
Seem reckless of our fate,
Of all the acts we've seen them do,
The vote's the thing we hate.

These are our fears, and this our dread,
They're based on grounds too true,
That slavery soon must yield its head,
And vanish like the dew;
The old "North Star" we've voted down,
And told him not to shine,
But still he gives Victoria's crown
These "things" from Southern clime.

We've work'd and toil'd, and rav'd and foam'd,
And hop'd to keep them down,
By prayers to Congress snugly roomed,
Unread, referred or known;
We've robbed the mail, and taken lives,
And then to fright the rest,
We've brandished rifles, bowie-knives,
Cold steel and Dupont's best.

What shall we do? O what, say what?
Our foes increase and rise,
Old slavery reels! the fever's hot,
She pants, she gasps, she dies;
What shall we do? we'll give it up,
And with the North agree,
To take the draught from freedom's cup,
Let all mankind be free.

Free Soil, pp. 205-206; and Freedom, pp. 205-206.

431. PARTY OF THE WHOLE

Author: E. Wright, Jr.
Tune: 'Tis Dawn, the Lark is Singing

Will ye despise the acorn,
Just thrusting out its shoot,
Ye giants of the forest,
That strike the deepest root?

Will ye despise the streamlets
Upon the mountain side;
Ye broad and mighty rivers,
On sweeping to the tide?

Wilt thou despise the crescent,
That trembles, newly born,
Thou bright and peerless planet,
Whose reign shall reach the morn?
Time now his scythe is whetting,
Ye giant oaks, for you;
Ye floods, the sea is thirsting,
To drink you like the dew.

That crescent, faint and trembling,
Her lamp shall nightly trim,
Till thou, imperious planet,
Shall in her light grow dim;
And so shall wax the Party,
Now feeble at its birth,
Till Liberty shall cover
This tyrant trodden earth.

That party, as we term it,
The Party of the Whole -
Has for its firm foundation,
The substance of the soul;
It groweth out of Reason,
The strongest soil below;
The smaller is its budding,
The more its room to grow!

Then rally to its banners,
Supported by the true -
The weakest are the waning,
The many are the few:
Of what is small, but living,
God makes himself the nurse;
While "Onward" cry the voices
Of all his universe.

Our plant is of the cedar,
That knoweth not decay:
Its growth shall bless the mountains,
Till mountains pass away.
God speed the infant party,
The party of the whole -
And surely he will do it,
While reason is its soul.

Free Soil, pp. 31-32; and Freedom, pp. 274-275.

Liberty, pp. 132-133, as "The Liberty Party," to the same tune.

432. SONG FOR THE ELECTION

Author: unspecified
Tune: Scots Wha Hae

Ye who know and do the right,
Ye who cherish honor bright,
Ye who worship love and light,
Choose your side today.
Succor freedom now you can,
Voting for a Free Soil man;
Let not slavery's blight and ban,
On your ballot lay.

Boasts your vote no higher aim,
Than between two blots of shame
That would stain our country's fame,
Just to choose the least?
Let it sternly answer no!
Let it straight for Freedom go;
Let it swell the winds that blow
From the north and east.

Blot! - the smaller - is a curse,
Blighting conscience, honor, purse;
Give us any, give the worse,
'Twill be less endured.
Freemen, is it God who wills
You to choose, of foulest ills,
That which only latest kills?
No; he wills it cured.

Do your duty, He will aid;
Dare to vote as you have prayed;
Who e'er conquered, while his blade
Served his open foes?
Right established would you see?
Feel that you yourselves are free;
Strike for that which ought to be -
God will bless the blows.

Free Soil, pp. 29-30; and Freedom, pp. 276-277, and p. 301,
with "honest" replacing "Free Soil" in verse one.

Liberty, p. 180, as "For the Election"; no tune specified.

433. [UNTITLED]

Sung at an Antislavery Convention at W. Winfield, N. Y.

Author: unspecified
Tune: unspecified

Just Heaven, and has it come to this,
Has slavery so mighty grown
That Northern men must be the hounds
To hunt the flying bondman down!

Liberator, March 14, 1851, p. 43.

434. THE BUFFALO SLAVE CASE

A Song for the Serviles and Lower Law Doctors.

Author: unspecified
Tune: unspecified

O, we're for law and order,
All along the Northern border
Of these free United States!
Yes, we wait your lordly pleasures;
Ye shall catch your ebon treasures,
While we stand to watch the gates.

Bring your chains, with clank and clatter;
If they're free, why, that's no matter;
One good word will make them yours;
Search our quiet homes, and hook them,
Knock them on the head, and cook them;
Northern patience long endures.

Never mind the race or color,
Be it white or something duller,
One's the rule for you and me;
Get some Southern foe to swear it -
Bring the thong, and we must wear it -
Where's the law to prove us free?

Friends can yield us no assistance;
If they make the least resistance,
Don't you hear it? "THEY'LL BE SHOT!"
Freedom's only a misnomer,
We must serve the South at home, or
In the rice swamps, damp and hot.

If your prey has proofs of freedom,
Break his skull, and he won't need 'em:
If you think his skin too white,
Drag him o'er some burning stove, or
From your own hearts tinge him over,
And the law will make it right.

Don't you see we're hushed and quiet?
Boast your power, - we can't deny it;
Each in turn his summons waits;
O, we go for law and order,
All along the Northern border
Of these free United States!

Liberator, October 3, 1851, p. 160.

435. AMERICAN UNION

Author: B. S. J.
Tune: Heavenly Union

Come ye who love the Union well,
And hear the slave his sorrows tell,
The bitter wo that him befell,
And made the earth a very hell,
All through this glorious Union.

Where Afric's spicy breezes blow,
Where Gambia's waters gently flow,
And golden sands in beauty glow,
A chieftain dwelt long time ago,
Before this glorious Union.

One day a Christian ship drew nigh,
And from its mast-head, floating high,
Was seen against the sunset sky
A flag with stripes of crimson dye,
And thirteen stars in Union.

At dead of night this chieftain woke
'Mid stifling clouds of flame and smoke,
And, ere the dawn of morning broke,
Himself and people wore the yoke
Of this slave-trading Union.

To Carolina's distant shore
The Christian thief his victims bore,
And husbands from their partners tore,
And doomed to slavery evermore,
Beneath the flag of Union.

My father was the chieftain brave,
Who vainly strove his tribe to save;
He sleeps within a bondman's grave,
And left his child a fettered slave,
Because so willed the Union.

For years and years I prayed to see
The blessed sun of liberty,
And hoped that I would yet be free,
In spite of all the "powers that be"
Of this slaveholding Union.

My daughters from my arms were torn,
And to the Orleans market borne;
A murdered wife I had to mourn,
And I was left alone, forlorn,
An offering to the Union.

Then felt I as a chieftain's son,
That death or freedom should be won,
Although the tyrant's blood must run,
And drench the soil he stood upon,
To glorify the Union.

I smote the spoiler to the earth,
And hurried from my bondage forth,
To seek within the colder North
A resting place, where man was worth
Far more than sinful Union.

The bloodhounds follow on my track,
And statesmen who in manhood lack,
And pious souls dressed up in black,
Declare the North must send me back,
To save this glorious Union.

And I, alas, too truly know
That you have sworn, it should be so,
Forgetful of the negro's wo,
And curses that must ever flow
From such unhallowed Union.

There's not a slave within the land
But has the wit to understand
It is the Northern people's hand
That rivet's fast oppression's band,
And thus preserves the Union.

O then take pity on our fate,
And with the fiery bolts of hate
The Union's altars desolate, -
Throw open wide glad Freedom's gate,
And sacrifice this Union.

And then, when every one is free,
A different union there will be,
A union God will love to see,
Of Justice, Freedom, Charity,
In truth, a GLORIOUS UNION.

Liberator, March 19, 1852, p. 48.

436. RESCUE OF JERRY

Sung at the Jerry Rescue Celebration
at Syracuse, N. Y.

Author: G. W. Putnam
Tune: Yankee Girl

Morn comes in the east, and the world is
awake,
And the bright sunshine gladdens the valley
and lake;
The silver dew glistens on hill side and tree;
Afar o'er the mountains the rising mists flee.
Now the yeomen go forth for the fruits of the
soil,
And the artisans hasten again to their toil;
But, hark! the wild cry which comes forth on
the air
Speaks of sadness and sorrow, of woe and
despair!
How the blood moves apace, how the beating
heart thrills,
As the low tolling bells echo out o'er the
hills!

Haste! haste! for the boaster hath set on his
hounds,
And Oppression has leaped o'er Humanity's
bounds!
Lo! the wolves from their covert have scented
their prey!
Their fetter is on his! they bear him away!
To his doom they will take him, o'er field and
o'er flood,
And the Tyrant's keen lash will drink deep of
his blood!
Up! up! to the rescue! O stalwart of limb!
From the salt-spring, and corn-field, and
workshop so dim,

Pass on the high summons, and, marshalled in
might,
Come forth, O ye people, for Freedom and
Right!

Hark! the uproar of voices! the tramping of
feet!
As they throng in their thousands the bridges
and street;
And their words like the voice of the ocean
arose,
As they murmured defiance and wrath to their
foes.
"Say, brothers! for this did the Patriots
toil?
For this did their life-blood once redden our
soil?"
And the hunters of men stood aghast at the
sound,
And trembled with fear as the watch-word went
round, -
"Come peaceful deliverance, or bloody affray,
The slave shall be free ere the dawning of
day!"

It was evening - the stars kept their watch in
the sky,
When through the still heaven rang, glorious
and high,
The cry of the PEOPLE - "Ho! down with the
wall!
Bring him out! bring him forth! set him free
from his thrall!"
Hark, the crash! it was done! with the
quickness of thought,
'Mid the fire of the foe, in the path of the
shot!
And the bright throng of heaven bent downward
to see,
When they brought forth the man, still in
fetters, but FREE!
And the shout that went up as proud Tyranny
fell,
Shook, with its deep thunder, the ramparts of
hell!

Bear him on by the altars unscarred by the
chain,
Where the Trumpet of Freedom e'er echoed in
vain;
Where the priest hath not taken the robber's
reward,
Or the man-thief once drank of the cup of the
Lord;

Where they ponder what God hath inscribed on
the sky:
"Man is great and immortal! the truth cannot
die!"
Where long hath been heard, through Faith's
open door,
The dash of Time's wave on Eternity's
shore;
Where was planted with tears, 'mid the tempest
of Sin,
The germ of the harvest this night gathered
in.

And still by the torch-light they bear him
along,
With words of rejoicing, with shout and with
song;
And the young city won, in that hour's mighty
strife,
An honor unfading - green laurels for life!
And pure-hearted WOMAN, high beauty and worth,
To cheer on the deed and the doers, came
forth.
And to him whose transgression would stain
ocean's flood,
They paid thirty pieces - the old price of
blood!
And a Boaster's vain threat, and a slave's
broken gyves,
Side by side have their place in a Nation's
archives!

He is gone - with no brand of the Slave on his
brow -
And the throne of a Monarch shall shelter him
now!
But, Freemen, O keep ye, forever and aye,
In honored remembrance, the deed and the day!
And Life's coming host shall tell proudly the
tale
How the plotters were baffled, the boasters
grew pale,
When the might of a PEOPLE, by Tyranny curst,
Gave their threats to the winds, and their
"LAW" to the dust!
And shall point where forever, on Time's
record broad,
The lofty deed beareth the signet of God!

Liberator, October 8, 1852, p. 162.

437. JERRY'S JUBILATE

Sung at the Jerry Rescue Celebration
at Syracuse, N. Y.

Author: Rev. John Pierpont
Tune: Oh, the Days are Gone, etc.

Oh! the days are gone when, looking back,
O'er worn-out plains,
I could see the hunter on my track,
With whip and chains;
No more I hear,
No more I fear
The blood-hound's open throat;
Oh! there's nothing makes my blood run cold,
Like his hoarse note!
Oh! it seems to come from the jaws of death;
That blood-hound's note!

Oh! the day I dreamed of, long ago,
Has come at last,
And the bondman's stripes, and tears, and woe,
For aye are past!
From links, that gall
The negro thrall,
My limbs and soul are free!
Oh! there's nothing in this world so sweet
As Liberty!
Oh! the blessed day, that I can say
I'm free! I'm free!

Oh! the Lord be praised, that there are men,
And women brave,
Who have rescued once, and will again,
The hunted slave!
The smile of Heaven,
From morn to even,
On all their sould shall shine!
And from them shall the prayers of the rescued
rise,
As now do mine.

Liberator, October 8, 1852, p. 162.

438. LITTLE TOPSY'S SONG

Author: Eliza Cook
Tune: original, by Henry Russell

"Topsy neber was born,
Neber had a moder;
'Spects I growed a nigger brat,
Jist like any oder.
Whip me till the blood pours down -
Ols missus used to do it;
She said she'd cut my heart right out,
But neber could get to it.
Got no heart, I don't belieb -
Niggers do widout em.
Neber heard of God or Love,
So can't tell much about 'em."
This is Topsy's savage song,
Topsy, cute and clever;
Hurrah, then, for the white man's right!
Slavery forever!

"I 'spects I'se very wicked,
That's jist what I am;
Ony you jist give me chance,
Won't I rouse Ole Sam?
'Taint no use in being good,
Cos I'se black, you see;
I neber cared for nothin' yet,
And nothin' cares for me.
Ha! ha! ha! Miss Feely's hand
Dun know how to grip me;
Neber likes to do no work,
And won't widout they whip me."
This is Topsy's savage song,
Topsy, cute and clever;
Hurrah, then, for the white man's right!
Slavery forever!

"Don't you die, Miss Evy,
Else I go dead too;
I knows I'se wicked, but I'll try
And be all good to you.
You hab taught me better things,
Though I'se nigger skin;
You hab found poor Topsy's heart,
Spite of all its sin.
Don't you die, Miss Evy dear,
Else I go dead too;
Though I'se black, I'se sure that God
Will let me go wid you."
This is Topsy's human song,
Under Love's endeavor;
Hurrah, then, for the white child's work -
Humanity forever!

Liberator, August 26, 1853, p. 136.

439. THE SLAVE-HOLDER'S HYMN
to be sung at evening prayers

Author: Joshua Simpson
Tune: short metre

"A charge to keep I have,"
A negro to maintain,
Help me, O Lord, whilst here I live,
To keep him bound in chain.

We thank Thee, Lord for Grace,
That's brought us safe this far,
While many of our dying race,
Were summoned to Thy bar.

No negroes have I lost -
Not one has run away;
I have been faithful to my trust,
Through this, another day.

Lord, we cannot lie down
'Till we implore Thy grace,
For if we do a mighty frown,
Will cover o'er Thy face.

Draw nigh, just now, O Lord,
And listen while we pray,
And each petition - every word -
Pray answer and obey.

Car, p. 104.

440. THE SLAVE-HOLDER'S MORNING SERVICE

Author: Joshua Simpson
Tune: any long metre

Come let us join our God to praise,
Who lengthens out our fleeting days;
The shade of one more night has passed,
Which has to many been the last.

And thus, kind Providence, it seems,
Has kept us through our midnight dreams,
Our dogs have guarded well the door,
And Lord, what could we ask thee more?

Thy promise, Lord, has been our stay;
Not e'en a slave has run away,
While scores have left on every side,
To seek Lake Erie's doleful tide.

O! grant us, Lord, a great display
Of thy rich mercies through this day,
May we, in strength, our work pursue,
"And love Thee as slave-holders do!"

Car, p. 101.

441. THE NEB-RASCALITY

As sung at the Concerts given by the Hutchinson Family.

Author: Hutchinsons
Tune: Tunes indicated, or Yankee Doodle throughout

Air - Dandy Jim:

Kind friends, with your permission, I
Will sing a few short stanzas,
About this new "Nebraska Bill,"
Including also Kansas;
All how they had it "cut and dried,"
To rush it through the Senate
Before the people rallied, and
Before they'd time to mend it.

Air - Yankee Doodle:

Iniquity so very great,
Of justice so defiant,
Of course could only emanate
From brain of mighty giant.
This giant now is very small,
As all of you do know, sirs,
But then there is no doubt at all
That he expects to grow, sirs.

There's one thing more I ought to say,
And that will make us even;
It is to mention by the way,
The giant's name is - Stephen.
GIANT'S BASS SOLO
"Fe, fi, fo, fe, fi, fum,
I smell the blood of freedom;
Fe, fi, fo, fe, fi, fum,
Dead or alive, I'll have some."

Oh, terribly the giant swore,
With awful oaths and curses,
And language such as I cannot
Engraft into my verses.
There was a giant once before,
And with a sling they slew him;
That Stephen could be slued with one,
No one would say who knew him.

Air - Burial of Sir John Moore

'Twas at the dead of night they met,
(So I'm informed the case is,)
Stephen in person leading on
The army of "dough-faces."
They voted, at the dead of night,
While all the land lay sleeping,
That all our sacred, blood-bought rights,
Were not worth the keeping.

Air - Yankee Doodle, double quick time

Oh! bless those old forefathers, in
Their Continental "trowsers,"
Who in their wisdom looked so far,
And organized two houses -
So let them shout, their time is short,
They'll very soon be stiller;
For in the house they'll find a boy
Called "Jack the Giant Killer."

Air - Scots Wha Hae

And now, kind friends, for once and all,
Let's swear upon the altar
Of plighted faith and sacred truth,
To fight and never falter -
That Liberty and Human Rights
Shall be a bright reality,
And we'll resist with all our might
This monstrous Neb-rascality!

Liberator, May 19, 1854, p. 80; and Freedom, pp. 310-312.

442. THE DYING SLAVE-HOLDER

Author: Joshua Simpson
Tune: any C. P. metre

O, death! I feel thy icy hand;
Cold drops of sweat now thickly stand
All o'er my trembling frame.
A gulf I see, both dark and drear,
While shrieks of fiends salute my ear,
And fill my soul with pain.

I look no way but what I see
His great Satanic Majesty
On fiery billows stand.
Beneath his feet red liquid rolls,
While all around ten thousand souls
Obey his dread command.

My pulse grows faint and fainter still -
And in my ears the infernal knell
Is tolling every breath.
My parched lips I scarce can move,
I cannot raise my thoughts above;
I'm not prepared for death.

Strange spirits passing to and fro
Say I must now to judgment go,
To stand before my God.
My mind is filled with doubt and gloom;
O, God! must I now meet my doom,
And feel thy chastening rod?

O! must my guilty soul be hurled
Before the judge of all the world;
All stained with human blood.
I cannot go, I'm not prepared,
Thus to receive my just reward,
In yonder fiery flood.

O, tell me fiends, must all my guilt -
Must all the blood that I have spilt,
Go with me to the bar?
O, yes! O yes! beyond a doubt,
My vital spark is almost out,
My sins will meet me there.

I was deceived - I did not think
That I was standing on the brink
"Of everlasting woe"
I hoped for many months and years,
But now the monster Death appears,
And I must shortly go.

O! must I meet those helpless slaves
Upon whose back my lash engraved
Those long and numerous scars?

While I shall writhe in endless pain,
And clank my hot and sluggish chains,
They'll wear a crown of stars.

I've killed, wronged and robbed my slaves,
Now I must fill a tyrant's grave -
A tyrant's Hell endure.
Now I must go! my friends, farewell;
I'm going now with fiends to dwell,
For my damnation's sure.

Car, pp. 67-69.

443. CALL TO KANSAS

Author: Lucy Larcom
Tune: Nelly Bly

Yeomen strong, hither throng!
Nature's honest men;
We will make the wilderness
Bud and bloom again.
Bring the sickle, speed the plough,
Turn the ready soil!
Freedom is the noblest pay
For the true man's toil.
Ho! brothers! come, brothers!
Hasten all with me,
We'll sing upon the Kansas plains
A song of Liberty!

Father, haste! o'er the waste
Lies a pleasant land;
There your firesides, altar-stones,
Fixed in truth, shall stand;
There your sons, brave and good,
Shall to freemen grow,
Clad in triple mail of right,
Wrong to overthrow.
Ho! brothers! come, brothers!
Hasten all with me,
We'll sing upon the Kansas plains
A song of Liberty!

Mother, come! here's a home
In the waiting West;
Bring the seeds of love and peace,
You who sow them best.
Faithful hearts, holy prayers,
Keep from taint the air;

Soil a mother's tears have wet,
Golden crops shall bear.
Come, mother! fond mother,
List! we call to thee!
We'll sing upon the Kansas plains
A song of Liberty!

Brother brave, stem the wave!
Firm the prairies tread!
Up the dark Missouri flood
Be your canvass spread.
Sister true, join us too,
Where the Kansas flows;
Let the Northern lily bloom
With the Southern rose.
Brave brother! true sister,
List! we call to thee!
We'll sing upon the Kansas plains
A song of Liberty!

One and all, hear our call
Echo through the land!
Aid us, with a willing heart,
And the strong right hand!
Feed the spark the pilgrims struck
On old Plymouth Rock!
To the watch-fires of the free,
Millions glad shall flock.
Ho! brothers! come, brothers!
Hasten all with me,
We'll sing upon the Kansas plains
A song of Liberty!

Liberator, February 23, 1855, p. 32.

Freedom, pp. 59-61, as "Ho! For Kansas," to the same tune.

444. RALLYING SONG

Sung at a Fremont meeting in New York City.

Author: unspecified
Tune: Marseilles Hymn

Behold! the furious storm is rolling,
Which Border-Fiends, confederates raise!
The Dogs of War, let loose, are howling,
And, lo! our infant cities blaze!

And shall we calmly view the ruin,
While lawless Force, with giant stride,
Spreads desolation far and wide,
In guiltless blood his hands imbruing?
Arise, arise, ye brave!
And let our war-cry be,
Free Speech, Free Press, Free Soil, Free Men,
A glorious Victory!

Oh! Liberty! can he resign thee,
Who once has felt thy generous flame?
Can threats subdue, or bolts confine thee, -
Or whips thy noble spirit tame?
No! by the heavens bright bending o'er us!
We've called our Captain to the van -
Behold the hour - behold the man!
Oh, wise and valiant, go before us!
Then let the shout again
Ring out from sea to sea,
Free Speech, Free Press, Free Soil, Free Men,
Our country shall be free.

Hurrah! hurrah! from hill and valley,
Hurrah! from prairie wide and free!
Around our glorious Chieftain rally,
For KANSAS and for LIBERTY!
Let him, who first her wilds exploring,
Her virgin beauty gave to fame,
Nor save her from the curse and shame
Which Slavery o'er her soil is pouring.
Arise, arise, ye brave!
And let our war-cry be,
Free Speech, Free Press, Free Soil, Free Men,
A glorious Victory!

Liberator, July 4, 1856, p. 106; and Freedom, pp. 320-321.

445. THE ARTFUL DODGER

Author: unspecified
Tune: The Frog He Would a Wooing Go

Bully Brooks he would a-fighting go,
Heigh ho! says Bully;
I'm full of valor and froth, you know,
Jusy give me a club and an unarmed foe,
With my roly-poly, gammon and dodging,
And I'll show them Brooks the Bully.

Bully Brooks crept into the Senator's hall,
Heigh ho! says Bully.
He found a man sitting not far from the wall;
He saw he was armed with nothing at all;
So he pounded his head till he saw him fall;
With his roly-poly, gammon and dodging;
Bravo for Brooks the Bully!

Up jumped a man named Burlingame,
Heigh ho! says Bully.
He said such things were a burning shame;
He called the deed by a cowardly name,
As a roly-poly, gammon and dodging;
And he showed up Brooks the Bully.

Quoth Brooks, "I wonder if he will fight?"
Heigh ho! for Bully.
"They say he won't, if I send outright;
At any rate, I'll venture to try't,
With my roly-poly, gammon and dodging;
We will get off Brooks the Bully."

But Burlingame he toed the mark,
Heigh ho! for Bully.
"We'll be off to Canada straight in the dark,
There's an underground road that's safe as the
ark,
No roly-poly, gammon or dodging,
But a rifle for Brooks the Bully."

Bully Brooks looked round as if he'd been
shot,
Heigh ho! says Bully;
The way is long, and the weather is hot,
There are bulls and bears, and the d--l knows
what;
If you catch me in Canada, I'll be shot,
Where my roly-poly, gammon and dodging
Won't save poor Brooks the Bully.

We talked and published, like flocks of geese,
Heigh ho! says Bully,
Till they bound us over to keep the peace;
And now I am feeling much more at my ease,
And my roly-poly, gammon and dodging,
Will pass in the State of the Bully.

Liberator, August 8, 1856, p. 128.

446. UNCLE TOM'S RELIGION

Author: unspecified
Tune: unidentified, from C. G. Howard

Far away from wife and children,
Still I plod my way along.
Massa Clare has gone to Eva,
Leaving friendless poor old Tom.
Yet with trust and strength in heaven,
I remain a faithful slave,
When the whip to me am given,
I'll think of Him who died to save.

Shall I turn against my brother,
Raise the hand of cruelty?
No: we must love one another,
Then we'll get where all am free.
Patience here, I'll go to glory,
There is comfort for the slave,
When the lash makes this flesh gory,
I'll pray to Him who died to save.

Good-bye, Chloe! farewell, children!
Poor old Tom you'll see no more:
Mind, be good, and have religion;
'Twill bear you to the faithful shore.
Do not weep, nor feel dejection, -
Suffering's over in the grave;
But at the glorious resurrection,
We'll meet with Him who died to save.

Freedom, pp. 62-63.

447. STRIKE FOR FREEDOM AND FOR RIGHT

Author: unspecified
Tune: Dan Tucker - slow and grave

From the bloody plains of Kansas,
From the Senate's guilty floor,
From the smoking wreck of Lawrence,
From our Sumner's wounds and gore,
Comes our country's dying call -
Rise for Freedom, or we fall! (Repeat.)

Hear ye not succeeding ages
From their cloudy distance cry?
See ye not the hands of nations
Lifted toward the threatening sky?
Now, or never, rise and gain
Freedom for this fair domain!

We have vanquished foreign tyrants -
Now the battle draws a-near;
Let not Despots have this boasting,
That a Freeman knows to fear.
By your Fathers' patriot graves,
Rise! nor be forever slaves!

Speak, ye Orators of Freedom -
Let your thunder shake these plains;
Write, ye Editors of Freedom -
Let your lightning rive their chains.
Up! ye sons of Pilgrims, rise!
Strike for Freedom, or she dies!

Give this land to future ages
Free, as God has made it free;
Swear, that not another acre
Shall be cursed with Slavery;
Strike for freedom and for right -
God himself is Freedom's might.

Freedom, pp. 312-313.

448. FREE KANSAS

Author: unspecified
Tune: original, by G. W. C.

Hark! on the winds we hear a cry,
To which the heavens and earth reply,
Our eagle, singing as she flies,
"Free Kansas."

Her pinions spread from shore to shore,
'Tis heard above the ocean's roar,
Now listen! would you hear it more?
"Free Kansas."

Shame! Ruffians, shame! to try to drown
With cannon's music, every sound,
As it is echoed round and round,
"Free Kansas."

The Northern hills re-echo shame!
Though well they know, 'twere more than vain,
To try to still the voice - again,
"Free Kansas."

Now speed thee on, thou noble bird,
Till every Freeman brave, has heard
You sing in loudest tones the words,
"Free Kansas."

And let the "Border Ruffians" hear,
And while they listen, note their fear,
As whispered round from ear to ear,
"Free Kansas."

Freedom, pp. 53-54.

449. SLAVERY IS A HARD FOE TO BATTLE

Author: Judson Hutchinson
Tune: Jordan is a Hard Road to Travel

I looked to the South, and I looked to the
West,
And I saw old Slavery a coming,
With four Northern doughfaces hitched up in
front,
Driving freedom to the other side of Jordan.
Then take off your coats and roll up your
sleeves,
Slavery is a hard foe to battle I believe.

Slavery and Freedom they both had a fight,
And the whole North came up behind 'em;
Hit Slavery a few knocks with a free
ballot-box,
Sent it staggering to the other side of
Jordan.
Then rouse up the North, the sword unsheath,
Slavery is a hard foe to battle I believe.

If I was the Legislature of these United
States,
I'd settle this great question accordin';
I'd let every Slave go free over land, and on
the sea,
And let them have a little hope this side of
Jordan.
Then rouse up the free, the sword unsheath,
Freedom is the best road to travel I believe.

The South have their school where the masters
learn to rule,
And they lord it o'er the free states
accordin';
But sure they'd better quit e'er they raise
the Yankee grit,
And we tumble 'em over 'tother side of Jordan.
Then wake up the North, the sword unsheath,
Slavery is a hard foe to battle I believe.

But the day is drawing nigh that Slavery must
die,
And every one must do his part accordin';
Then let us all unite to give every man his
right, (woman too!)
And we'll get our pay the other side of
Jordan.
Then wake up the North, the sword unsheath,
Freedom is the best road to travel I believe.

Freedom, pp. 315-316.

450. FREMONT AND VICTORY
THE PRIZE SONG

Author: Charles S. Weyman
Tune: Suoni la Tromba

Men of the North, who remember
The deeds of your sires, ever glorious,
Join in our paean victorious,
The paean of Liberty!
Hark! on the gales of November
Millions of voices are ringing,
Glorious the song they are singing -
Fremont and Victory!
Hurrah!
Join the great chorus they're singing,
Fremont and Victory!

Come from your forest-clad mountains,
Come from the fields of your tillage,
Come forth from city and village,
Join the great host of the free!

As from their cavernous fountains
Roll the deep floods to the ocean,
Join the great army in motion,
Marching to victory!
Hurrah!
Echo, from ocean to ocean,
Fremont and Victory!

Far in the West rolls the thunder,
The tumult of battle is raging,
Where bleeding Kansas is waging
Warfare with Slavery!
Struggling with foes who surround her,
Lo! she implores you to stay her!
Will you to Slavery betray her?
Never - she shall be free!
Hurrah!
Swear that you'll never betray her;
Kansas shall yet be free!

March! we have sworn to support her;
The prayers of the righteous shall speed us;
A chief never conquered shall lead us -
Fremont shall lead the free!
Then from those fields, red with slaughter
Slavery's hordes shall be driven,
Freedom to Kansas be given,
Fremont shall make her free!
Hurrah!
To Kansas shall freedom be given;
Fremont shall make her free!

Men of the North, who remember
The deeds of your sires, ever glorious,
Join in our paean victorious,
The paean of Liberty!
Hark! on the gales of November
Millions of voices are ringing,
Glorious the song they are singing -
Fremont and Victory!
Hurrah!
Join the great chorus they're singing,
Fremont and Victory!

Liberator, September 26, 1856, p. [156; printed as 150].

Freedom, pp. 115-116, as "The Prize Song," to the same tune,
with "Freedom" replacing "Fremont."

451. BULLY BROOKS'S SONG

As sung by himself, at a private meeting of his
friends in Washington, immediately after his attempted
assassination of Sumner. Old Uncle Butler presiding.

Author: unspecified
Tune: unspecified

O! my name is BULLY BROOKS,
Bully Brooks, Brooks, Brooks;
O! my name is Bully Brooks,
Ha-ha! ha-ha!
I've strength, if not good looks,
Know bludgeons, if not books,
And am the dirtiest of Brooks,
By far - by far!

And I likes to play the Coward,
Play the Coward, Coward, Coward;
O! I likes to play the Coward,
Ha-ha! ha-ha!
For I knocks a feller down,
Then raps him on the crown,
And does the "science" brown,
Ha-ha! ha-ha!

I'm the Nephew of my Uncle,
My Uncle, Uncle, Uncle;
Yes, the Nephew of my Uncle,
Ha-ha! ha-ha!
And I round the Senate lurk,
To do his dirty work,
Which all his niggers shirk,
Ha-ha! ha-ha!
And I have a brother Bully,
Brother Bully, Bully, Bully;
Ay, I have a brother Bully,
Ha-ha! ha-ha!
He, too, 's from Carolina,
And yesterday flogg'd Dinah,
His washerwoman Dinah,
Ha-ha! ha-ha!

Aren't we a pair of Dastards,
Of Dastards, Dastards, Dastards;
A precious pair of Dastards,
Ha-ha! ha-ha!
We flogs women, men, and niggers,
When there's no one near to twig us,
And there's no fear of triggers -
Ha-ha! ha-ha!

The Northrons, they despise us,
Despise, despise, despise us;
The Northrons, they despise us,
Ha-ha! ha-ha!
But tho' we flogg'd our mothers,
Stabb'd our sisters or our brothers,
We count upon the <u>South-ers</u>,
Ha-ha! ha-ha!

(Interrupted by drunken chorus from the
company:)

Then three cheers for Bully Brooks,
Bully Brooks, Brooks, Brooks!
And three for Bully Keitt,
Hip-hip-hurrah!
Tho' they flogg'd their very mothers,
Stabb'd their sisters or their brothers,
They could count upon the South-ers,
Hurrah! hurrah!

<u>Liberator</u>, July 4, 1856, p. 108.

452. WE'RE FREE

Author: John G. Whittier
Tune: Lucy Neal

The robber o'er the prairie stalks,
And calls the land his own;
And they who talk as Slavery talks,
Are free to talk alone.
But tell the knaves we are not slaves,
And slaves we ne'er will be;
Come weal or woe, the world shall know,
We're free, we're free, we're free!

Oh, watcher on the outer wall,
How wears the night away?
"I hear the birds of morning call,
I see the break of day!"
Rise, tell the knaves, etc.

The hands that hold the sword and purse
Ere long shall lose their prey;
And they who blindly wrought the curse,
The curse shall sweep away.
Then tell the knaves, etc.

The land again in peace shall rest,
With blood no longer stained:
The virgin beauty of the West,
Shall be no more profaned.
We'll teach the knaves, etc.

Then let the idlers stand apart,
And cowards shun the fight,
We'll band together, heart to heart,
Forget, forgive, unite.
And tell the knaves, etc.

Freedom, pp. 321-322.

453. DOWN WITH SLAVERY'S MINIONS

Author: E. W. Locke
Tune: Old Dan Tucker

Rouse ye, freemen, from your slumbers;
Seize your arms and count your numbers;
Now's the time for deeds of bravery,
Freedom grapples now with Slavery.
CHORUS:
Down with Douglas, Pierce and Shannon,
Down with Slavery and Buchanan!
Freedom's traitors - sing their dirges,
Long and loud as ocean surges.

In the halls of Congress pleading,
On the fields of Kansas bleeding,
Brothers true as steel implore us -
"Join the fight and join the chorus!"
CHORUS

Mark the flag of Slavery's minions -
"Bludgeons versus Free Opinions!"
"Rule or Ruin! Compacts Broken!"
"Choke Free Words, before they're spoken!"
CHORUS

Are we cowards now to falter?
Have we naught for Freedom's altar?
Shall our forces, by division,
Reap defeat and bold derision?

Never! never! all are ready!
Every column marching steady:
True as were our sires before us,
Marching steady to the chorus!
CHORUS

Freedom, pp. 316-317.

Liberator, September 28, 1860, p. 156, as "Rouse, Ye Freemen!"; no tune specified.

454. RISE, BROTHERS, ALL

Author: unspecified
Tune: Sparkling and Bright

A sound of arms, and of war's alarms,
Each breath from the South is bringing;
'Tis the charging van of oppression's clan,
To the breeze their dark flag flinging.
CHORUS:
Then rise, brothers, all, at duty's call,
Beat back our fierce assaulters,
And strike with might, for God and the right,
And the fires of freedom's altars!

Our brothers bold in the prairies cold,
In bloody shrouds are lying,
And their wives on high send the piercing cry,
And from burning homes are flying.
CHORUS

A noble hero is bleeding now,
In the halls of the nation falling;
And his crimson gore as it stains the floor,
Is for vengeance loudly calling.
CHORUS

Then on let us go to meet the foe,
Though above us the thunder rattles,
We stake our life, in the holy strife,
With our trust in the God of battles.
CHORUS

Liberator, October 3, 1856, p. 160.

Freedom, p. 319, as "A Sound to Arms," to the same tune.

455. THE SLAVEHOLDER'S PRAYER

Author: B. C., with chorus by G. W. C.
Tune: Dandy Jim, with variation

These slaves I now possess are mine,
Sanction'd by laws of earth and heaven;
I thank thee, oh! thou Great Divine,
That unto me this boon is given!
CHORUS:
My old master tells me so!
'Tis a blessed system O,
It came from heaven, this I know,
For my old master tells me so.

In Scripture thou hast bade us make
Slaves of the heathen and the stranger;
And if we heathen "niggers" take,
There is no harm nor any danger.
CHORUS

Sure in thy wisdom thou made us
The instruments to show thy power;
And thus fulfill on them the curse
Of "Cain," - nay, "Ham," until this hour.
CHORUS

What care we for the Northern fools,
Who talk about the rights of "niggers"?
WE know that we were made to rule,
And they ordained to be the diggers.
CHORUS

Besides, it can be seen at sight,
Our slaves, if freed, would turn out lazy;
And if the fanatics are right,
The Bible's wrong and we are crazy.
CHORUS

Then hold on, brethren of the South -
They tell me agitation's dying;
This cry's in almost every mouth,
Unless you think the rascal's lying.
CHORUS

Whether or not this "corner-stone"
Of our republic shall e'er crumble,
Our laws and niggers are our own,
So let the poor fanatics grumble.
CHORUS

Freedom, pp. 303-304.

456. THE BULLY BROOKS. HIS CANADA SONG

Author: Bryant
Tune: Cork Leg

To Canada Brooks was asked to go,
To waste of powder a pound or so,
He sighed as he answered, No, no, no,
They might take my life on the way, you know,
Ri tu di nu di nu di na,
Ri tu di ni nu, ri tu di nu di na.

There are savages haunting New York Bay,
To murder strangers that pass that way;
The Quaker, Garrison, keeps them in pay,
And they kill at least a score a day.
Ri tu di nu, etc.

Beyond New York, in every car,
They keep a supply of feathers and tar;
They daub it on with an iron bar,
And I should be smothered ere I got far.
Ri tu di nu, etc.

Those dreadful Yankees talk through the nose;
The sound is terrible, goodness knows,
And when I hear it, a shiver goes
From the crown of my head to the tip of my
toes.
Ri tu di nu, etc.

So, dearest Mr. Burlingame,
I'll stay at home, if 'tis all the same,
And I'll tell the world 'tis a burning shame
That we did not fight, and you're to blame.
Ri tu di nu, etc.

Freedom, pp. 64-65.

457. THE AMERICAN TRACT SOCIETY, AND ITS SOUTHERN MASTERS

Author: Justitia
Tune: Heavenly Union

Come, saints and sinners, hear me tell
What certain Pharisees befel,
Who did their Christian brothers sell,
And oft exclaimed - "God doth things well,"
And talked of Christian Union.

These "conservators" did agree
To publish tracts on Slavery, -
Enjoining masters kind to be, -
And send them wide o'er land and sea,
Through all this blessed Union.

But soon their Southern masters heard,
And all their pious wrath was stirred,
And they declared that not a word
From these "fanatics" should be heard,
Or they'd dissolve the Union.

They said, if we've a mind to steal,
And on our brothers place our heel,
What right have they to make appeal,
Pretending that they seek our weal, -
And thus create dis-Union?

We'll threaten, if they still persist,
We'll with our "funds" no more assist;
They for a time will squirm and twist,
But "money" soon will make them whist,
And keep them in the Union.

The tidings through the nation flew,
Which soon a host together drew,
Who asked their God what they should do;
Who said, Be to your master true,
With "thieves" if you'll have Union.

They said - Though slav'ry is a sin,
As we're in pressing want of "tin,"
WE will not brand th' accursed thing,
But to the winds our conscience fling,
And with the "thieves" keep Union.

We'll hence to "men-stealers" be true,
And always take a "South-Side View,"
For we're convinced it will not do
To part from such a "pirate" crew,
And thus break up our Union.

Then there arose some noble men,
Protesting both with tongue and pen,
Who spoke in language strong and plain,
And spurned the proffered gyve and chain,
And such unholy Union.

Divided thus they took the field,
Some to oppose, but more to yield;
DEXTER the shafts of truth did wield,
'Gainst which the cravens sought to shield
With thieves their cherished Union.

Next CHEEVER'S thundering voice was heard,
And all who'd life in them were stirred;
And many trembled 'neath his word; -
Some said - "It is the voice of God,"
With sin to have no Union.

Though we're informed the end's not yet,
The Right we're sure the victory'll get;
When "truth and mercy" once are met,
The sun upon no slave shall set,
And then shall we have Union.

O hasten, Lord, that joyous day,
When man on man no more shall prey,
When every wrong shall pass away,
And all who on the earth shall stay
Shall live in holy Union.

Liberator, June 25, 1858, p. 104.

458. DIRGE

Sung at a meeting in Concord, Mass., Dec. 2, 1859.

Author: unspecified
Tune: unspecified

Today, beside Potomac's wave,
Beneath Virginia's sky,
They slay the man who loved the slave,
And dared for him to die.

The Pilgrim Fathers' earnest creed,
Virginia's ancient faith,
Inspired this hero's noblest deed,
And his reward is - Death!

Great Washington's indignant shade
Forever urged him on -
He heard from Monticello's glade
The voice of Jefferson.

But chiefly on the Hebrew page
He read Jehovah's law,
And this from youth to hoary age
Obeyed with love and awe.

No selfish purpose armed his hand,
No passion aimed his blow;
How loyally he loved his land
Impartial Time shall show.

But now the faithful martyr dies,
His brave heart beats no more,
His soul ascends the equal skies,
His earthly course is o'er.

If this we mourn, but not for him, -
Like him in God we trust;
And though our eyes with tears are dim,
We know that God is just.

Liberator, December 9, 1859, p. 196.

459. JOHN BROWN IS GONE!

Author: E. W. T.
Tune: Auld Lang Syne

John Brown is gone, that good old man,
We'll see his form no more;
He gave his life to free the slave
On old Potomac's shore.

John Brown is gone, that good old man,
Whose heart was warm and true;
He scorned to ask of other men
More than for them he'd do.

John Brown is gone, that good old man,
Who ne'er the poor refused;
Like him of Nazareth, he set
At liberty the bruised.

John Brown is gone, that good old man,
Who sought th' oppressed to free,
For which the tyrants in their wrath
Condemned him to the tree.

John Brown, to help the helpless slave,
Counted all else but loss;
Henceforth that hateful gallows tree
Is glorious like the cross.

John Brown still lives! a martyr crowned,
He walks the peaceful spheres,
While Freedom's foes, who shed his blood,
Are quaking with their fears.

John Brown still lives! let us rejoice
That souls cannot be slain,
Nor listless lie in paradise,
But come to earth again.

Come, then, John Brown, inspire us all
With purpose true and strong,
And we will write our thoughts in deeds,
Till right shall conquer wrong!

Liberator, January 20, 1860, p. 12.

460. THE HERO'S HEART

Sung at the Music Hall, on the Twenty-Sixth
National Anti-Slavery Subscription Anniversary,
Jan. 26, 1860.

Author: Mrs. Lydia Maria Child
Tune: unspecified

A winter sunshine, still and bright,
The Blue Hills bathed with golden light,
And earth was smiling to the sky,
When calmly he went forth to die.

Infernal passions festered there,
Where peaceful Nature looked so fair;
And fiercely, in the morning sun,
Flashed glittering bayonet and gun.

The old man met no friendly eye,
When last he looked on earth and sky;
But one small child, with timid air,
Was gazing on his silver hair.

As that dark brow to his up-turned,
The tender heart within him yearned;
And, fondly stooping o'er her face,
He kissed her, for her injured race.

The little one, she knew not why
That kind old man went forth to die;
Nor why, mid all that pomp and stir,
He stooped to give a kiss to her.

But Jesus smiled that sight to see,
And said, "He did it unto me!"
The golden harps then sweetly rung,
And this the song the angels sung:

"Who loves the poor, doth love the Lord!
Earth cannot dim thy bright reward;
We hover o'er yon gallows high,
And wait to bear thee to the sky."

Liberator, February 3, 1860, p. 20, with the note, "When
he [John Brown] went from the jail to the gallows, he stooped
to kiss a colored child that stood near."

461. FREEDOM'S BATTLE-SONG

Written for and sung at the Framingham
A. S. Celebration, July 4.

Author: R. Thayer
Tune: Auld Lang Syne

A band of FREEMEN we go forth
To battle with the foe;
From East to West, from South to North,
We'll lay the monster low:
We'll lay the monster low, - hurrah!
We'll lay the monster low;
From East to West, from South to North,
We'll lay the monster low.

To lead us in this noble strife,
We're men who 're always true;
And we're resolved, come death or life,
We'll fight the battle through:
We'll fight the battle through, etc.

If to the fray our foes come forth,
Like Israel's foes of yore,
We'll show them there is yet a NORTH,
Which they must flee before:
Which they must flee before, etc.

> We'll push the battle till they cry -
> "To Freedom's hosts we yield!"
> Then shout - we've gained the victory!
> We're masters of the field!
> We're masters of the field, etc.

Liberator, July 13, 1860, p. 112.

462. [UNTITLED]

Written for the celebration of July 4 at North Elba,
and read by the Secretary, as it was not possible
to arrange music for it at the time.

Author: Mr. Sanborn
Tune: unspecified

> Eternal hills! that rise around
> To guard the consecrated ground;
> Ye ancient woods that o'er us wave,
> Oh, hear us! and for aye record,
> Till deeds redeem our plighted word,
> The vows we offer at the grave!
>
> We swear, by him who lies below, -
> Whose death the justice, sure and slow,
> Of God's great law shall yet repay, -
> Ever to hold his memory dear,
> And follow him in that career
> Where he, unfaltering, showed the way.
>
> Be ours the slave's neglected cause;
> No golden bribes, no godless laws,
> Shall taint our heart or cheek or hand;
> Firm to resist the tyrant's power,
> Swift to attack when dawns the hour,
> For righteous Liberty we stand.
>
> Too well we love our father's fame,
> Too keenly feel our country's shame,
> To vex with boasts this mountain air, -
> With pride we tell our glories past,
> On Thee our fears and cares we cast,
> Just God! by Thee our oaths we swear.

Liberator, July 27, 1860, p. 118; and Douglass, September,
1860, p. 332.

463. SONG FOR THE FOURTH OF JANUARY

Author: The Old Colony Bard
Tune: The Poachers

Come one and all, throughout the land, aside
your labors cast,
The "glorious" Union now to save, let's hold a
general fast;
From North to South, from East to West, pour
forth a rending wail,
And with a copious flood of tears allay the
rising gale -
And with a copious flood of tears allay the
rising gale.

The "glorious" Union trembles now;
alas! and woe the day,
That Dissolution e'er should think to cross
the UNION'S way!
The precedent is dangerous, we must in sadness
own;
Then on this fourth of January let us fast and
groan!
Then on this fourth of January let us fast and
groan!

Slaveholders, groan, lest ye may lose all hope
of Northern aid;
Groan, ye fire-eaters, ere ye reap the
whirlwind ye have made!
Buchanan, groan, between two fires, groan as
you feel the flames -
O, how impossible to play, at once, two
different games!
O, how impossible to play, at once, two
different games!

Groan, ye who once did worship Clay, and
Webster, and Calhoun -
Groan, lest the sun which they adored should
set in blood at noon!
A brilliant galaxy might shine, perhaps upon
their graves,
Did all men banish from their thoughts
millions of chattel slaves!
Did all men banish from their thoughts
millions of chattel slaves!

Then let us all together join to celebrate
this fast -
As great events come far between, this chance
may be our last;
Let's weep and howl, and rend our hair, and go
without our food,
Believing such a solemn fast must surely do
some good -
Believing such a solemn fast must surely do
some good!

Liberator, January 4, 1861, p. 4.

464. SIGNS OF THE TIMES
A PARODY

Author: Justitia
Tune: The Morning Light is Breaking

The signs, there's no mistaking,
Betoken judgments near,
The captive's chains are breaking,
Sweet Freedom's trump we hear:
Each hour the skies grow darker -
More bright the lightnings flash, -
Soon men in men who barter
Shall cease to wield the lash.

Each breeze that sweeps the Union
Brings tidings from the South,
That she has no communion
With Freedom's open mouth;
She threatens she will leave us,
Unless we will be dumb, -
But let this never grieve us,
Nor cause us to succumb.

Let us in Freedom's armor,
Undaunted, meet the foe, -
Mechanic - tradesman - farmer, -
All who can strike a blow;
For weapons, Truth's smooth pebbles,
With justice for our sling;
Ere long from all our troubles
A sweet release we'll bring.

The slave, from bondage leaping,
No more shall wear the chain, -
Our land rich blessings reaping,
Freed from her darkest stain;
Millions of voices sounding,
Shall then proclaim, "We're free!"
Through all the earth resounding -
"'Tis Freedom's jubilee."

Liberator, February 22, 1861, p. 32.

465. TIME TO START

Author: unspecified
Tune: Johnny Cope

O Jamie, are you sleeping yet?
O Jamie, are you sleeping yet?
You know 'tis time for you to get
Ready to start in the morning.

The Northern boys are rousing fast;
Inspired by memories of the past,
They vow that treason shall not last;
So you'd better start in the morning.

Bad government is heard to bear,
And robbery is far from fair;
As both have had your fostering care,
You'd better leave in the morning.

O Jamie, why did you not avoid
Blustering Toombs, and Cobb, and Floyd?
Your reputation they've destroyed,
And left you alone in the morning.

The patriot men of Seventy-Six
Would have scorned to favor rebel cliques;
But you say, smiling at their tricks,
"We'll make it all right in the morning!"

You thought the Major didn't do right
To leave poor Moultrie alone one night,
Because Fort Sumter was not quite
So pleasant to take in the morning.

No wonder, then, you talked so rough,
For he spoil'd your game of Southern bluff:
Ah! you didn't wake up soon enough
To catch Bob asleep in the morning!

Yes, pack your books; O, worst of all,
The O. P. F.'s that e'er had "a call," -
March Fourth is written on the wall,
And Abe will be "round" in the morning!

Liberator, March 1, 1861, p. 36, with an introduction quoting
a telegram to the Boston Journal: "'President Buchanan is
packing his library, and will leave for Lancaster on the morning of March 5th.'"

466. YANKEE LAND
A PARODY

Author: Justitia
Tune: Dixie's Land

The Yankees' love for man is rotten;
The Yankee land is ruled by Cotton;
Look around! look around! look around in
Yankee land!
In Yankee land which I was born in,
The "higher law" they treat with scorning.
Look around! look around! look around in
Yankee land!
CHORUS:
Yet I'm glad that I'm a Yankee - hooray!
hooray!
In Yankee land I'll take my stand,
To live an honest Yankee.
Away! away! such mock humanity!
Hooray! hooray! I'll be an honest Yankee!

Each day, as I around am walking,
I see vain men and women stalking,
Strutting round, etc.
They'll turn their nose up at a nigger,
They feel that they're a good deal bigger,
Strutting round, etc.
CHORUS

Yet when their Southern lord and master
Just snaps his whip, they'll travel faster,
Strutting round, etc.
As much his slaves, - in different station, -
As those at home on his plantation,
Strutting round, etc.
CHORUS

Though they may dress a little better,
They just as truly wear the fetter,
Sneaking round, etc.
They'll never be true men and women
Till they leave off this wholesale sinning:
Looking round, looking round, to give the
suffering slave their hand.
CHORUS

Liberator, April 12, 1861, p. 60.

467. HAIL, COLUMBIA!
RESPECTFULLY DEDICATED TO THE FOUNDERS
OF THE NEW SOUTHERN REPUBLIC

Author: M. J. V.
Tune: [Hail Columbia]

Hail, Columbia, traitors' land!
Hail, ye negroes, captive band,
Who toil each day in "massa's" cause,
Who toil each day in "massa's" cause;
And, when the weary task is done,
Sigh o'er the "unground peck" you've won,
Ne'er of independence boast,
Ever mindful what 't would cost;
But thank God, each night and morn,
That you were in thraldom born!
CHORUS:
Firm in this forever be,
Rallying round your slavery;
As a band of captives, then,
Ne'er remember you are men.

Sons of stolen sires of yore,
You know no rights, you have no power;
Bow ye to your master's hand,
Bow ye to your master's hand;
There the large deposit lies,
Earned by you with tears and sighs!
Believe he is sincere and just,
And place in Heaven your firmest trust,
That truth and justice soon may fail,
And each disunion scheme prevail.
CHORUS

Sound, sound the trump of fame!
Let Buck's dishonored name
Ring through the South with loud applause,
Ring through the South with loud applause;

Let every clime to Slavery dear
Listen with a joyful ear:
By prayers and tears he seeks the power
To rule the land in this dark hour,
"Yet plays the traitor's part with ease,
His masters of the South to please."
CHORUS

Behold him trying to command
A snarling, fighting, Southern land,
The land on which a curse shall rest,
The land on which a curse shall rest;
And flanked by traitors far and near,
He strives to sweep the Union clear.
But, should his good friends fall away -
Should Lincoln's star obscure his day -
Let us, with minds from changes free,
Resolve on Death to Slavery!
CHORUS

Liberator, April 19, 1861, p. 64, with the note, "The above
was written when Old Buck was dishonoring the chair of State."

468. THE OLD FOGY'S APPEAL;
OR, "DO NOT TOUCH THE NIGGER"

Author: Plebs
Tune: Yankee Doodle

Old fogies sing on every hand -
The little man and bigger:
Wage war against the rebel band,
But, do not touch "the Nigger!"

Strike any other martial blow,
And use extremest rigor;
But, lest you "irritate the foe,"
Oh, do not touch "the Nigger!"

Let every rifle drop a man,
Whene'er ye draw the trigger;
Aim at what vital part you can,
But, do not touch "the Nigger!"

'Tis true, their slaves a profit yield
Of the very "highest figger";
They work them hard in trench and field,
But, do not touch "the Nigger!"

What though they arm and drill the slave?
We do not care a fig, ah!
Let the Confederate banner wave,
But, do not touch "the Nigger!"

Ye seamen in the navy, toil,
From Commodore to rigger;
Bombard the forts, possess the soil,
But, do not touch "the Nigger!"

Ye fossils all, at Washington,
Who "Democrat" or "Whig" are,
Confiscate what the traitors own,
But, do not touch "the Nigger!"

A million dollars every day
Is a pretty costly "figger";
But any money let us pay,
Rather than touch "the Nigger!"

The war dyes red our country's dust,
And every hour grows bigger;
But part with dearest friends we must,
Sooner than touch "the Nigger!"

Down with the agitators, then,
Who running such a rig are,
The reckless Abolition men,
Who wish to touch "the Nigger!"

Thus sings the fogy; of the grave
Of freedom he's the digger,
Denies all justice to the slave,
And whines, touch not "the Nigger!"

But patriots, who, the war to end,
Would wage it with all vigor,
Cry, to the heart the arrow send!
Give freedom to "the Nigger!"

Liberator, January 3, 1862, p. 4, with the note, "Plebs does
not like the word 'Nigger,' which occurs so frequently above.
He never uses it of his own accord, and employs it now as a
quotation simply, it being a current word with the class
represented."

469. WAR

Author: G. W. Rogers
Tune: America

What blast blows o'er the land,
Through every isle and strand,
Sounding afar -
Booming through every vale,
Borne on the midnight gale,
Rending each hill and vale?
'Tis Civil War!

Our Country, 'tis for thee,
Land of the brave and free,
In this dark hour,
That War's loud trumpet bray,
Men meet in deadly fray;
Arms clash from day to day,
Mid cannons' roar.

They are no common foe,
Banded to overthrow
Fair Freedom's fane;
Rebels from "Dixie's Land,"
A traitorous, coward band,
Wasting with ruthless hand,
Greedy of gain.

What prompts this rebel crew
These wanton acts to do?
Who will reply?
Slavery! that fiend from hell,
Suffered on earth to dwell,
God's image buy and sell,
None can deny.

Shame on a nation's guilt,
Where this dread scourge is felt,
Draining its blood;
Come to the rescue, then,
From every mountain glen,
Acquit yourselves like men,
Trusting in God!

Congress has power today
For aye to wipe away
Slavery's foul stain;
In God's name, then, we say,
Do it! without delay,
Strike the blow while you may,
Break every chain!

Liberator, January 10, 1862, p. 8.

470. JONATHAN'S APPEAL TO CAROLINE;
OR, MR. NORTH TO MADAM SOUTH

Author: Mary Stoddard
Tune: Jeannette and Jeannot

You are going far away, far away, my little
pet;
There's no one left to love me now oh,
darling! you forget
How I've always bowed to you, let you always
have your way;
Now, dearest, don't ungrateful be, and tear
yourself away! -
Think of all I've sacrificed, just for you to
keep your slaves,
And to increase your wealth and power, and
make your children knaves; -
Think, too, how I have compromised, every time
you wished you know:
Carolina, 'tis a shame to treat your loving
Johnny so!

Only think the gold I paid, buying all your
lands and State,
And then pursued the Seminole with war and
deadly hate;
Texas, too, I bought with blood, besides a
heap of gold,
Because you mean that men should be like
cattle bought and sold:
Then I've carried all your mails, letters,
papers, all for you,
And from my pocket I have paid most of your
postage, too;
Then to think how you have ruled, in Congress,
Church and State,
And always had your President, nor cared to
please your mate.

Now because, for once, my votes outdo all your
swindling plan,
You mean to break the Union up, and do what
harm you can!
Think to please you how I worked, down upon my
knees I've toiled,
While for my sake you've never once your
dainty fingers soiled.
Then you've called me wicked names, Yankee
mudsill, farmer small,
And yet I have a Christian been, and borne in
meekness all;

Yes, you know I've borne all this, and a
thousand other ills,
Just to live in peace with you, and run my
cotton mills.

Then, you know, I've active been, mobbing
preachers; if they dared
Say aught against your darling sin, hard was
the fate they shared;
Then to think I've caught your slaves, when
they tried to run away,
And never let them stop to rest this side of
Canada!
Now it really makes me mad to think how
foolish I have been,
How for your sake I've lost my peace, and
steeped my soul in sin!
And yet you have a traitor proved, and stole
my guns away;
But as I have a few more left, I guess I'll
stop your play!

Madam, you will trouble see unless your temper
soon is mended,
And much you'll wish you'd stayed with me,
before the war is ended;
But as you the war have brought, blame
yourself for all the sorrow
That now enshrouds all hearts and homes, and
fills our land with horror.
Though I fight but for the laws, stand on the
Constitution,
Yet blame yourself if, midst the crash, down
comes your institution;
And devoutly good men pray for such a
consummation,
And wise ones say peace cannot come but by
emancipation.

Carolina, don't you see that we both have
blinded been
To think that God would always smile upon our
nation's sin?
Read the names of nations lost! - once they
built their Babel towers,
But sin hath swept them from the earth: will
justice pass by ours?
Madam, I am half inclined to think that good
men see aright,
That naught but justice to the slave will
bring our nation light.

God of justice, grant me sight, show to me thy
path more clear,
And grant me strength to walk therein,
untrammelled, too, by fear!

Liberator, January 24, 1862, p. 16.

471. SONG OF THE CONTRABAND

Author: J. C. Hagen
Tune: The Braes of Balquither

Let us sing, brothers, sing,
But no longer in sadness!
Let the old cabin ring
With the shouts of our gladness!
Our bondage is o'er,
To return again never;
We are chattels no more -
We are freemen forever!

The glad tidings we hear
Shall silence our grieving;
The glad tidings from fear
The crushed spirit relieving;
And it thrills through our hearts,
Like a song of salvation,
On the white cotton-field
And the sugar plantation.

When our enemies sought
In their pride to conceal it,
Oh! how little they thought
That their fears would reveal it!
And our hearts danced with glee,
Round our hearthstones assembled;
For we knew we were free
When our task-masters trembled!

Praise to God! praise to God!
For the word that was spoken;
'Twas by him that the red
Of the smiter was broken.
He has answered the prayer
Of the poor and forsaken;
To his sheltering care
The oppressed he has taken.

Oh! how gladly we'll toil
When the lash does not drive us;
Of the fruits of the soil
They no more can deprive us;
When husband and wife
Can no longer be parted,
Or robbed of their dear ones,
To die broken-hearted!

Then we'll sing, brothers, sing,
But no longer in sadness;
Let the old cabin ring
With the songs of our gladness!
Praise to God! praise to God!
For 'tis he who has done it;
Praise to him! praise to him!
For his mercy has won it.

Liberator, June 13, 1862, p. 96.

472. [UNTITLED]

Written for and sung by the audience at a meeting
of colored and white citizens of Buffalo commemorating
the Emancipation of Slavery in the District of Columbia.

Author: Mrs. Nancy M. Weir
Tune: unspecified

We meet, O Lord, to offer thee
Unnumbered thanks and praise;
The District of Columbia's free
Through thy prevailing grace.

The Morning Star of Liberty
In this great act we see;
Freedom's bright day is soon to be: -
Columbia's soil is free!

No more the scars of servile chains
On human limbs shall be,
Within the limits of thy bounds, -
Columbia's land is free!

God bless the Nation's honored Chief!
Thy servant may he be,
Who wisely has advised relief,
Columbia's soil to free.

May those who now in bondage sigh
Rejoice with us to see
The good old Stars and Stripes on high -
Thank God! Columbia's free!

Lord, with united heart and voice,
The praise we give to thee!
Let every one in truth rejoice!
Columbia now is free!

Liberator, June 27, 1862, p. 104.

473. ORIGINAL HYMN

Written for and sung at a July 4
celebration at Framingham.

Author: Caroline A. Mason
Tune: Old Hundred

Our fathers worshipped Thee, O God,
Of old, in forests green and dim:
And here, where erst their footsteps trod,
We raise to Thee our trembling hymn.

Oh, how their grand old anthems rung
In praise to Thee, for freedom given!
Their quivering notes, to gladness strung,
Made music that was heard in heaven.

Alas! a sadder strain we raise, -
Their children, heirs of liberty:
We dare not take their cup of praise,
And shout, "Thank God, the land is free!"

For fierce-eyed War and bitter feuds
Make red the sacred soil we love,
And the dark curse of SLAVERY broods,
Like thickest clouds, the land above.

And fettered hands lift up to heaven
Dumb cries for justice! - shall it stay?
Shall the dark cloud be never riven,
That broods above our land today?

O Sword of Truth, swift answer make!
Say to dead Freedom, "Up, arise!"
Then shall our lips glad anthems wake,
And shout them to the farthest skies.

<u>Liberator</u>, July 11, 1862, p. 112.

474. SONG FOR THE TIMES

Author: H.
Tune: Scots Wha Hae

From the lowly cabin, hear!
Sounds like these salute the ear:
"Bless the Lord, the time is near,
When we shall be free!"

Shall this aspiration fail?
Shall the captive still bewail?
Shall the tyrant's power prevail
O'er this fated land?

Powers of darkness! hence, away!
Ye that lead the mind astray,
Ye whose teachings will betray,
And in ruin end.

Will no sense of justice dawn?
Will no powers of light transform
Those who seem in error born,
By their senseless cry?

He who marks the sparrow's fall,
Judge supreme of great and small,
Hath ordained, alike for all,
Freedom's glorious boon.

Can we thwart His high decree,
Which would set the captives free,
When they humbly bend the knee,
To implore his aid?

How much longer shall we dare
To defy the Father's care?
He hath said, of this beware,
"Vengeance in mine own."

He hath said, "But for a span
Shall my spirit strive with man;
Yield in mercy while ye can,
Or in judgment bow."

Long has been his mercy shown,
Long, too long, the captive's moan
Hath ascended to his throne,
For his power to save.

Let the people then arouse,
And the bondman's cause espouse;
And sincerely plight their vows,
That all shall be free.

Liberator, July 18, 1862, p. 116.

475. THE NORTHERN STAR
PATRIOTIC SONG AND CHORUS

Author: E. H. G. Clark
Tune: [Bonnie Blue Flag?]

Oh! we're a band of brothers,
Arrayed at Freedom's call;
We're fighting for man's dearest rights,
Which God designed for all.
Our watchword is "THE UNION!"
We mean it shall be just;
We hail the Goddess Liberty,
And place it in her trust.
CHORUS:
Hurrah! hurrah! for Freedom's flag, hurrah!
The red, the white, the heavenly blue,
Where shines the Northern Star!

The haughty Southern traitors
Must fail before our might;
Their hearts are hot, their arms are strong,
But we are in the right.
We wish them nothing evil;
Our welfare is their gain:
But for our country and our God
We must break every chain.
CHORUS

Liberator, September 19, 1862, p. 150, with an introduction
indicating that the music "was originally attached to most
odious secession words. Mr. Clark deemed it too beautiful not

to press it into the service of freedom; and so he accompanies
it with the following verses."

476. THE MASSACHUSETTS JOHN BROWN SONG

Author: L. H.
Tune: [John Brown's Body]

Old John Brown's body is a-mouldering in the
dust,
Old John Brown's rifle's red with blood-spots
turned to rust,
Old John Brown's pike has made its last,
unflinching thrust,
His Soul is marching on!
Glory! Glory! Hallelujah!
"Forward!" calls the Lord, our Captain:
Glory! Glory! Hallelujah!
With Him we're marching on.

For treason hung because he struck at
treason's root,
When soon palmetto tree had ripened treason's
fruit,
His dust, disquieted, stirred at Sumter's last
salute -
His Soul is marching on!

Who rides before the army of martyrs to the
word?
The heavens grow bright as He makes bare his
flaming sword,
The glory fills the earth of the coming of the
Lord -
His Soul is marching on!

Thou soul the altar under, white-robed by
martyrdom!
Thy cry, "How long, O Lord?" no longer finds
me dumb;
"Come forth!" calls Christ, "the year of my
redeemed is come" -
His Soul is marching on!

"And ye on earth, my army! tread down God's
grapes till blood
Unto your horses' bridles hath out His
wine-press flowed!

The day of vengeance dawns, - the day of wrath of God" -
His Soul is marching on!

His sacrifice we slay! our sword shall victory crown!
For God and country strike the fiend Rebellion down!
For Freedom and the Right remember Old John Brown!
His Soul is marching on!

Liberator, October 17, 1862, p. 168.

477. EMANCIPATION HYMN FOR 1863

Sung by the vast assembly of colored people at the Great Emancipation Demonstration at Cooper Union.

Author: unspecified
Tune: unspecified

Hail to the brightness of Liberty's morning,
Join all the earth in an anthem of praise;
Freedom's glad day in its glory is dawning,
Light is dispensing its soul-cheering rays.
See how 'tis gilding both mainland and ocean,
Hark to the echoing songs of great joy;
Brighter is burning the flame of devotion,
Music far sweeter the angels employ.

Cry out and shout, all ye children of sorrow,
The gloom of your midnight is passing away;
Bright is the bow which now beams on our morrow,
[Fruition's] new glories o'ershadow today.
Let people and nations, aroused from their slumber,
Rejoice in the severance of slavery's chain,
While voices and instruments mighty in number,
Sound praises to him who removed the dark stain.

Glory to God in the highest be given,
Who hath through the carnage a highway up thrown,
Where those who like beasts to the market were driven,
Now walk, and in songs make their gratitude known.

Hail, then, all hail! to this glorious
morning,
Let Christians rejoice with the myriads
released;
Let those who have labored midst cursing and
scorning,
Now shout, for the night of oppression hath
ceased.

<u>Liberator</u>, January 16, 1863, p. 9.

478. THE YEAR OF JUBILEE

Author: S. L. L.
Tune: unspecified

Oh, saw ye the sun as he purpled the sky?
As he rose on the morning that SLAVERY must
die?
CHORUS:
Oh, happy New Year! Oh, happy New Year!
To good Abraham Lincoln a happy New Year!

Sixty-three, Sixty-three, Freedom's grand
jubilee!
From the proud Southern Pharaoh the people go
free!
CHORUS

He hath thundered His word! He is bathing his
sword
In the blood of Idumea! Oh, praise ye the
Lord!
CHORUS

The "high towers fall" - on the mountains they
call,
To be veiled from the wrath of the great Lord
of all!
CHORUS

Year of his redeemed, of which prophets have
dreamed,
How resplendently real on our sight thou hast
beamed!
CHORUS

As if from their graves, arise the poor
slaves,
While o'er them, ascending, the Star-banner
waves.
CHORUS

See, there is JOHN BROWN, with his rich martyr
crown;
And TORREY and LOVEJOY look radiantly down.
CHORUS

The crisis comes on - soon the battle is won -
From the temple comes forth the great voice,
"It is done!"
CHORUS

First beam of that day, first millennial ray,
All hail this New Year! we exultingly say.
CHORUS

From new ransomed men, from rock, hill and
glen,
Our shout is re-echoed - AMEN and AMEN!
CHORUS

Liberator, January 16, 1863, p. 12.

479. ODE
FOR EMANCIPATION DAY, JANUARY 1, 1863

Sung by the negroes on Emancipation Day in South Carolina.

Author: unspecified
Tune: Scots Wha Hae

Ye sons of burning Afric's soil,
Lift up your hands of hardened toil;
Your shouts from every hill recoil -
Today you are free!
A mighty arm has struck your chain,
The same that broke a tyrant's reign,
And took the Lion by beard and mane,
Beneath his knee.

Today you hear a nation's voice,
Today you have the glorious choice
Forever, ever to rejoice,
In FREEDOM'S reign;

Or, ground to earth as fearful slaves,
Your thirsting soul forever craves
To find dishonorable graves
From earthly pain.

The Sun of LIBERTY'S first ray
Reveals a shining throng's array;
Millions unborn to hail this day -
The day you are free!
They spread their shadowy hands to you;
"O, fathers, to your sons be true;
Snatch us the fruit that early grew
On LIBERTY'S tree!"

O, Abraham Lincoln, thanks to you,
From every Christian heart you drew
The grand, the beautiful, the true,
And sent it down
To gladden, to uplift our hearts,
To give the life that hope imparts,
The joy of dawn when night departs,
And veils its frown.

We hail this dawn of future days,
And God's right arm that still upstays
The cheering sun's perpetual rays,
Now makes us free.
WE thank the Lord, we thank the North,
Whose breath hath sent the tidings forth;
Today a people's glorious birth;
Today we're FREE!

Liberator, January 16, 1863, p. 10.

480. THE PRESIDENT'S PROCLAMATION

Author: Edna Dean Proctor
Tune: John Brown Song

John Brown died on a scaffold for the slave;
Dark was the hour when we dug his hallowed
grave;
Now God avenges the life he gladly gave -
Freedom reigns today!
Glory, glory, hallelujah,
Glory, glory hallelujah,
Glory, glory, hallelujah,
Freedom reigns today!

John Brown sowed, and his harvesters are we; -
Honor to his who has made the bondmen free!
Loved evermore shall our noble Ruler be -
Freedom reigns today!
Glory, etc.

John Brown's body lies mouldering in the
grave;
Bright, o'er the sod, let the starry banner
wave -
O! for the millions he periled all to save,
Freedom reigns today!
Glory, etc.

John Brown lives - we are gaining on our foes
Right shall be victor whatever may oppose -
Fresh, through the darkness, the wind of
morning blows -
Freedom reigns today!
Glory, etc.

John Brown's soul through the world is
marching on;
Hail to the hour when oppression shall be
gone!
All men will sing, in the batter age's dawn,
Freedom reigns today!
Glory, etc.

John Brown dwells where the battle-strife is
o'er;
Hate cannot harm him, nor sorrow stir him
more;
Earth will remember the crown of thorns he
wore -
Freedom reigns today!
Glory, etc.

John Brown's body lies mouldering in the
grave;
John Brown lives in the triumphs of the brave;
John Brown's soul not a higher joy can crave -
Freedom reigns today!
Glory, etc.

Liberator, January 23, 1863, p. 16.

481. EMANCIPATION

Author: F. M. Adlington
Tune: Auld Lang Syne

'Tis done! - the righteous deed is done!
Proclaim'd the jubilee!
Columbia hails her faithful son,
The Father of the free!
The Father, etc.

Aloft the signal flag is raised -
The swift wing'd tidings fly:
"Glory to God! his name be praised!"
Unnumber'd tongues reply.
Unnumber'd, etc.

Fair Freedom lifts her drooping head -
A smile her tears restrains;
Though mourning still her noble dead,
Who died to break her chains.
Who died, etc.

A blessing on our Chieftain's name,
Who gave the great command;
Engrave it on the rock of fame, -
HE FREED HIS NATIVE LAND!
He freed, etc.

And let the listening nations hear,
Throughout creation's bound,
That Freedom has her dwelling here -
Her land is holy ground!
Her land, etc.

A refuge for the suffering poor,
A home for the oppressed,
She opens wide her friendly door,
And feeds them from her breast.
And feeds, etc.

No more, his eyes with weeping dim,
The slave unpitied pines;
The Stripes and Stars now shelter him -
The sun of Freedom shines.
The sun, etc.

Huzza! proclaim the jubilee!
Let grateful anthems rise!
"Huzza! Columbia's land is free!"
Re-echoes through the skies.
Re-echoes, etc.

Now let the host of traitors come,
With foreign foes allied,
One tap on Freedom's larum drum,
The world is on our side!
The world, etc.

Liberator, January 30, 1863, p. 20.

482. SONG OF FREEDOM

Dedicated to Frederick Douglass.

Author: Mrs. W. D. G.
Tune: America

Come sing a cheerful lay,
And celebrate this day
Throughout the land:
Oh! let us joyful be,
For freedom's sons are we,
In this land now the free
At Thy command.

This day we celebrate,
Our works we consecrate,
Great God to Thee;
Accept our grateful praise
To thee our voices raise,
Grant that our future days
Be ever free.

Loud will the chorus round
Through all the world resound -
Blest glorious day;
Firmly unite our arts,
By love's most fertile hearts,
Let not vile traitorous darts,
Bring sad dismay.

Then shout aloud and sing,
Let the whole welkin ring
With praise to Thee:
For Freedom's rights are won,
And enslaved Afric's son
Has Southron's power o'ercome,
Hail! we are free.

Douglass, April, 1863, p. 831.

483. DAVIS'S ADDRESS

Rewritten for the South and English Southerners.

Author: Charles Mackay
Tune: Scots Wha Hae

Men who have your daughters sold,
Men whose sons have brought you gold,
For your trade in flesh be bold!
On for chains and slavery!

Now's the day and now's the hour;
See the front of battle lower,
See approach cursed freedom's power;
Down with all but slavery!

Who'd not be a Southern knave,
Who'll not fill a traitor's grave,
Who'd not own and lash a slave,
Yankee, let him turn and flee!

Who for hell our rights and law,
Slavery's sword will strongly draw,
Woman-whipper, stand or fa',
Brother, let him on with me!

By oppression's woes and pains,
By our sons in servile chains,
We will drain our dearest veins
But they shan't - they shan't be free!

Lay the vile men-freers low;
Freemen fall in every foe,
Slavery's in every blow,
Forward! let us do or die!

Roebuck hugs us to his heart!
Tories long to take our part!
Well their Clarkson's ghost may start!
Wilberforce must howl on high!

All the thrice-cursed crew who rant,
Freedom's friends, no longer cant:
Cotton - cotton's all they want;
That, and up with slavery!

On! that millions yet may groan!
Build your State on wrongs alone;
Slavery's its corner-stone;
On! "Our Chains!" our battle-cry.

Liberator, August 21, 1863, p. 136.

484. [UNTITLED]

Rewritten for the South and English Southerners.

Author: Charles Mackay
Tune: Rule, Britannia!

When Davis first, at hell's commands,
Dug, for a million, bloody graves,
This was the charter of his land,
And women-whippers sung the staves:
Rule, son-sellers,
Whoever at you raves,
Southerners ever, ever will have slaves.

The nations not so blest as we,
Must sell their daughters not at all,
Breeders of selling babes to be
To any brutes to whom they fall;
Rule, girl-sellers,
Whoever at you raves,
Southerners ever, ever will whip slaves.

Still more atrocious will we rise
The more all justice we defy,
The more black souls we brutalize,
And call all right and God a lie;
Rule, Jeff Davis,
Whoever at you raves,
Southerners ever, ever will burn slaves.

Us, God nor man shall ever shame;
All their attempts to put chains down
Shall make us think man-hunting fame,
And hold wife-lashing our renown.
Rule, wife-whippers,
Whoever at you raves,
Southerners ever, ever will whip slaves.

To us belongs the right to burn
The man who dares a man to be,
The man who dares our chains to spurn,
And be, as God would have him, free:

Rule, girl-whippers,
Whoever at you raves,
Southerners ever, ever will lash slaves.

All vices still with slavery found,
Shall to our cursed homes repair;
Lust - cruelty shall there abound;
Torture and murder shall be there;
Rule, child-sellers,
Whoever at you raves,
Southerners ever, ever will breed slaves.

And while both heaven and earth abhor
Our new-born rule that shames the day,
We'll boast of all they hate the more,
And women's backs their taunts shall pay;
Rule, girl-whippers,
Whoever at you raves,
Southerners ever, ever will have slaves.

Liberator, August 21, 1863, p. 136.

485. FAREWELL TO BEECHER

Author: unspecified
Tune: Jeanette and Jeannot

You are going far away,
Far away from the nigger folks;
They've no one left but Cheever now
Their white breth'ren to coax
Into the abolition scheme
And amalgamation dire,
Which he preaches from his pulpit's height
With true Ciceronean fire.   (Repeat)

But his eloquence is lost
On New York's arid soil;
We recognize the niggers' usefulness
When in cotton fields they toil.
We're sorry, too, to hear
That sometimes they're misused;
But marry our daughters to the blacks
We'd rather be excused.   (Repeat)

Then farewell, parson Beecher,
You spotless, stainless man;
Just stay away in foreign lands
As long as ever you can.

Our derision will be with you,
Wherever you may go,
And we only wish that you had taken
One Harriet Beecher Stowe.   ("Yes," repeat)

That nigger worshipper,
That rabid Republican,
Who'd be a second preacher Beecher
If she had been a man.
Now tell us, reverend parson,
And be sure you tell us true,
Does Harriet always talk in Greek,
And are her stockings blue?
Does she really talk in Greek,
And what's her stockings' hue?

I suppose we shall hear often
Of what you've done and said;
You'll write letters to some paper
That'll pay you nary red.
I hope a strong sea breeze
Will you o'er the waters waft,
(And - "lay the unction to your soul" -
You have escaped the draft.)   ("Yes," repeat)

'Tis true the New Yorkers
Do heartily despise
All your abolition sermons,
And your canting set likewise.
Oh! if I were uncle Abe,
Or, still better, William Seward,
I'd keep such men as you at home,
Nor let them go abroad.
For, if preachers will leave the Gospel,
And in politics take delight,
Why, then, they that made the quarrel
Should be the only ones to fight;
Yes, Beecher, and Cheever, and all the crew
Should be the only ones to fight.

By rights I ought to finish;
But a question I'd like to ask;
And I pray you, sporting Beecher,
Your feelings to unmask:
'Tis true, I have no right
Thus to interrogate you;
(For in your church I do not own
Nor even rent a pew.)   ("No," repeat)

I never sent you tea,
Nor anything nice to eat;
And never worked you slippers gay
To decorate your feet;

But some men do declare,
And I believe they're right,
That you've steered your bark to England's
isle
To see the Heenan fight;
Yes, you've thrown the black man overboard
To see the Heenan fight.

Liberator, October 2, 1863, p. 157.

486. ON THE CONQUEST OF ATLANTA BY THE UNION TROOPS

Author: Caroline A. Robbins
Tune: John Brown

Our flag o'er Atlanta waves triumphant today!
Its ample folds fall o'er the strong city's
walls;
While under it, marching, the Union soldiers
play,
And shout at her downfall!
O, glory! Hallelujah,
Glory, glory, Hallelujah!
Atlanta is our own!

For all our toils and trials we now have a
reward;
Rebellion cannot stand this deadly, dreadful
blow:
Be joyful, friends of Freedom, and every fear
discard -
Secession is laid low!
O, glory, etc.
The tyrants are o'erthrown!

The slaves will have their freedom, and the
Union be restored;
Not a compact with Satan, an agreement with
hell;
But a Constitution framed in the fear of the
Lord,
Who doeth all things well!
O, glory, etc.
The Lord is marching on!

All honor to the brave! - let them live in our
hearts;
And to Lincoln, our Pilot, who has hastened us
through the storms;

Our heroic armies have well sustained their
parts
In the fields they have fought and won!
O, glory, etc.
We see the rising sun!

Peace soon o'er our borders shall spread her
dove-like wings;
And harpies that would suck our nation's life
away,
Shall speedily become like other paltry things
Like a bubble shall vanish away!
Praise ye the Lord! Hallelujah! etc.
Who has saved our land today!

Liberator, October 7, 1864, p. 164.

487. O, SING OF LIBERTY!
A PARODY

Author: R. Thayer
Tune: There'll Be No Sorrow There

O, sing of Liberty
For all, both low and high;
When men in chains no more shall be
Obliged to live and die;
There'll be no sorrow then;
There'll be no sorrow then;
When every heart is filled with love
For all its fellow-men.

Then on our raptured ear
Shall fall, in sweetest strain, -
"No more shall man his brother fear,
Nor wear the galling chain";
There'll be, etc.

Then cruel war shall cease,
And peace on earth shall reign,
Our land enjoy a sweet release
From Slavery's damning stain:
There'll be, etc.

Our country then shall be
The pride of all the lands,
When North and South all men we see
Joining fraternal hands:
There'll be, etc.

The angels then shall sing
As at the Savior's birth -
"Glad tidings to the world we bring,
Sweet peace to men on earth":
There'll be, etc.

Liberator, February 10, 1865, p. 24.

488. THE JUBILEE HYMN OF THE REPUBLIC

Written for an Emancipation Jubilee
and reception of William Lloyd Garrison
at City Hall in Newburyport.

Author: Austin Dodge
Tune: unspecified

Lo! a swarthy nation rises
With the wale-stripes on their backs,
With their ankles scarred with fetters,
And the red blood in their tracks!
Lo! a host of coming columns,
Like the drops of driven rain,
Like the dusky leaves of autumn,
Like the thick mists on the main.
CHORUS:
Lo! Jehovah's trumpet sounding,
Sweeps the blast from sea to sea!
Hallelujah in the highest!
God hath set his people free!

Hark! the tramp of dark battalions,
Of a race four millions strong,
Keeping time to God's own music,
Grandly chanting Freedom's song!
Coming up from years of bondage,
From a night of misery,
To the Nation's Resurrection,
From the Hell of Slavery.
CHORUS

Out from under heel of iron,
From the brutal auctin-block,
Out from under teeth of blood-hound,
Freed Prometheus spurns the rock!
Thrown the Etna off the Giant,
See a Nation stands up free!
From the ravening beak of vulture
Springs the slave to liberty!
CHORUS

On the hills let lighted beacons
Blaze the news with tongues of fire!
Let the heavy church-bell, swinging,
Rock and jar the granite spire!
Speak, ye silver tongues of trumpets,
Like the storm-wind on the sea!
Shout, ye iron lips of cannon,
Boom out thunder-bursts of glee!
CHORUS

Praise God for Emancipation!
He hath bared His own right arm;
Let the thanks of all the nation
Swell in thunder like a psalm!
Fill the welkin full of banners,
Let them clap their hands on high,
Till high Heaven shouts wild hosannas,
Sending down its glad reply!
CHORUS

Liberator, March 3, 1865, p. 35.

489. HYMN

Written for an Emancipation Jubilee
and reception of William Lloyd Garrison
at City Hall in Newburyport.

Author: John G. Whittier
Tune: original, by C. P. Morrison

Not unto us who did but seek
The word that burned within to speak,
Not unto us this day belong
The triumph and exulting song.

Upon us fell in early youth
The burden of unwelcome truth,
And left us, weak and frail and few,
The censor's painful work to do.

Thenceforth our life a fight became,
The air we breathed was hot with blame;
For not with gauged and softened tone
We made the bondman's cause our own.

We bore, as Freedom's hope forlorn,
The private hate, the public scorn;
Yet held through all the paths we trod
Our faith in man and trust in God.

We prayed and hoped; but still, with awe,
The coming of the sword we saw;
We heard the nearing steps of doom,
And saw the shade of things to come.

We hoped for peace: our eyes survey
The blood-red dawn of Freedom's day;
We prayed for love to loose the chain:
'Tis shorn by battle's axe in twain!

Not skill nor strength nor zeal of ours
Has mined and heaved the hostile towers;
Not by our hands is turned the key
That sets the sighing captives free.

A redder sea than Egypt's wave
Is piled and parted for the slave;
A darker cloud moves on in light,
A fiercer fire is guide by night!

The praise, O Lord! be Thine alone,
In thy own way thy work be done!
Our poor gifts at Thy feet we cast,
To whom be glory, first and last!

Liberator, March 3, 1865, p. 35.

490. A FUNERAL ODE

Chanted in the Hopedale Chapel by the choir,
as the closing exercise of the general funeral service
solemnising the obsequies of President Lincoln,
April 19, 1865.

Author: Adin Ballou
Tune: unspecified

The Nation's noblest Chief we mourn,
Struck down by fiendish spite -
The People's second Washington,
Laid low in murd'rous plight!
And all the land bewails the blow,
O'erwhelmed in unexpected woe!

Thus Slavery's last, most hellish deed
Rebellion's dying rage -
Has made her clement Conqueror bleed,
And darker stained the age!
Down, writhing dragon, down the pit!
Thy native den, and tomb most fit!

To thee we turn, Almighty God,
Thou ever good and wise,
And pray thy grace-distilling rod
May soothe the bitter cries
That burst from household hearts bereaved,
And bless this cup to millions grieved!

We thank thee for illustrious worth,
So long sustained and spared;
For threatened lives still left on earth;
For Future Life declared;
For martyrdom in meekness crowned,
And merit wreathed with glory round.

And now, most gracious Father, teach
A groaning Nation peace -
To heal their gaping, bleeding breach
In Freedom's grand release;
May Justice rule, and Mercy plead,
And true repentance soon succeed!

To Thee, in hope, our prayers commend
The noble Chieftain's soul,
The weeping ones that sadly bend
Around his clay so cold,
The sable hosts that bless his name,
And all that prize his deathless fame.

Liberator, May 5, 1865, p. 72.

491. HYMN

Sung at the meeting at Peterboro', N. Y.,
on the day of the burial of President Lincoln.

Author: G. W. Putnam
Tune: unspecified

The song of spring-birds in the grove,
The unchained waters sweeping fast,
And signs below, around, above,
Proclaim that Winter's reign is past.

In vain to us the cheerful light,
In vain the unchained waters sing,
In vain the earth and sky so bright,
And happy spring-birds caroling.

Deep clouds and darkness shroud the land;
A cry of agony and woe
Goes up to Heaven - for MURDER'S hand
Hath laid our lofty Leader low.

But late yon shrouded banner flung
Its starry folds against the sky;
We sang the song that Miriam sung,
The unbound millions marching by.

Our Heaven with Hope was all aflame;
The cannon's voice, from shore to shore,
And shout of myriads, with acclaim,
Declared the bloody struggle o'er.

Today we bow 'neath sorrow's rod!
A Nation, in its hour of woe,
Pleads for Thy guidance: O, our God!
We cannot, will not let Thee go!

As once across the desert sand
Thy shaft of fire lit up the night,
So now reach down thy blessed hand,
And lead us onward to the LIGHT.

Liberator, May 5, 1865, p. 72.

492. [UNTITLED]

Sung at the New England Anti-Slavery Convention.

Author: unspecified
Tune: unspecified

Our nation's free! our nation's free!
All hail the land of liberty!
Loud swell the trump that sounds its fame,
No longer now an empty name.

For let the joyful tidings spread,
Where'er the feet of man can tread:
Waft it, ye breezes, o'er the sea,
And tell the world our nation's free.

Our nation's free! our nation's free!
Proclaim the glorious jubilee!
Sublimely let its echoes roll,
And thrill with music to the soul!

The oppressor's power at last is broke,
And millions, freed from slavery's yoke,
Their thankful hearts and voices raise,
To speak their great Deliverer's praise.

Our nation's free! our nation's free!
How bright its future destiny!
Within its bounds no clanking chain
Shall bind the human form again.

Liberator, May 19, 1865, p. 78.

Author Index

All numbers are song numbers.

Abbott, W. S., 78
Adlington, F. M., 256, 481
Alexander, S. R., 309
Atlee, E. A., 163
Atwood, M. P., 124

Bailey, Mrs. Dr., 324
Ball, Miss, 350
Ballou, Adin, 490
Blanchard, Rev. J., 331
Bradford, Claudius, 123
Brown, William Wells, 264
Bryant, 456
Burleigh, Charles C., 300, 398
Burleigh, George S., 99
Burns, Robert, 267

C., A. B., 363, 405
C., B., 455
C., H., 4
C., L. M., 327
C., S. G., 219, 222
Carrie, 397
Carter, Mrs. J. G., 173
Chandler, Elizabeth M., 36, 48, 86, 116, 336, 351, 358, 360
Chapman, Maria W., 22, 25 [same as 140], 46, 238
Chapman, Mrs. H. G., 32
Child, Lydia Maria, 460
Clark, E. H. G., 475
Clark, George W., 166, 172, 179, 180, 186, 258, 295?, 333, 392, 455 [chorus]
Collier, Mary Ann, 117, 155
Colored Man, A, 332
Cook, Eliza, 438

Title Index

All numbers are song numbers, and numbers in ( ) indicate alternate titles from sources other than those designated in the main entries. Titles are listed alphabetically, except that "Oh" is treated as "O."

Acres and Hands, 94
Advent of Christ, 31
African Girl, The, 370
Afric's Dream, The, 358
Albert Morris, 377
All Things Speak, 284
Am I Not a Man and Brother? 337
Am I Not a Sister? 338
America - A Parody, 130
American Female Slave, The, 116
American Slave's Address to the American Eagle, The, 363
American Tract Society, and its Southern Masters, The, 457
American Union, 435
And the Days of Thy Mourning Shall Be Ended, 289
Anniversary, 209
Anti-Slavery Call, The, 241
Anti-Slavery Hymn, 74, 96, 234
Anti-Slavery Ode, 81
Appeal for the Samaritan Asylum, (16)
Appeal to American Freemen, An. 226
Appeal to Woman, 354
Are Ye Truly Free? 156
Arming, But Not With Carnal Weapons, 62
Army Hymn, 98
Arouse! Arouse! 175
Arouse, New-England's Sons, 149
Artful Dodger, The, 445
Away to Canada, 366

Ballot, The, 412
Ballot-Box, The, 413

*A number of songs in <u>Melodies</u> are titled simply "Hymn" with a corresponding number for that collection. They are as follows:

Tune Index

Following are titles of tunes as they appear in the original sources. Brackets indicate alternate titles by which the tune is or was known. Question marks designate those cases in which the editor assigned the tune on the basis of pattern, meter, or other evidence. Tunes are listed alphabetically, except that "Oh" is treated as "O." All numbers are song numbers.

Alabama Again, 374
Alknomook, 118
All is Well, 284
America, 9, 13?, 39, 46, 77?, 85?, 120?, 130, 146, 187, 205?, 210, 211, 215?, 219, 226, 245?, 290?, 469, 482
And To Begging I Will Go, 406
Araby's Daughter, 315, 331
Auld Lang Syne, 41, 108, 136, 171, 183, 218, 240, 253?, 264, 280, 312, 404, 409, 459, 461, 481
Away the Bowl, 145

Bavaria, 294, 317, 354
Be Free, Oh, Man, Be Free, 195
Beatitude, 190
Belville, 59
Blue Juniata, 397
Blue-Eyed Mary, 234
Bonnie Blue Flag [The Irish Jaunting Car], 475?
Bonny Boat, 147
Bonny Doon, 259, 327, 412
Braes of Balquither, The, 471
Bride's Farewell, 337
Britannia Hath Triumphed [Sound the Loud Timbrel], 115
Burial of Sir John Moore, 441
Buy a Broom [Lieber Augustine], 368

Calvary, 26
Campbells are Coming, The, 174, 197, 298, 415

original (probably written specifically for the lyrics rather
    than borrowed): by G. W. C., 35, 44, 82, 83, 87, 95,
    119, 184, 194, 196, 257, 265, 270, 276, 278, 279, 292,
    295, 322, 336, 343, 344, 346, 349, 350, 390, 408, 410,
    411, 426, 448; by O. Dresel, 98; by L. Mason, 117, 232;
    by C. P. Morrison, 489; by H. Russell, 438; by C. M.
    Traver, 299; by S. S. Wardwell, 160; by T. Wood, 94
Ortonville, 38, 121
Our Flag is There, 221
Our Warrior's Heart, 176, 267, 416?, 422?
Over the Mountain, 352, 353?

Pilot of the Deep, 323
Pirate's Glee, The, 269
Poachers, The, 463
Poor Old Slave Has Gone to Rest, The, 395
Portuguese Hymn [Adeste Fidelis], 110

Rory O'More [Young Rory O'More], 188, 420, 423
Rose of Allandale, 360
Rose That All Are Praising, The, 271
Rosin the Bow [The Liberty Ball], 152, 166, 287
Rule, Britannia! 484

Sandy and Jenny, 66
Scots Wha Hae [Bruce's Address], 91?, 109, 114, 167, 169, 199,
    200, 202, 208, 213, 224, 248?, 387?, 400, 432, 441, 474,
    479, 483
Silver Moon, 339, 341
Slave Girl Mourning Her Father, 328
Somerville, 88
Sparkling and Bright, 74, 326, 454
Spider and the Fly, 7
Star-Spangled Banner, The, 163, 222?
Strike the Cymbal, 231
Suoni la Tromba, 225, 450
Sweet Afton, 273, 324
Sweet Alive Ben Bolt, 376
Sweet Birds Are Singing [The Merry May?], 209
Sweet Home, 5, 313, 414

There is a Happy Land, 384
There Was a Little Man, and He Woo'd a Little Maid, 401
There'll Be No Sorrow There, 487
There's a Good Time Coming, 275
'Tis Dawn, the Lark is Singing, 418, 431
To Greece We Give Our Shining Blades, 321
Troubadour, The, 192, 314, 405

Uncle Ned, 362

unidentified, 13, 21, 24, 27, 29, 30, 31, 35, 37, 38, 39, 43, 44, 48, 51, 52, 56, 60, 62, 63, 64, 65, 67, 69, 70, 86, 111, 116, 123, 140, 144, 146, 148, 149, 150, 152, 153, 154, 155, 157, 212, 233, 244, 246, 249, 250, 258, 272, 274, 283, 293, 317, 332, 333, 342, 351, 356, 391, 392, 394, 446
unspecified (only those songs for which no tune was ever specified), 1, 2, 3, 4, 6, 10, 11, 14, 15, 16, 17, 18, 20, 25, 32, 34, 40, 45, 49, 54, 55, 61, 68, 71, 75, 76, 79, 80, 81, 84, 92, 100, 101, 102, 104, 106, 107, 112, 113, 122, 124, 125, 126, 127, 128, 134, 139, 143, 175, 189, 193, 198, 201, 207, 217, 220, 227, 228, 235, 236, 237, 238, 239, 251, 261, 262, 281, 282, 301, 304, 307, 308, 309, 311, 316, 338, 359, 365, 372, 379, 393, 398, 417, 419, 433, 434, 439, 440, 442, 451, 458, 460, 462, 472, 477, 478, 488, 490, 491, 492
Uxbridge, 50, 246

Wake Isles of the South, 247
Watchman, Tell Us of the Night, 242
We Are All Noddin', 383
We Won't Give Up the Bible, 285
Wells, 28, 111
We're Traveling Home to Heaven Above, 377
What Fairy Like Music, 302
When I Can Read My Title Clear, 241
When the Trump of Fame, 133
Where Can the Soul Find Rest? 369
Wild Hunt of Lutzow, The, 159, 165, 180
Wind of the Winter Night, 345
Wreathe the Bowl, 181

Yankee Doodle, 181, 441, 468
Yankee Girl, 436
Yarmouth, 137

Zion, 19, 58, 232, 252

First Line Index

First lines are listed alphabetically, except that "Oh" is treated as "O." All numbers are song numbers.

Is this the land our fathers loved, 184
It comes! the joyful day, 244
I've heard them talk of a happy home, 378

John Brown died on a scaffold for the slave, 480
John Brown is gone, that good old man, 459
Just Heaven, and has it come to this, 433
Joy to the pleasant land we love, 185

"Keep it before the people," 95
Kind friends, with your permission, I, 441

Land of my sleeping fathers! 155
Land our fathers left to us, The, 80
Land was wrapped in moral night, The, 90
Let freeborn empires offer prayer, 67
Let mammon hold while mammon can, 233
Let others strive for fame and gold, 76
Let the floods clap their hands! 29
Let the trump of Fame, 133
Let us sing, brothers, sing, 471
Let waiting throngs now lift their voices, 268
Lift up a voice of gladness, 289
Lift up our country's banner high, 143
Lift up to God the shout of joy, 84
Lo! a swarthy nation rises, 488
Lo! in Southern skies afar, 400
Lo! the bondage of ages has ceased! 144
Lord Deliver! thou canst save, 30
Lord will come! the earth shall quake, The, 31
Loud he sang the psalm of David, 317
Loud Hosannas, Wave your banners, 126
Low in the west, see the sun now declining, 204

March on! march on! we love the Liberty flag, 269
March to the battlefield, 186
Memory of the faithful dead, The, 32
Men of the North, who remember, 450
Men of thought be up and stirring, 292
Men, who bear the Pilgrims' name, 208
Men who breathe New England air, 213
Men who have your daughters sold, 483
Men! whose boast it is that ye, 156
Merrily every bosom boundeth, 293
Minstrel Boy to the war has gone, The, 390
Moonless night! - the sky is clear, A, 398
Morn comes in the east, and the world is awake, 436
Morning is breaking, The, 209
Mother came, when stars were paling, A, 391
My country, shall thy honored name, 157
My country, 'tis for thee, Dark, 187
My country! 'tis for thee, Sad, 219

Oh, Thou, whose presence went before, 111
Oh, turn ye not displeased away, though I, 351
O weep, ye friends of Freedom, weep! 189
Oh! we're a band of brothers, 475
O, we're for law and order, 434
O whar is de spot what we were born on, 392
O, where has mother gone, papa? 379
Oh, who shall see that joyful day, 250
O'er the southern plains of darkness, 57
O'er this wide extended country, 93
Oft in the chilly night, 318
Old fogies sing on every hand, 468
Old John Brown's body is a-mouldering in the dust, 476
On Afric's land our fathers roamed, 309
On the earth the day is dawning, 294
On the mountain tops appearing, 58
Once more is heard the funeral knell, 127
Once poor Afric's day was shining, 230
One hundred years hence what a change will be made, 295
Onward, O ye sons of Freedom, 220
Oppression shall not always reign, 251
Our brother, lo! we come! 85
Our cause is just and holy, 285
Our countrymen are dying, 135
Our emblem is the Cedar, 418
Our Fathers fought on Bunker's Hill, 168
Our fathers worshipped Thee, O God, 473
Our fellow countrymen in chains, 190
Our flag o'er Atlanta waves triumphant today! 486
Our grateful hearts with joy o'erflow, 145
Our nation's free! our nation's free! 492
Our noble advocate and friend, 280
Our Pilgrim Fathers - where are they? 191
Out of the dark the circling sphere, 102
Over the mountain and over the moor, Comes, 352
Over the mountain, and over the moor, Hungry, 353
Over the mountain wave, 192
Over thy grassy grave, 290
Ox, that treadeth out the corn, The, 59

Pilgrims are launched on the wild winter main, The, 159
Poor wayfaring man of grief, A, 330
Praise for slumbers of the night, 86
Praise to God who ever reigns, 393
Praise we the Lord! let songs resound, 193
Pray who is Mr. Prejudice, 6
Press forward to hear him, the eloquent stranger, 305
Pride of New England! 160

Quick, fly to the covert, thou hunted of men! 273

Republic of the setting sun! 198
Ridden by the Slave Power, 301

Subject Index

This index includes persons, places, and other items from the songs which are not covered elsewhere; no general song topics have been indexed, however, since the volume itself is organized around those subjects. All numbers are song numbers and the item may be found in the title, heading, lyrics, or notes to the song. Unless otherwise specified, persons and places are subjects of songs and/or appear in lyrics, dedications, or notes. Composers are included in the TUNE INDEX under "original" and so are not repeated here, and Biblical references and single mention of relatively minor figures are not indexed. Names of organizations refer to their meetings at which songs were sung and can be found either in headings or footnotes. Organizations and their locations are cross-indexed when possible, but cities, states, and countries are not.

Abington, as location, 34, 42, 99, 182, 205, 229, 252, 304, 400
Adams, John Quincy, 237, 245, 253
Addison County, as location, 19
Akron, as location, 283
Alabama, 211, 365
Alabama River, 397
Albany, as location, 45
Albion, see England
Antigua, 127
Anti-Slavery League (England), 259
antislavery societies: Abington, 34, 42; Addison County, 19; American, 38, 100, 101, 102, 150, 190; Female (Plymouth County), 41; Massachusetts, 32, 182, 232, 233; New England, 6, 39, 96, 108 (intended), 109 (intended), 167 (intended), 492; Plymouth County, 18, 41, 120; Rhode Island, 22 (intended); Utica, 114 (intended); Vermont, 232; Western, 262; Westford, 123
Ashland, 407
Asia, 205, 259, 297

About the Author

VICKI L. EAKLOR is Assistant Professor of History in the Division of Human Studies, Alfred University. She has contributed articles to the *Journal of Research in Music Education, Selected Papers in Illinois History 1980,* and the *Bulletin of the Missouri Historical Society.*